Advancing Adaptive Education:

Technological Innovations for Disability Support

Eriona Çela
University of New York Tirana, Albania

Mathias Mbu Fonkam
Pennsylvania State University, USA

Narasimha Rao Vajjhala
University of New York Tirana, Albania

Philip Eappen
Cape Breton University, Canada

Vice President of Editorial	Melissa Wagner
Managing Editor of Acquisitions	Mikaela Felty
Managing Editor of Book Development	Jocelynn Hessler
Production Manager	Mike Brehm
Cover Design	Phillip Shickler

Published in the United States of America by
IGI Global Scientific Publishing
701 East Chocolate Avenue
Hershey, PA, 17033, USA
Tel: 717-533-8845
Fax: 717-533-8661
E-mail: cust@igi-global.com
Website: https://www.igi-global.com

Copyright © 2025 by IGI Global Scientific Publishing. All rights reserved. No part of this publication may be reproduced, stored or distributed in any form or by any means, electronic or mechanical, including photocopying, without written permission from the publisher.
Product or company names used in this set are for identification purposes only. Inclusion of the names of the products or companies does not indicate a claim of ownership by IGI Global Scientific Publishing of the trademark or registered trademark.

Library of Congress Cataloging-in-Publication Data

CIP Pending
ISBN: 979-8-3693-8227-1
EISBN: 979-8-3693-8229-5

British Cataloguing in Publication Data
A Cataloguing in Publication record for this book is available from the British Library.

All work contributed to this book is new, previously-unpublished material.
The views expressed in this book are those of the authors, but not necessarily of the publisher.
This book contains information sourced from authentic and highly regarded references, with reasonable efforts made to ensure the reliability of the data and information presented. The authors, editors, and publisher believe the information in this book to be accurate and true as of the date of publication. Every effort has been made to trace and credit the copyright holders of all materials included. However, the authors, editors, and publisher cannot assume responsibility for the validity of all materials or the consequences of their use. Should any copyright material be found unacknowledged, please inform the publisher so that corrections may be made in future reprints.

Eriona Çela

I would like to extend my heartfelt gratitude to my family. Its unwavering support and belief in me have been my guiding light throughout this journey. Thank you for standing by me, for your patience, and for always reminding me of the importance of this work. I am truly fortunate to have you in my life.

Narasimha Rao Vajjhala

I want to thank my family members, particularly my mother, Mrs. Rajeswari Vajjhala, for her blessings and for instilling in me the virtues of perseverance and commitment.

Mathias Fonkam

I would like to express my sincere gratitude to my beloved wife Antonia and our 2 younger ones – my 10-year old princess, Noella, and my 8-year old son, Asobo, for their endless love, patience, understanding and support as I have had to steal time off the dad schedule for this and other work. I also owe much gratitude to the many in this field who have structured and charted the course and on whose shoulders we mostly stand.

Philip Eappen

I want to take this opportunity to express my appreciation to Dr. Narasimha Rao Vajjhala for his support, encouragement and for sharing his experience, knowledge, and expertise throughout the completion of this book.

Thanks a million, to my wife, Figgi Philip, for her patience, encouragement, and endurance during my academic journey. I cannot thank you enough for your kind and unwavering support during my research activities. I am thankful to my son, Evan Eappen Philip: Your naughtiness, and cuteness made my life fun-filled and more enjoyable. To my parents, Eapen TP and Baby Eapen: Both of you made me feel smart, unique, and capable. Thank you for your kindness and encouragement. I would also like to thank my sister, brothers-in-law, and my in-laws for their encouragement and support during these years. All of you motivated and encouraged me during this journey, and I am what I am because of all your support.

Editorial Advisory Board

Albérico Travassos Rosário, *GOVCOPP - IADE - Universidade Europeia, Portugal*
Antonio Muñoz, *University of Málaga, Spain*
Ayodele A. Adebiyi, *Landmark University, Nigeria*
Denise Wright, *Howard University, United States*
Efosa Carroll Idemudia, *Arkansas Tech University, United States*
Figgi Sarah, *Nova Scotia Health Authority, Canada*
George Salu Thandekkattu, *American University of Nigeria, Nigeria*
Gregory Wajiga, *Modibbo Adama University, Nigeria*
Jasmine Jones, *Bill and Melinda Gates Foundation, Nigeria*
Jelena Vucetic, *Alpha Mission, Inc., United States*
João Conrado de Amorim Carvalho, *Centro de Ensino Superior Dom Bosco, Brazil*
Johnson James, *Central Michigan University, United States*
L lá Osawe, *Central Michigan University, United States*
Lohith Potluri, *University of California San Diego, United States*
Lori Annette Slater, *American InterContinental University, United States*
Maiendra Moodley, *State Information Technology Agency, South Africa*
Manuel Sousa Pereira, *Instituto Politécnico de Viana do Castelo, Portugal*
Mariano Carrera, *King Mongkut's University of Technology, Thailand*
Mohammed El Amine Abdelli, *University of Salamanca, Spain*
Maximiliano Korstanje, *University of Palermo, Argentina*
Mustafa Özer, *Anadolu University, Turkey*
Olumide Babatope Longe, *Academic City University College, Ghana*
Padma Pradhan, *Jawaharlal Nehru Technological University, India*
Paola Modesti, *University of Parma, Italy*
P.B. Zirra, *Federal University of Kashere, Nigeria*
Prabhakar Rontala, *University of Kwazulu-Natal, South Africa*
Ramgopal Kashyap, *Amity University, India*
Reshu Agarwal, *Amity University, India*
Sandip Rakshit, *Université Internationale de Rabat, Morocco*

Sanjiban Sekhar Roy, *Vellore Institute of Technology, India*
Tanushri Mukherjee, *Amity University, India*
Thenmozhi T, *KGISL Institute of Technology, India*
Vishnu Rajan, *Xavier Institute of Management, India*
Vijender Kumar Solanki, *CMR Institute of Technology, India*
Vivek Agrawal, *GLA University, India*
Yuri Shenshinov, *The American University of Kurdistan, Iraq*
Zhaohao Sun, *PNG University of Technology, Papua New Guinea*

Table of Contents

Foreword xv

Preface xvii

Chapter 1
Foundations of Adaptive Technologies in Inclusive Education 1
    Eriona Çela, University of New York Tirana, Albania
    Mathias M. Fonkam, Penn State University, USA
    Narasimha Rao Vajjhala, University of New York Tirana, Albania

Chapter 2
Artificial Intelligence in Adaptive Education: A Transformative Approach 21
    Sulagna Das, JIS University, India
    Indranil Mutsuddi, JIS University, India
    Nilanjan Ray, JIS University, India

Chapter 3
Adaptive Learning Technologies in Healthcare Education for Students With Disabilities 51
    Vismaya Annie Vinod, Cape Breton University, Canada
    Eriona Çela, University of New York, Tirana, Albania
    Philip Eappen, University of Toronto, Canada

Chapter 4
AI-Powered Innovations Transforming Adaptive Education for Disability Support 73
    Munikrishnaiah Sundara Ramaiah, Independent Researcher, San Antonio, USA
    Sevinthi Kali Sankar Nagarajan, Independent Researcher, San Antonio, USA
    Pawan Whig, VIPS, India
    Pushan Kumar Dutta, Amity University, Kolkata, India

Chapter 5
Data-Driven Solutions Enhancing Adaptive Education Through
Technological Innovations for Disability Support 101
    Sevinthi Kali Sankar Nagarajan, Independent Researcher, San Antonio,
        USA
    Munikrishnaiah Sundara Ramaiah, Independent Researcher, San
        Antonio, USA
    Pawan Whig, VIPS, India

Chapter 6
Assistive Technology and Accessibility Tools in Enhancing Adaptive
Education 125
    Tunde Toyese Oyedokun, Thomas Adewumi University, Oko-Irese,
        Nigeria

Chapter 7
The Role of Assistive Technology in Education: A Study of Four SADC
States 163
    William Chakabwata, University of South Africa, South Africa

Chapter 8
VR Interventions for Students With Intellectual Disabilities: Innovative
Approaches and Practical Applications 193
    Hüseyin Göksu, İstanbul University-Cerrahpaşa, Turkey
    Selami Eryilmaz, Gazi University, Turkey

Chapter 9
Exploring the Perspectives and Expectations of Special Educational Needs
Coordinators on the Use of Special iApps for Children 215
    Samiullah Paracha, Xi'an Jiaotong-Liverpool University, China
    Lynne Hall, University of Sunderland, UK
    Gillian Hagan-Green, University of Sunderland, UK
    Derek Watson, University of Sunderland, UK

Chapter 10
Digital Literacy Among Students With Disabilities in India: Pros and Cons.... 255
    Madhavi Kilaru, VNR Vignana Jyothi Institute of Engineering and
        Technology, India
    Rajasekhara Mouly Potluri, Kazakh-British Technical University,
        Kazakhstan

Compilation of References 271

About the Contributors 313

Index 323

Detailed Table of Contents

Foreword xv

Preface xvii

Chapter 1
Foundations of Adaptive Technologies in Inclusive Education 1
    Eriona Çela, University of New York Tirana, Albania
    Mathias M. Fonkam, Penn State University, USA
    Narasimha Rao Vajjhala, University of New York Tirana, Albania

This chapter lays the foundation for exploring the transformative potential of adaptive technologies in inclusive education. This chapter examines the principles of adaptive education, emphasizing its role in addressing the diverse needs of learners, particularly students with disabilities. The discussion highlights the integration of assistive technologies and artificial intelligence as critical tools for fostering equity, accessibility, and engagement in educational environments. By addressing key barriers such as cost, accessibility, and teacher preparedness, the chapter advocates for the adoption of innovative and inclusive practices to empower all learners. Grounded in interdisciplinary research and ethical considerations, this chapter sets the stage for understanding how adaptive technologies can reshape education systems to create a more inclusive and equitable future for students worldwide.

Chapter 2
Artificial Intelligence in Adaptive Education: A Transformative Approach 21
    Sulagna Das, JIS University, India
    Indranil Mutsuddi, JIS University, India
    Nilanjan Ray, JIS University, India

Integrating artificial intelligence (AI) in higher education has revolutionized how institutions design and enhance learning systems. Higher education institutions (HEIs) increasingly leverage adaptive learning techniques to create dynamic and personalized educational environments. These methods use teaching and learning data to tailor educational experiences to meet each student's unique needs and capabilities. AI-driven applications are at the core of this transformation, offering significant advantages such as improved learning experiences, flexible scheduling, immediate feedback, personalized educational management, and accelerated student progress. This chapter examines the multifaceted dimensions of adaptive learning within the education system, emphasizing the pivotal role of AI-driven technologies in enabling and advancing this innovative approach.

Chapter 3
Adaptive Learning Technologies in Healthcare Education for Students With
Disabilities 51
    Vismaya Annie Vinod, Cape Breton University, Canada
    Eriona Çela, University of New York, Tirana, Albania
    Philip Eappen, University of Toronto, Canada

This chapter explores the integration and impact of adaptive learning technologies in healthcare education, specifically for students with disabilities. By leveraging experiential technologies such as virtual reality (VR), mixed reality (MR), and augmented reality (AR), healthcare education can foster more immersive, interactive, and inclusive learning experiences. This narrative review identifies the unique challenges faced by students with disabilities, including accessibility issues, gaps in disability competency training, and inequities in educational opportunities. The chapter examines how adaptive learning, supported by artificial intelligence (AI) and machine learning (ML), can create personalized learning paths that enhance student engagement, confidence, and skill development. Additionally, it highlights the role of assistive technologies in improving accessibility and fostering inclusive educational practices.

Chapter 4
AI-Powered Innovations Transforming Adaptive Education for Disability
Support 73
    Munikrishnaiah Sundara Ramaiah, Independent Researcher, San
        Antonio, USA
    Sevinthi Kali Sankar Nagarajan, Independent Researcher, San Antonio,
        USA
    Pawan Whig, VIPS, India
    Pushan Kumar Dutta, Amity University, Kolkata, India

This chapter examines artificial intelligence's (AI) transformative impact on adaptive education for students with disabilities. This chapter explores how AI-driven technologies, including intelligent tutoring systems, speech recognition tools, and personalized learning algorithms, are reshaping educational experiences to be more inclusive and effective. By leveraging these innovations, educators can tailor content and support to meet individual learning needs, enhance accessibility, and overcome barriers to education. Drawing on case studies and practical examples, the chapter highlights the ability of AI to revolutionize traditional educational models by delivering customized, responsive support for diverse disabilities. Emphasizing the potential of AI to foster equity and inclusion, the chapter underscores its role in advancing opportunities for all learners and creating a more accessible educational landscape.

Chapter 5
Data-Driven Solutions Enhancing Adaptive Education Through
Technological Innovations for Disability Support 101
    Sevinthi Kali Sankar Nagarajan, Independent Researcher, San Antonio,
        USA
    Munikrishnaiah Sundara Ramaiah, Independent Researcher, San
        Antonio, USA
    Pawan Whig, VIPS, India

This chapter explores the transformative role of data-driven solutions in advancing adaptive education for students with disabilities. This chapter examines how advanced data analysis techniques enable the creation of personalized learning environments tailored to individual needs and challenges. Key topics include innovative data collection methods, such as learning analytics and behavioral data, and their application in designing customized educational tools and strategies. The chapter also presents real-world case studies showcasing the successful use of data-driven approaches to enhance accessibility and inclusivity in educational settings. By providing a comprehensive analysis, this chapter underscores the potential of data-driven solutions to improve educational outcomes, foster equity, and create more effective support systems for students with disabilities.

Chapter 6
Assistive Technology and Accessibility Tools in Enhancing Adaptive
Education 125
    Tunde Toyese Oyedokun, Thomas Adewumi University, Oko-Irese,
        Nigeria

The integration of assistive technology and accessibility tools is transforming education for students with disabilities. This chapter examines the development, significance, and future potential of these technologies within adaptive education frameworks. It analyzes tools such as wearable technology, virtual and augmented reality, artificial intelligence, and universal design, highlighting their role in fostering independent learning and personal growth. The discussion includes successful implementation strategies and case studies that demonstrate how assistive technology enhances self-advocacy and participation. Additionally, it addresses challenges, financial, logistical, and attitudinal that hinder adoption, along with proposed solutions. The chapter emphasizes the need for inclusive policies and partnerships to create a sustainable ecosystem for assistive technology deployment, ensuring equitable access to learning materials for all students as these tools evolve.

Chapter 7
The Role of Assistive Technology in Education: A Study of Four SADC
States 163
William Chakabwata, University of South Africa, South Africa

This chapter examines the availability and accessibility of assistive devices and technologies in four Southern African Development Community (SADC) states— Namibia, South Africa, Zambia, and Zimbabwe. While assistive devices hold great potential for enhancing learning and supporting people with disabilities, their accessibility remains limited due to high costs and reliance on imported products. Moreover, the distribution of these devices is predominantly focused in urban areas, leaving individuals with disabilities in rural settings without the essential educational and support tools they need. Grounded in the principles of Ubuntu and intersectionality, this chapter highlights the urgent need for governments to prioritize the development of locally produced assistive technologies. It also advocates increased investment in assistive devices to promote equitable access and advance the realization of inclusive education across the region.

Chapter 8
VR Interventions for Students With Intellectual Disabilities: Innovative
Approaches and Practical Applications 193
Hüseyin Göksu, İstanbul University-Cerrahpaşa, Turkey
Selami Eryilmaz, Gazi University, Turkey

This chapter explores the development and evaluation of a virtual reality (VR) application designed to enhance learning for students with mild intellectual disabilities. The application focuses on teaching eight foundational concepts—"few," "many," "large," "small," "far," "near," "long," and "short"—through an adaptive, sequential learning approach. Each concept is unlocked only after the student demonstrates mastery of the preceding one, ensuring a structured and progressive learning experience. Developed using Unity software, the application leverages immersive technology and was tested with the Oculus Quest 2 headset. A pilot test was conducted at a vocational high school in Antalya with the participation of a student with mild intellectual disabilities under the guidance and supervision of their teachers. The findings contribute to understanding how VR technology can support personalized and accessible education for students with special needs.

Chapter 9

Exploring the Perspectives and Expectations of Special Educational Needs
Coordinators on the Use of Special iApps for Children 215
    Samiullah Paracha, Xi'an Jiaotong-Liverpool University, China
    Lynne Hall, University of Sunderland, UK
    Gillian Hagan-Green, University of Sunderland, UK
    Derek Watson, University of Sunderland, UK

The digitalization of education has significantly transformed special education practices and the roles of Special Education Needs Coordinators (SENCOs). One area of rapid growth is the use of learning applications for children with severe intellectual disabilities, with many apps promising both new ways to engage and educational benefits. Despite this potential, research examining the impact of these tools remains limited. This chapter addresses this gap by exploring SENCOs' perspectives and expectations regarding learning apps, specifically Special iApps, for children with severe intellectual disabilities. Through qualitative research methods and an inductive approach, the study investigates the overarching question: "What do SENCOs perceive and expect from learning apps designed for children with severe intellectual disabilities?" The findings shed light on SENCOs' views on the educational effectiveness of these apps and offer critical recommendations to support the integration of mobile technologies in teaching practices.

Chapter 10

Digital Literacy Among Students With Disabilities in India: Pros and Cons.... 255
    Madhavi Kilaru, VNR Vignana Jyothi Institute of Engineering and
        Technology, India
    Rajasekhara Mouly Potluri, Kazakh-British Technical University,
        Kazakhstan

Digital literacy has emerged as a critical competency in the 21st century, particularly for students with disabilities in India. This chapter explores the unique challenges faced by this group and emphasizes the importance of adopting tailored strategies to integrate technology effectively into their education. Digital literacy empowers students with essential skills, enhancing their learning experiences, fostering independence, and improving access to information and services. Tools such as screen readers, voice recognition software, and accessible internet platforms enable greater engagement in academic and social activities, bridging gaps in learning and providing opportunities for remote education and specialized resources. Despite these advancements, the chapter highlights the significant barriers that persist, as many digital platforms in India remain inaccessible and fail to meet the needs of individuals with disabilities. Addressing these gaps is essential for creating an equitable and inclusive digital learning environment.

Compilation of References 271

About the Contributors 313

Index 323

Foreword

Education is a cornerstone of personal growth, societal progress, and economic development. Yet, for millions of individuals with disabilities, traditional educational systems have often fallen short in providing equitable access to learning opportunities. As the global discourse increasingly shifts toward inclusivity, the role of adaptive education technologies in bridging these gaps has emerged as a critical area of focus. Advancing Adaptive Education: Technological Innovations for Disability Support arrives at a pivotal moment, offering a comprehensive exploration of the transformative potential of technology in fostering inclusivity and equity in education. The book's emphasis on adaptive education and assistive technologies is particularly significant given the rapid pace of technological advancements in recent years. Tools such as artificial intelligence, virtual reality, and data-driven learning systems are no longer futuristic concepts but practical solutions reshaping classrooms and learning experiences. This volume captures the essence of these innovations, providing a roadmap for educators, policymakers, and technologists to harness their potential in addressing the diverse needs of learners with disabilities.

At the heart of this book lies a deep commitment to inclusivity. It goes beyond merely highlighting the possibilities of adaptive technologies and examines the real-world challenges of implementation. From cost barriers and accessibility issues to cultural stigmas and infrastructure limitations, the authors tackle the multifaceted hurdles that hinder the widespread adoption of these tools. By presenting thoughtful strategies and evidence-based recommendations, the book bridges the gap between theory and practice. One of the most striking aspects of this book is its interdisciplinary approach. The authors draw on expertise from education, technology, psychology, and public policy, creating a rich tapestry of perspectives that underscore the complexity of adaptive education. This collaborative effort highlights the importance of collective action in addressing systemic issues and fostering a culture of inclusivity.

The global scope of the book further enhances its relevance. By incorporating case studies and examples from diverse regions, the authors illuminate the universal nature of the challenges faced by learners with disabilities while also showcasing region-specific solutions. Whether discussing virtual reality applications in Europe, assistive technologies in Africa, or data-driven learning systems in Asia, the book offers valuable insights that resonate across contexts. This foreword would be incomplete without acknowledging the ethical considerations that permeate the book. The integration of adaptive technologies into education raises critical questions about data privacy, algorithmic bias, and equitable access. The authors' commitment to addressing these issues reflects a thoughtful and responsible approach to innovation, ensuring that technology serves as a tool for empowerment rather than exclusion.

One of the key strengths of this book is its forward-looking perspective. While it provides a thorough analysis of current practices and challenges, it also envisions a future where adaptive technologies are seamlessly integrated into education systems worldwide. This vision is not just aspirational but grounded in practical steps and actionable recommendations, making it a valuable resource for anyone invested in the future of education. The role of educators is central to the success of adaptive education technologies, and this book does an excellent job of highlighting their contributions. By emphasizing the importance of teacher training and professional development, it ensures that educators are not merely passive recipients of technology but active participants in shaping its use. This empowerment of educators is crucial for creating sustainable and impactful change. As you explore the chapters of Advancing Adaptive Education: Technological Innovations for Disability Support, you will find a wealth of knowledge, inspiration, and practical insights. Each chapter builds on the others, creating a cohesive narrative that underscores the transformative power of technology in education. The authors' passion for their subject matter is evident on every page, making this book not only informative but also deeply engaging.

This book is a timely and significant contribution to the fields of education and technology. It challenges us to rethink traditional approaches to learning and to embrace innovation as a means of achieving equity and inclusivity. For educators, policymakers, researchers, and advocates, this book offers both a call to action and a guide for navigating the evolving landscape of adaptive education. It is my privilege to introduce this inspiring and impactful work, and I hope it serves as a catalyst for positive change in the lives of learners with disabilities around the world.

Adeyemi Abel Ajibesin
Cape Peninsula University of Technology, South Africa

Preface

The field of education is undergoing a transformative evolution, driven by the integration of adaptive technologies and innovative strategies to support learners with disabilities. Advancing Adaptive Education: Technological Innovations for Disability Support presents a comprehensive exploration of how cutting-edge technologies, such as artificial intelligence, virtual reality, and assistive devices, are reshaping educational landscapes to foster inclusion and equity. This book brings together perspectives from researchers, educators, and practitioners across the globe, showcasing diverse approaches to addressing the unique challenges faced by students with disabilities. By delving into interdisciplinary methodologies, case studies, and actionable frameworks, it highlights the potential of technology to bridge accessibility gaps and create empowering learning environments.

The chapters in this volume cover a wide range of topics, from the development of adaptive learning systems to the implementation of assistive technologies in specialized educational settings. Each chapter is grounded in empirical research and enriched with practical insights, making the book an invaluable resource for educators, policymakers, technologists, and advocates of inclusive education. The authors critically examine key issues such as cost, accessibility, and ethical considerations, while also offering forward-looking solutions that emphasize sustainability and collaboration. This multifaceted approach ensures that the book not only addresses current challenges but also provides a roadmap for the future of adaptive education.

As we embark on an era where personalized and inclusive education is more achievable than ever before, Advancing Adaptive Education: Technological Innovations for Disability Support serves as both a call to action and a guide for fostering systemic change. By emphasizing the importance of innovation, equity, and shared responsibility, this book aims to inspire stakeholders across sectors to work together in creating educational systems that empower every learner. Whether you are a seasoned professional or new to the field of adaptive education, this book offers the tools, knowledge, and inspiration needed to make a meaningful impact.

CHAPTER OVERVIEW

In Chapter 1 – Foundations of Adaptive Technologies in Inclusive Education, Eriona Çela, Mathias Fonkam, and Narasimha Rao Vajjhala examine the transformative role of adaptive technologies in fostering inclusivity within educational environments. The chapter explores how adaptive education and assistive technologies work in tandem to address the diverse needs of learners, particularly students with disabilities. By examining the integration of artificial intelligence, adaptive teaching frameworks, and universal design principles, the authors provide a comprehensive understanding of how technology can empower learners while promoting equity and accessibility. The chapter also highlights the critical role of interdisciplinary research and ethical considerations in advancing the implementation of adaptive technologies. Grounded in global and regional perspectives, the authors discuss the key barriers to adopting assistive technologies, including high costs, insufficient training for educators, and cultural stigma. They emphasize the importance of addressing these challenges through targeted policy reforms, investment in infrastructure, and professional development programs. This chapter not only identifies the potential of adaptive technologies to reshape education systems but also advocates for collaborative strategies to create inclusive learning environments. By bridging gaps in accessibility and fostering engagement, the chapter underscores the need for a unified approach to transforming education for all learners.

In Chapter 2 – Artificial Intelligence in Adaptive Education: A Transformative Approach, Sulagna Das, Indranil Mutsuddi, and Nilanjan Ray examine the integration of artificial intelligence (AI) in higher education and its transformative impact on adaptive learning systems. This chapter explores how AI technologies such as machine learning, natural language processing, and adaptive algorithms are reshaping educational practices by enabling personalized learning, providing real-time feedback, and addressing individual student needs. By analyzing adaptive education's key components—content, sequencing, and assessment—the authors demonstrate how AI-driven applications empower educators and institutions to create dynamic, data-driven educational environments. The chapter also discusses critical challenges, including data privacy, implementation costs, and ethical considerations, offering solutions to maximize AI's potential in promoting equitable and inclusive education. Building on the background of adaptive education and the evolution of AI-driven tools, the chapter highlights practical applications such as AI-powered learning management systems, virtual tutoring, and advanced assessment methodologies. These technologies are framed as essential in bridging the gap between traditional pedagogical methods and the demands of the digital era. Through detailed case studies and research, the authors present insights into how adaptive learning frameworks can enhance student engagement, improve learning outcomes, and foster lifelong learning opportunities. This chapter serves as a comprehensive guide for educators, policymakers, and researchers, emphasizing the need for interdisciplinary collaboration and innovative strategies to integrate AI effectively into education systems globally.

In Chapter 3 – Adaptive Learning Technologies in Healthcare Education for Students with Disabilities, Vismaya Annie Vinod, Eriona Çela, and Philip Eappen investigate the integration of adaptive learning technologies into healthcare education to enhance inclusivity and accessibility for students with disabilities. This chapter examines how experiential technologies, such as virtual reality (VR), mixed reality (MR), and augmented reality (AR), can create immersive and interactive learning experiences. By addressing unique challenges like accessibility barriers, disability competency gaps, and inequities in educational opportunities, the authors emphasize the role of artificial intelligence (AI) and machine learning (ML) in developing personalized learning paths. The chapter also explores the use of assistive technologies to improve engagement and accessibility, offering actionable recommendations for educators, policymakers, and healthcare institutions to foster inclusive educational practices. The chapter highlights the ethical considerations tied to the use of adaptive technologies, including data privacy, algorithmic bias, and equitable access, and proposes strategies for their responsible implementation. Through a narrative review of literature, the authors synthesize insights from diverse healthcare contexts across the United States, Canada, and the UAE. By showcasing practical applications and challenges, the chapter provides a roadmap for integrating adaptive learning technologies into healthcare education to address the evolving needs of students with disabilities. The authors advocate for systemic reforms, collaborative efforts, and interdisciplinary research to create an inclusive and supportive learning environment that empowers students and prepares them for leadership roles in healthcare.

In Chapter 4 – AI-Powered Innovations Transforming Adaptive Education for Disability Support, Munikrishnaiah Sundara Ramaiah, Sevinthi Kali Sankar Nagarajan, Pawan Whig, and Pushan Kumar Dutta explore how artificial intelligence (AI) technologies are revolutionizing adaptive education for students with disabilities. The chapter examines the integration of AI-driven tools such as intelligent tutoring systems, speech recognition technologies, and personalized learning algorithms to enhance accessibility and inclusivity in educational practices. Through practical case studies and real-world applications, the authors demonstrate how these technologies are overcoming traditional barriers to education, fostering personalized learning experiences, and empowering educators to better support diverse learners. The chapter emphasizes the critical role of AI in creating equitable and responsive educational environments tailored to individual needs. The authors also address challenges and ethical considerations in implementing AI technologies in adaptive education. They highlight issues such as data privacy, algorithmic bias, and the digital divide, advocating for policies and strategies to mitigate these concerns. By combining technical advancements with an ethical framework, the chapter provides actionable recommendations for educators, policymakers, and researchers aiming to enhance adaptive education systems. Through a balanced discussion of opportunities and challenges, this chapter underscores the transformative potential of AI in fostering inclusive education and bridging gaps in accessibility for students with disabilities.

In Chapter 5 – Data-Driven Solutions: Enhancing Adaptive Education Through Technological Innovations for Disability Support, Sevinthi Kali Sankar Nagarajan, Munikrishnaiah Sundara Ramaiah, and Pawan Whig explore the transformative role of data-driven approaches in advancing adaptive education for students with disabilities. This chapter examines the integration of advanced data analytics and learning technologies to create personalized, inclusive educational experiences tailored to individual student needs. Key focus areas include the use of learning analytics, behavioral data, and artificial intelligence to develop adaptive systems that address challenges in accessibility and engagement. Through real-world case studies, the authors demonstrate how data-driven solutions have successfully improved educational outcomes, particularly for students requiring specialized support. The chapter also examines critical considerations, such as data privacy, ethical use of analytics, and strategies for ensuring equitable access to educational technologies. By highlighting the practical applications of data-driven innovations, the authors provide valuable insights for educators, policymakers, and technologists aiming to enhance inclusivity in educational settings. The chapter emphasizes the potential of combining advanced analytics with assistive technologies to foster more effective learning environments, advocating for systemic reforms and interdisciplinary collaboration to achieve equitable educational opportunities for all students.

In Chapter 6 - Assistive Technology and Accessibility Tools in Enhancing Adaptive Education, Tunde Oyedokun explores the pivotal role of assistive technologies (AT) and accessibility tools in fostering inclusive learning environments. This chapter examines the historical evolution of AT, its categorization into low-tech, mid-tech, and high-tech solutions, and its transformative impact on adaptive education. Through case studies and research, the author highlights how these tools enhance accessibility, self-advocacy, and academic performance for students with disabilities. Challenges such as financial constraints and attitudinal barriers are examined, alongside strategic solutions to overcome these obstacles. The chapter underscores the necessity of collaborative efforts among educators, policymakers, and families to create sustainable ecosystems for AT deployment. By advocating for inclusive policies and leveraging emerging technologies like artificial intelligence, augmented reality, and wearable devices, the author presents a forward-looking perspective on the evolution of adaptive education. The chapter emphasizes the importance of universal design principles and equitable access to AT, illustrating how these tools not only support learners with disabilities but also enrich educational practices for all students. Ultimately, it provides a comprehensive framework for understanding the integration of AT into diverse learning settings, ensuring that education remains accessible, equitable, and transformative.

In Chapter 7 - The Role of Assistive Technology in Education: A Study of Four SADC States, William Chakabwata critically examines the availability and accessibility of assistive technologies across Namibia, South Africa, Zambia, and Zimbabwe. This chapter highlights the transformative potential of assistive devices in supporting individuals with disabilities while addressing the significant barriers posed by high costs, reliance on imported technologies, and limited distribution in rural areas. Drawing on the principles of Ubuntu and intersectionality, the author calls for a shift toward local manufacturing of assistive devices and greater investment in inclusive education infrastructure. The chapter includes detailed case studies from each country, exploring how these technologies are being integrated into educational systems. These examples shed light on the disparities in access and the innovative approaches adopted by communities and organizations. By advocating for sustainable, locally driven solutions, this chapter provides actionable insights for policymakers, educators, and stakeholders committed to advancing inclusive education within the Southern African Development Community (SADC).

In Chapter 8 - VR Interventions for Students with Intellectual Disabilities: Innovative Approaches and Practical Applications, Hüseyin Göksu and Selami Eryilmaz investigates the use of virtual reality (VR) as an educational tool to support students with mild intellectual disabilities. The chapter presents the development and testing of a VR application designed to teach foundational concepts such as "few," "many," "large," and "small" through an adaptive, sequential approach. Leveraging Unity software and the Oculus Quest 2 headset, the application enables students to practice and master these concepts independently, offering repeated practice in immersive settings. The chapter highlights how VR can bridge educational gaps during disruptions like pandemics or natural disasters, empowering both students and parents in the learning process. By examining practical applications and user feedback, the chapter underscores VR's transformative potential in special education. It discusses challenges such as the high cost of VR equipment, technological barriers faced by teachers, and privacy concerns while offering solutions to these issues. The chapter concludes by advocating for the integration of VR into broader educational strategies, emphasizing its ability to create inclusive and engaging learning environments. This work provides educators, researchers, and policymakers with actionable insights into how VR technology can enhance learning outcomes for students with intellectual disabilities.

In Chapter 9, Exploring the Perspectives and Expectations of Special Educational Needs Coordinators on the Use of Special iApps for Children with Severe Intellectual Disabilities, Samiullah Paracha, Lynne Hall, Gill Hagan-Green, and Derek Watson examine the critical role of Special Educational Needs Coordinators (SENCOs) in integrating learning technologies within special education. This chapter focuses on SENCOs' perceptions of Special iApps, a platform designed to aid children with severe intellectual disabilities. Through qualitative research, the authors investigate how these apps are perceived in terms of educational effectiveness, engagement, and accessibility. The chapter highlights the potential of Special iApps to transform learning experiences for children with severe intellectual disabilities, while also addressing barriers such as lack of digital competence and the need for tailored, inclusive designs. Key recommendations include fostering interdisciplinary collaboration to improve app design and implementation and ensuring that SENCOs are equipped with the necessary training to harness digital tools effectively in their teaching practices. By providing a thorough examination of the challenges and opportunities in the digitalization of special education, the authors underscore the importance of play-based and engaging learning technologies for students with severe intellectual disabilities. This chapter serves as a resource for educators, policymakers, and researchers seeking to enhance the accessibility and impact of digital tools in special education settings. It advocates for innovations in the educational technology sector to better cater to the unique learning needs of this population while emphasizing the importance of inclusive practices that empower SENCOs as key stakeholders in advancing disability-inclusive education.

In Chapter 10 - Digital Literacy Among Students with Disabilities in India: Pros and Cons, Madhavi Kilaru and Rajasekhara Mouly Potluri, explore the role of digital literacy in empowering students with disabilities in India. The chapter examines the transformative impact of digital literacy in fostering inclusion, independence, and access to education and employment opportunities. Tools such as screen readers, voice recognition software, and accessible internet platforms are discussed as critical enablers for bridging learning gaps and ensuring equitable access to digital resources. The authors also highlight the significant barriers faced by this group, including inaccessible digital platforms, inadequate training, and financial constraints, while proposing strategies for overcoming these challenges. By addressing the broader context of the Digital India initiative, the chapter connects national efforts to the specific needs of students with disabilities, emphasizing the importance of adaptive technologies and inclusive practices. Case studies, including individual success stories, illustrate how tailored interventions can transform lives, while discussions on systemic barriers shed light on areas for policy improvement. This chapter serves as a valuable resource for educators, policymakers, and technologists seeking to promote digital inclusion and equity in education. It underscores the importance of collaborative efforts and innovative strategies in creating a truly inclusive digital learning environment for students with disabilities in India.

As educational systems worldwide strive to become more inclusive, the role of adaptive technologies in transforming learning for students with disabilities has never been more critical. Advancing Adaptive Education: Technological Innovations for Disability Support underscores the importance of leveraging innovation to address systemic barriers and create equitable opportunities for all learners. By showcasing practical applications, research-driven insights, and diverse global perspectives, this book highlights the progress being made while emphasizing the work that still lies ahead. It is a testament to the power of technology when combined with thoughtful implementation and collaboration among educators, technologists, and policymakers.

We hope this book serves as both a source of inspiration and a guide for those committed to advancing inclusive education. Whether you are an educator seeking new strategies, a researcher exploring adaptive solutions, or a policymaker aiming to foster systemic change, this volume offers a wealth of knowledge and practical insights. As you turn these pages, we invite you to join us in reimagining education for the 21st century—one that celebrates diversity, embraces innovation, and ensures that no learner is left behind. Together, we can build an educational future that is inclusive, empowering, and transformative for all.

Eriona Çela
University of New York Tirana, Albania

Mathias Mbu Fonkam
Pennsylvania State University, USA

Narasimha Rao Vajjhala
University of New York Tirana, Albania

Philip Eappen
Cape Breton University, Canada

Chapter 1
Foundations of Adaptive Technologies in Inclusive Education

Eriona Çela
 https://orcid.org/0000-0003-2710-5489
University of New York Tirana, Albania

Mathias M. Fonkam
 https://orcid.org/0000-0002-2776-1462
Penn State University, USA

Narasimha Rao Vajjhala
 https://orcid.org/0000-0002-8260-2392
University of New York Tirana, Albania

ABSTRACT

This chapter lays the foundation for exploring the transformative potential of adaptive technologies in inclusive education. This chapter examines the principles of adaptive education, emphasizing its role in addressing the diverse needs of learners, particularly students with disabilities. The discussion highlights the integration of assistive technologies and artificial intelligence as critical tools for fostering equity, accessibility, and engagement in educational environments. By addressing key barriers such as cost, accessibility, and teacher preparedness, the chapter advocates for the adoption of innovative and inclusive practices to empower all learners. Grounded in interdisciplinary research and ethical considerations, this chapter sets the stage for understanding how adaptive technologies can reshape education systems to create a more inclusive and equitable future for students worldwide.

DOI: 10.4018/979-8-3693-8227-1.ch001

INTRODUCTION

Adaptive education, commonly referred to as "adaptive teaching" or "adaptive instruction," is an instructional approach that tailors to educational experiences to meet the unique needs of individual learners. Rooted in advancements in technology and cognitive science, adaptive teaching has emerged as a critical aspect of educational innovation. It aims to ensure that all students, especially those on the margins, have equitable access to challenging content, thereby fostering an inclusive learning environment. The importance of adaptive education today cannot be overstated. As highlighted by Annie Jean-Baptiste, Head of Product Inclusion at Google, the proactive inclusion of diverse learners is essential to avoid unintentional exclusion. This approach recognizes that traditional methods often cater to a "middle majority," neglecting those who require additional support. By designing lessons and resources with flexibility, adaptive teaching allows learners to demonstrate their knowledge and skills in ways that resonate with their individual needs.

Inclusion is a central tenet of adaptive education, promoting a sense of belonging among students by considering diversity and equity during the instructional design process. It extends beyond supporting students with Special Educational Needs and Disabilities (SEND), encompassing all learners who may require temporary or permanent adjustments throughout their educational journey. By embedding these supports within the universal educational framework, schools empower students to become more autonomous and self-aware, facilitating self-advocacy and preparing them for future challenges in adulthood. As the prevalence of students with identified SEND continues to rise and becomes increasingly complex, adaptive teaching proves essential in addressing these diverse educational needs. By fostering an environment of belonging and engagement, adaptive education equips all students with the skills and knowledge necessary to thrive in their communities. Ultimately, well-implemented adaptive teaching not only enhances learning outcomes but also promotes a more inclusive and equitable society, preparing future generations for the complexities of modern life.

PRINCIPLES AND ADVANTAGES OF ADAPTIVE EDUCATION AND ASSISTIVE TECHNOLOGY

Assistive technology (AT) serves as a vital resource to enhance the independence and engagement of students with disabilities within educational settings. According to Viner et al., (2019), AT facilitates these children in participating more fully in learning activities alongside their peers, promoting a more inclusive classroom environment. The diverse needs of students with disabilities necessitate careful consideration and selection of appropriate assistive technology devices to support their educational success.

Other studies emphasize that when effectively integrated into the learning process, assistive technology devices can yield significant benefits for students with disabilities, impacting their ability to perform daily tasks. Specifically, technologies such as game-based learning and location-based services can assist users in navigating their environments, thereby enhancing their interaction with the world around them. Similarly, other scholars affirm that AT devices create motivating and constructive environments that promote independence and skill development among students with disabilities. They note that these devices enable children to leverage their strengths, thereby allowing them to overcome obstacles and reach their full potential (Viner et al., 2019).

The principles of adaptive education are paramount in creating opportunities for students with disabilities to succeed academically and transition effectively into postsecondary environments. Different scholars have conducted thorough literature reviews focusing on the use of technology, specifically assistive technology (AT), to facilitate this success. In this regard, it is essential to address funding resources for assistive technology during the transition process. Assistive technology can vary significantly in cost, often becoming a financial barrier for families or educational institutions. Early identification of the necessary devices is crucial to ensure that students have sufficient time for training and adaptation before entering postsecondary education. On the other hand, the selection of appropriate assistive technology should be guided by a comprehensive assessment of individual students' needs and the specific demands of their intended postsecondary environment. This alignment is critical in order to maximize the effectiveness of the technology in supporting student learning. Training in the use of assistive technology is another vital component. Proper training enhances students' educational gains by increasing their proficiency and confidence in utilizing the tools available to them (Alnahdi et al., 2014).

Moreover, the attitude of students towards assistive technology has been shown to influence not only their motivation but also that of their educators, as highlighted by Viner et al., (2019). Cultivating a positive mindset towards technology can significantly enhance the educational experience for both students and teachers, fostering an atmosphere conducive to learning. Therefore, a primary aim of education for students with disabilities should be to ensure their success within inclusive general education classrooms, this requires the provision of environments that empower all students to learn effectively.

Furthermore, the design of assistive technology should adhere to the principles of universal design, as outlined by The Trace Center. These principles advocate for equitable use, flexibility, simplicity, perceptible information, tolerance for error, low physical effort, and appropriate size and space for users. Adopting these principles ensures that assistive devices are accessible and user-friendly for all students, including those with disabilities. Despite these frameworks, several barriers hinder the widespread adoption of technological accommodations among students with disabilities. These include the perception of assistive technology as mere "cognitive prostheses," the high cost and limited availability of devices, abandonment of purchased technology by students, inadequate training, and questions regarding eligibility for assistance. Furthermore, expensive high-tech devices are often less utilized than more affordable low-tech options. Rather than seeking out specialized assistive technology, educators and families should consider leveraging existing general technology to meet the needs of students with disabilities. For instance, devices such as the iPod Touch can serve multiple educational purposes while being significantly more cost-effective than traditional high-tech solutions (Alnahdi et al., 2014).

Creating such positive learning spaces necessitates collaboration among classroom teachers, special education professionals, and educational leaders. Leaders play a crucial role in fostering a culture of diversity and inclusivity, which is essential for the successful integration of students with disabilities. Furthermore, they are involved in crucial decision-making processes related to the development and evaluation of a student's Individualized Education Plan (IEP) and must possess the knowledge and skills necessary for making informed decisions. Effective school leaders and educators should be proficient in several key areas to maximize the impact of assistive technology on learning. These include the ability to define assistive technology, understand applicable laws, participate in IEP teams, recognize available AT devices and services, identify funding sources, provide professional development, and adhere to ethical guidelines.

Importantly, while high-tech assistive devices, like computers and digital technologies, can have a profound effect, they can also be costly. Missteps in device selection can adversely impact a student's learning experience. Experts assert that the appropriateness of an assistive device is heavily dependent on the supporting staff and teachers' understanding, values, and educational philosophies. Thus, ensuring effective selection hinges on comprehensive training and support for those involved in the IEP process. By addressing these multifaceted challenges, educational settings can harness the full potential of assistive technology to benefit students with disabilities, leading to meaningful participation and success in their educational journeys (Viner et al., 2019).

INCLUSIVE EDUCATION AND ITS IMPORTANCE IN INTERCULTURAL VALUES

Inclusive education is an approach that emphasizes accommodating the diverse needs of all students, particularly those with special needs, to ensure their full participation in typical classroom activities. This philosophy encompasses various adaptations within the educational environment, including the integration of technological tools such as word prediction and sound synthesis, which facilitate learning for students facing challenges. As the vision of inclusion evolves, inclusive education focuses not only on removing barriers that hinder learning but also on fostering the holistic development of each student's potential. It prioritizes the accessibility of resources for all learners, recognizing that such adaptations enhance the educational experience not only for those with difficulties but also for their peers. Moreover, the concept of digital inclusion, or e-inclusion, has emerged, highlighting the role of digital technologies in dismantling obstacles to learning. These technologies empower students with disabilities to achieve greater autonomy while promoting collaboration and interaction, leading to enriched learning experiences (Bouajila, 2023).

On the other hand, research indicates that instilling intercultural values is essential for citizens to thrive in a democratic society. By fostering an understanding of diverse cultural experiences, students can enrich their learning and cultivate beneficial social habits and behaviors. This inclusive approach not only supports students' educational journeys but also contributes to a more cohesive school environment where all individuals are respected and valued. Intercultural coexistence is recognized as a necessary and enriching aspect of society. By promoting respect and understanding for others, this coexistence forms the foundation of human rights, which are universally applicable to all individuals, regardless of their cultural, social, or political backgrounds. The United Nations emphasizes that without the recognition of these rights, quality of life is compromised. Human rights, which encompass various values, establish a code of conduct that underpins the dignity of every person. Human rights are traditionally classified into three generations. The first generation consists of civil and political rights that encompass fundamental freedoms, including the rights to life, expression, personal autonomy, and equality. These rights fundamentally support the value of freedom, allowing individuals the authority to act without coercion. The second generation addresses economic, social, and cultural rights, such as the right to education, work, and social security, which are rooted in the values of equality and participation. Equality in this context means treating all individuals without discrimination, while participation emphasizes collaborative engagement in communal endeavors. The integration of intercultural values within inclusive education is essential for addressing cultural diversity in schools. By fostering respect, understanding, and cooperation among students, educational institutions can create a more inclusive and supportive environment, promoting the overall development and well-being of all learners, including those with disabilities. This emphasis on intercultural education not only enriches the educational experience but also prepares students to be responsible, engaged members of a diverse society (Manzano-García & Fernández, 2016).

USAGE OF AI TECHNOLOGIES FOR STUDENTS WITH DISABILITIES

The integration of technology in inclusive classrooms is instrumental in providing students with disabilities (SWD) the necessary support to access the general education curriculum effectively. As middle and high school students face rising academic demands, such as extracting information from textbooks and mastering complex writing skills, the use of technology becomes crucial. Three articles in a recent issue highlight the application of technological interventions in the areas of reading, writing, and note-taking (Boyle & Kennedy, 2019).

The first article explores how augmented reality tools, such as the HP Reveal app, can facilitate reading for students with Autism Spectrum Disorder (ASD) by linking printed words to video content that enhances comprehension and reading fluency. The second article presents technology-based graphic organizers designed to aid students with learning disabilities (LD) and emotional behavioral disorders (EBD) in their writing processes, illustrating how these tools can support various writing genres while fostering self-regulation skills through structured stages of writing. The third article focuses on smartpens, which help students with LD improve their note-taking abilities by recording audio and synchronizing it with written notes, allowing for a more effective review and retention of lecture materials (Boyle & Kennedy, 2019).

Additionally, technology is increasingly recognized for promoting student engagement among SWD. One article discusses the use of the Poll Everywhere app to enhance opportunities for response during lessons, fostering active participation in discussions. Similarly, the MotivAider device is introduced as a tool for increasing positive reinforcement from teachers. The potential of technology extends beyond student interaction, offering teachers insights through tools such as the Classroom Teaching (CT) Scan for real-time feedback on instructional practices (Boyle & Kennedy, 2019).

Key Insights into Adaptive Technologies in Inclusive Education

Adaptive technologies have revolutionized inclusive education by addressing the diverse needs of students with disabilities, enabling them to access equitable learning opportunities. Despite significant advancements, the accessibility and adoption of these technologies remain uneven across regions, as illustrated by global disparities. For example, as shown in Figure 1, North America and Europe report higher access rates to assistive devices (72% and 68%, respectively), compared to Asia (40%), Africa (25%), and Latin America (38%). These differences highlight the challenges faced in regions with limited resources and infrastructure, underscoring the need for targeted interventions to bridge these gaps.

The adoption of assistive devices also varies between high-tech and low-tech solutions, as shown in comparative data. Low-tech devices, such as magnifying glasses and communication boards, are more widely used (60%) than high-tech devices like screen readers and augmented reality tools (40%). This preference reflects the affordability and simplicity of low-tech solutions, particularly in under-resourced settings. However, high-tech solutions offer more advanced capabilities that can significantly enhance learning outcomes when appropriately implemented. Balancing affordability with functionality is a critical factor for increasing the adoption of high-tech assistive technologies globally.

Figure 1. Regional access to assistive technologies in education

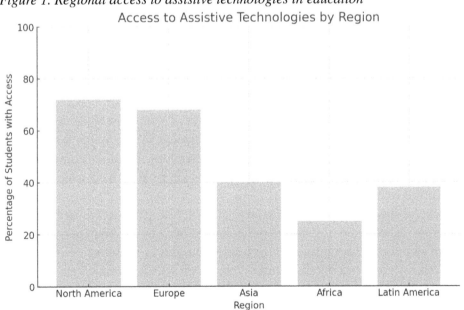

Barriers to the effective use of adaptive technologies are multifaceted, including high costs, insufficient training for educators, and inadequate infrastructure. For instance, the cost of assistive devices often limits their availability to wealthier regions or urban areas, leaving rural communities underserved. Additionally, the lack of professional development programs prevents educators from fully leveraging these technologies to support students with disabilities. Addressing these challenges requires a collaborative effort from governments, educational institutions, and technology providers to invest in capacity building and infrastructure development.

Figure 2 highlights the major barriers to the adoption of assistive technology in education, emphasizing their impact on inclusive education initiatives. Among these barriers, high costs emerge as the most significant, with an impact level of 85%. Assistive devices, particularly high-tech solutions, are often expensive, making them inaccessible to many schools, especially in low-income regions. The financial burden is exacerbated by limited funding allocations for inclusive education, making it difficult for educational institutions and families to afford these technologies. Addressing this issue requires increased government subsidies, the promotion of local production, and partnerships with non-profit organizations to reduce costs.

The lack of educator training is the second-most significant barrier, with an impact level of 70%. Many teachers are unfamiliar with assistive technologies or lack the necessary skills to integrate them effectively into their teaching practices. This gap often results in underutilization or misapplication of available resources, reducing their potential benefits for students with disabilities. Investing in professional development programs is crucial to equipping educators with the knowledge and skills required to maximize the impact of assistive technologies, thereby fostering more inclusive learning environments.

Insufficient infrastructure ranks as the third barrier, with an impact level of 65%. Many schools, particularly in rural or underdeveloped areas, lack the technological infrastructure needed to implement assistive technologies. Issues such as unreliable electricity, limited internet connectivity, and outdated equipment hinder the deployment and use of these tools. Infrastructure investments, such as improving internet access and equipping schools with modern technology, are vital to overcoming this challenge and ensuring that assistive devices can be effectively integrated into educational settings.

Cultural stigma, with an impact level of 50%, also plays a significant role in hindering the adoption of assistive technologies. In many communities, there is a lack of awareness or acceptance of the needs and rights of individuals with disabilities. This stigma not only discourages the use of assistive technologies but also perpetuates exclusion and discrimination. Public awareness campaigns, community engagement initiatives, and inclusive policies can help change societal attitudes, reducing stigma and fostering a more supportive environment for adopting these technologies. Together, these efforts can significantly improve access to and effectiveness of assistive technologies, enhancing learning opportunities for students with disabilities.

Figure 2. Major barriers to assistive technology adoption

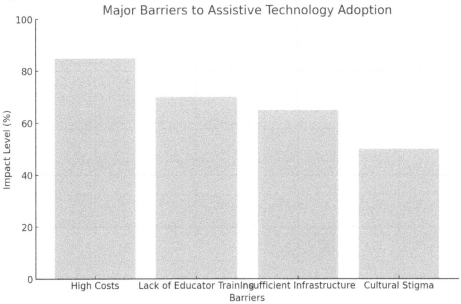

Creating inclusive educational environments demands strategic planning and the integration of universally designed technologies. Universal design principles, such as flexibility, simplicity, and equitable use, can ensure that adaptive technologies are accessible and user-friendly for all learners. These efforts must be supported by policy reforms, increased funding, and public awareness campaigns to reduce stigma and encourage the adoption of inclusive practices. By addressing these systemic barriers, adaptive technologies can play a pivotal role in fostering equity, engagement, and empowerment for students with disabilities, thereby transforming educational systems worldwide.

The heatmap in Figure 3 offers a consolidated visual representation of the major barriers to assistive technology adoption and the disparities in regional access, making it easier to identify patterns and relationships. By using a color gradient, the heatmap effectively conveys the intensity of each variable, with darker shades representing higher values. This intuitive design enables quick comparisons and highlights critical areas requiring intervention. For instance, high costs stand out as the most significant barrier, while Africa and Asia exhibit the lowest levels of access to assistive technologies.

Figure 3. Heatmap of barriers and regional access to assistive technologies

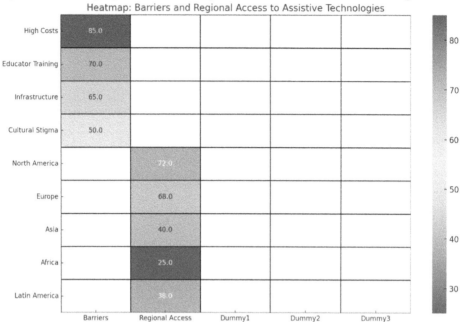

The data on barriers illustrates the substantial impact of systemic challenges such as high costs (85%), lack of educator training (70%), and insufficient infrastructure (65%). These dark-shaded cells emphasize the areas that contribute most to hindering the adoption of assistive technologies. Cultural stigma, while less impactful (50%), still plays a notable role, especially in regions with limited awareness or acceptance of disability rights. The heatmap visually underscores that addressing these barriers is pivotal to creating equitable access to assistive technologies.

In terms of regional access, the heatmap highlights stark disparities across different parts of the world. North America and Europe exhibit relatively high access levels (72% and 68%, respectively), signified by lighter shades, reflecting the availability of resources and supportive policies. Conversely, regions like Africa and Asia show significantly lower access levels (25% and 40%, respectively), represented by darker shades, pointing to systemic inequities such as insufficient funding and infrastructure. Latin America falls somewhere in between, demonstrating moderate access at 38%.

The juxtaposition of barriers and regional access in the heatmap provides a comprehensive view of the intertwined challenges in implementing assistive technologies. It reveals how the barriers disproportionately affect regions with already limited access, further widening the gap in educational opportunities for students with disabilities. This visualization underscores the need for targeted investments in infrastructure, cost reduction strategies, and professional development programs, particularly in under-resourced areas. By addressing these interconnected issues, educational systems can make meaningful strides toward achieving inclusive and equitable learning environments worldwide.

Advantages of Adaptive Learning

Assistive technology plays a critical role in empowering students with disabilities (SWD) to achieve greater independence and active participation in educational settings. By providing tools that enhance mobility, communication, visual, and auditory capabilities, assistive technology fosters greater engagement in learning activities. This not only supports individual rights but also bridges the gap between students with disabilities and their peers, enabling equitable access to educational, social, and recreational opportunities. The implementation of assistive technology has numerous benefits that extend beyond education. It enhances health and mobility, contributes to improved self-esteem, and can lead to reduced costs associated with educational services and personal support. Research has shown a clear correlation between the use of assistive technology and positive outcomes in both educational achievement and socioeconomic status for children with disabilities. Access to personalized learning experiences can significantly reduce the likelihood of school dropout, thereby enhancing employment prospects and decreasing reliance on social welfare systems. Moreover, early provision of assistive technology is crucial, as it can mitigate the development of secondary health conditions and enhance overall well-being. For instance, technologies such as foot orthoses can prevent the need for more invasive medical interventions later in life, showcasing the long-term value of timely support. Additionally, for those unable to attend traditional school settings, assistive technologies, including accessible information and communication technologies (ICTs) and cloud-based services, can provide avenues for remote learning and social interaction. The imperative to provide assistive technology is underscored by the Convention on the Rights of Persons with Disabilities (CRPD), which mandates that States Parties take actionable steps to promote the availability and use of technologies that cater to individuals with disabilities. Specific articles within the CRPD articulate the necessity of inclusive educational practices and reasonable accommodations to support the diverse needs of students. Notably, Article 24 asserts the right to accessible quality education, thereby reinforcing the obligation of governments to facilitate the use of assistive technologies. In summary, assistive technology is an essential component of educational strategies for students with disabilities, fostering independence, enhancing learning opportunities, and aligning with international mandates for inclusivity. Its benefits not only resonate within the classroom but extend into broader societal contexts, making it a fundamental investment in the future of individuals and communities alike (*Assistive Technology for Children with Disabilities*, 2015).

Empowering People with Disabilities Through Artificial Intelligence

The integration of information and communications technology (ICT) into educational strategies is pivotal for fostering social inclusion among students with disabilities. Several methodologies can be effectively implemented in school environments to ensure these students are actively involved in the educational process, enhancing their learning experiences and outcomes.

Firstly, Distance Learning stands out as a prominent approach, offering accessible educational opportunities for students with disabilities. Through distance learning, students can continue their studies from home, enabling them to partake in courses, share materials, collaborate on projects, and engage in presentations without the necessity of physical attendance at educational institutions. The use of computers, which is intrinsic to this format, facilitates a seamless transition into the learning environment, catering specifically to the diverse needs of students with varying disabilities. Another very efficient method can be Digital and Audio Libraries, which serve as another crucial resource for students facing intellectual, auditory, visual, or reading disabilities. These libraries provide access to a wealth of educational materials through digital formats, allowing students to engage with content online. By leveraging the Internet, learners can read or listen to necessary books and resources from home, thereby eliminating barriers associated with physical access to traditional libraries or educational facilities. This innovation is instrumental in providing equitable access to educational opportunities (Eid, n.d.).

Furthermore, the Internet and Broadband Connectivity play a significant role in empowering students with disabilities by facilitating communication and access to information. Through the Internet, students can connect with peers and educators, gather essential public information, engage in leisure activities, and manage day-to-day tasks independently. A reliable broadband connection enhances the ability of these individuals to participate actively in both educational and social contexts, promoting an inclusive environment conducive to independent living. Facilitated Communication is another method that can be implemented since through online platforms it enables students with disabilities to engage with instructors and peers effectively. Many learners, particularly those with mobility impairments or hearing difficulties, may encounter challenges in managing synchronous communication during online courses. To address these issues, course moderators or facilitators play an essential role in guiding discussions, clarifying information, and ensuring that all participants comprehend the content being presented. This supportive structure enhances the learning experience for students, ensuring that the communication barriers do not hinder their educational engagement (Eid, n.d.).

Implementing diverse methods of distance learning, such as digital libraries, Internet access, facilitated communication, and dedicated support centers, creates a more inclusive educational framework for students with disabilities. By prioritizing these approaches, educational institutions can foster greater engagement and academic success for all students, ensuring that barriers to learning are effectively addressed.

Future Challenges of Adaptive Technologies for Students With Disabilities

The adoption of adaptive technologies in educational settings for students with disabilities faces several significant challenges that must be addressed for successful implementation and efficacy. These challenges, elaborated upon by leading researchers in the field, include practical and technical hurdles related to developing accurate learner models, acquiring valid learner data, maximizing benefits while minimizing costs, managing learner control and privacy concerns, and addressing the requisite bandwidth for capturing learner interactions.

One of the core challenges lies in the creation of useful learner models (LMs). Experts like Judy Kay highlight the necessity of harnessing the vast amounts of learning trace data, which are currently underutilized within individual learning tools. Transforming this data into meaningful LMs involves interpreting the information to derive insights about learners' knowledge and preferences. This interpretation requires augmenting existing data with a knowledge layer that connects evidence from trace data to inferences about learner characteristics (Shute & Zapata-Rivera, 2012).

Acquiring reliable data from learners presents another obstacle, particularly when relying on self-reports. Such reports can be prone to inaccuracies due to deliberate misrepresentation or unintentional errors. Addressing these issues might involve creating separate views of the LMs and developing reconciliation mechanisms to integrate diverse learner perspectives. While gathering valid data could enhance diagnostic accuracy and foster greater learner agency, the imposition of additional data collection during learning can also lead to frustration and disengagement (Bouajila, 2023). The high costs associated with developing and deploying adaptive technologies, contrasted with unclear returns on investment, pose practical challenges for their integration. The lack of controlled evaluations exacerbates this issue, necessitating a focus on identifying specific contexts that require adaptation. Jameson suggests aligning adaptivity with cases where learners lack the familiarity or resources necessary for effective content selection, thereby enhancing the perceived value of adaptive systems (Alnahdi et al., 2014).

Learners often seek control over their educational experiences, which necessitates a careful balance between system-driven adaptations and learner agency. Strategies that invite learner participation in decision-making can alleviate concerns about feeling monitored or controlled. Furthermore, transparency is essential in managing data privacy, as adaptive systems may otherwise appear obtrusive. Implementing transparent mechanisms enables learners to understand and scrutinize how their data is managed and interpreted (Boyle & Kennedy, 2019). The capability to capture a comprehensive range of learner characteristics through interactions is hindered by bandwidth limitations. This encompasses both the volume and relevance of data transmitted over time. Although historic challenges associated with bandwidth persist, the current trend indicates increased interaction with technology by learners, facilitating the potential for richer data acquisition. Researchers like McCalla argue for adaptive systems that understand learners' evolving knowledge and motivations in real time, thus promoting ongoing adaptability (Shute & Zapata-Rivera, 2012). The future of AI adoption in education for students with disabilities hinges on overcoming these intertwined challenges, ensuring that adaptive technologies are effectively implemented and oriented around the unique needs of learners. Doing so will require a concerted effort from researchers, educators, and technologists to develop frameworks that prioritize accuracy, accessibility, privacy, and engagement in adaptive learning environments.

ETHICAL CONSIDERATIONS

The integration of AI into educational curricula for students with disabilities necessitates a rigorous examination of ethical considerations to safeguard the interests of all stakeholders involved. While AI technology is not yet capable of replicating human consciousness, ethical issues surrounding its application are pressing. Concerns arise over potential infringements on laws and the risks associated with AI-driven assessments, which may inadvertently reinforce systemic inequalities and discrimination against marginalized learner groups. As highlighted by Lim et al., (2023) as the likelihood of ethical missteps amplifies, there is an urgent need for the educational technology sector, including schools and educators, to focus on developing frameworks for ethical AI in learning contexts. Prioritizing ethical practices is essential to ensure the well-being and equitable treatment of students with disabilities, who may be particularly vulnerable to these risks.

The exploration of ethics in the adoption of AI in education can be understood through various philosophical lenses, including normative ethics, deontological ethics, and virtue ethics. Normative ethics provides the framework for establishing moral rules and standards that govern behavior in educational environments, ensuring fairness and equity are prioritized. Deontological ethics emphasizes the rights and duties of individuals, underscoring the importance of safeguarding privacy and aiming for unbiased educational practices. It positions moral obligation as a cornerstone of ethical decision-making in AI implementations. Conversely, virtue ethics focuses on the character and practical wisdom of stakeholders, positing that the cultivation of moral integrity leads to better ethical choices. Given the complexities of value plurality, ethics training for educators and technology implementers becomes critical to fostering an environment of phronesis, or practical wisdom, enabling them to navigate the challenges posed by AI-driven assessments effectively. Thus, a comprehensive ethical framework that encompasses these various dimensions is crucial for responsibly integrating AI into educational curricula for students with disabilities while ensuring equity, dignity, and respect for all learners (Lim et al., 2023).

CONCLUSION

In conclusion, the integration of adaptive education, assistive technology, and artificial intelligence within the educational curricula for students with disabilities represents a pivotal advancement towards achieving equity and inclusivity in learning environments. Adaptive education is not merely an instructional method; it is a commitment to recognizing and addressing the diverse needs of all learners, particularly those who are often marginalized. By tailoring educational experiences to each student's unique requirements and providing essential support through technologies such as assistive devices and AI-driven tools, educators can foster environments that not only enhance individual academic success but also promote a sense of belonging among peers. Moreover, the principles of universal design, which advocate for equitable and accessible instructional materials, further bolster the efficacy of these strategies, allowing students with disabilities to engage meaningfully in their education and prepare for future challenges.

However, the ethical implications of implementing AI and adaptive technologies must be critically examined to mitigate risks associated with systemic bias, discrimination, and privacy infringements. Establishing ethical frameworks guided by normative, deontological, and virtue ethics is crucial to ensuring that these innovations are harnessed responsibly and equitably. Educators and stakeholders must receive training that equips them with practical wisdom to navigate the ethical landscape of adaptive education and AI, thereby ensuring that the needs and rights of students with disabilities are prioritized. Thus, while the potential of adaptive technologies to transform educational experiences is significant, it is imperative that such innovations are developed and implemented with a keen focus on ethical considerations that uphold the dignity and well-being of all learners. By doing so, we can create a more inclusive and just educational system that empowers every student to realize their full potential.

REFERENCES

Alnahdi, G., Dean, V., & Box, P. O. (2014). Assistive technology in special education and the universal design for learning. *The Turkish Online Journal of Educational Technology*, 13(2), 18–23.

Assistive technology for children with disabilities: Creating opportunities for education, inclusion and participation: A discussion paper. (2015). UNICEF & WHO.

Bouajila, A. (2023). Technological innovation at the service of the educational inclusion of children with disabilities: Digital education. *International Journal of Disability and Education*, 1(1), 1–15.

Boyle, J. R., & Kennedy, M. J. (2019). Innovations in classroom technology for students with disabilities. *Intervention in School and Clinic*, 55(2), 67–70. DOI: 10.1177/1053451219837716

Eid, N. (n.d.). *Innovation and technology for persons with disabilities*. Retrieved from. [https://www.un.org/esa/socdev/egms/docs/2013/ict/innovation-technology-disability.pdf]

Lim, T., Gottipati, S., & Cheong, M. L. F. (2023). Ethical considerations for artificial intelligence in educational assessments. In Keengwe, J. (Ed.), (pp. 32–79). Advances in educational technologies and instructional design. IGI Global., DOI: 10.4018/979-8-3693-0205-7.ch003

Manzano-García, B., & Fernández, M. T. (2016). The inclusive education in Europe. *Universal Journal of Educational Research*, 4(2), 383–391. DOI: 10.13189/ujer.2016.040210

Shute, V. J., & Zapata-Rivera, D. (2012). Adaptive educational systems. In Durlach, P. J., & Lesgold, A. M. (Eds.), *Adaptive technologies for training and education* (1st ed., pp. 7–27). Cambridge University Press., DOI: 10.1017/CBO9781139049580.004

Viner, M., Singh, A., & Shaughnessy, M. F. (2019). Assistive technology to help students with disabilities. In Singh, A., Viner, M., & Yeh, C. J. (Eds.), *Advances in early childhood and K-12 education* (pp. 240–267). IGI Global., DOI: 10.4018/978-1-7998-1431-3.ch012

ADDITIONAL READING

Ingavélez-Guerra, P., Robles-Bykbaev, V. E., Perez-Muñoz, A., Hilera-González, J., & Otón-Tortosa, S. (2022). Automatic adaptation of open educational resources: An approach from a multilevel methodology based on students' preferences, educational special needs, artificial intelligence and accessibility metadata. *IEEE Access : Practical Innovations, Open Solutions*, 10, 9703–9716. DOI: 10.1109/ACCESS.2021.3139537

Istenic Starcic, A., & Bagon, S. (2014). ICT-supported learning for inclusion of people with special needs: Review of seven educational technology journals, 1970–2011. *British Journal of Educational Technology*, 45(2), 202–230. DOI: 10.1111/bjet.12086

Moltudal, S. H., Krumsvik, R. J., & Høydal, K. L. (2022, February). Adaptive learning technology in primary education: Implications for professional teacher knowledge and classroom management. [). Frontiers Media SA.]. *Frontiers in Education*, 7, 830536. DOI: 10.3389/feduc.2022.830536

Şahin, F., Kızılaslan, A., & Şimşek, Ö. (2024). Factors influencing the acceptance of assistive technology by teacher candidates in the context of inclusive education and special needs students. *Education and Information Technologies*, 29(10), 12263–12288. DOI: 10.1007/s10639-023-12383-3

Valeriaa Caretti, A., & Marije, N. (2024). Assessing Cognitive Flexibility: Quantitative Insights into the Impact of Adaptive Learning Technologies in Special Education. *International Journal of Religion*, 5(10), 1040–1054. DOI: 10.61707/phnszh92

KEY TERMS AND DEFINITIONS

Adaptive Education: An instructional approach that customizes learning experiences to meet the diverse needs of individual students, fostering inclusivity and equity in education.

Assistive Technology (AT): Tools or devices designed to support individuals with disabilities in performing tasks, enhancing their independence and learning outcomes.

Cultural Stigma: Negative societal attitudes and misconceptions about disabilities that hinder the acceptance and use of assistive technologies.

Inclusive Education: An educational philosophy and practice that ensures all students, regardless of abilities or disabilities, have equal access to learning opportunities.

Interdisciplinary Research: Collaborative studies that integrate methods and insights from multiple disciplines to address complex challenges, such as inclusive education.

Low-Tech Solutions: Simple and cost-effective tools, such as communication boards or magnifying glasses, used to support students with disabilities.

Universal Design: A framework for creating educational environments and tools that are accessible and usable by all individuals, regardless of their abilities.

High-Tech Devices: Advanced technologies, such as screen readers, augmented reality tools, and smartpens, used to provide specialized support for students with disabilities.

Teacher Training: Professional development programs that equip educators with the skills and knowledge to effectively integrate adaptive technologies into classrooms.

Equity in Education: Ensuring that all students, particularly those with disabilities, have the necessary resources and opportunities to achieve their full potential.

Chapter 2
Artificial Intelligence in Adaptive Education:
A Transformative Approach

Sulagna Das
https://orcid.org/0000-0003-4683-453X
JIS University, India

Indranil Mutsuddi
https://orcid.org/0000-0002-4202-8744
JIS University, India

Nilanjan Ray
https://orcid.org/0000-0002-6109-6080
JIS University, India

ABSTRACT

Integrating artificial intelligence (AI) in higher education has revolutionized how institutions design and enhance learning systems. Higher education institutions (HEIs) increasingly leverage adaptive learning techniques to create dynamic and personalized educational environments. These methods use teaching and learning data to tailor educational experiences to meet each student's unique needs and capabilities. AI-driven applications are at the core of this transformation, offering significant advantages such as improved learning experiences, flexible scheduling, immediate feedback, personalized educational management, and accelerated student progress. This chapter examines the multifaceted dimensions of adaptive learning within the education system, emphasizing the pivotal role of AI-driven technologies in enabling and advancing this innovative approach.

DOI: 10.4018/979-8-3693-8227-1.ch002

INTRODUCTION

The swift advancement of artificial intelligence (AI) technologies, especially generative AI, is transforming the global workforce and leading to significant changes in online and adult learning (OAL) practices (Costin et al., 2023; Goel et al., 2024; Holmes & Littlejohn, 2024; Shrivastava, 2023). The education system continues to rely on outdated methods. Despite flaws in current grading systems, the integration of AI tools and technology promises to initiate a new era of automation. AI has revolutionized education by enhancing personalized learning experiences, automating administrative tasks, and providing data-driven insights. AI-powered tools tailor content to individual student needs, offer adaptive tutoring, and introduce a range of innovations in educational technology (Chukhlomin, 2024). Educators should explore digital transformation strategies to effectively incorporate AI technologies and achieve the desired outcomes. Let's explore some of the primary applications of AI in education (Vincent-Lancrin & van der Vlies, 2020). Additionally, AI aids educators by managing administrative duties, optimizing schedules, and identifying students who may be at risk. Building on this understanding, this chapter aims to examine and discuss the different aspects of adaptive learning practices in contemporary education and the impact of artificial intelligence (AI)-driven technologies on these practices. It will provide valuable insights for educators and education policymakers to develop effective strategies for transforming the current education system to meet digital age demands.

Background of the Study: Adaptive Education

Adaptive education represents a pedagogical approach that leverages data to tailor learning experiences to the individual requirements and capabilities of each student. This methodology is frequently implemented in online and blended educational environments. Adaptive learning systems employ algorithms and advanced technologies to monitor various data points concerning students, including their progress, engagement levels, and performance metrics ("What is Adaptive Learning?", 2024). Subsequently, these systems utilize this data to personalize learning experiences by modifying the content, sequence, and assessments specific to each learner. For instance, the system may adjust the pace or complexity of practice exercises and assessments or incorporate additional resources to enhance areas of learning. Furthermore, it may offer timely feedback and guided pathways to assist students in addressing their distinct needs. Adaptive learning has the potential to empower educators in refining their instructional strategies and enriching the learning experiences of their students (Sharma, 2024). Research indicates that adaptive learning methodologies can yield significant advantages, such as increased pass rates, reduced dropout rates, and enhanced performance outcomes.

There exists a multitude of methodologies to assess learner behaviors and performance to effectively tailor courseware. These methodologies are referred to as adaptively factors — encompassing performance (the actions of the student and their historical performance), knowledge level (previously acquired or recently obtained), content preferences, misconceptions, demographic information, or various other data sources. Educational technology has the capacity to customize learning experiences for everyone based on an array of these factors. Adaptive factors can elicit distinct responses by employing various adaptive types. Depending on the student's learning history, should you advance them according to the established plan, help, or completely alter their learning trajectory? There are numerous strategies to cultivate an exceptional adaptive learning experience. Here are several instances of adaptive factors and categories of adaptability:

Adaptivity Factors: Learner information/profile, behaviors, and performance metrics that can be utilized to tailor a learning experience, for instance.
- *Performance:* Was the response accurate or inaccurate? How has the learner performed across a series of activities/lessons?
- *Behaviors:* What duration did the learner require to complete the task?
- *Information:* Learners may communicate their confidence levels regarding the material, preferences for content types, or personal data to influence subsequent actions.

Categories of Adaptability: The methods by which the lesson can be modified in response to the learner's performance. For instance:
- *Real-time Feedback:* Provide timely assistance when it is most crucial, such as offering hints related to identified misconceptions (akin to students receiving guidance from a tutor supervising their work).
- *Differentiated Pathways:* Present diverse sequences of content tailored to each student, for example, supplying additional support to a student for a specific concept prior to advancing to the subsequent topic, accelerating the progress of advanced learners, or permitting learners to determine their next area of study.

The domain of Adaptive Learning can be categorized into three distinct components: adaptive content, adaptive sequencing, and adaptive assessment:
- *Adaptive Content*: When a learner provides an answer to a question, the system delivers tailored feedback based on their specific response (e.g., hints, supplementary materials pertaining to the relevant skill, additional scaffolding) while maintaining the established sequence of

skills. This represents an enhancement over merely marking responses as correct or incorrect without providing an explanation.
- *Adaptive Sequence*: The process involves the continuous collection and analysis of student data to dynamically adjust the content presented to the learner; this includes modifications to the sequence of skills a student engages with as well as the type of material they receive.
- *Adaptive Assessment*: The method entails modifying the questions presented to a student based on their responses to prior questions. The complexity of the questions will escalate as a student demonstrates accuracy, whereas if the student encounters difficulties, the questions will become simpler. This approach is frequently employed to evaluate student comprehension or progress.

Adaptive Technology plays an important role in enhancing educational experience and broadening learning opportunities. It is improbable that class sizes will diminish, and it is equally improbable that educators will be able to provide individualized guidance to every student facing difficulties during each demanding lesson — this is where adaptive technology plays a pivotal role. Educators and instructional designers have the capability to formulate engaging, tailored learning experiences that accommodate varying educational requirements, ensuring that both at-risk and advanced learners receive the requisite attention consistently. This technology can be utilized to disseminate introductory resources, preparatory assignments, remedial instruction, case studies, and investigations of both novel and established concepts. When implemented with meticulousness and consideration, adaptive learning technology broadens an instructor's ability to enhance educational outcomes for every individual student. Education has evolved into a lifelong endeavor, pursued both formally and informally. It encompasses a wide array of learning experiences, including institution-based education, online courses, ongoing professional development, vocational training, and personal interests. Crafting adaptive learning experiences empowers learners to persist in their studies, obtain feedback, and navigate complex content even in the absence of immediate instructor support. Moreover, students are afforded the chance to take ownership of their learning journey, explore distinct learning pathways, and progress at their own pace.

Role of AI in Adaptive Education

Educational technologies harness artificial intelligence and adaptive learning algorithms to evaluate learners' performance and provide tailored feedback and recommendations (Akavova et al, 2023). This method helps identify areas for improvement and personalize learning experiences. Adaptive learning and artificial intelligence (AI) have emerged as transformative elements in education, radically altering traditional teaching approaches. Artificial Intelligence (AI) is transforming education by offering innovative tools and approaches for teaching and learning. "AI-driven adaptive learning functions akin to a dedicated tutor for each learner, steering them through their academic journey with tailored assistance and constructive feedback." AI algorithms facilitate adaptive learning by examining extensive datasets to discern patterns and trends in students' learning behaviors ("How does AI Impact on Education?", 2024). These algorithms subsequently utilize this information to forecast students' future performance and to propose tailored learning trajectories. For instance, if a student encounters difficulties with a specific concept, the AI system can offer supplementary practice problems or resources to assist them in mastering the content (Hwang et al., 2020; Moreno-Guerrero et al., 2020; Papamitsiou et al., 2018). AI-driven adaptive learning employs a diverse array of methodologies and techniques to customize the educational experience for each individual learner. Below are several prevalent methodologies:

Machine Learning Algorithms: Machine learning algorithms are employed to scrutinize data concerning students' learning behaviors, preferences, and performance metrics. These algorithms possess the capability to discern patterns and trends within the data, thereby enabling the formulation of predictions about students' future performance and the recommendation of tailored learning pathways.

Natural Language Processing (NLP): Natural Language Processing is utilized to evaluate students' written or verbal responses to inquiries and assignments. This facilitates the system's capacity to gauge students' comprehension of the material and furnish individualized feedback.

Bayesian Knowledge Tracing: Bayesian knowledge tracing represents a methodology employed to model the evolution of students' mastery of concepts over time. It leverages probabilistic models to monitor students' progress and modify the educational experience in accordance with their current knowledge state.

Cognitive Modeling: Cognitive modeling algorithms replicate the intricate cognitive mechanisms associated with the learning process to forecast the optimal learning modalities for students. By emulating the variances in individual learning styles and strategies, these algorithms are capable of offering tailored recommendations pertaining to educational activities.

Adaptive Assessment Algorithms: Adaptive assessment algorithms modulate the complexity of inquiries in accordance with the responses provided by students. This mechanism guarantees that each learner encounters challenges commensurate with their abilities and assists in pinpointing specific areas where additional academic support may be requisite.

Affective Computing: Affective computing algorithms assess students' emotional conditions by interpreting their facial expressions, gestures, or various physiological indicators. Such data can be leveraged to customize the educational experience by modifying the pace or content of instruction in alignment with the emotional states of students.

These methodologies collaboratively engender a personalized and adaptive learning environment (Gransden, et al, 2024) that caters to the distinct requirements of each student, ultimately fostering enhanced educational outcomes and heightened engagement. Adaptive learning systems grounded in artificial intelligence can be delineated into various categories, each embodying a unique methodology for tailoring the educational experience. The following enumerates some prevalent forms of AI-based adaptive learning:

o **Knowledge Tracing:** Algorithms designed for knowledge tracing meticulously monitor students' interactions with educational resources to deduce their present knowledge state. Informed by these deductions, the system is capable of offering personalized suggestions for subsequent study or remediation.
o **Content Sequencing:** Algorithms that govern content sequencing ascertain the sequence in which educational materials are dispensed to learners, predicated on their academic progression and performance metrics. This methodology guarantees that students encounter the appropriate material at an optimal temporal juncture.
o **Personalized Feedback:** Artificial intelligence algorithms possess the capability to scrutinize students' answers to inquiries and assignments, thereby supplying tailored feedback. Such feedback serves to elucidate students' errors and facilitates a more effective learning process.
o **Cognitive Modeling:** Algorithms focused on cognitive modeling emulate the cognitive processes integral to learning, enabling predictions regarding the most effective learning strategies for individual students. By accounting for variances in learning styles and methodologies, these algorithms can proffer personalized recommendations for educational activities.
o **Natural Language Processing (NLP):** NLP algorithms are adept at analyzing students' written or verbal responses to questions, facilitating an assessment of their comprehension of the subject matter. This capability aids in customizing the educational experience to rectify specific misconceptions or knowledge deficiencies.

These instances represent merely a subset of the various AI-based adaptive learning strategies that are currently being innovated and implemented within the educational sector. As advancements in artificial intelligence continue to unfold, one can anticipate the emergence of increasingly sophisticated and individualized adaptive learning systems, thereby further transforming pedagogical practices and learning outcomes. The efficacy of AI-driven adaptive learning is fundamentally rooted in its capacity to customize the educational journey for each individual learner. The following delineates several pivotal dimensions of its efficacy:

o **Personalization:** AI-driven adaptive learning possesses the capability to customize the educational experience in accordance with the distinct needs, preferences, and competencies of each learner. This tailored methodology has the potential to yield enhanced educational outcomes and foster greater engagement.

o **Accessibility:** Adaptive learning is especially advantageous for learners with specific needs or learning disabilities, as it can furnish bespoke support and accommodations to address their individual requirements.

o **Data-Driven Insights:** Adaptive learning systems generate a substantial corpus of data pertaining to students' learning behaviors, which can be utilized to discern patterns and trends in both learning and pedagogical practices. Such data can inform enhancements to the curriculum, instructional methodologies, and educational resources.

o **Engagement:** Adaptive learning can sustain learner engagement by offering a customized educational experience that aligns with their interests and competencies. This alignment can culminate in elevated levels of motivation and satisfaction with the educational endeavor.

o **Scalability:** AI-driven adaptive learning can be expanded to serve large cohorts of learners, rendering it a financially viable solution for delivering personalized education on a broad scale.

o **Continuous Improvement:** Adaptive learning systems are capable of continual adaptation and enhancement predicated on feedback from both learners and educators. This iterative refinement can contribute to ongoing advancements in the effectiveness of the educational experience.

In addition, the efficacy of AI-driven adaptive learning is predicated on its capacity to deliver personalized, efficient, and effective educational experiences that empower students to realize their utmost potential. Despite the numerous advantages associated with AI-driven adaptive learning, there exist challenges and considerations that warrant attention. These encompass:

- o **Privacy Concerns:** Adaptive learning systems accumulate extensive data on learners, engendering apprehensions regarding privacy and data security.
- o **Implementation Costs:** The deployment of AI-driven adaptive learning systems may incur significant expenses, necessitating investment in technology, training, and infrastructure.
- o **Equity:** There exists a potential risk that adaptive learning systems could exacerbate pre-existing disparities in education, as learners with access to superior technology or resources may gain an advantage over their counterparts.

AI Powered Learning Tools

The advent of AI has fundamentally transformed the educational landscape, leading to a paradigm shift in the methodologies through which students engage with and assimilate knowledge, thereby significantly enriching their overall learning experiences in a multitude of ways that were previously unimaginable. By leveraging sophisticated machine learning algorithms, AI possesses the remarkable capability to tailor educational content and experiences to align with the distinct needs of individual learners (Kabudi, et al, 2021), thereby offering personalized learning pathways that are meticulously designed to accommodate their unique learning preferences and requirements. Beyond the provision of customized instructional methodologies, AI-driven tools have also succeeded in making educational resources more universally accessible than ever before, allowing students who experience disabilities or who possess varying learning styles to take full advantage of AI-powered assistive technologies that deliver specifically tailored support and necessary accommodations conducive to their success.

Furthermore, AI harbors the potential to significantly enhance student engagement and intrinsic motivation, as evidenced by the emergence of virtual tutors that are powered by AI technology and capable of interacting with students, offering them personalized feedback and guidance that fosters deeper understanding and mastery of the subject matter. However, it is essential to acknowledge that despite the immense promise and transformative potential that AI holds within the realm of education, it is imperative that it does not supplant the irreplaceable role of human educators. The function of teachers remains a cornerstone of the educational process, as they are instrumental in guiding and mentoring students, nurturing critical thinking abilities, and providing crucial emotional support that is vital for holistic development. AI should be conceptualized as a powerful adjunct that complements and enriches the educational experience, rather than a mere substitute for the invaluable human interactions that underpin effective teaching and learning practices. AI technologies have indeed revolutionized the educational domain by facilitating personalized learning experiences for students, enhancing accessibility to educational materials, and significantly boosting student engagement levels through interactive and responsive tools. As advancements in AI technology continue to progress at a remarkable pace, the future of education is imbued with substantial promise and potential, as it evolves and adapts to meet the ever-changing and diverse needs of the student population in a dynamic educational landscape.

One of the most significant advantages that artificial intelligence (AI) brings to the educational landscape is its highly specialized and targeted approach to instruction, which is tailored to meet the unique needs of individual learners. In contrast, traditional educational environments often find themselves grappling with the challenge of addressing the wide-ranging and diverse learning requirements of their student bodies, which can lead to a one-size-fits-all approach that may not benefit every learner. Nevertheless, the advent of AI technologies has revolutionized this dynamic, allowing students to engage with and comprehend intricate concepts in a manner that is both effective and self-paced, thereby fostering a deeper understanding of the material presented.

The remarkable adaptive capabilities inherent in AI algorithms empower students to receive customized instructional experiences, which are designed to ensure that they have a comprehensive understanding of the subject matter before progressing to more advanced topics. This personalized pedagogical approach has been empirically demonstrated to yield substantial improvements in both academic performance and retention rates among students, as they are able to master content at a rhythm that suits their individual learning trajectories. Moreover, the incorporation of AI into educational frameworks holds considerable promise for enhancing levels of student engagement and motivation, which are crucial elements in the learning process. For instance, virtual tutoring systems that are powered by artificial intelligence can facilitate interactive dialogues with students, providing them with personalized feedback and insightful guidance tailored to their specific educational needs and challenges. An AI-driven tutoring platform for students has the inherent capability to modify its instructional techniques to align with the distinct learning styles and preferences of each individual, thereby transforming the educational experience into one that is not only more engaging but also considerably more enjoyable for learners. By integrating interactive components, such as gamification and virtual reality technologies, AI can cultivate immersive learning experiences that effectively capture the attention of students, while simultaneously instilling a genuine passion for learning and exploration in their academic pursuits. Students now have access to a variety of AI technologies that are specifically made to help them on their educational adventures. These AI learning aids for pupils not only improve the educational process but also offer insightful analysis and individualized assistance. In order to help you select the ideal AI tools for your requirements, let's examine some of the most widely used categories of AI tools for students:

AI-Enhanced Learning Management Systems (LMS): The emergence of AI-enhanced Learning Management Systems has fundamentally transformed the manner in which students engage with educational content and evaluate their academic progress through assessments. These innovative systems employ sophisticated artificial intelligence algorithms that meticulously analyze a vast array of student performance data, ultimately yielding actionable insights that can inform both teaching and learning strategies. By leveraging the capabilities afforded by machine learning algorithms, Learning Management Systems are now equipped to recommend personalized learning resources that are specifically tailored to meet the unique needs of each learner, simultaneously identifying and emphasizing areas where students may require additional practice or support, all while continuously tracking their progress over extended periods of time. This sophisticated approach enables students to experience a more individualized and effective learning journey that is customized to their particular strengths and weaknesses, thereby fostering a deeper understanding of the material.

AI-Driven Tutoring Technologies for Students: The utilization of virtual tutors powered by artificial intelligence has witnessed a significant surge in popularity among students seeking additional academic support. These AI-driven tutoring technologies serve as personalized mentors, delivering customized lessons, providing detailed explanations, and offering constructive feedback designed to enhance the learning process. Through the careful analysis of student responses and ongoing progress, AI tutors possess the capability to pinpoint areas where learners may require extra assistance and subsequently deliver targeted support that addresses those specific needs.

AI Innovations in Language Acquisition: Acquiring proficiency in a new language presents a myriad of challenges; however, the advent of AI innovations has rendered this process significantly more accessible and engaging for learners of all ages. Contemporary AI technologies are being harnessed to create interactive language learning experiences that captivate and motivate students. These advanced tools are capable of: Simulating authentic conversations that mimic real-life interactions, Analyzing and providing feedback on pronunciation to enhance speaking skills, Adapting lessons in real-time based on individual progress and performance metrics.

AI technologies are being utilized in education more and more for creative purposes. AI chatbots provide students with immediate assistance, speeding up response times and increasing accessibility. Large-scale educational data can be analyzed by AI algorithms to find patterns and trends that improve teaching methods. AI tools have endless potential in education as technology advances. These resources support students on their educational journeys and give teachers the tools they need to design individualized learning spaces. Even with today's tools, learning experiences can be transformed to provide better outcomes more quickly and readily. Herein lies a meticulously curated list of recommendations for ten of the most exceptional artificial intelligence tools that have been specifically designed to assist students in their academic endeavors:

Grammarly: Grammarly is an advanced writing assistant that operates on the principles of artificial intelligence, which aids students in honing and refining their writing capabilities to a greater extent than they might have previously thought possible. This innovative tool possesses the remarkable ability to identify and rectify a myriad of errors related to grammar, spelling, punctuation, and stylistic inconsistencies in real time, thereby providing immediate feedback that is invaluable. As such, this resource proves to be particularly beneficial for students engaged in the composition of essays, term papers, and various other academic assignments that require meticulous attention to detail and clarity of expression.

Syntea: Syntea is an innovative tool that harnesses the power of artificial intelligence and has been developed by the esteemed IU International University of Applied Sciences for the express purpose of assisting students in their educational journeys. Available in English across all courses, this groundbreaking advancement in the realm of online education allows students to tailor their study experiences to align with their individual needs at any given moment, thereby maximizing the efficacy of their learning efforts through the utilization of cutting-edge technological advancements. As a student at IU, one can capitalize on the advantages afforded by AI tools, which ultimately prepares them more thoroughly for prospective career opportunities. Currently, Syntea provides two primary features: the ability to pose inquiries pertaining to course content and the Pre-Assessment feature that evaluates one's skills and knowledge prior to commencing a course. This dual functionality not only aids in identifying which units require focused attention but also assists in establishing an effective study plan tailored to specific academic requirements. Furthermore, Syntea offers the capability to assess one's knowledge in preparation for the final exam, thereby highlighting areas that necessitate improvement and optimizing the overall exam preparation process. For additional information regarding Syntea, interested individuals are encouraged to request complimentary informational materials available at the top of this page.

Gradescope: Gradescope embodies an artificial intelligence-driven grading solution that significantly streamlines the grading process for both students and educators by facilitating the online submission of assignments, automatically grading a variety of question types, including multiple-choice, fill-in-the-blank, and coding questions, while simultaneously providing instantaneous feedback that enhances the learning experience. This efficiency not only alleviates the workload of instructors but also ensures that students receive timely evaluations of their performance.

Chat-GPT: Chat-GPT is a sophisticated web application powered by artificial intelligence, developed by the renowned organization OpenAI, which is designed to simulate conversations that mimic human interactions and effectively respond to inquiries spanning a diverse array of topics. This application is particularly adept at furnishing students with immediate answers to their questions, clarifying complex concepts, and facilitating engaging and interactive study sessions that can significantly enhance the learning experience. As a leading figure in the realm of AI tools tailored for students, Chat-GPT serves to enrich their educational journey while providing swift access to a wealth of information, thus rendering it an invaluable resource for all learners.

Tutor.ai: Tutor.ai represents a groundbreaking platform that harnesses artificial intelligence to connect students with qualified tutors who possess the expertise necessary to provide targeted assistance. This innovative service enables students to schedule virtual tutoring sessions at their convenience, receive personalized guidance tailored to their unique learning needs, and ultimately improve their comprehension of challenging subjects or assignments, thereby offering essential support and direction that can lead to academic success.

Copyscape: Copyscape is an advanced plagiarism detection tool powered by artificial intelligence that plays a crucial role in assisting students in ensuring that their work is both original and appropriately sourced. By meticulously scanning documents for any instances of duplicate content, this tool generates comprehensive reports that highlight any matches discovered online, thereby serving as a safeguard against unintentional instances of plagiarism that could undermine academic integrity.

Otter.ai: It is an innovative transcription tool specifically designed to convert spoken language into written text with remarkable accuracy, making it an ideal resource for students who require the transcription of lectures, interviews, or class discussions. This capability not only facilitates easy review of recorded audio files but also enables efficient search functions that enhance the overall accessibility of information, thereby supporting students in their academic pursuits.

DALL-E: It represents a groundbreaking artificial intelligence tool that proves to be exceptionally beneficial for individuals engaged in graphic design and visual arts disciplines, particularly students who are keen on exploring innovative avenues in their creative endeavors. Functioning as a specialized iteration of the renowned OpenAI machine learning framework, known as GPT, DALL-E is meticulously engineered to generate intricate images that correspond to specific textual descriptions provided by users. Upon receiving a text prompt, DALL-E leverages its advanced, trained artificial intelligence capabilities to meticulously construct images that align as closely as possible with the articulated request, thus showcasing its remarkable proficiency in this domain. This extraordinary capacity to produce distinctive and imaginative images derived from textual cues signifies a momentous advancement in the realms of artificial intelligence and machine learning algorithms, thereby unlocking a plethora of potential applications across various sectors, notably in the fields of art and design where visual creativity is paramount.

Mendeley: This sophisticated software facilitates the seamless importing and categorization of references, the generation of citations, and promotes collaborative efforts among peers, which ultimately streamlines the research process. The functionalities offered by Mendeley not only save invaluable time but also ensure adherence to proper citation practices, which is crucial in academic writing and integrity. Furthermore, these tools provide a multitude of additional benefits, including the enhancement of writing skills, the improvement of organizational capabilities and productivity levels, the provision of tailored tutoring experiences, the identification of potential plagiarism, the conversion of spoken language into written text, the optimization of study habits, and the effective management of research documents.

When selecting artificial intelligence (AI) tools for educational purposes, numerous factors warrant careful consideration. The selection process transcends merely identifying an aesthetically pleasing tool; it necessitates thorough evaluation to ascertain that it adequately fulfills the requirements of your educational institution. Some critical aspects to contemplate when undertaking this significant choice are

Compatibility is Essential: Primarily, one must assess the compatibility of the AI tool with the pre-existing systems in place. It is imperative to confirm that the tool can integrate effortlessly with the infrastructure of your educational institution. Opting for a tool that aligns with your current systems mitigates potential complications and facilitates a smooth transition. This compatibility promotes efficient implementation and utilization of the AI tool, ultimately conserving time and resources.

Effectiveness and Dependability are Important: In the realm of AI tools, their effectiveness and dependability are paramount. Prior to reaching a decision, it is vital to engage in comprehensive research and scrutinize user testimonials to gauge the tool's performance history and standing in the field. Seek out AI tools that boast a documented history of yielding favorable educational outcomes and delivering precise assessments and personalized feedback, preferably developed by reputable organizations, such as Open AI.
Recognizing the Constraints: Although AI tools present a multitude of advantages, it is crucial to acknowledge their limitations. They should not be viewed as replacements for human interaction or critical analysis. Instead, AI tools ought to be perceived as enhancements to conventional pedagogical approaches, rather than substitutes. Striking an equilibrium between the deployment of AI tools and traditional teaching methodologies is essential to ensure a comprehensive and well-rounded educational experience for learners.

The process of selecting an appropriate AI tool necessitates meticulous consideration of compatibility, effectiveness, dependability, and an awareness of limitations. By accounting for these factors, one can make an enlightened choice that will enrich the educational experience for both students and educators. The advantages of utilizing an advanced AI learning platform are increasingly evident (Campbell, 2024).

o   Firstly, automation facilitates the execution of routine workflows, permitting professionals to concentrate on more complex L&D responsibilities.
o   Secondly, AI-driven personalized course recommendations address skill deficiencies effectively within the organization.
o   Thirdly, sophisticated machine learning models expedite course design, thereby conserving valuable time and resources.
o   Additionally, real-time analytics from AI systems provide crucial metrics for assessing the efficacy of reskilling initiatives.
o   Ultimately, these innovations lead to significant cost and time savings, enabling strategic resource deployment aligned with educational goals.

Moreover, generative AI enables prompt-controlled authoring, allowing subject-matter experts to efficiently create training content. AI coaching tools further support learners in grasping essential concepts while assessing their progress. Additionally, skills management is optimized through AI analytics, targeting specific skill gaps effectively, and automated enrollments tailor training recommendations based on individual learner profiles. Finally, modern platforms employ machine learning algorithms to anticipate learner needs and identify areas for improvement proactively.

Assessment in Adaptive Education

Emerging technologies are causing a major upheaval in the education sector, which is why remote exams for admission and semester-ending exams are becoming more and more popular. Online assignments have taken the place of exams in universities as a result of the COVID-19 shutdown of schools. Students can take the GRE and TOEFL examinations from home under the supervision of a proctor thanks to ETS. On a broad scale, this strategy is not practical. Remote proctoring can be used to guarantee security, practicality, and ease of use for teachers and students. Artificial intelligence (AI)-driven remote proctoring and invigilation systems can stop unfair exam practices and cheating ("Remote Proctoring Using Ai – Enabling Seamless Management Of Online Examinations", 2024). The integration of manual and AI-based technologies presents several advantages, such as the ability for students to take exams from any location with the necessary technical setup and the removal of the requirement for physical testing locations.

In simpler terms, candidates are not required to physically attend a designated venue; instead, they can undertake examinations from the comfort of their residences. In conventional examination settings, the presence of an invigilator at the examination center is imperative for monitoring candidates participating in the assessment. To supervise a cohort of 30-40 candidates, one invigilator is necessary. Conversely, the administration of an examination involving over 1000 candidates necessitates the engagement of more than 25 invigilators to oversee the examination proceedings. Online proctoring can be executed via the internet utilizing the candidate's web camera. This system is capable of recording the entirety of the examination session from inception to conclusion, encompassing not only video footage but also capturing desktop screens, chat logs, and images. Proctoring can be categorized into several distinct types, which include the following:

> **Proctoring via Video:** Video proctoring is particularly beneficial for high-stakes examinations, wherein a candidate is monitored through continuous video streaming. Throughout the entirety of the examination, the candidate's video is recorded, and the assessment controller scrutinizes the footage to ascertain any instances of academic dishonesty or unethical behavior exhibited by the candidate.
>
> **Image-Based Proctoring:** Image proctoring is advantageous in scenarios where internet connectivity is suboptimal. This form of proctoring is designed to verify remote candidates' multiple times at random intervals. The system captures images of the candidate at predetermined moments, such as the commencement and conclusion of the examination, the questions attempted, and every 30 to 45 seconds thereafter. Educational institutions can

utilize these images to confirm that a legitimate candidate has undertaken the online examination and that no instances of malpractice have occurred. Furthermore, image proctoring is considered more cost-effective relative to video streaming options.

Self-Proctoring: For those seeking to perform monitoring and analytical activities automatically for remote candidates, auto proctoring serves as an appropriate solution. This method involves the continuous streaming of candidates situated in remote locations during online assessments. It conducts an analysis of videos and images to detect any potential cheating behaviors, such as the use of mobile devices during the examination, external assistance, or the utilization of notes or reference materials.

Verification of the Candidate ID: In this form of proctoring, the verification of the candidate's identity occurs prior to the initiation of the online examination. The candidate is required to present an identification card and examination hall ticket in front of the camera. The proctor, situated in a remote location, validates the candidate's identity card and subsequently either approves or rejects the candidate based on the submitted documentation.

Adaptive Learning and Pedagogical Style

The interplay between adaptive learning and pedagogical style is symbiotically beneficial, with adaptive learning serving as a mechanism to tailor and enhance diverse instructional methodologies. Pedagogical styles, whether they adhere to traditional frameworks or adopt a student-centered orientation, lay the groundwork for the underlying philosophy and methodological approach to instruction, while adaptive learning furnishes the technological capabilities necessary to customize that instruction in real-time. Within student-centered or constructivist pedagogical frameworks, adaptive learning facilitates individualized learning trajectories by modifying both content and pace to align with the unique requirements of each learner, thereby fostering greater engagement. Even within more conventional, teacher-centric paradigms, adaptive learning has the potential to improve differentiation, providing targeted interventions or enrichment opportunities predicated on real-time assessment data. Fundamentally, adaptive learning enhances and amplifies the efficacy of any pedagogical style by leveraging technology to synchronize instruction with the distinct abilities, progress, and learning preferences of individual students. This integration culminates in a more dynamic, responsive, and effective educational experience.

Automated proctoring is among the most effective ways to employ a webcam and screen-sharing software when compared to the other methods mentioned above. Computer algorithms that can identify suspicious activity take the role of a human proctor in this type of proctoring. AI-enabled remote proctoring systems are able to learn, adapt, and get wiser over time using machine learning. By assisting humans in spotting nuances such as low sound levels, whispers, reflections, shadows, etc., artificial intelligence (AI) is intended to enhance proctoring accuracy rather than replace human labour. The following three areas are the emphasis of remote proctoring:

- Find identity theft.
- Examine the conduct of those who cheat.
- Learn about content theft.

Thousands of iterations are required to build, train, and fine-tune each event in the AI-based remote proctoring process. These occurrences may be isolated incidents or signposts of dishonesty, identity theft, or content theft. The process proceeds once the quantity of data points exhibiting the same behavior surpasses a predetermined threshold. Every incident is labelled as possibly involving fraud, theft, or cheating, and the session is flagged as possibly involving an integrity breach. A variety of AI technologies can be applied to improve remote proctoring services and give educational institutions an effective means of arranging exams.

DISCUSSIONS AND APPLICATIONS

AI Technologies Utilized in the Domain of Remote Proctoring

Identification of Patterns: The phenomenon of academic dishonesty, often referred to as cheating, is inherently predicated upon a series of specific behavioral patterns that can be detectable and analyzable. Advanced Artificial Intelligence (AI) systems possess the remarkable capability to discern and identify various patterns embedded within a diverse array of data sets. Through meticulous examination of the information at their disposal, these systems strive to uncover any prevailing regularities or deviations that may signify the presence of illicit activities. The concept of pattern recognition itself can be elucidated as the systematic classification and categorization of data points, which is grounded in previously acquired knowledge or statistical insights that have been amassed from the observation and analysis of recurring patterns and their respective representations.

Voice Recognition: The sophisticated technology of Voice Recognition plays a crucial role in enhancing the integrity of examination environments by effectively capturing sound waves and correlating them with ambient background noise, thereby mitigating instances of potential cheating through the identification of unique speech patterns (Cohen, 2024). This cutting-edge technological advancement proves to be particularly advantageous in distinguishing between audio signals that are deemed appropriate and congruent with a legitimate testing context, as opposed to those that are extraneous or anomalous, which should not be present in such settings.

Facial Recognition: Facial Recognition technology serves a multifaceted purpose, ranging from the verification of a candidate's identity to the identification of unfamiliar faces present within a given testing environment, thus demonstrating its versatility in application. This innovative technology is capable of simultaneously recognizing and processing multiple facial attributes, which allows it to ascertain whether any unauthorized individuals are providing assistance to the candidate during the course of an online examination, thereby ensuring the fairness of the assessment process.

Eye Movement Detection: The integration of AI-driven Eye Movement Detection systems can significantly enhance the monitoring of candidates by facilitating the recognition and analysis of their eye movement patterns, which in turn helps in determining whether the examinee is maintaining direct focus on the examination screen or is instead diverting their attention towards any external objects, books, or electronic devices such as mobile phones. Data regarding eye movements that may indicate potential misconduct are meticulously collected and analyzed to ascertain if the candidate is engaging in any form of dishonest behavior or utilizing unfair means to gain an advantage in the examination setting. It is certainly used in neural marketing for consumer behavior.

Mouth Detection: Mouth Detection technology operates on principles akin to those employed in eye detection, wherein key facial points are utilized, and it is imperative that test-takers maintain an upright posture during the examination process. This technology meticulously monitors the spatial distance between key points on the lips over an extended series of frames and should there be any significant increase in the distance between these lip points beyond a predetermined threshold, such an infringement is systematically recorded and reported, thereby contributing to the overarching goal of maintaining academic integrity within remote assessment contexts.

How Can Artificial Intelligence Enhance the Efficacy of Remote Proctoring Services in the Realm of Online Assessments?

Artificial Intelligence functions as an invaluable supplementary resource that operates akin to a second set of vigilant eyes for human proctors, as it possesses the remarkable capability to generate alerts for any anomalous activity that it detects, thereby enabling it to identify behaviors or indicators that human proctors might not be able to recognize effectively or promptly during the high-pressure environment of real-time assessments. Again, increased scalability efficiencies gained through the augmented accuracy in the identification of unusual behaviors allow remote proctoring software to conduct thorough oversight of online assessments without sacrificing the critical security advantages that stem from human intervention, thus creating a more robust and scalable system that can accommodate a larger number of candidates simultaneously without a decrease in the quality of oversight. Unparalleled Security is another aspect that the automated system identifies negative behaviors or the utilization of unapproved resources that could potentially elude the attention of a human proctor, the remote proctoring system possesses the capability to initiate immediate corrective measures against the candidate in question, thereby instilling an additional layer of confidence in the integrity of high-stakes examinations where the prevention or remediation of academic misconduct is of paramount importance. An Artificial Intelligence model is directly correlated with its accuracy; hence, for the system to function optimally, it necessitates the acquisition of hundreds, if not thousands, of data points that will contribute to its learning process. Consequently, the more comprehensive the dataset available for analysis, the more sophisticated and intelligent the AI system will become, resulting in enhanced performance and reliability in the context of remote proctoring.

The implementation of remote proctoring technologies that utilize artificial intelligence has the profound potential to revolutionize the entire educational landscape, enabling a plethora of activities and interactions to take place in a fully virtual environment that was previously deemed impossible. These advanced AI-integrated computer systems are designed to meticulously verify the integrity of examinations by actively preventing candidates from engaging in dishonest practices or utilizing unfair advantages during their assessments, thereby fostering a fair and equitable testing atmosphere. Furthermore, with the advent of remote proctoring solutions, educational institutions are afforded the remarkable opportunity to maintain the continuity of their examination schedules without the need to delay or defer assessments, even amidst the unprecedented challenges posed by the COVID-19 pandemic, which has significantly disrupted traditional educational practices. Consequently, this innovation not only enhances the security and reliability of the examination process but also exemplifies a critical adaptation to the evolving demands of modern education in a rapidly changing global context.

Artificial Intelligence Contributing to the Field of Education in Contemporary Society: Applications

The phenomenon of Artificial Intelligence, commonly referred to as AI, has emerged as a pivotal catalyst for innovation across an extensive range of industries on a global scale, and it is imperative to recognize that the education sector is no exception to this transformative trend. In recent years, numerous educational institutions have begun to implement a diverse array of learning management tools, which are increasingly being leveraged to enhance the educational experience for both educators and students alike. However, it is important to note that our traditional education system has been relatively sluggish in embracing AI-powered solutions that could significantly enhance the learning process. Nevertheless, the unprecedented circumstances brought about by the pandemic have dramatically altered this conventional approach, compelling educational institutions to rely heavily on technology to facilitate virtual learning environments. As a result of this shift, it has become increasingly evident that a significant majority of educators now contend that technology should be regarded as an integral and indispensable component of the modern education system. Among the myriad of advantages that Artificial Intelligence brings to the realm of education, several key benefits stand out and warrant comprehensive examination:

Personalization: The concept of personalization has emerged as a fundamental aspect of contemporary education, underscoring the necessity for tailored educational experiences that cater to the unique needs of individual learners. In this context, AI plays a crucial role by enabling students to customize their approach to learning in accordance with their personal preferences and learning styles.

Tutoring: It is not uncommon for students to require additional assistance beyond the confines of the classroom setting, a need that is frequently unmet due to the constraints of time faced by many educators. In light of this reality, it is Artificial Intelligence that steps in to provide essential support and guidance to students who seek extra help. Consequently, the emergence of AI-driven Chabot's and virtual tutors offers a viable solution, allowing students to access the assistance they require without necessitating the presence of a traditional educator.

Quick Response: The phenomenon of delayed responses to student inquiries, particularly when students pose the same questions days after a topic has been concluded, can be a source of significant frustration for both students and faculty alike.

Universal 24/7 Access to Learning: Above all other considerations, it is imperative to acknowledge that Artificial Intelligence significantly enhances the educational landscape by providing AI-powered tools that facilitate universal access to learning opportunities for all students. Furthermore, these technological advancements simplify the process for students to delve into and explore knowledge in their areas of interest, thereby fostering a more engaging and enriching educational experience.

Is Artificial Intelligence Unable to Replace the Teachers?

A pressing question that arises among educators pertains to the potential trajectory of our educational landscape—specifically, are we on the brink of a reality in which large computer screens and AI systems supplant the role of human teachers? The answer to this inquiry is not as straightforward as it may seem, as educators need not harbor concerns that Artificial Intelligence will render their roles obsolete. This is primarily due to the fact that AI is fundamentally limited in its capacity to effectively teach students complex concepts and nuanced skills; it simply cannot replicate the multifaceted attributes of a human being.

The most salient distinction between Artificial Intelligence and in-person instruction lies in the fact that AI lacks the inherent qualities of a real human being. When students engage with AI instructors, they are acutely aware that they are interacting with a mere text-based system or a digital interface, which inherently diminishes the potential for genuine empathy and emotional connection. Consequently, this absence of human interaction precludes the development of the same level of engagement and rapport that can be fostered through interactions with human educators. Moreover, it is essential to recognize that computers and AI systems do not possess the capacity to genuinely care for students in the same manner that their teachers do, highlighting a fundamental difference between the experiences afforded by AI and those provided by human educators. In a similar vein, it is important to note that robots and AI systems are fundamentally incapable of inspiring students to undertake specific tasks or motivating them in the way that dedicated teachers can. In addition, the process of learning transcends the mere accumulation of information or factual knowledge; rather, it is fundamentally about the creation of meaning and understanding derived from that information, which is an aspect that human educators excel at facilitating.

Ways to Utilize Artificial Intelligence in the Field of Education

The influence that artificial intelligence exerts upon the educational sector is indeed extensive and far-reaching. It is fundamentally reshaping the methodologies employed by educators, as well as the strategies adopted by educational institutions, thereby creating a paradigm shift in pedagogical practices. Moreover, artificial intelligence is not only altering the instructional approaches but is also significantly transforming the manner in which students engage with the learning process. As indicated by the Market Research Engine, "Artificial Intelligence (AI) for numerous applications within the education sector to reinforce teachers' and students' experience and improve their knowledge and growing want for multilingual translators integrated with the AI technology are expected to drive the expansion of the AI in the education market." This assertion highlights the burgeoning demand for AI technologies in educational settings, which are anticipated to enhance both the teaching experience for educators and the learning experience for students, while simultaneously addressing the increasing need for multilingual capabilities within the educational framework. Consequently, it is imperative to explore several fundamental approaches through which AI technology is significantly contributing to the transformation of instructional methodologies:

Task Automation: Through the implementation of artificial intelligence, it becomes possible to automate various administrative responsibilities and managerial duties that are typically associated with educational institutions and professors. The deployment of AI technologies facilitates the effective management of classroom environments and alleviates the burden of numerous organizational tasks that educators are often tasked with. In a similar vein, artificial intelligence streamlines the evaluation processes related to homework assignments, grading examinations, and an array of other academic assessments, thereby enhancing overall efficiency.

Smart Content: The development of innovative content represents another critical avenue through which artificial intelligence is making substantial contributions to the field of education. By introducing novel methodologies and solutions tailored to student needs, AI plays a pivotal role in enabling the educational system to achieve remarkable outcomes. This creative content encompasses a diverse array of digital resources, including electronic textbooks, video lectures, and virtual conferencing tools, among others. Furthermore, artificial intelligence empowers educators to deliver customized learning experiences, thereby providing students with the opportunity to optimize their academic performance and attain exceptional grades through the application of these innovative techniques.

Personalized Learning: It is essential to acknowledge that each student possesses unique learning strategies and approaches that differ significantly from one another. The traditional educational framework often struggles to accommodate the diverse needs of individual learners, which is where artificial intelligence can offer a transformative solution. AI technologies can be utilized to provide tailored assistance to students based on the specific challenges and difficulties they encounter in their educational journey, thus facilitating a more personalized learning experience that aligns with each student's unique requirements.

Virtual Learning Environment: Artificial intelligence plays a crucial role in digitizing educational platforms by offering access to digital textbooks and resources that students can utilize from virtually any location and on any device of their choosing. This functionality significantly enhances the learning experience by enabling students to participate in classes and access educational materials regardless of their physical presence within the traditional school environment. As a result, students are afforded unprecedented flexibility in their educational pursuits, which can lead to improved learning outcomes.

Secure Online Exams: A multitude of educational institutions and universities across the globe are increasingly turning to artificial intelligence assessment tools to facilitate the administration of examinations. These tools not only provide students with a pre-established question bank to aid in their test preparation but also ensure the integrity of the examination process. Most importantly, AI technologies offer an intelligent framework that enhances the security and reliability of online assessments, thereby safeguarding the academic integrity of the evaluation process.

How is Artificial Intelligence Influencing the Realm of Education and Learning Processes?

With the advent of artificial intelligence technology, students are no longer constrained to the physical confines of traditional classrooms, enabling them to engage in their educational pursuits from the comfort of their homes or any location of their choice. The integration of artificial intelligence into the educational landscape facilitates the utilization of various virtual learning tools that enhance the overall learning experience for students. Furthermore, the availability of learning materials is significantly increased as long as students possess reliable internet access, thus democratizing education and making it accessible to a broader audience. Consequently, the following delineates some of the profound impacts that AI has on the field of education:

The Capability to Deliver High-Quality Educational Content to Students Around the Globe: Artificial intelligence has revolutionized the accessibility of education, ensuring that learners from diverse geographical locations can partake in high-quality educational opportunities. In other words, AI serves as a catalyst that empowers educators and academic institutions to disseminate comprehensive and sound knowledge to their students through the implementation of AI-powered educational tools and platforms. As a result, the barriers that traditionally hindered access to education are effectively dismantled, and with the aid of artificial intelligence, the process of acquiring knowledge becomes significantly more straightforward and efficient.

The Provision of Customized and Personalized Educational Content: Artificial intelligence possesses the remarkable ability to curate intelligent and high-quality educational content tailored specifically to the needs of individual students, thereby optimizing their potential to achieve superior academic outcomes. Nevertheless, the efficiency of AI in aggregating and presenting quality educational material within a condensed timeframe proves to be immensely advantageous for students seeking to enhance their learning experience and academic performance.

The Delivery of Specialized Information Tailored to Meet Individual Academic Requirements: In accordance with the unique queries posed by each student, artificial intelligence is adept at furnishing precise and relevant answers that cater specifically to their academic inquiries. Moreover, by identifying the various challenges and obstacles encountered by students during their learning journey, AI is capable of offering targeted solutions that effectively address and resolve their academic dilemmas.

FUTURE ASPECTS OF AI-BASED ADAPTIVE LEARNING

The prospective trajectory of AI-based adaptive learning is optimistic, characterized by several noteworthy advancements on the impending horizon. The following delineates critical future dimensions that warrant attention:

Augmented Personalization: As AI algorithms attain greater sophistication, adaptive learning frameworks will be capable of delivering increasingly tailored educational experiences. This may encompass individualized learning pathways, customized content, and assessments meticulously designed to align with each student's unique requirements and preferences.

Convergence with Virtual Reality (VR) and Augmented Reality (AR): The convergence of adaptive learning with VR and AR technologies holds the potential to engender immersive educational experiences that replicate authentic environmental contexts. Such advancements could enhance educational outcomes by affording students experiential learning opportunities within a virtual milieu.

Amplified Data Analytics: Progressions in data analytics will empower adaptive learning systems to scrutinize more extensive and intricate datasets, facilitating more precise forecasts concerning students' learning necessities and behavioral patterns. This capability may assist educators in making more enlightened decisions regarding the customization of instructional approaches to cater to individual student requirements.

Lifelong Learning: Adaptive learning transcends conventional educational frameworks. In the foreseeable future, it is plausible that adaptive learning systems will be employed to bolster lifelong learning endeavors, aiding individuals in the acquisition of new competencies and knowledge throughout their lifespans.

Global Reach: AI-driven adaptive learning possesses the capacity to extend its influence to a worldwide audience, thereby affording access to high-quality educational resources for students situated in remote or marginalized regions. This potential could contribute to the mitigation of educational disparities and enhance the availability of learning opportunities for all individuals.

Ethical Considerations: As the prevalence of adaptive learning escalates, there will be a heightened emphasis on ethical considerations, encompassing data privacy, algorithmic bias, and the ramifications of automation on the role of educators. Addressing these concerns will be imperative to guarantee that AI-based adaptive learning serves to benefit all students in an equitable manner.

CONCLUSION

The future of AI-based adaptive learning holds great promise, with the potential to transform education and offer more personalized and effective learning experiences for students globally. This chapter has highlighted that AI-driven applications have empowered adaptive learning systems, intelligent mechanisms, and adaptive learning platforms to become the most commonly proposed and employed solutions for addressing the challenges encountered by students and teachers. Their significance was especially evident during the pandemic, as these systems aided teachers in providing high-quality instruction and enhancing learning design. As an increasing number of higher education institutions (HEIs) embrace hybrid education models, the relevance of AI-driven adaptive learning for educators and HEI policymakers will continue to grow in the coming years.

REFERENCES

Akavova, A., Temirkhanova, Z., & Lorsanova, Z. (2023). Adaptive learning and artificial intelligence in the educational space. In *E3S Web of Conferences* (Vol. 451, p. 06011). EDP Sciences. DOI: 10.1051/e3sconf/202345106011

Chukhlomin, V. (2024). Conceptualizing AI-Driven Learning Strategies for non-IT Professionals: From EMERALD Framework to a Sample Course Design. *Available at SSRN* 4820332. DOI: 10.2139/ssrn.4820332

Costin, D. S., Cristian, A. F., Georgian, D. I., Ionu , C. S., & Alexandru, M. S. (2023). The implications of leveraging machine learning and artificial intelligence for the transformation of adult education and vocational training. Journal of Management and Quality, 14-20. DOI: 10.1002/aaai.12157

Goel, A., Dede, C., Garn, M., & Ou, C. (2024). AI-ALOE: AI for reskilling, upskilling, and workforce development. *AI Magazine*, 45(1), 77–82. DOI: 10.1002/aaai.12157

Gransden, C., Hindmarsh, M., Lê, N. C., & Nguyen, T.-H. (2024). Adaptive learning through technology: A technical review and implementation, *Higher Education. Skills and Work-Based Learning*, 14(2), 409–417. DOI: 10.1108/HESWBL-05-2023-0121

Holmes, W., & Littlejohn, A. (2024). 10. Artificial intelligence for professional learning. Handbook of Artificial Intelligence at Work: Interconnections and Policy Implications, p. 191.

How does AI Impact on Education? Top Ways to Use AI in Education. (n.d.) https://yourtechdiet.com/blogs/how-does-ai-impact-on-education-top-ways-to-use-ai-in-education/, accessed on 20.08.2024

Hwang, G. J., Xie, H., Wah, B. W., & Gašević, D. (2020). Vision, challenges, roles and research issues of Artificial Intelligence in Education, Computers & Education. *Artificial Intelligence*, 1, 100001.

Kabudi, T., Pappas, I., & Olsen, D. H. (2021). AI-enabled adaptive learning systems: A systematic mapping of the literature, Computers and Education: Artificial Intelligence, Volume 2, 2021, 100017, ISSN 2666-920X, https://doi.org/DOI: 10.1016/j.caeai.2021.100017

Lin, M., Baykasoglu, A., & Dominici, G. (2024). Artificial Intelligence Technology in Education, International Journal of Intelligent Computing and Cybernetics, https://emeraldgrouppublishing.com/calls-for-papers/artificial-intelligence-technology-education

Moreno-Guerrero, A. J., López-Belmonte, J., Marín-Marín, J. A., & Soler-Costa, R. (2020). Scientific development of educational artificial intelligence in web of science. *Future Internet*, 12(8), 124. DOI: 10.3390/fi12080124

Papamitsiou, Z., Economides, A. A., Pappas, I. O., & Giannakos, M. N. (2018). Explaining learning performance using response-Time, self-Regulation and satisfaction from content: An fsQCA approach, ACM international conference proceeding series (2018), pp. 181-190

Remote Proctoring Using Ai – Enabling Seamless Management of Online Examinations. (n.d.) https://www.leewayhertz.com/remote-proctoring-using-ai/#What-are-the-AI-technologies-used-for-Remote-Proctoring. Accessed on 28.08. 2024

Sharma, S. (2024) AI-Based Adaptive Learning: Revolutionizing Education. https://www.linkedin.com/pulse/ai-based-adaptive-learning-revolutionizing-education-shobha-sharma-ufrec/

Shrivastava, R. (2023). Role of artificial intelligence in future of education. *International Journal of Professional Business Review*, 8(1), 2. DOI: 10.26668/businessreview/2023.v8i1.840

Vincent-Lancrin, S., & van der Vlies, R. (2020). Trustworthy Artificial Intelligence (AI) in Education: Promises and Challenges. OECD Education Working Papers, No. 218. *OECD Publishing*.

ADDITIONAL READING

Jaiswal, A., & Arun, C. J. (2021). Potential of Artificial Intelligence for transformation of the education system in India. *International Journal of Education and Development Using Information and Communication Technology*, 17(1), 142–158.

Kumar, K. (2023). Artificial Intelligence in Education: Transforming Learning Through Adaptive Technologies. *Educational Administration: Theory and Practice*, 29(3), 791–798.

Olatunde-Aiyedun, T. G. (2024). Artificial Intelligence (AI) in Education: Integration of AI Into Science Education Curriculum in Nigerian Universities. *International Journal of Artificial Intelligence for Digital*, 1(1).

Rane, N., Choudhary, S., & Rane, J. (2023). Education 4.0 and 5.0: Integrating artificial intelligence (AI) for personalized and adaptive learning. *Available at SSRN 4638365*. DOI: 10.2139/ssrn.4638365

Samuel, Y., Brennan-Tonetta, M., Samuel, J., Kashyap, R., Kumar, V., Krishna Kaashyap, S., Chidipothu, N., Anand, I., & Jain, P. (2023). Cultivation of human centered artificial intelligence: Culturally adaptive thinking in education (CATE) for AI. *Frontiers in Artificial Intelligence*, 6, 1198180. DOI: 10.3389/frai.2023.1198180 PMID: 38106981

KEY TERMS AND DEFINITIONS

Adaptive Learning: A teaching method that uses AI and data analytics to tailor educational content and pacing to the unique needs and progress of each student.

Artificial Intelligence (AI): The simulation of human intelligence in machines, enabling them to perform tasks such as learning, reasoning, and problem-solving.

Data-Driven Insights: Analysis and interpretation of student performance data to improve educational outcomes and decision-making.

Educational Technology (EdTech): The use of digital tools and platforms to enhance teaching, learning, and administrative processes in education.

Learning Management System (LMS): Software platforms designed to administer, document, track, and deliver educational courses and training programs.

Personalized Learning: An educational approach that customizes learning experiences based on individual student preferences, abilities, and progress.

Scalability: The capability of an educational technology or system to efficiently support an increasing number of users or expand to meet growing demands.

Virtual Learning Environment (VLE): A digital platform for delivering and managing educational content and interactions remotely.

Natural Language Processing (NLP): An AI technique that enables machines to understand and respond to human language through text or speech.

Ethical AI: The responsible development and deployment of AI technologies, ensuring fairness, transparency, and accountability in educational applications.

Chapter 3
Adaptive Learning Technologies in Healthcare Education for Students With Disabilities

Vismaya Annie Vinod
https://orcid.org/0000-0001-8727-6736
Cape Breton University, Canada

Eriona Çela
https://orcid.org/0000-0003-2710-5489
University of New York, Tirana, Albania

Philip Eappen
https://orcid.org/0000-0002-8120-8449
University of Toronto, Canada

ABSTRACT

This chapter explores the integration and impact of adaptive learning technologies in healthcare education, specifically for students with disabilities. By leveraging experiential technologies such as virtual reality (VR), mixed reality (MR), and augmented reality (AR), healthcare education can foster more immersive, interactive, and inclusive learning experiences. This narrative review identifies the unique challenges faced by students with disabilities, including accessibility issues, gaps in disability competency training, and inequities in educational opportunities. The chapter examines how adaptive learning, supported by artificial intelligence (AI) and machine learning (ML), can create personalized learning paths that enhance student engagement, confidence, and skill development. Additionally, it highlights

DOI: 10.4018/979-8-3693-8227-1.ch003

the role of assistive technologies in improving accessibility and fostering inclusive educational practices.

INTRODUCTION

The emergence of technological innovations has significantly advanced the healthcare sector, particularly in response to the changing demands of patient care. A critical challenge healthcare management professionals face is adapting to these advancements effectively. Ryan et al. (2022) found that knowledge gained through experiential technologies—such as virtual, mixed, and augmented reality—can be as beneficial or even more advantageous than traditional educational methods. These technologies offer immersive, interactive experiences that simulate real-world situations. The study assessed the impact of these technologies on health education at the university level compared to conventional educational modalities. According to Ryan et al. (2022), immersive technology provides a more engaging learning experience, increasing student satisfaction, confidence, and participation. Implementing problem-based learning can be especially helpful for students with disabilities. This approach presents students with complex, real-world problems, helping them develop medical expertise through expert knowledge. It also fosters disciplinary thinking, promotes collaboration and articulation, and reduces cognitive load (Jinn & Bridges, 2014).

The 2022 Canadian Survey on Disability provides extensive data across ten disability categories, focusing on limitations in activities related to hearing, sight, movement, flexibility, hand coordination, learning, mental well-being, and developmental impairments (Pianosi et al., 2023). Individuals with physical disabilities face numerous environmental challenges in medical facilities, such as examination rooms lacking sufficient space for mobility and patient examination tables that are not adjustable to accommodate wheelchairs (Gault et al., 2020). Despite the availability of technologies and accommodations aimed at enhancing their participation, students with sensory and physical disabilities remain underrepresented in medical schools. Many institutions have established technical standards that focus more on deficiencies than the skills required to perform essential tasks effectively (Mckee et al., 2016). This chapter highlights the unique challenges faced by students with disabilities and emphasizes the urgent need for more inclusive practices in medical education.

METHODS

This chapter is based on a narrative review of literature conducted between July and November 2024. Without a predefined protocol, we performed unstructured searches across common literature databases such as PubMed, PsycINFO, CINAHL, Scopus, and Google Scholar. While recent publications were prioritized due to their relevance to the subject, no filters were applied to restrict the publication dates. The review intentionally included sources from various health-related disciplines and favoured review articles over individual studies to ensure a broader, synthesized perspective rather than narrow, specific viewpoints. The search strategy encompassed keywords such as technological innovations, healthcare management, experiential technology, immersive learning, virtual reality (VR), mixed reality (MR), augmented reality (AR), and problem-based learning (PBL). We reviewed multiple studies, including systematic reviews, scoping reviews, qualitative studies, and survey analyses. The settings of interest in the sources reviewed included schools, secondary educational institutions, universities, and healthcare institutions. The included sources were from the United States (US), the United Arab Emirates (UAE), and Canada. The search was not intended to be exhaustive but aimed to provide an overview of common provider perspectives.

MAIN FOCUS OF THE CHAPTER

Unique Challenges Faced by Students with Disabilities

The discrepancies in disability curriculum in medical education are a significant concern as there is a lack of clear consensus on the required disability topics to be covered. Competency training for disability appears to differ among multiple medical programs, where very few cover a comprehensive understanding of disability. A constrained period to cover the curriculum topics makes delivering comprehensive training on disability-related issues challenging, which will harm the initiatives to prioritize students with disabilities (Lee et al., 2023). Many funding programs do not focus on limitations instead of competency and depend on predefined classifications and descriptors. Policies on expulsion and suspension are established inflexibly, overlooking the specific circumstances of individual pupils. Discriminatory attitudes in the education system towards students with disabilities prevail, and the narrow-minded approach can hinder their equal access to services offered by the institution by faculty and fellow students (Ontario Human Rights Commission, 2024). It is imperative to consider that the limited knowledge of healthcare professionals regarding the experiences and requirements of people with disabilities leads to inequities in healthcare (Lee et al., 2023). Most institutions educate students about disability to shape viewpoints without providing in-depth knowledge and skill procurement. This reflects a widespread issue in healthcare education where the focus is on shifting perceptions without looking for the structural changes that aid effective learning (Loerger et al., 2019).

According to the Association of American Medical Colleges & University of California, San Francisco report (2021), there are pressing concerns associated with disability in medical education. Medical schools demonstrated notable variations in communicating disability status resulting from a lack of standardization. Self-disclosed practices varied widely, with no definitive guidelines to standardize them. A lack of proper training in supporting pupils with disabilities was reported. The report identified the constrained knowledge of administrators regarding the law and legislation to facilitate the conduct of students with disabilities.

Acquiring Diverse Skills

Learning Health Systems (LHS) underscored the pertinence of developing varied skills at multiple levels of healthcare ecosystems, involving patients, healthcare professionals, and within the broader systems (McDonald et al., 2022). At the patient level, attaining knowledge and skills to deliver information within the implemented system and engage with technological tools is essential. Considering the healthcare professional level, proficiency in evidence-based practice, leadership skills, self-awareness, collaborative work, and analytical and technical abilities are considered (McDonald et al., 2022). As LHS continues to advance, additional research is required to identify inclusive competency requirements and address both individual and organizational requirements for the balanced development of skills in healthcare management (McDonald et al., 2022).

Individuals with disabilities and older adults who encounter challenges with access to health care are most likely to require assistance from other people. Tackling healthcare inequalities necessitates the acknowledgement of perceptions from patients and healthcare providers as well (Ramšak et al., 2023). Critical elements that determine the hostility experienced by pupils with disabilities are culture and climate. Programs that emphasize legal compliance regarding the accommodations generally overlook the significance of including disability-related topics in education (Association of American Medical Colleges & University of California, San Francisco, 2021).

The competencies with the health policies domains emphasize taking leadership initiatives and evolving healthcare at political levels. Programs that blend coursework and clinical practice exhibit the potential to develop leadership skills in the clinical and systems domains (Heinen et al., 2019). Competency-based medical education programs (CBME) established at both undergraduate and graduate levels may enable early graduation, considering competency attainment. On the other hand, this perceived advantage might be outweighed by challenges in teaching (Hawkins et al., 2015).

Meeting Rigorous Academic Standards

Supportive educational services involve modifying teaching or evaluation strategies to uphold fundamental content, ensuring students with disabilities access the essential materials (Lovette, 2021). Parity in education means providing non-discriminatory access to everyone instead of ensuring uniform outcomes for all. Despite services being provided, students with disabilities may experience lower performances compared to students without disabilities. Even though accessibility services can enhance performance and narrow the disparity in outcomes, their purpose differs from the goal of enhancing performance. Accommodations enhance accessibility to educational opportunities but do not ensure success in specific academic tasks (Lovette, 2021).

Many accommodation strategies are designed to meet distinct needs, supporting students with physical, cognitive, and sensory disabilities (Vats & Dey, 2022). Presentation accommodations enable students to access educational resources in alternative formats, like audio recordings. Response accommodations allow pupils to deliver answers that align with their comfort level. These involve tools such as spell checkers, calculators to solve mathematical problems, and other technological resources to aid students with disabilities. Timing accommodations help students by providing additional time to finish their tasks and assignments. Setting accommodations is known to comprehend academic growth with the aid of exams. Organizational Skills Accommodations provide students with clear instructions on improving their learning abilities (Vats & Dey, 2022).

According to the study conducted by Lipka et al. (2020), students with mental disabilities showed low adjustment scores in significant domains such as personal, social, academic, and institutional areas compared to other disability groups. Students with physical and sensory disabilities experienced challenges in personal adjustment. The study advises that assistance services address the needs and challenges faced by students with disabilities, as these may differ across various disability groups.

Adaptive Technologies: Overcoming Barriers to Access

Online education necessitates the tutor strengthening competencies in three core areas: pedagogy, technology, and content knowledge. Additionally, digital education helps ensure better content delivery and provides evidence-based medicine (Nimavat et al., 2021). The efforts to foster the inclusion of students with disabilities have driven the adoption of assistive technology in education. To delve deep into the role of assistive technologies in students with disabilities, it is necessary to explore the concept of disability. Assistive technology is generally classified into two categories: 1) The lower technology category uses magnifiers, which do not require programming. 2) The higher technology category employs computers that rely on programming (Fernández-Batanero et al., 2022). Students with disabilities face multiple challenges from psychological and social perspectives. Assistive technologies claim to ensure them with social engagement and academic involvement (McNicholl et al., 2019).

Personalized Learning Paths with AI and ML

Personalized learning is centered on tailoring educational needs to align with each learner's interests, preferences, and pace. The universally accepted conventional teaching is known to have a multitude of limitations as it overlooks the differences in context and requirements. With the increase in digitalized classrooms and learning paths, technologists and educators were prompted to explore the role of AI in revolutionizing education. Artificial intelligence (AI) learning has evolved as a catalyst in tailoring learning opportunities, leading to a pertinent shift from conventional teaching methods (Jian & Maher, 2023). AI refers to the ability of a machine to execute tasks that generally require human intelligence, comprising speech-to-text technology, language interpretation, and decision-making processes (Soori et al., 2023). When AI is said to mimic human intellect, it is crucial to know the capacity of human intellect, which is to extrapolate from experience, work with abstract ideas, and derive conclusions from suppositions (Procházková, 2014). AI systems analyze large database sets and extract insights, providing an exceptional opportunity to obtain an in-depth understanding of the learner (Jian & Maher, 2023).

AI-Driven Learning Pathways

The merged application of AI and technology in healthcare is an effective way to address resource allocation challenges. The increased availability of multi-channel data covering genomics, demographic, clinical, and phenotypic information combined with the innovations in mobile technology and data security signal a turning point in aligning healthcare and technology to radically transform healthcare provision frameworks through AI-powered healthcare systems (Bajwa et al., 2021). Considering the 2018 AI board report summary from the American Medical Association (2018), the policy frame emphasizes the need for research regarding the efficiency of AI in medical education that results in better clinical outcomes. Dumić-Čule et al. (2020)

assessed practitioners' perspectives regarding introducing artificial intelligence in the medical curriculum, where the dominant group strongly welcomed the approach.

AI-driven tools facilitate interactive learning environments by providing quick feedback, digital simulations, and engaging education of AI materials. Many applications are available that aid learning in classrooms and digital learning environments directly and indirectly (Dash & Bhoi, 2024). Cognitive neuropsychology helps understand how the brain processes information and assists in diagnosing brain dysfunction. It evaluates brain development and learning processes, contributing to refining teaching methods to enhance learning outcomes (Halkiopoulos & Gkintoni, 2024). Machine learning algorithms help forecast multiple phenotypes ranging from traits such as eye colour to more complex ones such as drug response and susceptibility to medicines (Alowais et al., 2023). Findings by Wang & Avillach (2021) suggest that deep learning methods aid in recognizing genetic factors associated with autism spectrum disorder (ASD). The study revolutionized the scene by predicting the ASD status with genomic data alone. This application of AI aids in identifying disabilities, which could aid in personalizing education for students.

Dynamic Adjustments: How ML Algorithms Modify Content Delivery

The technical approaches involved with AI, including Machine learning (ML), Deep learning (DL), Rule-based techniques, and neural networks (Narayan et al., 2023), are highly efficient and effective in the field of education. ML, a subset of AI, is focused on designing algorithms that enable machines to learn and perform tasks autonomously by developing analytical models (França et al., 2021). This strategic and anticipatory approach in healthcare education, where big data is utilized to analyze learning patterns, predict outcomes, and personalize educational content and user interactions (Song et al., 2024), is a testament to the value of these technologies. ML enables a data-centric approach to analyzing individual learning patterns, examining extensive datasets to detect similar patterns, and refining instructional methods to align with the personalized educational journey of each student (Gligorea et al., 2023).

The incorporation of AI and ML in adaptive learning is a student-centered approach that is supported by a multitude of advantages. It ensures students have a tailored learning experience that enhances their learning journey. As a result, students can progress at their own pace with immediate feedback, which improves retention. Adaptive techniques and technologies are incorporated into online courses and platforms. The platforms employ algorithms and AI to interpret student data, including their interactions, reports, and progress. The system then builds on the data analyzed to tailor the content, structure, and delivery of learning materials to address the specific needs of each student (Gligorea et al., 2023).

Assistive Technologies in Healthcare Simulations

Adaptive Learning Systems

AI-powered adaptive learning systems assist students with physical disabilities by decreasing physical barriers to their education (Chalkiadakis, 2024). The curriculum is personalized, considering the students' strengths and weaknesses (Dash & Bhoi, 2024). Harvard Medical School is proactively integrating generative AI (GenAI) into its curriculum (Gehrman, 2024).

Natural Language Processing (NLP)

Natural Language Processing describes the field that focuses on equipping the computer to comprehend and analyze human language in a manner that parallels human understanding (Chary et al., 2019). When AI and NLP are harnessed, virtual teaching assistants can analyze and provide feedback on code snippets, mathematical equations, and statistical models. Additionally, they interpret and react to visual inputs in diverse educational settings (Sajja et al., 2024). NLP comprises systems that integrate speech with natural language, collaborative interfaces for databases, knowledge bases simulating human interaction, multilingual platforms, machine translational technologies, and message comprehension (Joshi, 1991).

Chatbots

Chatbots are pertinent in medical education as they can help students by automating repetitive tasks and retaining information (Ghorashi et al., 2023). ChatGPT, which is an AI language model, has notably impacted radiology education by generating learning assignments, developing lesson plans, performing as a 24/7 virtual tutor, facilitating critical thinking, summarizing large volumes of information, and offering immediate feedback for a multitude of subjects, including radiology (Meşe et al., 2024). Ghorashi et al. (2023) advise chatbots to be programmed so that they consult evidence-based medical resources and generate accurate and dependable content that complies with medical standards, scientific writing guidelines, and ethical principles.

Intelligent tutoring system (ITS): ITS provides personalized instructions to students, replicating the strategies used by human teachers. Collaborative Medical Tutor (COMET) is an ITS that employs Bayesian networks to represent the knowledge activities of individual students and groups (Suebnukarn, 2009). The incorporation of AI in ITS facilitates the learning of students with disabilities, providing personalized learning paths, conducting success forecasting, and analyzing learning patterns (Seung, 2024).

VR and AR Simulations

Virtual reality (VR) generates an interactive, three-dimensional environment using computer technology, where objects appear to have a sense of spatial presence. It is generally connected to immersive effect-producing experiences using head-worn virtual reality devices (Lioce et al., 2020). Virtual reality is leveraged in healthcare education and emergency medicine to simulate rare or difficult-to-create scenarios. Screen-based virtual reality simulations train technical skills, specifically in laparoscopic and robot-assisted surgeries, within fields such as gastroenterology and urology (Bracq et al., 2019). The application of VR in education enhances the learning methodologies and techniques used, particularly in simulating the challenges experienced by individuals with disabilities. VR technology is centred on visual and auditory stimuli, though it covers a limited sensory change. Physical accessories and stimulators are generally incorporated to provide an enriched experience (Zwoliński et al., 2023).

Augmented reality (AR) is a technology that integrates digital information and real-world environments to facilitate user experience and perception (Lioce et al., 2020). Gil et al. (2021) explore the application of VR-AR as a complementary tool in physiotherapy and rehabilitation. By implementing multiple educational strategies, AR technologies support students with special educational needs, particularly those with autism spectrum disorder (Fernández-Batanero et al., 2022). As a blended and enhanced reality, AR holds pertinent educational potential, which is then augmented by developing AR systems that include multiple technologies (Wu et al., 2012). AR components are introduced to pupils with the help of smartphones and tablets (Köse & Güner-Yildiz, 2021).

Students who have dyslexia find it challenging to write without spelling mistakes, which often coincide with other language-related challenges. These challenges can act as constraints that limit the ability of pupils to efficiently use writing as a tool for learning, which in turn limits their social participation (Bäck et al., 2024). Speech-to-text technology involves transforming speech to text on a screen without requiring the student to type the spoken words manually. This technology requires students to speak into the appliance with speech recognition characteristics, where the speech-to-text software translates the speech into text on the screen. Speech-to-text technology supports students with memory problems by navigating cognitive changes associated with writing tasks (Liu et al., 2019). Individuals with reading disabilities encounter notable challenges in reading and its associated skills, which include decoding and fluency. These challenges associated with reading disabilities are considered to have a neurobiological emergence and are characterized by the inability to respond to instructions. Text-to-speech technology enhances reading comprehension for people with reading disabilities (Wood et al., 2018).

Data-Driven Approaches to Assessment and Feedback

Song et al. (2024) describes the Dynamic Feedback-Driven Learning Optimization Framework (DFDLOF) that revolutionizes education by employing machine learning to tailor educational settings to individual needs. It evaluates real-time data from students' performance and interactions; according to the information collected, the content, method, and difficulty level are continually altered. The system comprises short-term feedback to correct errors and long-term feedback for more comprehensive educational adjustments. This approach thereby ensures a personalized learning experience.

Educational data mining is known for its ability to facilitate student learning outcomes. Feedback mechanisms have long served as a pertinent component in education evaluation. The value of feedback depends on the approaches employed along with students' engagement (Tepgec et al., 2024). Feedback practices have been revolutionized with the emergence of Learning Analytics (LA). Educators find it easier to track students' performance, detect gaps in learning, and generate feedback mechanisms to foster student performance (Tepgec et al., 2024). Tepgec et al. (2024) claim that a research gap remains despite the widespread acknowledgment of LA in emerging adaptive learning settings. The study specifies the shortage of empirical education to explore the association between feedback systems and LA-powered learning.

The swift integration of online learning platforms has reshaped education practices, creating new opportunities for inclusive learning. The biggest boon of online learning is its ability to accommodate students by enabling them to access learning resources without geographical and physical barriers. Students with physical disabilities benefit from this shift to online learning platforms without the need for special support (Panggabean et al., 2024). Customized assessments support students with disabilities access to online learning platforms. Alternative formats such as visual presentations, oral presentations, and extended timelines enable students with disabilities to demonstrate their skills in a way that caters to their strengths. Adaptive learning technologies generate a loop of feedback where continued support is delivered to the students by using real-time data from their interactions with the platform (Panggabean et al., 2024).

Inclusive Curriculum Design

Curriculum Flexibility: The shift towards curriculum flexibility in education showcased by platforms such as VetCloud and approaches like flipped classrooms delivers a promising path to facilitating experiences. These approaches promote diverse learners by providing flexible and modular content and fostering active student participation (Singh et al., 2024).

Holistic Approaches: Integrating case-based, experiential, and collaborative education promotes inclusion. In healthcare education, experiential learning enables students to develop practical skills within interprofessional settings, fostering their competencies for interprofessional collaboration. Kolb's experiential theory proposes that learning is an ongoing and cyclic process driven by experience. This theory emphasizes the significance of reflection and active participation in enhancing learning (Nagel et al., 2024). Case-based learning is an established strategy that engages students in real-world scenarios to improve their learning experience. Collaborative learning fosters active engagement, where pupils collaborate with peers and experts to develop a sound understanding of the resource. This leads to enhanced productivity (Xiao et al., 2008).

ETHICAL CONSIDERATIONS IN USING AI AND DATA IN EDUCATION

Ethical considerations in using AI in education involve multiple ethical dilemmas that require scrutiny and thoughtful resolution (Elendu et al., 2023). Risks to safety and security must be identified, addressed, and mitigated throughout the AI system to ensure the safety of humans, the environment, and the ecosystem (UNESCO, 2022). Data processing and usage must adhere to privacy and security principles (Huang, 2023).

Bias and Fairness

Data can include bias during the process, from production to management. As a result, data ethics is vital in mitigating challenges and unintentional consequences from poorly managed data (Ball Dunlap et al., 2024). Equity in machine learning is acquired through fairness, and notable efforts have been centred on standardizing this concept in machine learning algorithms (Wesson et al., 2022). Addressing responsibility attrition challenges involves evaluating structural and temporal relationships between humans and technology, ensuring transparency and traceability of AI systems (Jeyaraman et al., 2023).

RECOMMENDATIONS AND FUTURE DIRECTIONS

Medical AI should prioritize supporting students in collecting pertinent medical information and streamlining tasks accurately and quickly (Li et al., 2023). Diversity and inclusiveness should be respected, protected, and promoted at every level of the AI system's life cycle in line with international law, including human rights law (UNESCO, 2022). It is advisable to integrate case studies and industrial collaboration with many teaching methods to foster the understanding of AI in healthcare (Crotty et al., 2024). Medical organizations should educate tutors and administrators on leveraging the impact of AI in teaching, assessment, and management (Narayanan et al., 2023). Implementation of uniform standards and frameworks necessitates the combined activities of organizations and regulatory bodies to ensure the responsible use of AI (Mir et al., 2023). It is crucial to conduct research in collaboration with AI specialists, scientists, healthcare professionals, and individuals with disabilities to design AI solutions tailored to address the personal needs of students with disabilities in the healthcare sector.

CONCLUSION

The integration of adaptive learning technologies in healthcare education offers transformative opportunities to create more inclusive and effective learning environments for students with disabilities. By leveraging innovations such as artificial intelligence, virtual reality, and assistive technologies, educators can address long-standing challenges related to accessibility, equity, and competency training in medical and healthcare education. These technologies provide personalized learning experiences that empower students to overcome barriers and thrive academically, professionally, and personally. This chapter highlights the importance of embracing adaptive learning technologies as a pathway to enhancing student engagement, confidence, and skill development. It underscores the role of educators, policymakers, and healthcare institutions in fostering inclusive practices that go beyond mere compliance with legal requirements, focusing instead on meaningful educational reforms. By addressing gaps in disability competency training and ensuring equitable access to resources, stakeholders can create an environment where every student can succeed.

Ethical considerations remain at the forefront of this transformation, requiring vigilance to ensure that the use of data and AI technologies is transparent, fair, and respectful of individual privacy. Collaborative efforts among educators, technologists, and healthcare professionals are crucial to designing systems that not only accommodate but also empower students with disabilities. As the healthcare sector continues to evolve, integrating adaptive learning technologies can help prepare a diverse generation of leaders equipped to navigate the complex challenges of modern healthcare. This vision requires a commitment to innovation, inclusivity, and a shared responsibility to create a future where education and technology work in harmony to improve lives and communities.

REFERENCES

Alowais, S. A., Alghamdi, S. S., Alsuhebany, N., Alqahtani, T., Alshaya, A. I., Almohareb, S. N., Aldairem, A., Alrashed, M., Saleh, K. B., Badreldin, H. A., Yami, M. S. A., Harbi, S. A., & Albekairy, A. M. (2023). Revolutionizing healthcare: The role of artificial intelligence in clinical practice. *BMC Medical Education*, 23(1), 689. Advance online publication. DOI: 10.1186/s12909-023-04698-z PMID: 37740191

Ankam, N. S., Bosques, G., Sauter, C., Stiens, S., Therattil, M., Williams, F. H., Atkins, C. C., & Mayer, R. S. (2019). Competency-Based Curriculum Development to Meet the Needs of People with Disabilities: A Call to Action. *Academic Medicine*, 94(6), 781–788. DOI: 10.1097/ACM.0000000000002686 PMID: 30844926

Bäck, G. A., Mossige, M., Svendsen, H. B., Rønneberg, V., Selenius, H., Gøttsche, N. B., Dolmer, G., Fälth, L., Nilsson, S., & Svensson, I. (2024). Speech-to-text intervention to support text production among students with writing difficulties: A single-case study in Nordic countries. *Disability and Rehabilitation. Assistive Technology*, 19(8), 1–20. DOI: 10.1080/17483107.2024.2351488 PMID: 38776244

Bajwa, J., Munir, U., Nori, A., & Williams, B. (2021). Artificial intelligence in healthcare: Transforming the practice of medicine. *Future Healthcare Journal*, 8(2), e188–e194. DOI: 10.7861/fhj.2021-0095 PMID: 34286183

Chalkiadakis, A., Seremetaki, A., Kanellou, A., Kallishi, M., Morfopoulou, A., Moraitaki, M., & Mastrokoukou, S. (2024). Impact of Artificial Intelligence and Virtual Reality on Educational Inclusion: A Systematic Review of Technologies Supporting Students with Disabilities. *Education Sciences*, 14(11), 1223. DOI: 10.3390/educsci14111223

Chary, M., Parikh, S., Manini, A., Boyer, E., & Radeous, M. (2018). A Review of Natural Language Processing in Medical Education. *The Western Journal of Emergency Medicine*, 20(1), 78–86. DOI: 10.5811/westjem.2018.11.39725 PMID: 30643605

Crotty, E., Singh, A., Neligan, N., Chamunyonga, C., & Edwards, C. (2024). Artificial intelligence in medical imaging education: Recommendations for undergraduate curriculum development. *Radiography*, pp. *30*, 67–73. DOI: 10.1016/j.radi.2024.10.008

Dash, S., & Bhoi, C. (2024). Exploring the Intersection of Education and Artificial Intelligence: A Comprehensive Review. *International Journal of Multidisciplinary Approach Research and Science*, 2(02), 601–610. DOI: 10.59653/ijmars.v2i02.637

Dumić-Čule, I., Orešković, T., Brkljačić, B., Tiljak, M. K., & Orešković, S. (2020). The importance of introducing artificial intelligence to the medical curriculum – assessing practitioners' perspectives. *Croatian Medical Journal*, 61(5), 457–464. DOI: 10.3325/cmj.2020.61.457 PMID: 33150764

Dunlap, P. B., & Michalowski, M. (2024). Advancing artificial intelligence data ethics in nursing: Future directions for nursing practice, research, and education (Preprint). *JMIR Nursing*, 7, e62678. DOI: 10.2196/62678 PMID: 39453630

Elendu, C., Amaechi, D. C., Elendu, T. C., Jingwa, K. A., Okoye, O. K., Okah, M. J., Ladele, J. A., Farah, A. H., & Alimi, H. A. (2023). Ethical implications of AI and robotics in healthcare. *Revista de Medicina (São Paulo)*, 102(50), e36671. DOI: 10.1097/MD.0000000000036671 PMID: 38115340

Fernández-Batanero, J. M., Montenegro-Rueda, M., & Fernández-Cerero, J. (2022). Use of Augmented Reality for Students with Educational Needs: A Systematic Review (2016–2021). *Societies (Basel, Switzerland)*, 12(2), 36. DOI: 10.3390/soc12020036

França, R. P., Monteiro, A. C. B., Arthur, R., & Iano, Y. (2021). An overview of deep learning in big data, image, and signal processing in the modern digital age. In *Elsevier eBooks* (pp. 63–87). DOI: 10.1016/B978-0-12-822226-3.00003-9

Ghorashi, N., Ismail, A., Ghosh, P., Sidawy, A., & Javan, R. (2023). AI-Powered Chatbots in Medical Education: Potential Applications and Implications. *Cureus*. Advance online publication. DOI: 10.7759/cureus.43271 PMID: 37692629

Gil, M. J. V., Gonzalez-Medina, G., Lucena-Anton, D., Perez-Cabezas, V., Del Carmen Ruiz-Molinero, M., & Martín-Valero, R. (2021). Augmented Reality in Physical Therapy: Systematic Review and Meta-analysis. *JMIR Serious Games*, 9(4), e30985. DOI: 10.2196/30985 PMID: 34914611

Gligorea, I., Cioca, M., Oancea, R., Gorski, A., Gorski, H., & Tudorache, P. (2023a). Adaptive Learning Using Artificial Intelligence in e-Learning: A Literature Review. *Education Sciences*, 13(12), 1216. DOI: 10.3390/educsci13121216

Gligorea, I., Cioca, M., Oancea, R., Gorski, A., Gorski, H., & Tudorache, P. (2023b). Adaptive Learning Using Artificial Intelligence in e-Learning: A Literature Review. *Education Sciences*, 13(12), 1216. DOI: 10.3390/educsci13121216

Halkiopoulos, C., & Gkintoni, E. (2024). Leveraging AI in E-Learning: Personalized Learning and Adaptive Assessment through Cognitive Neuropsychology—A Systematic Analysis. *Electronics (Basel)*, 13(18), 3762. DOI: 10.3390/electronics13183762

Harmon, G. E. (2019). *Health care augmented intelligence: Where the AMA stands.* https://www.ama-assn.org/system/files/2019-08/ai-2018-board-policy-summary.pdf

Hawkins, R. E., Welcher, C. M., Holmboe, E. S., Kirk, L. M., Norcini, J. J., Simons, K. B., & Skochelak, S. E. (2015). Implementation of competency-based medical education: Are we addressing the concerns and challenges? *Medical Education*, 49(11), 1086–1102. DOI: 10.1111/medu.12831 PMID: 26494062

Healthcare Simulation Dictionary. (2020). *Agency for Healthcare Research and Quality eBooks.*, DOI: 10.23970/simulationv2

Heinen, M., Van Oostveen, C., Peters, J., Vermeulen, H., & Huis, A. (2019). An integrative review of leadership competencies and attributes in advanced nursing practice. *Journal of Advanced Nursing*, 75(11), 2378–2392. DOI: 10.1111/jan.14092 PMID: 31162695

Hersh, M., & Mouroutsou, S. (2015). Learning Technology and Disability: Overcoming Barriers to Inclusion: Evidence from a Multi-Country Study. *IFAC-PapersOnLine*, 48(24), 83–88. DOI: 10.1016/j.ifacol.2015.12.061

Huang, L. (2023). Ethics of Artificial Intelligence in Education: Student Privacy and Data Protection. *Science Insights Education Frontiers*, 16(2), 2577–2587. DOI: 10.15354/sief.23.re202

Ioerger, M., Flanders, R. M., French-Lawyer, J. R., & Turk, M. A. (2019). Interventions to Teach Medical Students About Disability. *American Journal of Physical Medicine & Rehabilitation*, 98(7), 577–599. DOI: 10.1097/PHM.0000000000001154 PMID: 30730327

Jeyaraman, M., Balaji, S., Jeyaraman, N., & Yadav, S. (2023). Unraveling the Ethical Enigma: Artificial Intelligence in Healthcare. *Cureus*. Advance online publication. DOI: 10.7759/cureus.43262 PMID: 37692617

Jian, M. J. K. O. (2023). Personalized learning through AI. *Advances in Engineering Innovation*, 5(1), 16–19. DOI: 10.54254/2977-3903/5/2023039

Jin, J., & Bridges, S. M. (2014). Educational Technologies in Problem-Based Learning in Health Sciences Education: A Systematic Review. *Journal of Medical Internet Research*, 16(12), e251. DOI: 10.2196/jmir.3240 PMID: 25498126

Joshi, A. K. (1991). Natural Language Processing. *Science*, 253(5025), 1242–1249. DOI: 10.1126/science.253.5025.1242 PMID: 17831443

Köse, H., & Güner-Yildiz, N. (2020). Augmented reality (AR) as a learning material in special needs education. *Education and Information Technologies*, 26(2), 1921–1936. DOI: 10.1007/s10639-020-10326-w

Lee, D., Pollack, S. W., Mroz, T., Frogner, B. K., & Skillman, S. M. (2023). Disability competency training in medical education. *Medical Education Online*, 28(1), 2207773. Advance online publication. DOI: 10.1080/10872981.2023.2207773 PMID: 37148284

Li, Q., & Qin, Y. (2023). AI in medical education: Medical student perception, curriculum recommendations and design suggestions. *BMC Medical Education*, 23(1), 852. Advance online publication. DOI: 10.1186/s12909-023-04700-8 PMID: 37946176

Lipka, O., Sarid, M., Zorach, I. A., Bufman, A., Hagag, A. A., & Peretz, H. (2020). Adjustment to Higher Education: A Comparison of Students with and Without Disabilities. *Frontiers in Psychology*, 11, 923. Advance online publication. DOI: 10.3389/fpsyg.2020.00923 PMID: 32670127

Liu, K. K., Thurlow, M. L., Press, A. M., Dosedel, M. J., & University of Minnesota, National Center on Educational Outcomes. (2019). *A Review of the Literature on Computerized Speech-to-Text Accommodations* (Report No. 414). University of Minnesota, National Center on Educational Outcomes. https://files.eric.ed.gov/fulltext/ED600670.pdf

Lovett, B. J. (2021). Educational Accommodations for Students with Disabilities: Two Equity-Related Concerns. *Frontiers in Education*, 6, 795266. Advance online publication. DOI: 10.3389/feduc.2021.795266

Main barriers to education for students with disabilities (fact sheet) | Ontario Human Rights Commission. (n.d.). https://www3.ohrc.on.ca/en/main-barriers-education-students-disabilities-fact-sheet

McDonald, P. L., Phillips, J., Harwood, K., Maring, J., & Van Der Wees, P. J. (2022). Identifying requisite learning health system competencies: A scoping review. *BMJ Open*, 12(8), e061124. DOI: 10.1136/bmjopen-2022-061124 PMID: 35998963

McKee, M., Case, B., Fausone, M., Zazove, P., Ouellette, A., & Fetters, M. D. (2016). Medical Schools' Willingness to Accommodate Medical Students with Sensory and Physical Disabilities: Ethical Foundations of a Functional Challenge to "Organic" Technical Standards. *AMA Journal of Ethics*, 18(10), 993–1002. DOI: 10.1001/journalofethics.2016.18.10.medu1-1610 PMID: 27780023

McNicholl, A., Casey, H., Desmond, D., & Gallagher, P. (2019). The impact of assistive technology use for students with disabilities in higher education: A systematic review. *Disability and Rehabilitation. Assistive Technology*, 16(2), 130–143. DOI: 10.1080/17483107.2019.1642395 PMID: 31335220

Meeks, L. M., Jain, N. R., & Association of American Medical Colleges. (2018). Accessibility, Inclusion, and Action in Medical Education: Lived Experiences of Learners and Physicians with Disabilities. In *Association of American Medical Colleges*. https://sds.ucsf.edu/sites/g/files/tkssra2986/f/aamc-ucsf-disability-special-report-accessible.pdf

Meşe, İ., Taşlıçay, C. A., Kuzan, B. N., Kuzan, T. Y., & Sivrioğlu, A. K. (2023). Educating the next generation of radiologists: A comparative report of ChatGPT and e-learning resources. *Diagnostic and Interventional Radiology (Ankara, Turkey)*, 30(3), 163–174. DOI: 10.4274/dir.2023.232496 PMID: 38145370

Mir, M. M., Mir, G. M., Raina, N. T., Mir, S. M., Mir, S. M., Miskeen, E., Alharthi, M. H., & Alamri, M. M. S. (2023). Application of Artificial Intelligence in Medical Education: Current Scenario and Future Perspectives. *PubMed*, 11(3), 133–140. DOI: 10.30476/jamp.2023.98655.1803 PMID: 37469385

Mosia, P. A., & Phasha, N. (2017). Access to curriculum for students with disabilities at higher education institutions: How does the National University of Lesotho fare? *African Journal of Disability*, p. 6. DOI: 10.30476/jamp.2023.98655.1803 PMID: 37469385

Nagel, D. A., Penner, J. L., Halas, G., Philip, M. T., & Cooke, C. A. (2024). Exploring experiential learning within interprofessional practice education initiatives for pre-licensure healthcare students: A scoping review. *BMC Medical Education*, 24(1), 139. Advance online publication. DOI: 10.1186/s12909-024-05114-w PMID: 38350938

Narayanan, S., Ramakrishnan, R., Durairaj, E., & Das, A. (2023). Artificial Intelligence Revolutionizing the Field of Medical Education. *Cureus*. Advance online publication. DOI: 10.7759/cureus.49604 PMID: 38161821

Nimavat, N., Singh, S., Fichadiya, N., Sharma, P., Patel, N., Kumar, M., Chauhan, G., & Pandit, N. (2021). Online Medical Education in India – Different Challenges and Probable Solutions in the Age of COVID-19. *Advances in Medical Education and Practice*, 12, 237–243. DOI: 10.2147/AMEP.S295728 PMID: 33692645

Panggabean, T. E., Paramansyah, A., Halim, C., & Maliha, S. (2024). Assessing the Effect of Online Learning Platforms in Promoting Inclusive Education for Students with Disabilities. *International Education Trend Issues*, 2(2), 287–297. DOI: 10.56442/ieti.v2i2.696

Pianosi, R., Presley, L., Buchanan, J., Lévesque, A., Savard, S.-A., & Lam, J. (2023). Canadian Survey on Disability, 2022: Concepts and Methods Guide. In *Canadian Survey on Disability* (Report Catalogue no. 89-654-X). Statistics Canada. https://www150.statcan.gc.ca/n1/en/pub/89-654-x/89-654-x2023004-eng.pdf?st=UVRCv8XU (Original work published 2022)

Procházková, D. (2014). The Human Factor and Its Handling. In *Elsevier eBooks* (pp. 199–223). DOI: 10.1016/B978-0-12-397199-9.00007-0

Recommendation on the ethics of artificial intelligence. (n.d.). https://unesdoc.unesco.org/ark:/48223/pf0000381137

Ryan, G. V., Callaghan, S., Rafferty, A., Higgins, M. F., Mangina, E., & McAuliffe, F. (2021). Learning Outcomes of Immersive Technologies in Health Care Student Education: Systematic Review of the Literature. *Journal of Medical Internet Research*, 24(2), e30082. DOI: 10.2196/30082 PMID: 35103607

Sajja, R., Sermet, Y., Cikmaz, M., Cwiertny, D., & Demir, I. (2024). Artificial Intelligence-Enabled Intelligent Assistant for Personalized and Adaptive Learning in Higher Education. *Information (Basel)*, 15(10), 596. DOI: 10.3390/info15100596

Seung, Y., & Seung, Y. (2024, October 17). Inclusive Intelligence Chapter 4: Envisioning AI's Impact on Special Education Research - CIDDL. *CIDDL - Center for Innovation, Design, and Digital Learning.* https://ciddl.org/inclusive-intelligence-chapter-4-envisioning-ais-impact-on-special-education-research/

Singh, A. A., Shapter, F. M., Bernard, A., Whitworth, D. J., Holt, M. G., Waller, P. S., & Bond, S. L. (2024). Applying Iterative Student Feedback across Flipped Classroom and Flexible Teaching Approaches: Impact on Veterinary Students' Learning Experience. *Animals (Basel)*, 14(16), 2335. DOI: 10.3390/ani14162335 PMID: 39199869

Song, C., Shin, S., & Shin, K. (2024). Implementing the Dynamic Feedback-Driven Learning Optimization Framework: A Machine Learning Approach to Personalize Educational Pathways. *Applied Sciences (Basel, Switzerland)*, 14(2), 916. DOI: 10.3390/app14020916

Soori, M., Arezoo, B., & Dastres, R. (2023). Artificial intelligence, machine learning and deep learning in advanced robotics, a review. *Cognitive Robotics*, 3, 54–70. DOI: 10.1016/j.cogr.2023.04.001

Tepgec, M., Heil, J., & Ifenthaler, D. (2024). Feedback literacy matters: Unlocking the potential of learning analytics-based feedback. *Assessment & Evaluation in Higher Education*, •••, 1–17. DOI: 10.1080/02602938.2024.2367587

Vats, A. & Sharmistha Dey. (2022). Accommodation Strategies for Students with Disabilities in the Classroom. In G D Goenka University & Chandigarh University, *Technoarete Transactions on Applications of Information and Communication Technology (ICT) in Education: Vol. Vol-1* (Issue Issue-4, pp. 25–26). https://technoaretepublication.org/information-communication-technology/article/accommodation-strategies-students.pdf

Wang, H., & Avillach, P. (2021). Diagnostic Classification and Prognostic Prediction Using Common Genetic Variants in Autism Spectrum Disorder: Genotype-Based Deep Learning. *JMIR Medical Informatics*, 9(4), e24754. DOI: 10.2196/24754 PMID: 33714937

Wesson, P., Hswen, Y., Valdes, G., Stojanovski, K., & Handley, M. A. (2021). Risks and Opportunities to Ensure Equity in applying Big Data Research in Public Health. *Annual Review of Public Health*, 43(1), 59–78. DOI: 10.1146/annurev-publhealth-051920-110928 PMID: 34871504

Wood, S. G., Moxley, J. H., Tighe, E. L., & Wagner, R. K. (2017). Does the Use of Text-to-Speech and Related Read-Aloud Tools Improve Reading Comprehension for Students with Reading Disabilities? A Meta-Analysis. *Journal of Learning Disabilities*, 51(1), 73–84. DOI: 10.1177/0022219416688170 PMID: 28112580

Wu, H., Lee, S. W., Chang, H., & Liang, J. (2012). Current status, opportunities and challenges of augmented reality in education. *Computers & Education*, 62, 41–49. DOI: 10.1016/j.compedu.2012.10.024

Xiao, L., Carroll, J. M., Clemson, P., & Rosson, M. B. (2008). Support of Case-Based authentic learning activities: a collaborative case commenting tool and a collaborative case builder. *Proceedings of the 41st Annual Hawaii International Conference on System Sciences (HICSS 2008)*, pp. 19, 6. DOI: 10.1109/HICSS.2008.417

Zwoliński, G., Kamińska, D., Haamer, R. E., Coelho, L. F., & Anbarjafari, G. (2023). Enhancing empathy through virtual reality: Developing a universal design training application for students. *Medycyna Pracy*. Advance online publication. DOI: 10.13075/mp.5893.01407 PMID: 37695933

ADDITIONAL READING

Alzghoul, A. M. (2024). Implementation of Adaptive Technology Tools and Applications for Accessible Physics Education with Deaf and Handicapped Students. *Nanotechnology Perceptions*, •••, 777–791.

Chopra, A., Patel, H., Rajput, D. S., & Bansal, N. (2024). Empowering Inclusive Education: Leveraging AI-ML and Innovative Tech Stacks to Support Students with Learning Disabilities in Higher Education. In *Applied Assistive Technologies and Informatics for Students with Disabilities* (pp. 255–275). Springer Nature Singapore. DOI: 10.1007/978-981-97-0914-4_15

Jumaa, Y. M., Moussa, S. M., & Khalifa, M. E. (2017, December). The main aspects of adaptive educational games for normal and disabled/disordered learners: A comprehensive study. In *2017 Eighth International Conference on Intelligent Computing and Information Systems (ICICIS)* (pp. 348-355). IEEE. DOI: 10.1109/INTELCIS.2017.8260061

Papanastasiou, G., Drigas, A., Skianis, C., Lytras, M., & Papanastasiou, E. (2018). Patient-centric ICTs based healthcare for students with learning, physical and/or sensory disabilities. *Telematics and Informatics*, 35(4), 654–664. DOI: 10.1016/j.tele.2017.09.002

Skourlas, C., Tsolakidis, A., Belsis, P., Vassis, D., Kampouraki, A., Kakoulidis, P., & Giannakopoulos, G. A. (2016). Integration of institutional repositories and e-learning platforms for supporting disabled students in the higher education context. *Library Review*, 65(3), 136–159. DOI: 10.1108/LR-08-2015-0088

KEY TERMS AND DEFINITIONS

Adaptive Learning Technologies: Educational tools and systems that use data-driven algorithms and AI to personalize learning experiences based on individual student needs and progress.

Assistive Technologies: Devices or software designed to support individuals with disabilities by enhancing their functional capabilities and access to educational resources.

Augmented Reality (AR): A technology that overlays digital content onto the real world, creating interactive and immersive learning experiences.

Experiential Learning: A hands-on approach to education that emphasizes learning through real-world experiences, often enhanced by virtual or augmented reality.

Healthcare Education: The process of training students in medical and healthcare fields to develop skills, knowledge, and competencies for professional practice.

Immersive Learning: An instructional method that uses technologies such as virtual reality (VR) and AR to create highly engaging and interactive educational environments.

Inclusive Education: Educational practices that ensure all students, regardless of ability or disability, have equal access to learning opportunities and resources.

Machine Learning (ML): A subset of artificial intelligence that enables computers to learn from data and improve their performance on specific tasks without explicit programming.

Personalized Learning: An educational approach that tailors teaching methods, content, and pacing to the unique needs and preferences of each student.

Virtual Reality (VR): A simulated environment created using computer technology that provides an immersive, three-dimensional experience for educational purposes.

Chapter 4
AI-Powered Innovations Transforming Adaptive Education for Disability Support

Munikrishnaiah Sundara Ramaiah
 https://orcid.org/0009-0007-9855-9214
Independent Researcher, San Antonio, USA

Sevinthi Kali Sankar Nagarajan
 https://orcid.org/0009-0005-4684-0384
Independent Researcher, San Antonio, USA

Pawan Whig
 https://orcid.org/0000-0003-1863-1591
VIPS, India

Pushan Kumar Dutta
 https://orcid.org/0000-0002-4765-3864
Amity University, Kolkata, India

ABSTRACT

This chapter examines artificial intelligence's (AI) transformative impact on adaptive education for students with disabilities. This chapter explores how AI-driven technologies, including intelligent tutoring systems, speech recognition tools, and personalized learning algorithms, are reshaping educational experiences to be more inclusive and effective. By leveraging these innovations, educators can tailor content and support to meet individual learning needs, enhance accessibility, and overcome barriers to education. Drawing on case studies and practical examples, the

DOI: 10.4018/979-8-3693-8227-1.ch004

chapter highlights the ability of AI to revolutionize traditional educational models by delivering customized, responsive support for diverse disabilities. Emphasizing the potential of AI to foster equity and inclusion, the chapter underscores its role in advancing opportunities for all learners and creating a more accessible educational landscape.

INTRODUCTION

In recent years, the field of education has witnessed unprecedented transformations driven by technological advancements. Among these innovations, artificial intelligence (AI) and data-driven solutions have emerged as powerful tools, particularly in the realm of adaptive education for students with disabilities. The integration of these technologies into educational frameworks promises to address longstanding challenges and provide tailored support to enhance learning experiences for all students. This chapter explores the profound impact of AI and data-driven innovations on adaptive education, focusing on their potential to revolutionize support for students with disabilities. Adaptive education refers to educational practices and systems designed to accommodate the diverse needs of learners, particularly those who face unique challenges due to disabilities. Traditional educational models often fall short in providing equitable opportunities for students with disabilities, as they tend to adopt a one-size-fits-all approach. This lack of personalization can hinder the academic progress and overall well-being of students who require specialized support.

The Individuals with Disabilities Education Act (IDEA) emphasizes the importance of providing individualized instruction to ensure that students with disabilities receive a free and appropriate public education. Despite this mandate, achieving true inclusivity in education remains a complex challenge. Educational institutions are increasingly seeking innovative solutions to bridge this gap, and technology has emerged as a key enabler in this quest. Data-driven solutions have revolutionized various sectors, and education is no exception. By harnessing the power of data analytics, educators can gain valuable insights into students' learning behaviors, strengths, and areas for improvement. This wealth of information enables the creation of personalized learning experiences that are tailored to the specific needs of each student, including those with disabilities. Learning analytics is a field dedicated to analyzing data collected from educational environments to improve teaching and learning. For students with disabilities, learning analytics can provide a detailed understanding of how they interact with educational content, the challenges they face, and their progress over time. By analyzing this data, educators can design targeted interventions, adjust instructional strategies, and implement adaptive technologies that better support individual learning needs.

Artificial intelligence, with its ability to simulate human intelligence and learn from data, has made significant strides in various applications. In education, AI has the potential to transform how support is delivered to students with disabilities. AI-powered technologies, such as intelligent tutoring systems and speech recognition tools, offer innovative solutions that address specific learning challenges. Intelligent tutoring systems (ITS) are AI-driven platforms that provide personalized instruction and feedback to students. These systems adapt to the learning pace and style of each student, offering targeted support and interventions based on their individual needs. For students with disabilities, ITS can offer customized learning experiences that cater to their unique requirements, whether it be through alternative input methods, specialized content, or tailored feedback. Speech recognition technology is another AI-powered innovation that has significantly impacted adaptive education. For students with physical disabilities or those who struggle with traditional input methods, speech recognition provides an alternative way to interact with educational content. This technology allows students to dictate their responses, navigate learning materials, and engage with educational tools through voice commands, thereby reducing barriers to participation and enhancing accessibility.

The integration of data-driven solutions and AI into adaptive education has already yielded promising results in various educational settings. Case studies and real-world applications illustrate how these technologies have improved educational outcomes for students with disabilities. One notable example is the use of AI-powered assistive technology in inclusive classrooms. Schools and institutions have implemented tools that use AI to support students with visual impairments, such as text-to-speech software and screen readers. These tools not only enhance accessibility but also promote greater independence and engagement in the learning process. Another case study highlights the use of data analytics to improve personalized learning for students with learning disabilities. By analyzing data on students' performance and engagement, educators have been able to identify patterns and tailor instructional strategies to better meet individual needs. This approach has led to improved academic outcomes and increased student satisfaction.

While the potential benefits of data-driven solutions and AI in adaptive education are substantial, there are also challenges and considerations that must be addressed. Data privacy and security are critical concerns, as the collection and analysis of student data raise questions about how this information is stored, used, and protected. Additionally, the implementation of AI and data-driven technologies requires careful consideration of equity and accessibility. It is essential to ensure that these innovations do not exacerbate existing inequalities or create new barriers for students with disabilities. Educators and policymakers must work collaboratively to address these challenges and ensure that technology is used in a way that promotes inclusivity and supports all learners. Looking ahead, the continued evolution of AI and data-driven solutions promises to bring even more advancements to adaptive education. As technology continues to advance, new tools and applications will emerge, offering increasingly sophisticated ways to support students with disabilities. The integration of AI and data analytics into educational systems holds the potential to create more personalized, inclusive, and effective learning environments. In conclusion, the intersection of AI, data-driven solutions, and adaptive education represents a significant opportunity to enhance support for students with disabilities. By leveraging these technologies, educators can create personalized learning experiences that address individual needs and promote equitable educational opportunities. As we continue to explore and develop these innovations, it is crucial to remain mindful of the challenges and work towards solutions that ensure all students benefit from the advancements in educational technology.

LITERATURE REVIEW: AI AND ADAPTIVE TECHNOLOGIES IN EDUCATION

The integration of artificial intelligence (AI) and adaptive technologies into education has been a focal point of recent research, highlighting both the transformative potential and the ongoing challenges associated with these innovations. This literature review synthesizes findings from various studies on AI applications in education, focusing on their impact on inclusivity, personalization, and adaptive learning. Recent literature underscores the role of AI and innovative technology stacks in promoting inclusive education, particularly for students with learning disabilities. Chopra et al. (2024) discuss how AI-ML can empower inclusive education by supporting students with learning disabilities in higher education. They emphasize the importance of leveraging AI to provide personalized learning experiences that address individual needs. Similarly, Neha et al. (2024) explore pioneering assistive technologies that facilitate the inclusion of students with learning disabilities, highlighting advances in AI that make educational content more accessible.

Almufareh et al. (2024) propose a conceptual model for inclusive technology, advancing disability inclusion through AI. Their model aims to bridge gaps in accessibility and ensure that technological advancements benefit all students. This is echoed by Almufareh et al. (2023), who provide an AI perspective on intellectual disability, offering a framework for integrating technology to support students with diverse needs. AI's role in personalized learning is a recurrent theme in the literature. Aggarwal (2023) explores the integration of innovative technological developments and AI with education to create an adaptive learning pedagogy. This approach tailors educational experiences to individual student needs, enhancing engagement and learning outcomes. Singh (2023) further emphasizes the transformative power of AI in higher education, illustrating how AI can revolutionize learning environments through personalization.

Tan (2023) discusses the harnessing of AI for innovation in education, focusing on how AI-driven systems can provide personalized and adaptive learning opportunities. This is supported by Denga and Denga (2024), who highlight the power of technology in revolutionizing education and enhancing learning experiences through computational thinking and problem-solving. Khalid et al. (2024) examine the impact of AI-powered solutions in the rehabilitation process, noting recent improvements and future trends. Their research underscores the potential of AI to aid in rehabilitative education, enhancing support for students with special needs. Mohammad Abedrabbu Alkhawaldeh (2023) also explores how AI can be harnessed for personalized assistive technology, emphasizing its potential to address learning disabilities effectively. Despite the promising advancements, several challenges persist. Zdravkova (2022) discusses the potential and limitations of AI for assistive technology in education, emphasizing the need for accurate and reliable systems. Rane et al. (2023) address the complexities of integrating AI into educational frameworks, highlighting the need for effective change management and technical support.

Aldoseri et al. (2024) investigate the key pillars and industry impact of AI-powered innovation in digital transformation, pointing out the significant impact of AI on various industries, including education. Mehta et al. (2023) focus on the inclusion of children with special needs, discussing AI-assisted special education and its implications for students with exceptional needs. The integration of AI and adaptive technologies in education presents significant opportunities for enhancing inclusivity, personalization, and overall learning experiences. The reviewed literature demonstrates that while AI can provide substantial benefits in terms of personalized learning and support for students with disabilities, there are ongoing challenges related to data privacy, ethical considerations, and technical complexity. Addressing these challenges and continuously evaluating the effectiveness of AI-driven solutions are crucial for realizing the full potential of these technologies in education.

DATA-DRIVEN SOLUTIONS IN ADAPTIVE EDUCATION

1. **Understanding Learning Analytics**

Learning analytics refers to the collection, analysis, and application of data related to student learning and educational processes. This field leverages data to gain insights into learning behaviors, performance trends, and educational outcomes.

The core objective of learning analytics is to improve teaching and learning by providing actionable insights that can drive decision-making and enhance the overall educational experience.

Learning analytics leverages diverse data sources, including student assessments, classroom interactions, attendance records, and engagement metrics, to provide a comprehensive view of the learning environment and student progress. By employing descriptive analytics, educators can summarize historical data, such as average grades and attendance rates, to understand past performance. Predictive analytics builds on this by using historical data to forecast future outcomes, such as identifying students at risk of falling behind based on patterns in their performance and engagement. Prescriptive analytics further enhances this process by offering recommendations to improve educational practices, suggesting targeted interventions to address specific challenges and optimize learning outcomes. Practical applications of learning analytics include early warning systems that detect students needing additional support, data-driven curriculum design that ensures content relevancy, and instructional strategies tailored to individual learning needs, enabling educators to modify teaching methods and provide targeted resources effectively.

2. Collecting and Analyzing Educational Data

Effective data collection and analysis are crucial for deriving meaningful insights from educational data. This process involves gathering data from various sources, ensuring its accuracy, and using analytical tools to interpret it.

Data collection in education involves gathering various types of information to gain a comprehensive understanding of student performance and engagement. Student assessments, such as test scores, quizzes, and assignments, provide quantitative data that tracks progress and highlights areas for improvement. Engagement metrics, including student interactions with digital learning platforms, participation in class discussions, and time spent on tasks, offer valuable insights into engagement levels. Behavioral data, derived from observing participation patterns and responses to feedback, helps in understanding learning dynamics. Additionally, qualitative data collected through feedback and surveys provides insights into student satisfaction and their opinions on educational experiences.

Once the data is collected, it undergoes a thorough analysis process. Data cleaning is the first step, ensuring accuracy by addressing missing values, inconsistencies, and errors, which is crucial for reliable analysis. Statistical analysis follows, applying techniques like regression analysis, clustering, and factor analysis to identify trends, correlations, and significant differences within the data. Visualization tools are then used to create charts, graphs, and dashboards, making complex information more accessible and easier to interpret. Finally, data interpretation involves drawing meaningful conclusions from the analyzed data, contextualizing the findings, and considering their implications for educational practices to inform decision-making.

3. **Personalization through Data Insights**

Personalization is a key goal of adaptive education, aiming to tailor learning experiences to the individual needs of each student. Data-driven insights play a crucial role in achieving this level of personalization by providing a detailed understanding of each student's unique learning profile.

Personalized learning approaches leverage data to create tailored educational experiences that cater to individual student needs. Adaptive learning technologies play a significant role in this by using data to adjust the learning path for each student, offering customized content and activities based on their performance and preferences. Teachers can implement differentiated instruction by utilizing data to provide varied learning materials and strategies that accommodate diverse learning styles and abilities. Individual learning plans, informed by data insights, help address specific learning goals and challenges for each student. Additionally, data-driven platforms can offer real-time feedback, allowing students to understand their progress and identify areas for improvement instantly. The benefits of personalized learning are substantial. Enhanced engagement is a key advantage, as personalized learning experiences are more engaging for students by aligning with their interests and learning styles. This tailored approach often leads to improved outcomes, with students more likely to succeed when learning experiences are matched to their individual needs and abilities. Moreover, personalized approaches can increase student motivation by providing relevant and meaningful learning opportunities.

However, challenges exist in implementing personalized learning. Ensuring data privacy is critical, particularly when handling sensitive student information. Integration of data-driven solutions into existing educational systems requires careful planning and coordination to be effective. Scalability is another significant challenge, as personalizing learning on a large scale can be difficult, especially in educational institutions with diverse and large student populations.

Data-driven solutions offer significant potential to enhance adaptive education by providing insights that inform personalized learning experiences. Understanding and implementing learning analytics, collecting and analyzing educational data, and leveraging data for personalization are critical components in creating effective and inclusive educational environments.

Artificial Intelligence in Adaptive Education

Artificial Intelligence (AI) encompasses a range of technologies designed to simulate human intelligence and perform tasks that traditionally require human cognition. In the context of education, AI technologies are used to enhance and personalize learning experiences, making them more adaptive and responsive to individual student needs.

Key AI technologies are transforming education by providing innovative ways to enhance learning experiences and streamline educational processes. Machine Learning (ML), a subset of AI, involves algorithms that allow systems to learn from data and improve over time without explicit programming. In education, ML can be used to analyze student data, predict learning needs and outcomes, and enablr more personalized instruction. Natural Language Processing (NLP) is another essential AI technology that allows computers to understand, interpret, and generate human language. This technology is widely used in educational applications, such as chatbots and automated feedback systems, to facilitate communication and support learning. Computer Vision, which enables machines to interpret and understand visual information, can be utilized in education to analyze students' interactions with educational materials through visual inputs, providing insights into engagement and comprehension. Additionally, Robotics plays a crucial role in education, with AI-equipped educational robots interacting with students and assisting in learning activities, offering hands-on experiences and personalized support.

These AI technologies have several applications in education. Personalized Learning is a significant application, where AI can analyze student performance and adapt learning materials to meet individual needs, ensuring each student receives a tailored educational experience. Automated Assessment is another vital application, where AI technologies can grade assignments and provide feedback, reducing the workload for educators and offering students immediate responses, enhancing the learning process.

2. Intelligent Tutoring Systems (ITS)

Intelligent Tutoring Systems (ITS) are AI-driven platforms designed to provide personalized instruction and feedback to students. These systems mimic the functions of a human tutor by adapting to each student's learning style and pace.

Intelligent Tutoring Systems (ITS) are advanced educational technologies designed to provide personalized and adaptive learning experiences. One of the key features of ITS is Personalization, where AI algorithms tailor lessons and activities according to individual student performance, preferences, and learning styles. This helps address specific learning gaps and strengths, making education more effective.

Adaptive Feedback is another crucial feature, where the system offers real-time feedback on student performance, providing explanations, hints, and additional resources as needed to guide learning. ITS also excel in Progress Tracking, monitoring student progress over time, and adjusting the difficulty of tasks to match the student's evolving needs. Interactive Learning is a hallmark of ITS, engaging students through interactive exercises and simulations that make the learning process more dynamic and effective.

The benefits of ITS are significant. They provide Individualized Attention by delivering personalized instruction that is often difficult to achieve in traditional classroom settings. ITS are also Scalable, capable of serving large numbers of students simultaneously, which offers scalable solutions for educational institutions. The focus on personalized support leads to Improved Learning Outcomes, enhancing overall educational performance and retention by addressing specific learning needs. However, there are challenges associated with ITS. Complexity of Implementation is a significant hurdle, as developing and deploying ITS requires substantial resources and expertise, including data collection, algorithm design, and integration with existing educational systems. Additionally, Student Engagement remains a challenge, as it's crucial to ensure that students stay engaged with AI-driven systems without feeling isolated from human interaction, which is vital for effective learning.

3. **Speech Recognition and Assistive Technologies**

Speech recognition technology enables computers to interpret and process human speech, offering significant benefits for students with disabilities or those who struggle with traditional input methods.

Speech recognition technology has several valuable applications in education, enhancing accessibility and independence for students. Voice-Activated Commands allow students to navigate educational platforms, complete assignments, and interact with digital content using their voices, making learning more accessible. Speech-to-Text technology converts spoken language into written text, assisting students with physical disabilities or learning difficulties who may find typing challenging. Additionally, Language Translation through speech recognition systems supports multilingual education by translating spoken language into different languages, aiding non-native speakers. These applications offer significant Benefits, including enhanced accessibility for students with physical disabilities, dyslexia, or other learning challenges, and increased independence by empowering students to interact with learning materials and complete tasks autonomously. However, challenges such as ensuring Accuracy and Reliability in recognizing diverse accents and speech patterns, as well as addressing Privacy Concerns related to handling and storing voice data, must be carefully managed to protect student information.

4. **AI-Powered Educational Tools**

AI-powered educational tools encompass a broad range of applications designed to enhance learning experiences and support educators. These tools leverage AI to provide intelligent features and functionalities that improve educational outcomes.

AI-powered tools in education, such as Adaptive Learning Platforms, Virtual Classrooms, and Content Creation Tools, represent significant advancements in creating personalized and interactive learning experiences. Adaptive Learning Platforms use AI to tailor educational content and resources based on individual student performance and preferences, delivering a highly customized learning journey. Virtual Classrooms leverage AI to provide immersive and interactive environments, supporting remote and hybrid learning models. Content Creation Tools assist in generating quizzes, summarizing texts, and curating relevant materials, streamlining the educational content development process. The benefits of these AI-powered tools are substantial, including increased Efficiency in handling various educational tasks, Enhanced Learning Experiences that cater to diverse learning styles, and Data-Driven Insights that help educators make informed decisions about student performance and engagement. However, challenges such as Integration into existing educational systems and the need for Training and Support for educators must be addressed to ensure effective implementation. In conclusion, AI technologies offer promising solutions for adaptive education, providing scalable, personalized, and accessible learning experiences while necessitating careful management of accuracy, privacy, and system integration to fully realize their potential.

Integration of Data-Driven Solutions and AI

1. **Combining Data Analytics with AI**

Combining data analytics with AI represents a powerful synergy that enhances educational technologies by integrating data-driven insights with advanced AI capabilities. This integration aims to create a more responsive and personalized learning environment.

The integration of data analytics with AI in education encompasses several key aspects that significantly enhance learning experiences. Data Integration involves gathering and analyzing diverse educational data, such as student performance metrics, engagement levels, and behavioral patterns. AI systems utilize this data to make predictions and recommendations, offering actionable insights for educators by identifying trends and forecasting learning outcomes. Personalization is a major advantage of AI, as it customizes educational content and experiences based on individual student data, tailoring learning paths, suggesting relevant resources, and adjusting task difficulty to meet specific needs. Predictive Analytics further leverages historical data to forecast future learning trends and outcomes, identifying students who may require additional support and predicting the effectiveness of educational interventions. Real-Time Adjustments are enabled by combining data analytics with AI, allowing platforms to modify instructional strategies on-the-fly based on current data and providing immediate, relevant feedback to students.

The benefits of this integration are substantial. Improved Accuracy in predictions and recommendations results in more effective and personalized learning interventions. Scalability allows educational technologies to efficiently support large numbers of students with personalized assistance. Additionally, Enhanced Decision-Making provides educators with data-driven insights that inform instructional strategies and improve educational outcomes. However, challenges persist, including ensuring Data Quality, as inaccurate or incomplete data can undermine the reliability of AI systems. Complexity of Integration also poses a challenge, requiring expertise and careful coordination to effectively merge data analytics with AI technologies.

2. Implementing Adaptive Technologies in Classrooms

Implementing adaptive technologies in classrooms involves incorporating AI and data-driven solutions to create dynamic and responsive learning environments that adjust to individual student needs.

When integrating adaptive technologies into education, several key considerations must be addressed to ensure their effectiveness and alignment with educational goals. Technology Selection is a critical step, involving the choice of suitable tools such as intelligent tutoring systems, adaptive learning platforms, or AI-powered educational tools. The selection should be guided by the specific needs of students and the overarching educational objectives of the institution. Integration with Existing Systems requires that new adaptive technologies be seamlessly incorporated into current classroom technologies and curricula, ensuring compatibility and enhancing rather than disrupting existing practices. Teacher Training is essential for the successful implementation of these technologies. Educators need comprehensive professional development programs focused on leveraging these tools to enrich teaching and support student learning. Equally important is Student Involvement; students must be introduced to adaptive technologies and understand how these tools can enhance their personalized learning experiences.

The benefits of implementing adaptive technologies are significant. Personalized Learning is achieved as these tools tailor instruction to individual student needs, leading to more engaging and effective learning experiences. Efficient Use of Resources is another advantage, as adaptive technologies can optimize resource allocation by focusing interventions where they are most needed and automating routine tasks.

Additionally, Enhanced Learning Outcomes result from the personalized support these technologies provide, improving student performance and learning achievements. However, challenges such as Cost and Technical Issues must be addressed. The expense of acquiring and maintaining adaptive technologies, along with the costs associated with training, can be substantial. Furthermore, technical problems such as system malfunctions or integration difficulties can hinder the effectiveness of these technologies and disrupt the educational process.

3. **Enhancing Accessibility and Inclusivity**

Enhancing accessibility and inclusivity through adaptive technologies ensures that all students, including those with disabilities or diverse learning needs, can benefit from personalized education.

To effectively integrate adaptive technologies in education, several key strategies should be considered. Assistive Technologies play a crucial role in supporting students with disabilities by incorporating tools such as speech recognition, text-to-speech, and screen readers. These technologies help make educational content accessible and usable for all learners. Universal Design for Learning (UDL) principles should be implemented to create flexible learning environments that cater to diverse learning styles and needs. Adaptive technologies can support UDL by providing multiple means of representation, expression, and engagement, thus accommodating a broad range of learning preferences. Customizable Interfaces are essential, allowing students to adjust the learning environment to their preferences and needs. This includes options for modifying text size, color schemes, and navigation tools, which help tailor the educational experience. Feedback and Support are also critical, as adaptive technologies can offer real-time, tailored guidance and resources to assist students in overcoming challenges and improving their learning outcomes.

The benefits of adopting these strategies are significant. Increased Accessibility is achieved as adaptive technologies improve access to educational materials for students with disabilities, fostering an inclusive learning environment. Enhanced Engagement is another benefit, as these technologies accommodate diverse learning needs, thereby increasing student participation and interaction. Furthermore, Equitable Learning Opportunities are promoted by ensuring that all students have access to personalized learning experiences, helping to level the playing field and support equitable educational outcomes. However, challenges such as Implementation Costs and Ongoing Support must be addressed. Implementing adaptive technologies can be expensive, particularly for institutions with limited budgets. Additionally, providing continuous support and maintenance is essential to ensure these technologies remain effective and usable over time.

4. **Challenges and Considerations**

Integrating data-driven solutions and AI into education presents several challenges and considerations that must be addressed to ensure successful implementation and effectiveness.

The integration of data-driven solutions and AI in education presents numerous opportunities for enhancing learning experiences and outcomes, but it also involves several key challenges. Data Privacy and Security is a primary concern, as protecting student information and complying with regulations such as GDPR and FERPA are critical. Institutions must implement robust security measures to safeguard sensitive data. Ethical Considerations also come into play, with questions surrounding fairness, bias, and the potential misuse of AI systems. Ensuring that AI applications are designed and utilized ethically is essential to maintain trust and integrity. Additionally, Technical Complexity is a significant hurdle, as developing and integrating AI-driven and data-driven solutions involves intricate technical processes and requires specialized expertise. Institutions must be prepared to manage these complexities effectively. Change Management is another challenge, as adopting new technologies necessitates strategies to address resistance, facilitate smooth transitions, and support both educators and students throughout the implementation process.

For successful integration, several considerations are vital. Stakeholder Involvement is crucial; engaging educators, students, and parents in the planning and implementation stages ensures that the technologies meet their needs and expectations. Continuous Evaluation is necessary to regularly assess the effectiveness of adaptive technologies and data-driven solutions, allowing for adjustments and improvements to meet desired outcomes. Scalability must also be considered to ensure that technologies can be effectively implemented across diverse educational settings and institutions. While the integration of data-driven and AI technologies in education holds significant promise for improving learning experiences and outcomes, addressing challenges related to privacy, ethics, technical complexity, and changing management is essential. By focusing on stakeholder involvement, continuous evaluation, and scalability, institutions can maximize the benefits of these technologies and support all students effectively.

ETHICAL AND PRIVACY CONSIDERATIONS

Data Privacy and Security Issues

Data privacy and security are paramount concerns when implementing data-driven and AI technologies in education. These systems handle vast amounts of sensitive information, including students' personal details, academic records, and behavioral data. To ensure data privacy, educational institutions must implement stringent measures for data collection, storage, and usage. This includes employing robust encryption techniques, access controls, and secure storage solutions to protect against unauthorized access and breaches. Institutions should be transparent about their data practices, clearly communicating to students and parents what data is collected, how it is used, and with whom it may be shared. Consent is a critical aspect; obtaining informed consent from students and their guardians is essential before collecting and using their data. Institutions must also have protocols in place for responding to data breaches, including notifying affected individuals promptly and taking steps to mitigate any potential damage. Adopting a privacy-by-design approach, conducting regular audits, and providing ongoing training to staff are effective strategies for maintaining data security and privacy.

Ethical Implications of AI in Education

The integration of AI in education brings several ethical considerations that must be carefully addressed. One significant concern is the potential for AI systems to perpetuate or even exacerbate biases present in the data they are trained on. Biases in AI algorithms can lead to unfair treatment of students, influencing educational outcomes in ways that disproportionately affect certain groups. Ensuring fairness requires rigorous testing of AI systems to identify and mitigate biases. Transparency is another critical issue; AI decision-making processes can often be opaque, making it challenging to understand how and why certain recommendations or decisions are made. Educational institutions should strive for transparency by providing clear explanations of how AI systems operate and who is responsible for their decisions. Additionally, the use of AI should respect student autonomy and agency, supporting rather than replacing human decision-making. Informed consent is vital; students and parents should be well-informed about how AI systems will be used and how they might impact the learning experience. Establishing ethical guidelines for AI usage in education can help navigate these issues responsibly.

The ethical implications of artificial intelligence (AI) in education are profound and multifaceted, affecting students, educators, institutions, and society at large. As AI technologies become increasingly integrated into educational environments, it is essential to critically examine the ethical dimensions to ensure that these technologies are used responsibly and equitably. Below is a detailed exploration of the key ethical considerations associated with AI in education.

1. Equity and Access

    Digital Divide: AI technologies in education have the potential to exacerbate existing inequalities. Students from low-income backgrounds, rural areas, or underfunded schools may not have access to the necessary digital tools or internet connectivity to benefit from AI-driven educational resources. This digital divide can widen the gap between those who have access to high-quality education and those who do not.

    Bias in AI Algorithms: AI systems are trained on data that may reflect societal biases. If the data used to train educational AI systems is biased, the resulting algorithms can perpetuate and even amplify these biases, leading to unequal treatment of students based on race, gender, socioeconomic status, or other factors. For instance, an AI-powered grading system might unfairly disadvantage certain groups of students if it is trained on biased data.

    Personalized Learning: While AI has the potential to provide personalized learning experiences, there is a risk that it could reinforce existing disparities. If AI systems are primarily designed with a certain demographic in mind, students from different backgrounds may not receive the same level of customization or support, leading to unequal educational outcomes.

2. Privacy and Data Security

    Data Collection: AI systems in education often rely on vast amounts of data about students, including their academic performance, behavior, and even personal characteristics. The collection and storage of this data raise significant privacy concerns, particularly if the data is sensitive or if students are unaware of the extent of the data being collected.

    Consent and Transparency: It is crucial that students, parents, and educators are fully informed about what data is being collected, how it is being used, and who has access to it. Obtaining informed consent is a key ethical requirement, but it can be challenging to ensure that all parties fully understand the implications of data collection in AI systems.

    Data Security: Ensuring the security of student data is critical, as breaches could lead to serious consequences, including identity theft, discrimination, or other forms of harm. Educational institutions and AI developers must implement robust security measures to protect student data from unauthorized access or misuse.

3. Autonomy and Agency

Decision-Making: AI systems in education can make decisions that significantly impact students' academic trajectories, such as determining grades, recommending learning paths, or even identifying students for disciplinary action. There is a concern that these systems could undermine students' autonomy and agency by making decisions without sufficient human oversight or input.

Teacher Autonomy: The use of AI in education can also impact teachers' autonomy, potentially reducing their role to that of a facilitator or monitor of AI-driven content. This could diminish the value of teachers' professional judgment and expertise, and may lead to a loss of job satisfaction or professional identity.

Student Empowerment: While AI can support personalized learning, there is a risk that students might become overly reliant on AI systems, reducing their ability to think critically or make independent decisions. Ensuring that AI enhances rather than diminishes students' ability to learn and think for themselves is a key ethical consideration.

4. Accountability and Transparency

    Algorithmic Transparency: AI systems often operate as "black boxes," making decisions based on complex algorithms that are not easily understood by students, teachers, or even developers. This lack of transparency can make it difficult to hold AI systems accountable for their decisions, particularly if those decisions have negative consequences for students.

    Responsibility for Errors: When AI systems make mistakes, it is often unclear who is responsible—the developers, the educators using the system, or the institution that implemented it. Establishing clear lines of accountability is essential to ensure that errors are addressed and that those affected by them have recourse.

    Ethical AI Design: Developers of AI systems for education must be committed to ethical design principles, ensuring that their systems are fair, transparent, and accountable. This includes regularly auditing algorithms for bias, involving diverse stakeholders in the design process, and being transparent about the limitations of AI systems.

5. Impact on Educational Practices

    Standardization vs. Creativity: AI systems are often designed to optimize efficiency and standardize educational practices. However, this focus on standardization can stifle creativity and innovation in teaching and learning. There is a risk that AI could encourage a one-size-fits-all approach to education, reducing opportunities for creative and critical thinking.

Human Interaction: Education is not just about the transmission of knowledge; it is also about human interaction, emotional support, and the development of social skills. The increasing use of AI in education could reduce the amount of human interaction in the learning process, potentially impacting students' social and emotional development.

Teacher-Student Relationships: AI-driven education tools may alter the traditional teacher-student relationship. While AI can provide additional support, it cannot replace the empathy, understanding, and mentorship that human teachers provide. Maintaining a balance between AI tools and human interaction is crucial to preserving the integrity of the educational experience.

6. Long-Term Societal Implications

   Future Workforce: The integration of AI in education is preparing students for a future where AI plays a significant role in the workforce. However, there is a risk that the focus on AI-driven education could lead to a workforce that lacks critical thinking skills, creativity, or the ability to challenge AI-driven decisions.

   Social Inequality: If AI in education is not implemented equitably, it could contribute to increasing social inequality. Students who have access to the best AI tools and resources may gain a significant advantage, while others could be left behind, exacerbating existing social and economic disparities.

   Cultural Impacts: The global adoption of AI in education could lead to the homogenization of educational content and practices, potentially eroding cultural diversity. It is important to consider how AI systems can be designed and implemented in ways that respect and preserve cultural differences.

The ethical implications of AI in education are complex and far-reaching. While AI has the potential to revolutionize education by providing personalized learning experiences, enhancing access to knowledge, and supporting educators, it also poses significant ethical challenges. Addressing these challenges requires a commitment to equity, transparency, accountability, and the preservation of human dignity in the educational process. Policymakers, educators, and AI developers must work together to ensure that AI in education is used in ways that are ethical, inclusive, and beneficial to all students.

Ensuring Equity and Accessibility

Ensuring equity and accessibility is crucial when deploying data-driven and AI technologies in education. These technologies must be designed to accommodate a diverse range of learning needs and abilities to provide equitable educational opportunities for all students. Inclusive design principles should guide the development of educational technologies, incorporating features that support students with disabilities, such as customizable interfaces, speech recognition, and assistive tools. It is also essential to address disparities in access to technology; all students should have access to the necessary devices, internet connectivity, and technical support to benefit from these advancements. Cultural sensitivity is another key aspect; educational technologies should reflect and respect the diverse backgrounds and experiences of students, providing content and support in multiple languages and considering cultural differences. Additionally, providing comprehensive support and training for educators, students, and parents is vital to ensure effective use of these technologies. By focusing on these aspects, educational institutions can enhance accessibility and inclusivity, ensuring that all students have the opportunity to succeed.

Policy and Regulatory Considerations

Navigating the complex landscape of policies and regulations is essential for the responsible use of data-driven and AI technologies in education. Compliance with data privacy regulations, such as the General Data Protection Regulation (GDPR) and the Family Educational Rights and Privacy Act (FERPA), is mandatory to protect student information and uphold legal standards. Educational institutions must develop clear policies and guidelines that address data privacy, security, ethical use, and accessibility of educational technologies. Staying current with evolving legislation and industry standards is crucial, as regulations and best practices in the field of educational technology are continually changing. Institutions should engage with regulatory bodies and industry associations to stay informed and ensure compliance. Regularly reviewing and updating policies to reflect new developments and emerging issues is also necessary. Providing training and resources to staff and stakeholders helps promote adherence to these policies and regulations, ensuring that the integration of data-driven and AI technologies aligns with legal and ethical standards.

CASE STUDY: IMPLEMENTING AI-DRIVEN ADAPTIVE LEARNING SYSTEMS IN A HIGH SCHOOL

Background

A high school in the United States, "Techville High," sought to improve student engagement and learning outcomes through the integration of an AI-driven adaptive learning system. The goal was to personalize education by using data analytics to tailor instruction to individual student needs, thereby enhancing academic performance and addressing diverse learning styles.

Implementation

The adaptive learning system, "EduAI," was introduced to Techville High's math and science departments. The system utilized AI algorithms to analyze student performance data and provide personalized learning resources and feedback. Key components of the implementation included:

- **Data Collection:** EduAI collected data from student interactions with the platform, including quiz scores, time spent on tasks, and participation in interactive exercises.
- **Personalization Engine:** The AI engine analyzed the data to identify each student's strengths and weaknesses, adapting instructional materials and practice exercises accordingly.
- **Teacher Integration:** Teachers received insights and recommendations based on the AI analysis, allowing them to focus on targeted interventions and support for students who needed it.

Quantitative Results

1. Improvement in Academic Performance

Over the course of one academic year, Techville High tracked the impact of EduAI on student performance in math and science. The results were as follows:

- **Math Scores:** The average math test scores improved by 15% compared to the previous year. The percentage of students scoring in the top quartile increased by 25%.

- **Science Scores:** Science test scores showed a 12% improvement in average scores. The number of students achieving proficiency in science increased by 20%.

2. Student Engagement and Participation

EduAI's adaptive features aimed to increase student engagement. The following metrics were observed:

- **Quiz Participation:** The number of quizzes taken by students increased by 30%, indicating higher engagement with the learning material.
- **Time on Task:** Students spent an average of 20% more time interacting with the platform compared to the previous year, suggesting increased involvement and interest in learning.

3. Teacher Efficiency and Effectiveness

The integration of EduAI also impacted teaching efficiency:

- **Time Spent on Administrative Tasks:** Teachers reported a 25% reduction in time spent on grading and administrative tasks, as EduAI automated these processes.
- **Targeted Interventions:** Teachers used the data insights from EduAI to implement targeted interventions, resulting in a 10% increase in the number of students receiving personalized support.

4. Student Satisfaction

Student feedback was collected to gauge satisfaction with the adaptive learning system:

- **Satisfaction Rating:** 85% of students reported a positive experience with EduAI, citing the personalized learning approach as a major factor in their satisfaction.
- **Feedback on Learning Materials:** 78% of students found the personalized practice exercises and resources to be helpful and relevant to their learning needs.

Challenges and Lessons Learned

While the implementation of EduAI yielded positive results, several challenges were encountered:

Data Privacy Concerns: Ensuring the privacy and security of student data was a significant concern. The school had to implement robust data protection measures and communicate transparently with students and parents.
Technology Integration: Integrating the adaptive learning system with existing classroom technologies required additional training and support for teachers.
Continuous Improvement: The system required ongoing updates and refinements based on user feedback and evolving educational needs.

Case Study Conclusion

The implementation of the AI-driven adaptive learning system at Techville High demonstrated significant improvements in academic performance, student engagement, and teacher efficiency. The data-driven insights provided by EduAI enabled personalized instruction and targeted interventions, leading to enhanced learning outcomes. Despite challenges, the positive impact of the system highlights the potential of AI-driven technologies to transform education by addressing diverse learning needs and improving overall educational experiences. Future efforts should focus on addressing privacy concerns, refining system integration, and ensuring continuous adaptation to meet the evolving needs of students and educators.

The quantitative results from the implementation of the AI-driven adaptive learning system at Techville High, presented in tabular form:

Table 1. The improvements observed in academic performance

Metric	Before Implementation	After Implementation	Change (%)
Average Math Test Scores	72%	87%	+15%
Percentage of Students in Top Quartile (Math)	20%	25%	+25%
Average Science Test Scores	68%	76%	+12%
Percentage of Students Achieving Proficiency (Science)	30%	36%	+20%
Number of Quizzes Taken per Student	5	6.5	+30%
Average Time Spent on Platform (per week)	1 hour	1.2 hours	+20%
Reduction in Time Spent on Administrative Tasks (Teachers)	-	25%	-
Increase in Targeted Interventions	-	10%	-

continued on following page

Table 1. Continued

Metric	Before Implementation	After Implementation	Change (%)
Student Satisfaction Rating (%)	-	85%	-
Percentage of Students Finding Personalized Resources Helpful	-	78%	-

This table 1 presents the improvements observed in academic performance, engagement, and teacher efficiency following the implementation of the AI-driven adaptive learning system as shown in Figure 1.

Figure 1. Count of metric by before implementation

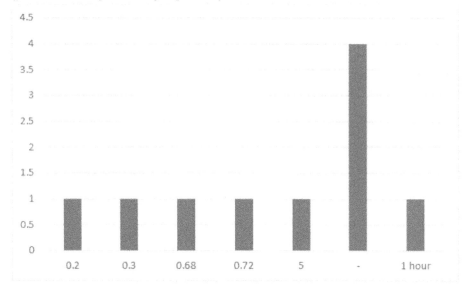

CONCLUSION

The implementation of the AI-driven adaptive learning system at Techville High has yielded significant improvements in academic performance, student engagement, and teacher efficiency. The data reveals a marked increase in average test scores for both math and science, with notable gains in the percentage of students achieving top quartile performance and proficiency. Student engagement metrics also show positive trends, including higher quiz participation and increased time spent on learning platforms. Additionally, the reduction in time spent on administrative tasks and the enhancement of targeted interventions underscore the effectiveness of the system in supporting educators. These results highlight the potential of AI-driven technologies to transform education by providing personalized learning experiences that cater to individual student needs. The positive feedback from students further emphasizes the effectiveness of personalized resources and the overall satisfaction with the adaptive learning system. However, the implementation also highlighted challenges such as data privacy concerns, technology integration, and the need for continuous system improvements.

Future Scope

Looking ahead, there are several avenues for further development and research in the field of AI-driven adaptive learning systems:

1. **Enhanced Personalization:** Future advancements could focus on refining AI algorithms to provide even more personalized learning experiences. Incorporating additional data sources, such as behavioral and emotional indicators, could further tailor educational content and support to individual student needs.
2. **Integration with Emerging Technologies:** Integrating AI-driven systems with emerging technologies, such as virtual and augmented reality, could offer immersive and interactive learning experiences. Exploring these integrations can provide new ways to engage students and enhance their understanding of complex subjects.
3. **Addressing Equity and Accessibility:** Continued efforts are needed to ensure that adaptive learning technologies are accessible to all students, regardless of their socio-economic background. Developing solutions to bridge the digital divide and provide equitable access to technology will be crucial for maximizing the benefits of these systems.
4. **Longitudinal Studies:** Conducting longitudinal studies to assess the long-term impact of AI-driven adaptive learning systems on student outcomes is essential. Research should focus on understanding how these systems influence students' academic trajectories, retention rates, and overall educational success over extended periods.
5. **Policy and Ethical Frameworks:** Developing comprehensive policy and ethical frameworks to guide the use of AI in education will be important for addressing privacy, security, and fairness concerns. Establishing clear guidelines and best practices will help ensure responsible and equitable deployment of these technologies.

6. **Professional Development for Educators:** Providing ongoing professional development for educators will be critical for effectively integrating AI-driven systems into the classroom. Training programs should focus on equipping teachers with the skills and knowledge needed to leverage these technologies and make data-driven decisions.

By exploring these future directions, educational institutions can continue to harness the power of AI and data-driven technologies to enhance learning experiences, improve educational outcomes, and address the diverse needs of students in a rapidly evolving educational landscape.

REFERENCES

Aggarwal, D. (2023). Integration of innovative technological developments and AI with education for an adaptive learning pedagogy. *China Petroleum Processing and Petrochemical Technology*, 23(2), 709–714.

Aldoseri, A., Al-Khalifa, K. N., & Hamouda, A. M. (2024). AI-Powered Innovation in Digital Transformation: Key Pillars and Industry Impact. *Sustainability (Basel)*, 16(5), 1790. DOI: 10.3390/su16051790

Almufareh, M. F., Kausar, S., Humayun, M., & Tehsin, S. (2024). A conceptual model for inclusive technology: Advancing disability inclusion through artificial intelligence. *Journal of Disability Research*, 3(1), 20230060. DOI: 10.57197/JDR-2023-0060

Almufareh, M. F., Tehsin, S., Humayun, M., & Kausar, S. (2023). Intellectual disability and technology: An artificial intelligence perspective and framework. *Journal of Disability Research*, 2(4), 58–70. DOI: 10.57197/JDR-2023-0055

Ayeni, O. O., Al Hamad, N. M., Chisom, O. N., Osawaru, B., & Adewusi, O. E. (2024). AI in education: A review of personalized learning and educational technology. *GSC Advanced Research and Reviews*, 18(2), 261–271. DOI: 10.30574/gscarr.2024.18.2.0062

Chisom, O. N., Unachukwu, C. C., & Osawaru, B. (2023). Review of AI in education: Transforming learning environments in Africa. *International Journal of Applied Research in Social Sciences*, 5(10), 637–654. DOI: 10.51594/ijarss.v5i10.725

Chopra, A., Patel, H., Rajput, D. S., & Bansal, N. (2024). Empowering Inclusive Education: Leveraging AI-ML and Innovative Tech Stacks to Support Students with Learning Disabilities in Higher Education. In *Applied Assistive Technologies and Informatics for Students with Disabilities* (pp. 255–275). Springer Nature Singapore. DOI: 10.1007/978-981-97-0914-4_15

Denga, E. M., & Denga, S. W. (2024). Revolutionizing Education: The Power of Technology. In *Revolutionizing Curricula Through Computational Thinking, Logic, and Problem Solving* (pp. 167-188). IGI Global.

Faresta, R. A. (2024). AI-Powered Education: Exploring the Potential of Personalised Learning for Students' Needs in Indonesia Education. *Traektoriâ Nauki*, 10(5), 3012–3022. DOI: 10.22178/pos.104-19

Khalid, U. B., Naeem, M., Stasolla, F., Syed, M. H., Abbas, M., & Coronato, A. (2024). Impact of AI-powered solutions in rehabilitation process: Recent improvements and future trends. *International Journal of General Medicine*, 17, 943–969. DOI: 10.2147/IJGM.S453903 PMID: 38495919

Mehta, P., Chillarge, G. R., Sapkal, S. D., Shinde, G. R., & Kshirsagar, P. S. (2023). Inclusion of Children With Special Needs in the Educational System, Artificial Intelligence (AI). In *AI-Assisted Special Education for Students With Exceptional Needs* (pp. 156-185). IGI Global.

Mohammad Abedrabbu Alkhawaldeh, M. A. S. K. (2023). Harnessing The Power of Artificial Intelligence for Personalized Assistive Technology in Learning Disabilities. *Journal of Southwest Jiaotong University*, 58(4).

Neha, K., Kumar, R., & Sankat, M. (2024). AI Wizards: Pioneering Assistive Technologies for Higher Education Inclusion of Students with Learning Disabilities. In *Applied Assistive Technologies and Informatics for Students with Disabilities* (pp. 59–70). Springer Nature Singapore. DOI: 10.1007/978-981-97-0914-4_4

Nuary, M. G., Judijanto, L., Nurliyah, E. S., Muriyanto, M., & El-Farra, S. A. (2022). Impact of AI in Education and Social Development through Individual Empowerment. *Journal of Artificial Intelligence and Development*, 1(2), 89–97.

Singh, R. J. (2023). Transforming higher education: The power of artificial intelligence. *International Journal of Multidisciplinary Research in Arts. Science and Technology*, 1(3), 13–18.

Srinivasa, K. G., Kurni, M., & Saritha, K. (2022). Harnessing the Power of AI to Education. In *Learning, teaching, and assessment methods for contemporary learners: pedagogy for the digital generation* (pp. 311–342). Springer Nature Singapore. DOI: 10.1007/978-981-19-6734-4_13

Tan, S. (2023). Harnessing Artificial Intelligence for innovation in education. In *Learning intelligence: Innovative and digital transformative learning strategies: Cultural and social engineering perspectives* (pp. 335–363). Springer Nature Singapore. DOI: 10.1007/978-981-19-9201-8_8

Whig, P., Battina, D. S., Venkata, S., Bhatia, A. B., & Alkali, Y. J. (2024). Role of Intelligent IoT Applications in Fog Computing. *Fog Computing for Intelligent Cloud IoT Systems*, 99-118. DOI: 10.1007/978-981-19-9201-8_8

Whig, P., Kouser, S., Bhatia, A. B., Purohit, K., & Modhugu, V. R. (2024). 9 Intelligent Control for Energy Management. *Microgrid: Design, Optimization, and Applications*, 137. Rane, N., Choudhary, S., & Rane, J. (2023). Education 4.0 and 5.0: Integrating artificial intelligence (AI) for personalized and adaptive learning. *Available atSSRN* 4638365.

Whig, P., Kouser, S., Bhatia, A. B., Velu, A., & Alkali, Y. J. (2024). Internet of Things (IoT) in the Agriculture Sector toward Urban Greening. *Changing Competitive Business Dynamics Through Sustainable Big Data Analysis*, 21. DOI: 10.1007/978-981-19-9201-8_8

Whig, P., Madavarapu, J. B., Yathiraju, N., & Thatikonda, R. (2024). Interdisciplinary Data Analytics Transforming Influencer Marketing Strategies. In *Advances in Data Analytics for Influencer Marketing: An Interdisciplinary Approach* (pp. 103–124). Springer Nature Switzerland. DOI: 10.1007/978-3-031-65727-6_7

Whig, P., Yathiraju, N., Modhugu, V. R., & Bhatia, A. B. (2024). 13 Digital Twin for. *AI-Driven Digital Twin and Industry 4.0: A Conceptual Framework with Applications*, 202. DOI: 10.1007/978-981-19-9201-8_8

Zdravkova, K. (2022). The potential of artificial intelligence for assistive technology in education. In *Handbook on Intelligent Techniques in the Educational Process: Vol 1 Recent Advances and Case Studies* (pp. 61-85). Cham: Springer International Publishing. DOI: 10.1007/978-3-031-04662-9_4

Chapter 5
Data-Driven Solutions Enhancing Adaptive Education Through Technological Innovations for Disability Support

Sevinthi Kali Sankar Nagarajan
https://orcid.org/0009-0005-4684-0384
Independent Researcher, San Antonio, USA

Munikrishnaiah Sundara Ramaiah
https://orcid.org/0009-0007-9855-9214
Independent Researcher, San Antonio, USA

Pawan Whig
https://orcid.org/0000-0003-1863-1591
VIPS, India

ABSTRACT

This chapter explores the transformative role of data-driven solutions in advancing adaptive education for students with disabilities. This chapter examines how advanced data analysis techniques enable the creation of personalized learning environments tailored to individual needs and challenges. Key topics include innovative data collection methods, such as learning analytics and behavioral data, and their application in designing customized educational tools and strategies. The

DOI: 10.4018/979-8-3693-8227-1.ch005

chapter also presents real-world case studies showcasing the successful use of data-driven approaches to enhance accessibility and inclusivity in educational settings. By providing a comprehensive analysis, this chapter underscores the potential of data-driven solutions to improve educational outcomes, foster equity, and create more effective support systems for students with disabilities.

INTRODUCTION

In today's rapidly evolving educational landscape, the integration of technology has become a cornerstone for enhancing learning experiences. This chapter focuses on a critical aspect of this technological revolution: the use of data-driven solutions to advance adaptive education for students with disabilities. As education systems strive to accommodate diverse learning needs, the role of data analysis and technological innovation has emerged as a powerful tool for fostering inclusivity and accessibility. Adaptive education refers to educational strategies and technologies designed to tailor learning experiences to the individual needs of each student. For students with disabilities, these adaptations are crucial for ensuring equitable access to educational opportunities. Historically, educational institutions have faced significant challenges in providing effective support for students with disabilities. These challenges have included a lack of resources, insufficient understanding of individual needs, and limited access to specialized tools and technologies. However, recent advancements in data analysis and technology have paved the way for more personalized and effective approaches to addressing these challenges.

The advent of data-driven solutions in education marks a paradigm shift from traditional, one-size-fits-all methods to more nuanced and individualized approaches. Data analysis allows educators to gain deeper insights into student performance, learning behaviors, and engagement patterns. By harnessing the power of data, educators can identify specific needs and tailor their instructional strategies accordingly. One of the key benefits of data-driven education is the ability to collect and analyze vast amounts of information about student learning processes. Learning analytics, which involves the systematic collection and analysis of educational data, provides valuable insights into how students interact with educational content. This information can be used to develop adaptive learning systems that adjust to the individual needs of students in real-time.

Technological innovations play a crucial role in enhancing support for students with disabilities. Assistive technologies, such as speech recognition software, screen readers, and adaptive input devices, have revolutionized the way students with disabilities engage with educational content. These tools enable students to overcome barriers to learning and participate more fully in the educational experience. Data-driven approaches further amplify the impact of these technologies by providing a more detailed understanding of how students use them. For example, data on how frequently and effectively students utilize assistive technologies can inform the development of new tools and features that better meet their needs. Additionally, the integration of artificial intelligence (AI) and machine learning algorithms into educational technologies has the potential to create highly personalized learning experiences. AI-powered systems can analyze data on student performance and provide real-time feedback, recommendations, and adjustments to instructional content.

Personalized learning is a central concept in adaptive education, emphasizing the importance of tailoring educational experiences to the individual needs of students. Data-driven solutions enable educators to create personalized learning plans based on detailed behavioral data. This data includes information on student engagement, progress, and areas of difficulty. Behavioral data can be collected through various means, including online learning platforms, classroom interactions, and assessments. By analyzing this data, educators can identify patterns and trends that reveal insights into each student's unique learning style and challenges. This information can then be used to design customized instructional materials and interventions that address specific needs. To illustrate the practical applications of data-driven solutions in adaptive education, this chapter examines several case studies where these approaches have been successfully implemented. These case studies highlight the transformative impact of data analysis and technological innovation on educational outcomes for students with disabilities.

For instance, one case study may focus on a school that implemented a data-driven adaptive learning platform designed to support students with dyslexia. By analyzing data on student reading habits and performance, the platform was able to provide tailored reading interventions and resources. The results demonstrated significant improvements in reading comprehension and overall academic achievement. Another case study might explore the use of AI-powered tools in a classroom setting to support students with autism. By analyzing data on student behavior and interaction patterns, the AI system was able to provide real-time feedback and adjust instructional strategies to better meet the needs of these students. The outcomes of this approach included increased engagement and improved social skills. While data-driven solutions offer numerous benefits, there are also challenges and considerations to address. Privacy and security concerns are paramount when handling sensitive student data. Educators and institutions must ensure that data is collected and used in compliance with relevant regulations and ethical guidelines.

LITERATURE REVIEW

In recent years, the integration of data-driven technologies and artificial intelligence (AI) in education and related fields has gained significant traction. This literature review explores the diverse applications and implications of data-driven approaches, focusing on enhancing learning experiences, supporting special needs education, advancing sustainable development goals, and fostering innovation. Liu et al. (2017) emphasizes the potential of data-driven personalization in higher education, where learning support can be tailored to individual student needs through advanced analytics. This approach is crucial for improving student outcomes, as it allows educators to identify and address specific learning gaps. Guan, Mou, and Jiang (2020) extend this discussion by analyzing two decades of AI innovation in education, underscoring the transformative impact of AI in enhancing educational methodologies and accessibility.

Assistive technologies powered by AI are particularly beneficial for students with special needs. Nakarmi et al. (2024) discuss how data-driven approaches empower assistive technologies, making education more accessible for learners with disabilities. Similarly, Almufareh et al. (2024) propose a conceptual model for inclusive technology, highlighting the role of AI in advancing disability inclusion. Mehta et al. (2023) further explore AI's contribution to special education, focusing on the inclusion of children with special needs. Baneres, Rodríguez, and Guerrero-Roldán (2020) explore the engineering of data-driven adaptive e-assessment systems, which enhance trust and reliability in educational evaluations. Miundy, Zaman, and Nordin (2017) review assistive digital learning technologies for dyscalculia learners, demonstrating how data-driven preliminary studies can support the development of effective learning tools.

Bresciani et al. (2021) highlights the role of big data in co-innovation processes, particularly in educational settings. Their work maps the field of data-driven innovation, proposing theoretical developments and setting a research agenda. This is complemented by Bachmann et al. (2022), who examine how data-driven technologies contribute to achieving sustainable development goals, illustrating the broader societal impact of these innovations. The paradigm of Industry 4.0, characterized by data-driven technologies, is systematically reviewed by Klingenberg, Borges, and Antunes Jr (2021). They discuss the implications for education, particularly in preparing students for the demands of a data-driven society. Ciolacu et al. (2017) extend this by discussing Education 4.0, which focuses on developing "tall thin" engineers equipped to thrive in a data-driven world.

Bibri and Krogstie (2020) explore the concept of data-driven smart cities, using London and Barcelona as case studies. They discuss how these cities leverage innovative solutions for sustainability, drawing parallels with educational environments that increasingly rely on data to enhance learning and operational efficiency. Koedinger et al. (2013) investigate the potential of data-driven intelligent tutoring systems (ITS), which optimize learning experiences by adapting to individual student needs. These systems are a testament to the power of AI in creating personalized and effective educational tools. Kumar and Nagar (2024) discuss AI-based language translation and interpretation services that improve accessibility for visually impaired students. Their work highlights the importance of making educational content accessible to all learners, regardless of their physical or cognitive abilities. Saaida (2023) concludes the review by discussing the broader challenges and opportunities presented by AI-driven transformations in higher education. While AI offers numerous benefits, including personalized learning and improved accessibility, it also poses challenges related to ethics, data privacy, and the digital divide. The reviewed literature underscores the transformative potential of data-driven and AI technologies in education and beyond. These innovations offer significant opportunities for enhancing learning experiences, supporting special needs education, advancing sustainable development, and fostering co-innovation. However, as these technologies continue to evolve, ongoing research is essential to address the associated challenges and maximize their benefits.

Additionally, the effectiveness of data-driven solutions depends on the quality of the data collected and the accuracy of the analysis. Inaccurate or incomplete data can lead to ineffective or even harmful interventions. It is essential for educators to use data thoughtfully and to continuously evaluate and refine their approaches based on feedback and results. The integration of data-driven solutions and technological innovations represents a significant advancement in adaptive education for students with disabilities. By leveraging data analysis and emerging technologies, educators can create more personalized, inclusive, and effective learning experiences. This chapter explores the various ways in which data-driven approaches are transforming education and highlights the potential for continued innovation in this field. As technology continues to evolve, the opportunities for enhancing support for students with disabilities will expand, paving the way for a more equitable and accessible educational landscape.

THE EVOLUTION OF DATA-DRIVEN SOLUTIONS IN EDUCATION

Historical Context

The integration of data-driven solutions into education has been a gradual evolution, driven by advances in technology and a growing understanding of the potential benefits of data analysis. Historically, educational methods were predominantly based on traditional teaching practices, which often employed a standardized approach to instruction. This one-size-fits-all method, while effective for many students, struggled to address the diverse needs of individual learners, particularly those with disabilities or unique learning requirements. The early 20th century saw the introduction of educational assessments and standardized testing, which provided some insight into student performance but were limited in scope. As technology advanced, the 1980s and 1990s brought about the use of computers in education, including early software programs designed to assist with learning. However, these tools were still relatively simplistic and did not fully leverage the potential of data analysis.

The turn of the 21st century marked a significant shift with the rise of digital technologies and the internet. The proliferation of online learning platforms, educational software, and digital resources provided educators with new tools to collect and analyze data. The concept of learning analytics began to take shape, as educators and researchers started to recognize the value of systematically collecting data on student learning processes.

The Rise of Learning Analytics

Learning analytics represents a key milestone in the evolution of data-driven solutions in education. It involves the systematic collection, analysis, and reporting of data related to student learning and educational environments. The goal of learning analytics is to gain actionable insights that can improve teaching and learning outcomes.

The rise of learning analytics can be attributed to several factors:

1. **Increased Data Availability:** The growth of digital education tools and platforms has led to a wealth of data on student interactions, behaviors, and performance. This data can be used to track progress, identify patterns, and assess the effectiveness of educational strategies.
2. **Advanced Data Analysis Techniques:** The development of sophisticated data analysis techniques, including statistical methods, machine learning, and artificial intelligence (AI), has enabled educators to gain deeper insights from

educational data. These techniques can identify trends, predict outcomes, and provide personalized recommendations.
3. **Focus on Student-Centric Approaches:** There has been a growing emphasis on personalized learning and student-centric approaches in education. Learning analytics supports these approaches by providing data-driven insights that help tailor instruction to meet the needs of individual students.
4. **Support for Evidence-Based Decision Making:** Learning analytics provides evidence-based insights that support decision-making processes in education. Educators and administrators can use data to make informed decisions about curriculum design, teaching strategies, and resource allocation.

Benefits of Data-Driven Approaches

Data-driven approaches offer numerous benefits for enhancing educational experiences and outcomes. These benefits are particularly significant for students with disabilities, as data-driven solutions can help create more inclusive and supportive learning environments. Some key benefits include:

1. **Personalized Learning:** Data-driven approaches enable educators to tailor instruction to the individual needs of each student. By analyzing data on student performance, learning styles, and engagement, educators can design customized learning experiences that address specific strengths and challenges.
2. **Early Intervention:** Data analysis can help identify students who may be at risk of falling behind or facing difficulties. Early detection of potential issues allows for timely interventions and support, which can prevent academic struggles and improve overall outcomes.
3. **Enhanced Engagement:** Data-driven solutions can provide real-time feedback and adaptive learning tools that keep students engaged and motivated. Personalized learning experiences can help maintain students' interest and enthusiasm for learning.
4. **Improved Resource Allocation:** By analyzing data on student needs and performance, educational institutions can make more informed decisions about resource allocation. This ensures that resources are directed towards areas that will have the greatest impact on student success.
5. **Evidence-Based Improvements:** Data-driven approaches provide a solid foundation for evaluating the effectiveness of educational strategies and interventions. Educators can use data to assess what works and what doesn't, leading to continuous improvement in teaching methods and learning outcomes.

6. **Informed Policy Making:** Educational policymakers can use data-driven insights to shape policies and initiatives that address the diverse needs of students. Data-driven decisions can lead to more equitable and effective educational practices.
7. **Enhanced Accessibility:** For students with disabilities, data-driven technologies can offer tailored support and accommodations. Assistive technologies and adaptive learning systems can be refined based on data to better meet the needs of these students.

The evolution of data-driven solutions in education represents a significant advancement in how we approach teaching and learning. From its historical roots to the rise of learning analytics and the benefits of data-driven approaches, this evolution highlights the transformative potential of data in creating more personalized, inclusive, and effective educational experiences. As technology continues to advance, the role of data in education will likely become even more integral, offering new opportunities for enhancing learning outcomes and supporting students with diverse needs.

TECHNOLOGICAL INNOVATIONS FOR DISABILITY SUPPORT

Assistive Technologies

Assistive technologies are devices or systems designed to aid individuals with disabilities in performing tasks that might otherwise be challenging or impossible. These technologies play a crucial role in creating inclusive educational environments, enabling students with disabilities to engage with learning materials and participate in classroom activities effectively.

Types of Assistive Technologies:
Screen Readers: For visually impaired students, screen readers convert text on a screen into spoken words. Software such as JAWS (Job Access with Speech) and NVDA (NonVisual Desktop Access) help students access digital content, including textbooks, websites, and educational software.
Speech Recognition Software: Tools like Dragon NaturallySpeaking allow students with physical disabilities or difficulties with written expression to dictate text and control their computers using voice commands. This technology helps with writing assignments, taking notes, and navigating software.

- **Alternative Input Devices**: For students who have limited motor control, alternative input devices such as adaptive keyboards, trackballs, and eye-tracking systems provide alternative methods for intcracting with computers and other digital tools. These devices can be customized to meet individual needs.
- **Text-to-Speech (TTS) Systems**: TTS technology converts written text into spoken words. Tools like NaturalReader and Google's Read Aloud feature support students with reading difficulties by reading textbooks, articles, and other written materials aloud.
- **Electronic Math Worksheets**: Software such as ModMath helps students with dysgraphia (difficulty with handwriting) complete math assignments by providing digital worksheets that can be filled out using a touchscreen or other input methods.

AI AND MACHINE LEARNING IN EDUCATION

Artificial Intelligence (AI) and Machine Learning (ML) are transforming the educational landscape by offering sophisticated tools and techniques for personalizing learning and supporting students with disabilities. These technologies leverage data to create adaptive and responsive educational environments that cater to individual learning needs.

Applications of AI and Machine Learning

AI-driven platforms like DreamBox and Knewton analyze student performance data to provide personalized learning experiences. These platforms adjust the difficulty of exercises, offer targeted feedback, and recommend additional resources based on the individual needs and progress of each student. Machine learning algorithms can predict students' future performance based on historical data, helping educators identify students at risk of falling behind and providing timely interventions. AI-powered assessment tools adjust the difficulty of questions based on student responses, ensuring that assessments are appropriately challenging and providing a more accurate measure of student understanding. AI-driven communication aids, such as text-to-speech and speech-to-text applications, help students with speech and language impairments communicate more effectively. Tools like Google's Live Transcribe provide real-time transcription of spoken language, supporting students with hearing impairments. AI can assist in the creation of educational content by generating customized learning materials based on student needs. For instance, AI tools can create simplified summaries of complex texts or generate practice questions tailored to individual learning gaps.

Benefits of AI and Machine Learning

AI and ML solutions can be scaled to support a large number of students, providing consistent and individualized support across diverse educational settings. These technologies enable highly personalized learning experiences by analyzing data on student performance and tailoring instruction to meet each student's unique needs. AI-powered systems provide immediate feedback on student performance, allowing for rapid adjustments and continuous improvement in learning.

By automating routine tasks and providing actionable insights, AI and ML can help educators allocate resources more effectively and focus on areas where their expertise is most needed. AI-driven tools can enhance accessibility by providing support for a wide range of disabilities, including visual, auditory, and cognitive impairments.

Technological innovations in assistive technologies and AI/machine learning are driving significant advancements in disability support within education. Assistive technologies provide essential tools for overcoming barriers to learning, while AI and ML offer powerful solutions for personalizing and optimizing educational experiences. Together, these technologies create more inclusive and supportive learning environments, helping students with disabilities achieve their full potential and engage more effectively in their educational journeys. As technology continues to evolve, the potential for further innovations in disability support remains vast, promising continued improvements in accessibility and educational outcomes.

PERSONALIZED LEARNING AND BEHAVIORAL DATA

Defining Personalized Learning

Personalized learning is an educational approach that tailors learning experiences to the individual needs, preferences, and strengths of each student. Unlike traditional, one-size-fits-all education models, personalized learning seeks to create a more dynamic and responsive educational environment that addresses the unique requirements of each learner. The goal is to ensure that all students have the opportunity to achieve their full potential by providing learning experiences that are customized to their individual needs.

Key Characteristics of Personalized Learning:
1. **Learner-Centered:** Personalized learning shifts the focus from the teacher's delivery of content to the learner's engagement and progress. It considers the individual's prior knowledge, learning style, and pace.

2. **Flexible Pathways:** Students have the flexibility to choose their learning paths, including the pace and sequence of learning activities. This approach allows students to explore subjects that interest them and engage with material in a way that suits their learning style.
3. **Competency-Based:** Personalized learning often emphasizes mastery of competencies or skills rather than time spent in class. Students progress based on their ability to demonstrate understanding and proficiency.
4. **Data-Driven:** Personalized learning relies on data to inform instructional decisions. This data includes assessments, behavioral insights, and feedback, which helps educators understand each student's needs and adjust their teaching strategies accordingly.
5. **Supportive Learning Environment:** Personalized learning environments provide support structures, such as mentorship, tutoring, and resources tailored to individual needs, to help students succeed.

Collection and Analysis of Behavioral Data

Behavioral data refers to information collected on how students interact with educational content, engage in learning activities, and perform in assessments. This data is crucial for understanding student behavior and performance, which informs the personalization of learning experiences.

1. Types of Behavioral Data:
    Engagement Metrics: Data on how actively students participate in learning activities, including time spent on tasks, frequency of logins, and interaction with educational tools.
    Performance Data: Information on student performance in assessments, quizzes, assignments, and projects. This includes scores, completion rates, and error patterns.
    Learning Preferences: Insights into students' preferred learning styles and methods, such as visual, auditory, or kinesthetic learning. This data can be gathered through surveys, self-reports, or observation.
    Behavioral Patterns: Analysis of patterns in student behavior, such as attention span, frequency of distractions, and participation in collaborative activities.
2. Methods of Data Collection:
    Learning Management Systems (LMS): LMS platforms track student interactions with digital content, including progress, time spent on tasks, and engagement levels.

Educational Software: Tools and applications used for teaching and assessment can collect data on student performance and behavior.

Surveys and Questionnaires: Direct feedback from students about their learning preferences, challenges, and experiences can provide valuable insights.

Observations and Logs: Educators can collect observational data on student behavior during classroom activities and review logs from digital tools.

3. Data Analysis Techniques:

    Descriptive Analytics: Summarizes data to provide an overview of student performance and engagement. This includes averages, frequencies, and trends.

    Predictive Analytics: Uses statistical models and algorithms to forecast future student performance and identify potential challenges. This can help in anticipating areas where students may need additional support.

    Diagnostic Analytics: Examines the causes of specific performance issues or behavioral patterns. This analysis helps identify underlying factors that may affect student learning.

    Prescriptive Analytics: Provides recommendations based on data analysis to improve instructional strategies and learning experiences. This can include personalized learning paths, targeted interventions, and resource allocation.

Designing Customized Learning Experiences

Designing customized learning experiences involves creating educational activities and materials that are tailored to the individual needs and preferences of each student. This process is informed by the insights gained from behavioral data and aims to provide a more effective and engaging learning environment.

1. Steps in Designing Customized Learning Experiences:

    Identify Individual Needs: Use behavioral data to understand each student's strengths, weaknesses, and learning preferences. This includes analyzing performance trends, engagement levels, and feedback.

    Set Learning Goals: Establish clear, personalized learning objectives based on the data. These goals should be specific, measurable, achievable, relevant, and time-bound (SMART).

- **Develop Personalized Content**: Create or curate educational materials and activities that align with each student's needs and learning style. This may include interactive exercises, multimedia resources, and differentiated assignments.
- **Implement Adaptive Learning Technologies**: Utilize adaptive learning platforms that adjust the difficulty of content and provide real-time feedback based on student performance. These technologies can offer personalized recommendations and resources.
- **Provide Targeted Support**: Offer additional support, such as tutoring, mentoring, or specialized resources, to address specific challenges identified through data analysis.
- **Monitor and Adjust**: Continuously monitor student progress and engagement using data analytics. Adjust learning experiences and interventions as needed to ensure that students are meeting their goals and making progress.

2. Benefits of Customized Learning Experiences:
   - **Enhanced Engagement**: Personalized learning experiences are more likely to engage students by aligning with their interests and learning styles.
   - **Improved Learning Outcomes**: Tailored instruction helps address individual learning gaps and supports mastery of competencies, leading to better academic performance.
   - **Increased Motivation**: Students are more motivated when they have control over their learning paths and receive feedback that is relevant to their needs.
   - **Efficient Use of Resources**: Customized learning experiences help allocate educational resources more effectively by targeting areas where they are most needed.

Personalized learning, supported by the collection and analysis of behavioral data, represents a transformative approach to education. By tailoring learning experiences to individual needs and preferences, educators can create more effective and engaging educational environments. The integration of data-driven insights into instructional design ensures that students receive the support they need to succeed, making personalized learning a powerful tool for enhancing educational outcomes and fostering a more inclusive learning experience.

CASE STUDY: IMPLEMENTING PERSONALIZED LEARNING THROUGH BEHAVIORAL DATA IN A HIGH SCHOOL MATHEMATICS PROGRAM

XYZ High School, located in a suburban district, serves a diverse student population with varying academic abilities. The school has recently adopted a personalized learning approach in its mathematics program to address the diverse needs of its students. The initiative aims to enhance student engagement, improve academic performance, and support individualized learning paths.

The name of the school is not mentioned due to privacy considerations. However, the findings and insights from this case study are applicable to a wide range of educational settings and can serve as a valuable reference for other institutions looking to implement personalized learning initiatives.

Objective

The primary objectives of the personalized learning initiative were to:

1. Increase student engagement and motivation in mathematics.
2. Improve academic performance in standardized math assessments.
3. Provide tailored support to meet the diverse needs of students.

Approach

1. Implementation of Personalized Learning:
    Behavioral Data Collection: The school utilized a Learning Management System (LMS) and educational software to collect data on student interactions, performance, and engagement. Data included time spent on assignments, quiz scores, and participation in online discussions.
    Data Analysis: The collected data was analyzed using descriptive and predictive analytics to identify patterns and trends in student behavior and performance. This analysis helped in understanding individual learning needs and preferences.
    Customized Learning Paths: Based on the analysis, personalized learning paths were designed for each student. These paths included customized assignments, targeted practice exercises, and adaptive learning modules that adjusted difficulty based on student performance.
    Targeted Interventions: Students who were identified as at risk of falling behind received additional support through tutoring sessions, personalized feedback, and extra practice materials.

Quantitative Results

1. Student Engagement:
   - **Pre-Implementation Data:** Prior to implementing personalized learning, student engagement in the mathematics program was measured through classroom participation and completion rates for assignments. The average participation rate was 65%, and assignment completion rates averaged 70%.
   - **Post-Implementation Data:** After the implementation of personalized learning, engagement metrics showed a significant increase. The average participation rate rose to 85%, and assignment completion rates improved to 90%. The percentage of students actively using adaptive learning tools also increased by 30%.
2. Academic Performance:
   - **Pre-Implementation Data:** Standardized test scores in mathematics were analyzed for the year preceding the personalized learning initiative. The average test score was 72%, with 40% of students scoring below the proficiency threshold.
   - **Post-Implementation Data:** In the year following the implementation, standardized test scores improved markedly. The average test score increased to 80%, and the percentage of students scoring below the proficiency threshold decreased to 25%. Additionally, 50% of students demonstrated a gain of at least 10 percentage points in their test scores.
3. Personalized Learning Impact:
   - **Student Feedback:** Surveys conducted at the end of the academic year revealed that 80% of students felt that personalized learning had positively impacted their understanding of mathematical concepts. 75% reported feeling more motivated and engaged in their math classes.
   - **Teacher Feedback:** Teachers noted a significant improvement in student participation and enthusiasm. 70% of teachers reported that personalized learning tools helped them better address individual learning needs and provided valuable insights into student progress.
4. Resource Allocation:
   - **Efficiency:** The data-driven approach allowed the school to allocate resources more effectively. Additional support was provided to students who needed it most, and the use of adaptive learning technologies optimized the distribution of instructional time and materials.

The implementation of personalized learning through behavioral data analysis at XYZ High School led to notable improvements in student engagement and academic performance in mathematics. The quantitative results demonstrated significant gains in participation rates, assignment completion, and standardized test scores. Additionally, feedback from students and teachers indicated positive experiences with the personalized learning approach.

By leveraging data to create customized learning paths and providing targeted interventions, the school successfully addressed the diverse needs of its students and enhanced the overall learning experience as shown in Table 1. This case study highlights the effectiveness of personalized learning strategies in improving educational outcomes and supporting individual student success.

Table 1. educational outcomes and supporting individual student success

Metric	Pre-Implementation	Post-Implementation	Change (%)
Average Student Engagement Rate	65%	85%	+20%
Assignment Completion Rate	70%	90%	+20%
Percentage of Students Using Adaptive Learning Tools	N/A	30%	N/A
Average Standardized Test Score	72%	80%	+8%
Percentage of Students Below Proficiency Threshold	40%	25%	-15%
Percentage of Students Showing a Gain of ≥10 Percentage Points	N/A	50%	N/A
Student Satisfaction with Personalized Learning	N/A	80%	N/A
Teacher Reports of Improved Engagement	N/A	70%	N/A

Figure 1. Bar Graph representation for pre and post implementation of data

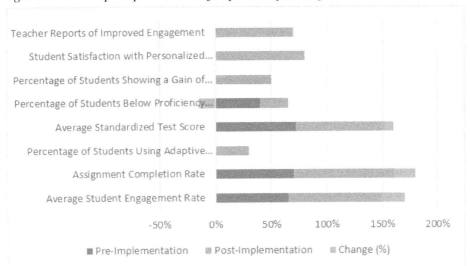

Table 1 provides a clear comparison of key metrics before and after the introduction of personalized learning, highlighting the impact of the initiative on student engagement, performance, and overall satisfaction as shown in Figure 1.

CONCLUSION

The introduction of personalized learning at XYZ High School has yielded substantial improvements in student engagement and academic performance. By leveraging behavioral data to tailor educational experiences, the school has successfully addressed individual student needs, resulting in a notable increase in participation rates and assignment completion. The average standardized test scores also showed a significant rise, and fewer students fell below the proficiency threshold. These positive outcomes were supported by favorable feedback from both students and teachers, highlighting increased motivation, better understanding of mathematical concepts, and more effective instructional practices. The successful integration of adaptive learning tools has demonstrated the potential of personalized learning to create a more engaging and responsive educational environment, ultimately contributing to enhanced student achievement and satisfaction. There are several promising avenues for expanding and refining personalized learning initiatives. One key area is the broadening of personalized learning models to encompass other subjects and educational levels. This expansion could provide valuable insights into the applicability and effectiveness of personalized learning across different contexts. Additionally, the integration of advanced artificial intelligence and machine learning technologies could further enhance the precision and adaptability of personalized learning experiences. Longitudinal studies will be essential to evaluate the long-term impact of these approaches on student outcomes and engagement. Ensuring scalability and accessibility of personalized learning initiatives, particularly in underserved areas, is crucial for achieving widespread benefits. Furthermore, investing in professional development for educators on data analytics and personalized learning tools will support the effective implementation and management of these strategies. Engaging students and parents more deeply in the personalized learning process and addressing ethical considerations related to data privacy are also vital for the success and sustainability of personalized learning initiatives. By pursuing these areas of development, educational institutions can continue to advance personalized learning and create more inclusive and impactful learning environments.

REFERENCES

Almufareh, M. F., Kausar, S., Humayun, M., & Tehsin, S. (2024). A conceptual model for inclusive technology: Advancing disability inclusion through artificial intelligence. *Journal of Disability Research*, 3(1), 20230060. DOI: 10.57197/JDR-2023-0060

Bachmann, N., Tripathi, S., Brunner, M., & Jodlbauer, H. (2022). The contribution of data-driven technologies in achieving the sustainable development goals. *Sustainability (Basel)*, 14(5), 2497. DOI: 10.3390/su14052497

Baneres, D., Rodríguez, M. E., & Guerrero-Roldán, A. E. (2020). *Engineering Data-Driven Adaptive Trust-based e-Assessment Systems*. Springer International Publishing. DOI: 10.1007/978-3-030-29326-0

Bibri, S. E., & Krogstie, J. (2020). The emerging data–driven Smart City and its innovative applied solutions for sustainability: The cases of London and Barcelona. *Energy Informatics*, 3(1), 5. DOI: 10.1186/s42162-020-00108-6

Bresciani, S., Ciampi, F., Meli, F., & Ferraris, A. (2021). Using big data for co-innovation processes: Mapping the field of data-driven innovation, proposing theoretical developments and providing a research agenda. *International Journal of Information Management*, 60, 102347. DOI: 10.1016/j.ijinfomgt.2021.102347

Channa, A., Sharma, A., Singh, M., Malhotra, P., Bajpai, A., & Whig, P. (2024). Original Research Article Revolutionizing filmmaking: A comparative analysis of conventional and AI-generated film production in the era of virtual reality. *Journal of Autonomous Intelligence*, 7(4).

Ciolacu, M., Svasta, P. M., Berg, W., & Popp, H. (2017, October). Education 4.0 for tall thin engineer in a data driven society. In *2017 IEEE 23rd International Symposium for Design and Technology in Electronic Packaging (SIITME)* (pp. 432-437). IEEE.

Guan, C., Mou, J., & Jiang, Z. (2020). Artificial intelligence innovation in education: A twenty-year data-driven historical analysis. *International Journal of Innovation Studies*, 4(4), 134–147. DOI: 10.1016/j.ijis.2020.09.001

Jain, A., Kamat, S., Saini, V., Singh, A., & Whig, P. (2024). Agile Leadership: Navigating Challenges and Maximizing Success. In Practical Approaches to Agile Project Management (pp. 32-47). IGI Global.

Kasula, B. Y., Whig, P., Vegesna, V. V., & Yathiraju, N. (2024). Unleashing Exponential Intelligence: Transforming Businesses through Advanced Technologies. International Journal of Sustainable Development Through AI. *ML and IoT*, 3(1), 1–18.

Klingenberg, C. O., Borges, M. A. V., & Antunes, J. A. V.Jr. (2021). Industry 4.0 as a data-driven paradigm: A systematic literature review on technologies. *Journal of Manufacturing Technology Management*, 32(3), 570–592. DOI: 10.1108/JMTM-09-2018-0325

Koedinger, K. R., Brunskill, E., Baker, R. S., McLaughlin, E. A., & Stamper, J. (2013). New potentials for data-driven intelligent tutoring system development and optimization. *AI Magazine*, 34(3), 27–41. DOI: 10.1609/aimag.v34i3.2484

Kumar, A., & Nagar, D. K. (2024). AI-Based Language Translation and Interpretation Services: Improving Accessibility for Visually Impaired Students. *As the editors of Transforming Learning. Power and Education*, 178.

Liu, D. Y. T., Bartimote-Aufflick, K., Pardo, A., & Bridgeman, A. J. (2017). Data-driven personalization of student learning support in higher education. *Learning analytics: Fundaments, applications, and trends: A view of the current state of the art to enhance e-learning*, 143-169.

Mehta, P., Chillarge, G. R., Sapkal, S. D., Shinde, G. R., & Kshirsagar, P. S. (2023). Inclusion of Children With Special Needs in the Educational System, Artificial Intelligence (AI). In *AI-Assisted Special Education for Students With Exceptional Needs* (pp. 156-185). IGI Global.

Mittal, S., Koushik, P., Batra, I., & Whig, P. (2024). AI-Driven Inventory Management for Optimizing Operations With Quantum Computing. In Quantum Computing and Supply Chain Management: A New Era of Optimization (pp. 125-140). IGI Global.

Miundy, K., Zaman, H. B., & Nordin, A. (2017). Review on data driven preliminary study pertaining to assistive digital learning technologies to support dyscalculia learners. In *Advances in Visual Informatics: 5th International Visual Informatics Conference, IVIC 2017, Bangi, Malaysia, November 28–30, 2017* [Springer International Publishing.]. *Proceedings*, 5, 233–246.

Moinuddin, M., Usman, M., & Khan, R. (2024). Strategic Insights in a Data-Driven Era: Maximizing Business Potential with Analytics and AI. *Revista Española de Documentación Científica*, 18(02), 117–133.

Nakarmi, S., Ouazzane, K., Yu, Q., Gill, M., & Khemka, S. (2024). Leveraging data driven approach to empower assistive technology.

Pansara, R. R., Mourya, A. K., Alam, S. I., Alam, N., Yathiraju, N., & Whig, P. (2024, May). Synergistic Integration of Master Data Management and Expert System for Maximizing Knowledge Efficiency and Decision-Making Capabilities. In 2024 2nd International Conference on Advancement in Computation & Computer Technologies (InCACCT) (pp. 13-16). IEEE. DOI: 10.1109/InCACCT61598.2024.10551152

Saaida, M. B. (2023). AI-Driven transformations in higher education: Opportunities and challenges. *International Journal of Educational Research and Studies*, 5(1), 29–36.

Sehrawat, S. K., Dutta, P. K., Bhatia, A. B., & Whig, P. (2024). Predicting Demand in Supply Chain Networks With Quantum Machine Learning Approach. In Quantum Computing and Supply Chain Management: A New Era of Optimization (pp. 33-47). IGI Global. DOI: 10.4018/979-8-3693-4107-0.ch002

Shafiq, W. (2024). Optimizing Organizational Performance: A Data-Driven Approach in Management Science. *Bulletin of Management Review*, 1(2), 31–40.

Whig, P., Bhatia, A. B., Nadikatu, R. R., Alkali, Y., & Sharma, P. (2024). 3 Security Issues in. Software-Defined Network Frameworks: Security Issues and Use Cases, 34.

Whig, P., Bhatia, A. B., Nadikatu, R. R., Alkali, Y., & Sharma, P. (2024). GIS and Remote Sensing Application for Vegetation Mapping. In *Geo-Environmental Hazards using AI-enabled Geospatial Techniques and Earth Observation Systems* (pp. 17–39). Springer Nature Switzerland. DOI: 10.1007/978-3-031-53763-9_2

Whig, P., Kasula, B. Y., Yathiraju, N., Jain, A., & Sharma, S. (2024). Transforming Aviation: The Role of Artificial Intelligence in Air Traffic Management. In New Innovations in AI, Aviation, and Air Traffic Technology (pp. 60-75). IGI Global.

Whig, P., & Kautish, S. (2024). VUCA Leadership Strategies Models for Pre-and Post-pandemic Scenario. In VUCA and Other Analytics in Business Resilience, Part B (pp. 127-152). Emerald Publishing Limited. DOI: 10.1108/978-1-83753-198-120241009

Whig, P., Mudunuru, K. R., & Remala, R. (2024). Quantum-Inspired Data-Driven Decision Making for Supply Chain Logistics. In Quantum Computing and Supply Chain Management: A New Era of Optimization (pp. 85-98). IGI Global. DOI: 10.4018/979-8-3693-4107-0.ch006

Whig, P., Remala, R., Mudunuru, K. R., & Quraishi, S. J. (2024). Integrating AI and Quantum Technologies for Sustainable Supply Chain Management. In Quantum Computing and Supply Chain Management: A New Era of Optimization (pp. 267-283). IGI Global. DOI: 10.4018/979-8-3693-4107-0.ch018

Whig, P., Silva, N., Elngar, A. A., Aneja, N., & Sharma, P. (Eds.). (2023). Sustainable Development through Machine Learning, AI and IoT: First International Conference, ICSD 2023, Delhi, India, July 15–16, 2023, Revised Selected Papers. Springer Nature. DOI: 10.1007/978-3-031-47055-4

Yandrapalli, V. (2024, February). AI-Powered Data Governance: A Cutting-Edge Method for Ensuring Data Quality for Machine Learning Applications. In *2024 Second International Conference on Emerging Trends in Information Technology and Engineering (ICETITE)* (pp. 1-6). IEEE. DOI: 10.1109/ic-ETITE58242.2024.10493601

ADDITIONAL READING

Bibri, S. E., & Krogstie, J. (2020). The emerging data–driven Smart City and its innovative applied solutions for sustainability: The cases of London and Barcelona. *Energy Informatics*, 3(1), 5. DOI: 10.1186/s42162-020-00108-6

Liu, D. Y. T., Bartimote-Aufflick, K., Pardo, A., & Bridgeman, A. J. (2017). Data-driven personalization of student learning support in higher education. *Learning analytics: Fundaments, applications, and trends: A view of the current state of the art to enhance e-learning*, 143-169. DOI: 10.1186/s42162-020-00108-6

Munagandla, V. B., Dandyala, S. S. V., & Vadde, B. C. (2024). Improving Educational Outcomes Through Data-Driven Decision-Making. *International Journal of Advanced Engineering Technologies and Innovations*, 1(3), 698–718.

Roy, B., Ghosh, S., Sarkar, S. K., Sen, A., & Choudhury, N. R. (2025). Implications of Artificial Intelligence for Special Education Technology. In *Transforming Special Education Through Artificial Intelligence* (pp. 401–430). IGI Global.

KEY TERMS AND DEFINITIONS

Adaptive Learning: An educational approach that uses technology and data to personalize learning experiences based on individual student needs and progress.

Assistive Technology: Devices or software designed to support individuals with disabilities, enhancing their ability to access and engage with educational content.

Behavioral Data: Information collected on how students interact with educational materials, tools, and environments, used to inform personalized learning strategies.

Data-Driven Solutions: Methods and technologies that utilize data analytics to improve decision-making, learning outcomes, and accessibility in education.

Inclusive Education: Educational practices that ensure equal access and opportunities for all students, regardless of their abilities or disabilities.

Learning Analytics: The collection, analysis, and reporting of data about learners and their contexts to optimize learning experiences and outcomes.

Personalized Learning: An instructional approach that customizes educational content, pacing, and strategies to align with each student's unique needs and abilities.

Real-Time Feedback: Immediate responses provided by educational systems or tools based on student performance, enabling adjustments to improve learning outcomes.

Student Engagement: The level of interest, participation, and emotional investment that students exhibit in the learning process.

Technological Innovation: The development and application of new technologies to enhance educational practices, particularly for students with disabilities.

Chapter 6
Assistive Technology and Accessibility Tools in Enhancing Adaptive Education

Tunde Toyese Oyedokun
 https://orcid.org/0000-0001-5306-038X
Thomas Adewumi University, Oko-Irese, Nigeria

ABSTRACT

The integration of assistive technology and accessibility tools is transforming education for students with disabilities. This chapter examines the development, significance, and future potential of these technologies within adaptive education frameworks. It analyzes tools such as wearable technology, virtual and augmented reality, artificial intelligence, and universal design, highlighting their role in fostering independent learning and personal growth. The discussion includes successful implementation strategies and case studies that demonstrate how assistive technology enhances self-advocacy and participation. Additionally, it addresses challenges, financial, logistical, and attitudinal that hinder adoption, along with proposed solutions. The chapter emphasizes the need for inclusive policies and partnerships to create a sustainable ecosystem for assistive technology deployment, ensuring equitable access to learning materials for all students as these tools evolve.

DOI: 10.4018/979-8-3693-8227-1.ch006

INTRODUCTION

The integration of assistive technology (AT) and accessibility tools in educational settings represents a transformative shift in how students with disabilities experience and engage with learning environments. Historically, education systems were not designed with accessibility in mind, often marginalizing students who required alternative methods to access curriculum content. However, as societal understanding of inclusivity has evolved, so too has the drive to make education accessible for all learners, regardless of physical, sensory, cognitive, or learning challenges. Adaptive education is a method used nowadays to accommodate a range of learning demands. It mostly depends on cutting-edge technologies to support students with disabilities' educational opportunity, autonomy, and involvement. As society has evolved toward inclusivity, adaptive education has emerged as a vital approach to meet diverse learning needs. Assistive technology tools encompass a variety of resources designed to enhance accessibility and support diverse learning needs. Low-tech options, such as graphic organizers, pencil grips, and color overlays, assist students with organizational skills and fine motor challenges. High-tech devices, including screen readers for visually impaired students, speech-to-text applications for those with writing difficulties, and communication devices for non-verbal learners, further improve accessibility. Additionally, AI-powered learning aids personalize educational experiences based on individual student needs and progress. Integrating these assistive technologies into educational settings, educators can foster dynamic and inclusive classrooms that enable all students to thrive academically and personally, benefiting not only those with disabilities but enriching the overall learning environment for everyone.

Assistive technology in education spans a wide spectrum, from low-tech tools like graphic organizers to high-tech devices and software such as screen readers, speech-to-text applications, and even AI-powered learning aids. The value of assistive technology lies not only in academic improvement but also in fostering self-advocacy, independence, and personal growth, enabling students to take charge of their own learning and daily interactions. Assistive technology, by making classrooms more adaptive, supports educators in developing inclusive teaching practices that resonate with a range of learning preferences and abilities, creating environments where all students can thrive. Moreover, assistive technology enhances students' ability to access curriculum content, thereby improving their academic performance (Satapathy, 2019). For instance, tools like text-to-speech (TTS) software can aid students with reading difficulties by reading text aloud, which helps improve comprehension and retention. With the right assistive technologies, students can perform tasks they might otherwise struggle with, promoting a sense of autonomy (Raffoul & Jaber, 2023). For example, speech recognition software allows students with writing difficulties to express their thoughts verbally, which are then transcribed into text. Teachers can create inclusive teaching methods that cater to different learning styles and abilities with the use of assistive technology. Regardless of their unique difficulties, this flexibility guarantees that every learner can interact with the content in a meaningful way. Assistive technology enables students to speak up for their own learning preferences and demands by providing them with tools tailored to their individual needs. This is essential for helping them develop a sense of autonomy and self-assurance in their academic endeavors. In the end, assistive technology ensures that students with disabilities have equal access to education and opportunities as their classmates without impairments.

Despite the significant advantages that assistive technology (AT) offers, challenges to its widespread implementation remain, including financial constraints, inadequate resources, limited professional training, and attitudinal barriers that hinder effective adoption in educational institutions. To address these issues, this chapter explores viable solutions such as increased advocacy efforts, policy support, and collaborative initiatives among educators, students, families, and policymakers. In order to guarantee that all students may take advantage of these vital resources in their educational settings, these tactics seek to create long-lasting frameworks for the implementation of assistive technology. This chapter aims to investigate the function of accessibility tools and assistive technology in adaptive education, providing information on their types, definitions, and historical background. This chapter attempts to highlight the educational advantages of assistive technology and offer practical suggestions for incorporating these tools in ways that optimize their impact through a thorough examination of recent research, case studies, and implementation strategies. By doing this, it hopes to enable educators, administrators, and legislators to make well-informed choices that maximize learning outcomes for every kid and give priority to inclusivity. In examining the future of assistive technology within adaptive education, this chapter also considers emerging trends and policy shifts that may influence the continued evolution of accessibility in educational settings.

Definition and Classification of Assistive Technology

According to Vincent, Okeowo, and Ariyo (2024), assistive technology (AT) is a broad category of instruments, equipment, and services intended to improve the functional capacities of people with impairments, especially in educational contexts. It makes it possible for kids who struggle with learning, physical, cognitive, or sensory issues to interact with the curriculum and take part in class activities, encouraging academic success alongside their peers. Assistive technology aims to empower users and foster independence, self-advocacy, and a sense of inclusion by giving users the ability to complete tasks that might otherwise be challenging or impossible (Fernández-Batanero, Montenegro-Rueda, Fernández-Cerero & Garcia-Martinez, 2022). Related accessibility tools include mechanisms and interfaces that facilitate access in both digital and physical environments, such as screen readers, closed captioning for multimedia content, ramps, and adjustable seating arrangements. These tools are essential for creating supportive environments that accommodate a diverse range of learners and ensure equitable educational opportunities for all. Assistive technology can address various educational needs across domains such as communication, mobility, sensory processing, and academic skills (Lynch, Singal & Francis, 2022). Communication devices, for example, allow non-verbal students to express their thoughts, while screen magnification software assists students with low vision in accessing digital content (Ozor, Dodo & Bana, 2024). Whether low-tech or high-tech, these tools all serve a common purpose: to enhance accessibility and quality of life, providing equitable opportunities and allowing students to actively participate in educational experiences.

Figure 1. Assistive technology

Assistive technologies are often classified as low-tech, mid-tech, or high-tech, depending on their complexity, functionality, and cost (Kirboyun, 2020). Low-tech assistive technology consists of simple, non-electronic tools that require minimal specialized training to use. These devices are generally inexpensive, accessible, and effective in helping students with specific challenges gain greater independence in performing everyday tasks (Erdem, 2017). Examples of low-tech assistive technology include graphic organizers that help students organize their thoughts and ideas visually, ergonomic writing tools designed for students with fine motor difficulties, communication boards that allow non-verbal students to express their basic needs, and visual schedules and timers that provide structure for students with autism or ADHD. Though these tools lack the sophistication of more advanced technology, they are highly adaptable and often serve as the foundation for developing essential skills (Viner, Singh & Shaughnessy, 2020).

Mid-tech assistive technology, on the other hand, includes devices that incorporate basic electronics or battery-operated systems. These tools often require moderate training to be used effectively but remain relatively cost-effective compared to more advanced high-tech solutions (Muhsin, Qahwaji, Ghanchi & Al-Taee, 2024). Audio recorders, for instance, allow students to record lectures or discussions, enabling them to review content at their own pace, which is especially beneficial for students with memory or attention difficulties. Talking calculators announce numbers and operations, helping students with visual impairments or dyscalculia engage in math tasks. Other examples of mid-tech assistive technology include portable word processors that assist students with writing difficulties and basic speech-generating devices (SGDs) that allow non-verbal individuals to communicate by selecting symbols or icons. These tools offer a middle ground for students who need more support than low-tech devices can provide but do not require the extensive functionalities of high-tech solutions (Nkomo & Daniel, 2021).

High-tech assistive technology (AT) includes sophisticated electronic or computerized systems that often utilize advanced software and artificial intelligence to deliver highly personalized support for students with complex needs (Zdravkova, Krasniqi, Dalipi & Ferati, 2022). Although these devices tend to be more expensive and require comprehensive training, they provide powerful functionality that enables full participation in educational settings. Examples include screen readers and magnification software, which offer spoken descriptions or enlarged views of on-screen content for students with visual impairments. Through the use of visuals, symbols, or text that the device converts into voice, non-verbal people can communicate via augmentative and alternative communication (AAC) technologies. Furthermore, students with physical limitations or dyslexia benefit greatly from speech-to-text software like Dragon NaturallySpeaking, which enables them to finish assignments and participate in class discussions by dictating their comments (Kambouri, Simon & Brooks, 2023). Some high-tech tools even include eye-tracking technology, which increases the independence of people with severe physical limitations when accessing digital resources by allowing them to manage a computer with their eye movements (Hsieh, 2022). All things considered; advanced assistive technology is a significant step in developing inclusive learning environments that accommodate a range of learning requirements.

The division of assistive technology into low-, mid-, and high-tech categories provides administrators, parents, and teachers with a useful framework for choosing the best resources for each student's need. This classification facilitates the evaluation of elements including price, usability, and possible influence on learning objectives. In order to optimize the advantages of assistive technology, it also offers schools and other organizations a guidance for allocating resources and developing training initiatives. These categories might broaden to incorporate new instruments and frameworks that improve accessibility in education as technology develops. Schools may create more inclusive classrooms where every student can fulfill their potential and interact meaningfully with their classmates by fostering an atmosphere that supports accessibility tools and assistive technology.

Historical Context and Evolution of Assistive Technology

The development of assistive technology (AT) in educational settings has a rich history that reflects broader societal shifts toward inclusivity, equity, and empowerment for individuals with disabilities. Over the years, advancements in technology have intersected with legislative changes, educational policies, and public awareness, leading to increasingly robust frameworks for supporting students with disabilities. Initially, students with disabilities were largely excluded from mainstream educational settings due to a lack of resources, appropriate tools, and societal understanding of their potential. However, significant milestones in the evolution of assistive technology have transformed the educational landscape, opening doors for adaptive education and individualized learning opportunities. Early in the 20th century, the first efforts to develop assistive tools focused primarily on low-tech solutions, such as Braille materials and hearing aids, to accommodate students with visual and hearing impairments (Viner, Singh & Shaughnessy, 2020). In 1918, the American Foundation for the Blind was established, leading to a growing awareness and development of resources tailored for students with blindness or low vision (Willings, 2022). Around the same time, researchers and educators began advocating for classroom accommodations, setting the foundation for future assistive technology developments. By the mid-20th century, advances in medical and psychological research led to a better understanding of cognitive disabilities, prompting educators to explore additional strategies for students who required more than basic accommodations (Hayes & Bulat, 2017).

The 1970s marked a pivotal era in the history of assistive technology, as advocacy groups and legislative efforts began to emphasize the importance of inclusive education. The right of students with disabilities to receive a free and appropriate public education (FAPE) in the least restrictive setting was established in 1975 with the passage of the Education for All Handicapped Children Act (EAHCA), which was later renamed the Individuals with Disabilities Education Act (IDEA) (Yell, Rogers & Rogers, 1998). Since teachers and schools were now legally obligated to provide resources and tools that would meet each student's specific learning needs, this act encouraged the use of assistive technology in classrooms. Additionally, the law established the idea of Individualized Education Programs (IEPs), which allowed teachers, parents, and experts to determine which assistance and assistive technology were required to meet each child's learning objectives.

In the 1980s and 1990s, rapid technological advancements contributed to significant growth in assistive technology availability and diversity. Microcomputers became more accessible and affordable, providing new ways for students to engage with academic content (Shanker, 2022). Early iterations of screen magnifiers and text-to-speech software became available, providing crucial assistance for students with learning challenges and visual impairments. The United States saw a significant advancement in the availability of assistive technology during this period with the enactment of the Technology-Related Assistance for Individuals with Disabilities Act of 1988, also known as the "Tech Act," which gave states federal funding to create and implement assistive technology programs (D'Andrea & Siu, 2015). In order to emphasize the significance of accessibility and inclusion in all areas of life, including education, the Tech Act further expanded the definition of assistive technology to encompass any tool or service that helps people with disabilities (Simeoni, R., Pirrera, A., Meli, P., & Giansanti, 2023). The early 2000s saw an expansion of digital assistive technology tools with the rise of the internet and advances in computing power, allowing for the development of increasingly sophisticated technologies that could support a broader range of disabilities (Weck & Afanassieva, 2023). The Accessibility for Ontarians with Disabilities Act (AODA) of 2005 and the Americans with Disabilities Act Amendments Act (ADAAA) of 2008 reinforced the importance of accessible education by mandating that public spaces and resources, including educational materials, be accessible to people with disabilities. These legislative shifts inspired the adoption of more advanced tools like speech-to-text software, portable communication devices, and computer-based learning programs that could be customized for individual students (Ontario Human Rights Commission, 2018).

The incorporation of mobile technology, machine learning, and artificial intelligence (AI) into educational resources has sped up the development of assistive technology in recent years. Students with disabilities can now interact with learning materials in previously unthinkable ways thanks to these innovations, which have made assistive technology more context-sensitive, adaptive, and personalized (Ogundaini & Mlitwa, 2024). AI-driven solutions, such as predictive text, voice recognition software, and adaptive learning platforms, have enhanced accessibility and engagement for students with cognitive, sensory, and motor impairments (Eziamaka, Odonker & Akinsulire, 2024). Additionally, the prevalence of mobile devices has democratized access to assistive technology, as students can now access a variety of educational resources directly from smartphones and tablets. Cloud-based assistive technology platforms also support real-time collaboration and integration with classroom technology, enabling seamless transitions between physical and digital learning environments.

Every significant development in assistive technology has aided in the growth of adaptable education, which creates learning environments that are customized to accommodate a range of demands. A growing understanding of the importance of inclusivity in education is reflected in the development of AT, which has shifted the emphasis from basic accessibility to all students' empowerment and independence. The accessibility and personalization of educational experiences could be further improved in the future by new technologies like virtual reality (VR), augmented reality (AR), and even more advanced AI-driven platforms. These advancements underscore the role of AT not only as a tool for accommodation but as a dynamic field that continues to shape educational practices and redefine what is possible for students with disabilities. Through continued innovation and advocacy, assistive technology is poised to play an even more integral role in creating equitable and inclusive learning environments in the years to come.

In a nutshell, important turning points in the development of assistive technology (AT) in education are reflected in its historical background. A free suitable public education for people with disabilities was ensured by the Individuals with Disabilities Education Act (IDEA), which was passed in 1975, marking the beginning of the journey. The phrases "assistive technology device" and "assistive technology service" were not, however, officially used in educational settings until the 1991 modifications. This marked a pivotal shift, as discussions about AT became integral to Individualized Education Program (IEP) meetings following the 1997 amendments. The Assistive Technology Act, enacted in 1998, further expanded access and funding for AT, making it more available to families and schools. According to a comprehensive analysis of research conducted between 2009 and 2020, the use of AT increased significantly beginning in 2017, underscoring its increasing acceptance and incorporation into adaptive education. A dedication to increasing accessibility for children with special educational needs (SEN) is demonstrated by recent initiatives, such as government training programs designed to improve staff awareness of assistive technology. These historical advancements highlight the continuous attempts to establish inclusive learning settings where all students can succeed as technology advances.

IMPACT OF ASSISTIVE TECHNOLOGY ON LEARNING OUTCOMES

Assistive technology (AT) has had a revolutionary effect on the learning outcomes of students with disabilities, fostering increased independence, better academic achievement, and stronger self-advocacy. Various research studies have highlighted the effectiveness of assistive technology tools in bridging educational gaps, demonstrating that when students have access to the right technological supports, they can engage more meaningfully with their coursework and develop critical skills for lifelong learning. Through focused interventions, AT has helped students with disabilities flourish in inclusive environments by promoting both academic success and personal development. Several research have demonstrated how AT improves academic performance. For example, a systematic review found that students with severe reading difficulties can improve their reading and writing skills by using text-to-speech (TTS) and speech-to-text (STT) programs. Although no traditional reading remediation was offered, students who received AT training in one study with 149 participants demonstrated improvements in their reading skills comparable to those of their peers without disabilities (Svensson, Nordström, Lindeblad, Gustafson, Björn, Sand, Almgrem-Back & Nilsson, 2019). This implies that AT can successfully close the achievement gap between kids with disabilities and their peers without impairments.

Additionally, computer-assisted instruction has proven beneficial for students with learning disabilities, particularly in areas such as spelling and math. Research indicates that this type of instruction provides immediate feedback, which is crucial for skill development. Students using computer-assisted tools demonstrated improved performance in memorizing math facts and expressed more positive attitudes toward the subject compared to those who did not use such technologies (Young & MacCormack, 2014). The ability of assistive technology to support diverse learning needs underscores its critical role in promoting academic success. Beyond academic performance, AT plays a vital role in fostering independence and self-advocacy among students with disabilities. Tools like communication boards and speech-generating devices empower non-verbal learners to express their needs and participate actively in classroom discussions. This increased ability to communicate not only enhances their social interactions but also builds confidence in their capabilities.

Case studies illustrate how assistive technology has transformed the educational experiences of individual students. For example, a student with dyslexia who utilized TTS software was able to engage with complex texts independently, leading to improved comprehension and a greater sense of ownership over their learning process. Similarly, students using portable word processors reported feeling more confident in their writing abilities, as they could focus on content rather than struggling with the mechanics of writing (McNicholl, Casey, Desmond, & Gallagher, 2021). Moreover, the use of AT encourages self-advocacy by allowing students to identify their strengths and weaknesses. As they become more adept at using these technologies, they learn to articulate their needs and preferences in educational settings. This empowerment is essential for fostering a sense of agency, enabling students to take charge of their learning journeys.

Students' experiences with AI-powered assistive technology reveal a range of feelings about the personalized learning opportunities these tools provide. The integration of such technologies into educational settings has transformed how students with disabilities engage with their learning environments, fostering independence and enhancing academic performance. Many students express enthusiasm about the personalized learning experiences enabled by AI-powered assistive technologies (Ellikkal & Rajamohan, 2024). For instance, a high school student shared, "Using my AI-driven learning app has made studying so much easier. It adapts to my pace and helps me focus on the areas where I struggle the most." This sentiment reflects the general consensus among students who appreciate the tailored support these technologies offer, allowing them to learn at their own speed and according to their individual needs (Seo, Tang, Roll, Fels & Yoon, 2021). Another student, who uses a speech-to-text application, noted, "It's like having a personal assistant. I can just talk, and it writes everything down for me. I feel more confident sharing my ideas in class." This highlights how AI-powered tools not only facilitate academic tasks but also empower students to participate more actively in discussions, fostering a sense of belonging and self-advocacy. AI-powered assistive technology significantly enhances students' independence (Almgren Bäck, et al., 2024). A parent of a child with autism remarked, "Since my son started using an AI-based communication device, he can express his thoughts without relying on others. It has been a game-changer for him." Such devices allow non-verbal students to communicate effectively, promoting their ability to advocate for themselves in educational settings (Li, Zarei, Alibakhshi, & Labbafi, 2024). Additionally, students report feeling more in control of their learning processes. For example, a student stated, "With the personalized feedback I get from my learning software, I can see exactly where I need to improve. It makes me feel like I'm in charge of my education." This sense of ownership is crucial for fostering self-confidence and motivation among learners (Lim, Dawson, Gašević, Joksimović, Fudge, Pardo & Gentili, 2020).

Despite the positive feedback, some students and parents have raised concerns regarding the reliance on technology. A student expressed hesitation, "Sometimes I worry that I depend too much on my assistive tech. What if it fails during an important test?" This concern underscores the need for balance in using technology while ensuring that students also develop traditional skills (McNicholl, 2022). Parents also highlight challenges related to implementation. A parent noted that,

"While the technology is fantastic, school struggles with providing adequate training for teachers. My son's progress could be even better if his teachers were fully equipped to use these tools effectively." This points to the necessity of professional development alongside technological integration to maximize the benefits of AI-powered assistive technologies (Osorio-Saez, Eryilmaz & Sandoval-Hernandez, 2021). Most importantly, students generally feel positively about the personalized learning experiences provided by AI-powered assistive technology. These tools not only enhance academic performance but also foster independence and self-advocacy among learners. However, it is essential to address concerns regarding over-reliance on technology and ensure that educators are adequately trained to implement these tools effectively. Educational institutions, by way of creating a balanced approach that combines technology with traditional learning methods, can further enhance the learning experiences of all students, particularly those with disabilities.

Implementation Strategies for Educators

Implementing assistive technology (AT) in educational settings requires well-considered strategies that are responsive to the diverse needs of students and the demands placed on educators. Selecting the right assistance for each learner is a critical first step in this process, as it ensures that the technology used genuinely enhances learning experiences and fosters independence (Theresa, 2023). However, the successful integration of assistive technology also depends heavily on educators' understanding of these tools. Therefore, professional development programs that focus on AT usage are essential, equipping educators with the skills to implement these technologies effectively and sustainably. Together, thoughtful AT selection and comprehensive educator training form the foundation of effective AT integration in classrooms, allowing students to maximize their academic and personal potential (Schaaf, 2018). Choosing appropriate assistive technology for diverse learners requires a nuanced approach that considers each student's unique strengths, challenges, and learning goals (Zwarych, 2023). The selection process often begins with a thorough assessment of individual needs, typically conducted by special education specialists, assistive technology consultants, or multidisciplinary teams who have a deep understanding of both the available technologies and the specific demands of each learning disability. While a student with ADHD could find organizing tools like digital planners or task management apps more helpful, a student with dyslexia might benefit more from text-to-speech software that helps with reading comprehension. Aligning assistive technology with specific learning objectives and educational tasks helps ensure that students are equipped with tools that provide direct support in their areas of need. This tailored approach not only makes assistive technology more effective but also empowers students to engage more fully in their educational experiences (Keelor, Creaghead, Silbert & Horowitz-Kraus, 2020; Hecker, Burns, Katz, Elkind & Elkind, 2002).

Educators also play a vital role in selecting assistive technology that is appropriate and adaptable to classroom environments. Given the rapid pace of technological advancements, it's important for educators to stay informed about new tools and updates to existing assistive solutions. When selecting tools, educators should consider factors such as ease of use, compatibility with other classroom resources, and scalability. For instance, some assistive technology devices are portable and can be used across multiple classes or even at home, which is particularly helpful for students who benefit from consistent support. Additionally, educators should be mindful of the level of support that each tool requires. Low-tech devices, such as pencil grips or graphic organizers, may require minimal training and can be easily integrated, while high-tech options like speech-to-text software or communication devices may need a more structured introduction. Educators, by carefully evaluating these factors can choose assistive technology tools that not only support learning but also fit seamlessly into the classroom environment, minimizing disruptions and maximizing effectiveness (Viner, Singh & Shaughnessy, 2019).

Professional development programs for educators are essential for the successful implementation of assistive technology, as these programs provide educators with the necessary skills and knowledge to use AT tools effectively. Training programs can take many forms, including workshops, online modules, peer mentoring, and ongoing professional learning communities focused on AT. These programs should begin with a foundational overview of AT, covering the types of tools available, the specific needs they address, and practical considerations for classroom use. Building from this base, educators benefit greatly from hands-on experience, where they can learn to navigate different AT devices and troubleshoot common issues that may arise. This experiential learning empowers educators to feel confident in using AT, making them better prepared to guide students in using these tools effectively (Alsolami, 2022).

An effective professional development program should also emphasize instructional strategies that incorporate assistive technology into daily teaching practices. For example, educators can learn to integrate text-to-speech tools into reading activities, helping students with reading challenges follow along with class materials. Similarly, teachers might incorporate visual supports, such as graphic organizers or visual timers, into their lesson plans to help students with executive functioning difficulties stay organized and on task. Educators, by weaving AT into the fabric of daily instruction create a more inclusive environment that normalizes the use of technology for learning, reducing stigma and promoting broader acceptance among students (Wood, Moxley, Tighe & Wagner, 2018). Another critical component of AT-focused professional development is training educators to support self-advocacy and independence in students who use assistive technology. As students become more comfortable with assistive technology tools, it's essential for educators to foster self-reliance by encouraging students to use these tools autonomously and to advocate for their needs in educational settings. For example, educators can teach students how to set up and customize their AT devices to suit their preferences, whether that means adjusting text size on screen readers or setting reminders on organizational apps. Educators can also guide students on how to request technical support when needed and encourage them to communicate openly about the accommodations that work best for them. This approach not only empowers students to take ownership of their learning but also prepares them for future transitions, whether that's moving to higher education or entering the workforce.

Collaboration with AT specialists and other educational support staff further strengthens the effectiveness of AT implementation in schools. Educators benefit from the expertise of AT consultants, occupational therapists, and special education coordinators, who can provide insights into specific tools and share best practices for their use. This collaborative approach ensures that AT strategies are tailored to the needs of each student and that educators have access to a network of support for guidance and troubleshooting. Schools can also establish learning communities or peer-support groups where educators share experiences and insights related to AT, creating an environment of ongoing professional growth (Chow, de Bruin & Sharma, 2024). Sustainable implementation of AT also requires a strong infrastructure within schools. Administrators play a key role in supporting AT integration by allocating resources for training, purchasing technology, and maintaining devices over time. Effective administrative support allows for consistent access to AT resources, making it easier for educators to incorporate these tools into their classrooms without interruption. Administrators contribute to a positive environment where AT can be reliably used to support student learning by ensuring that AT devices and software are regularly updated, and that technical support is available.

In essence, the successful implementation of assistive technology relies on strategic selection of tools and comprehensive professional development for educators. With careful assessment, educators can choose AT solutions that directly support the diverse needs of learners, enabling students to overcome barriers and reach their potential. Educators, by participating in robust professional development programs gain the skills and confidence needed to integrate AT effectively, creating inclusive classrooms where students with disabilities can thrive. This dual focus on thoughtful AT selection and educator training ensures that assistive technology becomes a powerful asset in promoting equitable, empowering education for all students.

Best Practices in Assistive Technology Deployment

Table 1. Best practices in assistive technology

Comprehensive Training for Educators	Provide structured training sessions for teachers to effectively use assistive technologies, enhancing their understanding and confidence.
Personalized Technology Inclusion Plans	Develop individualized plans that outline specific assistive technologies tailored to each student's unique needs and goals.
Ongoing Assessment and Feedback	Conduct regular assessments to evaluate the effectiveness of assistive technologies and make necessary adjustments based on student progress.
Collaboration with Families	Involve families in the AT planning and implementation process, providing training to help them support their children at home.
Creation of AT Support Teams	Establish teams composed of educators, administrators, families, and students to discuss progress, challenges, and customization of AT tools.
Integration into School Policies	Embed assistive technology use within broader school policies that promote inclusivity and accessibility for all students.
Co-Teaching Models	Implement co-teaching strategies where general and special education teachers collaborate to integrate AT into classroom instruction.
Technology-Rich Classrooms	Equip classrooms with adaptive software and devices to facilitate personalized learning experiences for students with disabilities.
Peer Mentoring Programs	Create programs where proficient students assist peers in using assistive technologies, fostering a collaborative learning environment.
Engagement in Decision-Making	Involve students in selecting and using assistive technologies to foster ownership over their learning experiences.
Professional Learning Communities (PLCs)	Encourage educators to participate in PLCs focused on AT use to share best practices and collaboratively address challenges.
Structured Collaborative Activities	Design group tasks that ensure active participation from all students while effectively utilizing assistive technologies.

This table provides a succinct overview of the best practices in the deployment of assistive technologies, making it easier for educators to reference and implement these strategies effectively in their classrooms.

Best practices in the deployment of assistive technology (AT) are essential for maximizing its effectiveness and ensuring meaningful outcomes for students with disabilities. Successful AT models in various educational environments demonstrate the importance of tailoring tools and strategies to each student's unique needs while integrating these tools seamlessly into the broader learning environment (Alam & Mohanty, 2023). Schools that excel in assistive technology deployment often foster collaborative efforts among students, educators, and families, creating a support network that reinforces the use of AT in all aspects of a student's life. Such practices not only enhance the immediate learning experience but also promote long-term success, self-advocacy, and independence for students who rely on assistive technology (Vincent, Okeowo & Ariyo, 2024). One effective model in assistive technology deployment emphasizes the personalization of technology to suit the individual needs and goals of each student. In inclusive educational environments, it is increasingly common to find "technology inclusion plans" that outline specific AT tools, settings, and usage guidelines tailored to individual learners (Fernández-Batanero, Montenegro-Rueda, Fernández-Cerero & Garcia-Martinez, 2022). For example, a student with visual impairment may be equipped with screen reader software, Braille displays, and auditory cues, while a student with ADHD might benefit from digital planners and visual scheduling aids that help with time management and organization (Ozor, Dodo & Bana, 2024). Schools that follow this individualized approach often pair assistive technology tools with learning objectives, ensuring that each technology aligns with the student's specific academic and personal development goals. This personalization makes assistive technology more effective, as students receive the support they need in real time and can access learning resources that might otherwise be unavailable.

An essential component of successful assistive technology deployment involves ongoing assessment and feedback. Many schools conduct regular assessments to evaluate how well AT tools are meeting students' needs, making adjustments as necessary to improve effectiveness. This iterative approach allows educators to adapt AT solutions as students' abilities, learning goals, and classroom demands evolve. For instance, as a student with dyslexia progresses in reading skills, their AT needs may shift from intensive text-to-speech support to tools focused on fluency and comprehension, such as auditory feedback for writing or spelling support applications. Schools, by consistently reviewing and updating AT tools, can ensure that students continue to receive relevant, impactful support throughout their educational journey (Erdem, 2017).

Collaboration among students, educators, and families is fundamental in making assistive technology deployment effective and sustainable. Schools that actively involve families in AT planning and implementation often see better outcomes, as students receive consistent support both at school and at home. Families are often given training sessions to understand how AT tools work, enabling them to support their children's use of technology beyond the classroom (Okoye, 2024). For example, if a student uses a speech-generating device in school, their family members can learn how to set up and customize it at home, facilitating smoother communication in both environments. This consistency helps students build confidence in using AT, making it a natural part of their daily lives rather than an isolated school-based intervention. Educators and support staff are also critical to collaborative AT deployment, as they provide guidance, instruction, and troubleshooting support that reinforce students' learning. Professional development workshops that focus on AT encourage educators to view AT tools as integral parts of their teaching practice rather than external add-ons. Teachers trained in AT can embed technology into classroom activities, allowing students who use AT to participate fully in the same assignments and projects as their peers (Mhlongo, Mbatha, Ramatsetse & Dlamini, 2023). This inclusive approach reduces the stigma often associated with AT, as students see it as a valuable tool for learning and communication rather than a marker of difference. Furthermore, educators who are well-versed in AT usage can act as mentors for their students, helping them explore new ways to leverage technology to meet their academic goals and develop self-advocacy skills.

In addition to classroom teachers, assistive technology specialists and technology coordinators play a valuable role in supporting the deployment of assistive technology. These specialists can provide tailored recommendations based on their expertise, helping educators select the most suitable assistive technology solutions for each student. In some successful school models, AT specialists collaborate closely with teachers to provide hands-on demonstrations and troubleshoot issues that may arise in the classroom. For instance, they may work with teachers to find the best settings on a particular device or provide tips for encouraging student engagement with AT. Schools ensure that both students and teachers have access to knowledgeable resources, by involving AT specialists in the implementation process, thereby making AT deployment more efficient and less stressful for everyone involved (Lahm, 2003).

One exemplary assistive technology deployment model is found in schools that have created "AT support teams" composed of educators, administrators, family members, and, when possible, students. These teams meet regularly to discuss each student's progress with assistive technology, address any challenges, and share insights on how the technology can be further customized or integrated. Such teams serve as a collaborative support system, giving each stakeholder a voice in the deployment process. For example, during team meetings, parents can share observations about how a particular AT tool is used at home, while teachers can discuss its application in classroom activities. This collaborative feedback loop allows for continuous improvement, ensuring that AT remains responsive to the students' changing needs and circumstances. Another best practice in assistive technology deployment is embedding AT within broader school policies and culture. Schools with inclusive policies and cultures that promote diversity and accessibility often have more successful AT outcomes, as these environments encourage acceptance and understanding among students and staff (Fernández-Batanero, Montenegro-Rueda, Fernández-Cerero & Garcia-Martinez, 2022). When AT use is normalized within the school, students with disabilities feel more comfortable using these tools openly, and their peers are more likely to view AT as part of the natural learning landscape. Schools that embrace inclusivity may also set up peer-support programs where students who use AT are paired with classmates who can help them navigate challenges or celebrate achievements. Such programs foster a supportive atmosphere, reducing stigma and promoting a culture of mutual understanding and assistance.

Effective models and cooperative strategies including students, teachers, and families are essential for the successful implementation of assistive technology (AT) in educational settings. Schools may optimize the advantages of AT and provide inclusive learning opportunities for all students by implementing best practices. The Universal Design for Learning (UDL) paradigm is a successful approach that prioritizes offering diverse learners a variety of engagement, representation, and action/expression options. All students can access learning materials in ways that meet their individual requirements thanks to the seamless integration of AT into curricula by schools that use UDL principles (Priyadharsini & Mary, 2024). For instance, to help pupils with varying learning styles, a school may employ text-to-speech (TTS) software in conjunction with visual aids and practical exercises. Co-teaching, in which general education and special education teachers work together to offer instruction, is another successful strategy. All students gain from the integration of AT made possible by this arrangement. To enable students with disabilities to fully participate alongside their peers, a co-teaching team could, for example, use interactive whiteboards with AT tools to encourage group conversations.

Technology-rich classrooms also play a significant role in enhancing student engagement levels among those with disabilities. Classrooms equipped with tablets and adaptive software allow for personalized learning experiences. For example, one school implemented a "tech corner" where students could explore various AT tools during independent study time, fostering both autonomy and skill development. Additionally, after-school programs designed to provide extra support can effectively utilize AT to enhance learning outcomes. For instance, a tutoring program might incorporate speech-to-text applications to assist students with writing assignments, allowing them to complete tasks they might struggle with during the school day. Collaboration between educators and families is crucial for successful AT deployment. Engaging students in the selection and use of AT fosters a sense of ownership over their learning. When students are part of the decision-making process regarding which technologies to use, they are more likely to embrace these tools and utilize them effectively. For example, a student with dyslexia might choose TTS software based on their comfort level and preferences. Schools can also host workshops or informational sessions to educate families about available technologies and how they can support their children's learning at home. This partnership empowers families to reinforce the use of AT in everyday situations, enhancing its effectiveness (Halpin, 2024).

Implementing peer mentoring programs can significantly enhance the effectiveness of assistive technology as well. Students who are proficient in using specific technologies can assist their peers in navigating these tools, fostering a collaborative learning environment. Peer-assisted learning has been shown to enhance students' social abilities in addition to their academic performance. Participating in professional learning communities (PLCs) centered on the use of assistive technology can also be advantageous for educators (Bhat, Gurung, Gupta, Dhungana & Thapa, 2022). These networks give educators the chance to exchange best practices, talk about difficulties, and work together to develop tech-integration methods. Effective collaborative learning requires careful planning and structure. Educators should design group tasks that ensure all students participate actively while utilizing AT tools effectively. Research shows that small groups (3-5 students) working towards a shared goal tend to achieve better outcomes when supported by structured collaborative activities (Le, Janssen & Wubbels, 2017). Educators, and families, schools can create inclusive classrooms where every student has the opportunity to thrive academically and socially by adopting these best practices in assistive technology deployment, leveraging successful models from various educational environments and fostering collaborative approaches among students. The thoughtful integration of AT not only enhances learning outcomes but also empowers students with disabilities to become self-advocates in their educational journeys.

Challenges to Implementing Assistive Technology

Implementing assistive technology (AT) in educational settings, though invaluable for students with disabilities, comes with various challenges that impact its widespread adoption and effectiveness. Financial, logistical, and attitudinal barriers all play significant roles in limiting access to assistive technology, posing obstacles for schools, educators, and families seeking to support students' learning and independence (Copley & Ziviani, 2004). Addressing these challenges requires a proactive approach that combines targeted solutions, advocacy efforts, and policy initiatives. Educational institutions, by understanding and tackling the barriers to assistive technology adoption, can work toward creating inclusive environments where all students can thrive. One of the most prominent challenges in implementing assistive technology is financial. Many AT devices and software are costly, placing a burden on schools with limited budgets. High-tech AT, such as screen readers, speech-generating devices, and interactive learning platforms, often come with significant expenses, not only for initial purchase but also for ongoing maintenance, upgrades, and technical support (Kirboyun, 2020). For underfunded schools or those in economically disadvantaged communities, securing these resources can be especially difficult, resulting in unequal access to AT across different educational settings. Additionally, because AT needs to be tailored to individual students, schools may require a range of devices, which can further strain budgets. In some cases, the expense of AT may discourage school administrators from pursuing it altogether, depriving students of critical support.

To address financial barriers, schools can explore various funding strategies, including grants, partnerships, and donations. Many public and private organizations offer grants specifically for the purpose of purchasing assistive technology. Schools can also apply for government funding through programs like the Individuals with Disabilities Education Act (IDEA) in the United States, which allocates funds for special education, including assistive technology. Partnerships with technology companies or local businesses can provide additional financial support, either through direct funding or through donations of devices and software. Moreover, advocating for increased funding from local, state, and national governments can help to raise awareness of the importance of AT and encourage budget allocations that prioritize inclusive education (Tay-Teo, Bell & Jowett, 2021).

Logistical challenges also pose significant obstacles to the effective implementation of AT. The process of selecting, installing, and maintaining assistive technology requires time, expertise, and ongoing support, which can be challenging for schools with limited resources (Oldfrey, et al., 2023). For instance, teachers and support staff need adequate training to understand how to use and integrate AT into their daily practices effectively. Without this training, AT can go underutilized, and students may not receive the full benefit of the technology available to them. Further, logistical issues arise when considering compatibility and infrastructure, as certain AT devices require specific hardware or software to function effectively, which may not be available in all classrooms or schools. These logistical challenges can create inconsistencies in AT deployment, leaving some students better supported than others. Addressing logistical barriers involves investing in professional development for educators and technical support staff. Comprehensive training on AT should be an integral part of professional development programs, equipping teachers and support staff with the knowledge and skills necessary to effectively integrate these tools into the classroom (Boot, Owuor, Dinsmore & MacLachlan, 2018). Ongoing training sessions and support from AT specialists can make a significant difference, allowing educators to troubleshoot issues and adapt tools as needed. Schools can also establish partnerships with AT vendors or specialists who offer technical support and regular device updates, ensuring that technology remains functional and relevant. When AT is treated as an integral part of school infrastructure, with sufficient resources allocated to support it, logistical barriers become less obstructive.

Attitudinal barriers, including misconceptions about assistive technology, also play a critical role in limiting its successful implementation. Some educators, parents, or administrators may hold outdated views that AT is only for students with severe disabilities or that it fosters dependency rather than independence. Such misconceptions can create reluctance to invest in or encourage the use of AT, even in situations where it would clearly benefit students (Ahmed, 2018). Additionally, there may be social stigma associated with using AT, with some students feeling embarrassed or singled out due to their reliance on technology, especially if their peers do not understand the purpose of AT or view it as a sign of difference. These attitudinal challenges can lead to underutilization of AT or a lack of motivation among students who would otherwise benefit greatly from it (Parette & Scherer, 2004). Overcoming attitudinal barriers involves awareness campaigns, inclusive policies, and education about the benefits of AT for students of all abilities. Schoolwide initiatives that educate staff, students, and families on the purpose and value of AT can help normalize its use and reduce stigma (Molina Roldán, Marauri, Aubert & Flecha, 2021). For instance, schools can implement awareness programs or workshops that demonstrate how AT promotes independence and supports diverse learning needs. Schools, by promoting a culture that views AT as a resource for all students can foster greater acceptance, encouraging students to embrace AT without feeling different. Additionally, integrating AT into classroom practices as a universal learning tool, rather than solely as an accommodation for disabilities, can promote inclusivity and reduce stigma. When all students have the opportunity to interact with AT, whether through shared tools or exposure to peers' devices, it reinforces the idea that AT is part of the educational experience.

Advocacy for policy change is another crucial strategy in overcoming barriers to assistive technology adoption. Educators, administrators, and families can work together to push for policies that mandate and fund AT in educational institutions. National and state-level advocacy efforts can help influence education policy, increasing funding for AT and ensuring that schools prioritize inclusive practices (Fteiha, Al-Rashaida, Elsori, Khalil & Al Bustami, 2024). Policymakers can be encouraged to establish clearer guidelines on AT funding, make professional development on AT a standard for educators, and promote the inclusion of AT in Individualized Education Programs (IEPs) and 504 Plans (National Academies of Sciences, Engineering, and Medicine, 1997). Through lobbying efforts, partnerships with advocacy organizations, and public awareness campaigns, stakeholders can work to elevate AT as a priority within education systems, creating a more supportive environment for students with disabilities. In essence, while financial, logistical, and attitudinal challenges to AT implementation are significant, they are not insurmountable. Schools can address financial limitations by securing funding through grants, partnerships, and advocacy. Logistical barriers can be minimized by prioritizing professional development and technical support, enabling educators to use AT effectively and confidently. Meanwhile, attitudinal barriers can be overcome through awareness campaigns and inclusive practices that destigmatize AT and promote it as a tool for all learners. Collectively, these solutions and advocacy efforts create a pathway for greater AT adoption, fostering an inclusive educational environment where all students have the resources and support, they need to succeed.

Successful Strategies for the Adoption of Assistive Technologies in Schools

The adoption of assistive technologies (AT) in educational settings has been a focal point of research, highlighting both the potential benefits and the challenges faced by schools. Several schools and institutions have successfully navigated the challenges of adopting assistive technologies (AT), addressing financial, logistical, and attitudinal barriers through specific strategies. Notable among others is Howard County Public Schools in Maryland that have effectively implemented assistive technologies (AT) through structured training programs for special education staff, aimed at enhancing their understanding and confidence in using these tools. Despite initial feedback indicating that staff felt under-trained, the introduction of comprehensive training sessions has significantly improved their capabilities. Additionally, the establishment of an assistive technology department has provided ongoing support, ensuring educators have access to specialists for implementation and troubleshooting of AT devices. A survey revealed that 83% of staff rated the effectiveness of assistive technologies highly, noting improvements in communication, socialization, and independence among students with disabilities, which reflects a positive shift in attitudes towards AT when adequate support and training are provided (HCPSS, 2024).

Also, schools in Zanzibar have made notable progress in providing assistive technologies, such as hearing aids and braille materials, although they face challenges related to resource distribution, which has led to strategies that involve grouping students for shared use of these resources. The schools have also adopted inclusive education practices that emphasize the significance of assistive technologies in engaging students with disabilities in regular classroom activities, with teachers creatively utilizing AT to support learning across various subjects. Despite the logistical challenges and limited availability of resources, schools reported significant positive impacts on student engagement and performance when assistive technologies were effectively employed, underscoring the importance of a commitment to inclusivity even amidst these constraints (Juma & Ntulo, 2024). Moreover, Kenya Institute of Special Education has prioritized infrastructure development to enhance the use of assistive technologies (AT) by ensuring that physical environments are conducive to their implementation. This initiative includes a strong emphasis on staff training and competency building through workshops and hands-on sessions designed to equip educators with the necessary skills for effective technology integration. As a result of these efforts, there has been improved access to information for students with disabilities, demonstrating that targeted training and infrastructure enhancements can significantly facilitate the adoption of assistive technologies in educational settings (KISE, 2024).

The literature consistently emphasizes that successful implementation of assistive technologies is contingent upon addressing both logistical and attitudinal barriers within educational institutions. For instance, studies have shown that teachers often lack familiarity with available assistive devices, which can lead to underutilization or ineffective application in classrooms (Chukwuemeka & Samaila, 2020; Loveys & Butler, 2023). Therefore, fostering an environment where educators are encouraged to explore and experiment with AT is crucial for maximizing its benefits. Additionally, integrating technology into teacher training programs can create a more supportive framework for educators, enabling them to feel more confident in using these tools. Succinctly, the literature suggests that while assistive technologies hold great promise for enhancing educational outcomes for students with disabilities, significant challenges remain. These include the need for comprehensive training programs for educators, adequate resource allocation, and ongoing support mechanisms to facilitate effective technology integration in classrooms. Addressing these issues is vital for ensuring that all students can benefit from the advancements made possible through assistive technology.

Future Directions in Assistive Technology and Accessibility Tools

The future of assistive technology (AT) and accessibility tools is shaped by rapid advancements in emerging technologies and a growing commitment to inclusive policies that support students with disabilities. These developments hold the potential to make adaptive education more effective, personalized, and accessible. New innovations, such as artificial intelligence (AI), virtual and augmented reality (VR/AR), and wearable devices, are transforming the landscape of AT, while policy changes are driving systemic support for accessible education and equitable opportunities (UNICEF, 2022). Together, these advancements indicate a future where AT and accessibility tools are seamlessly integrated into the educational experience, enabling all students to achieve academic success and independence. One of the most promising directions in assistive technology is the integration of artificial intelligence (AI) to create more responsive, adaptive learning tools. AI-powered AT can analyze individual learning behaviors and automatically adjust content or presentation methods to suit each student's needs (Gligorea, Cioca, Oancea, Gorski, Gorski & Tudorache, 2022). For instance, AI can enhance text-to-speech software, making it more accurate and responsive to different reading speeds, tones, and accents. AI-driven predictive text tools can also help students with motor disabilities or language impairments by suggesting words and phrases, reducing typing effort and enhancing communication. Additionally, AI can help develop customized learning pathways that adjust to a student's progress, providing real-time feedback and recommendations. As AI continues to evolve, its potential to provide nuanced, personalized support will enable AT to be even more effective in fostering academic growth and independence.

In adaptive education, virtual reality (VR) and augmented reality (AR) are also becoming transformative tools. While AR overlays digital information onto the physical world, offering additional context or visual aids that can help students with visual or cognitive impairments process information more easily, VR and AR are both useful tools for hands-on learning, making abstract concepts more tangible and accessible. Students with learning disabilities, for instance, can practice real-world skills in a safe, simulated environment, which can reduce anxiety and increase engagement. As VR and AR technologies become more affordable and widespread, they will likely play an increasingly central role in AT, offering new ways for students to interact with educational content and building a more inclusive classroom environment (Zhao, Ren & Cheah, 2023).

Wearable devices represent another trend that could significantly impact adaptive education. Devices such as smart glasses, wristbands, and haptic feedback devices are being used to provide sensory feedback and assist students with sensory processing challenges or mobility issues (Moon, Baker & Goughnour, 2019). For instance, wearable devices equipped with haptic technology can give physical prompts to guide students through tasks, aiding in motor skills development and attention management. For students with hearing impairments, smart glasses that display subtitles or sign language interpretation in real-time are a valuable tool that makes verbal communication more accessible. The integration of wearable technology into AT highlights the growing focus on creating unobtrusive, everyday tools that blend seamlessly into students' lives. As wearable devices continue to evolve, they are likely to provide even more personalized support, adapting to individual preferences and environmental needs.

Another important direction in assistive technology is the development of universal design principles, which seek to create accessible learning tools that benefit all students, regardless of their abilities. Universal design aims to make learning more inclusive by embedding accessibility features in standard educational technology, thus reducing the need for specialized, separate AT. For instance, many educational platforms are now incorporating features like closed captioning, adjustable text size, and voice commands, which were initially intended for students with disabilities but have since proven useful for all users. This inclusive approach to design not only improves access for students with disabilities but also normalizes AT as a standard part of the educational experience. Moving forward, universal design will likely become a foundational principle in AT development, promoting inclusivity and reducing the stigma often associated with specialized AT (Sharma, Thakur, Kapoor & Singh, 2023).

Policy changes are equally critical in supporting the evolution of assistive technology and ensuring its accessibility in educational settings. Legislation that mandates funding and resources for AT can create a more supportive framework for its implementation. For example, policies like the Individuals with Disabilities Education Act (IDEA) and the Americans with Disabilities Act (ADA) in the United States have already established legal requirements for accommodations and support in education. However, as AT becomes more advanced and integral to learning, these policies may need updates to reflect the current technology landscape. Ensuring that policies are adaptable and encompass emerging technologies will be essential to maintain equity and access. For instance, regulations could be expanded to include funding for cutting-edge tools like AI-powered devices and VR, recognizing these as vital components of adaptive education. Advocacy for policy change is essential to push for broader recognition of AT in national and state-level educational frameworks. Educators, families, and disability advocates play a crucial role in raising awareness about the importance of AT and urging policymakers to increase funding and prioritize accessibility in education. Promoting policy initiatives that mandate inclusive technology training for educators, advocate for dedicated AT funding, and push for universal design standards, stakeholders can create a more inclusive educational environment. Furthermore, policy changes that support interoperability standards for AT devices can also encourage greater collaboration among technology developers, educators, and institutions, leading to more cohesive and effective AT ecosystems (Karki, Rushton, Bhattarai & De Witte, 2021).

In the future, partnerships between educational institutions and technology companies will be key to advancing AT solutions. Collaborative efforts can lead to the development of specialized tools that are tailored to the needs of students and tested in real classroom environments. Many tech companies are already working closely with schools to pilot new assistive technology products, and expanding these partnerships could accelerate innovation while also ensuring that AT tools are both practical and effective. Such collaborations can help bridge the gap between research and practice, allowing AT developers to receive valuable feedback and educators to stay informed about the latest technological advancements (Viner, Singh & Shaughnessy, 2020). Schools and districts that prioritize these partnerships will likely be at the forefront of AT adoption, leading the way in creating inclusive learning environments. The future of assistive technology in education is rich with potential, driven by advancements in AI, VR/AR, wearable devices, and universal design. These emerging technologies promise to make AT more responsive, immersive, and accessible, transforming how students with disabilities engage with learning. Meanwhile, evolving policies that prioritize inclusivity and equitable funding will play a critical role in supporting the implementation of AT and ensuring that it remains available to all students who need it. Through the combined efforts of technological innovation, policy reform, and collaborative partnerships, the future of AT and accessibility tools in adaptive education looks bright, paving the way for a more inclusive and supportive educational experience for students with diverse needs.

Ethical Implications of Implementing Assistive Technology in Educational Contexts

The integration of assistive technology (AT) in educational contexts holds immense potential to foster inclusivity, empower learners with disabilities, and ensure equitable access to education. However, it also raises a range of ethical considerations that stakeholders, including educators, administrators, policymakers, and technologists must address to ensure that the implementation of AT aligns with principles of fairness, dignity, and respect. One of the foremost ethical concerns is equity and access. It is crucial that the implementation of AT guarantees equal access to educational resources for all students, regardless of their disabilities (Elfaizi & El Aouri, 2024). This necessitates addressing disparities in the availability and quality of assistive technologies across different schools and districts. Moreover, while personalized learning applications can enhance engagement, there are concerns about whether these systems inadvertently track and sort students in a discriminatory manner, raising questions about fairness in educational assessments and the potential for exacerbating existing inequalities.

Another significant ethical consideration is privacy and data security. The collection and use of student data by assistive technology systems must be conducted transparently. Students and their guardians should be informed about what data is collected, how it will be used, and who has access to it. Ethical practices dictate that data collection should only occur with explicit consent from students or their guardians (Creel & Dixit, 2022). Additionally, only necessary information should be collected to fulfill the intended purpose of the technology, adhering to the principle of data minimization. This approach helps protect students' privacy and ensures that sensitive information is not misused. The role of educators also raises important ethical questions regarding professional expertise versus technology. There is a concern that reliance on assistive technology may diminish the role of educators in assessing and supporting students' needs. While technology can provide valuable assistance, it cannot replace the nuanced understanding that educators have regarding their students' unique challenges (Kunka & Wahome, 2021). Therefore, it is essential to maintain a balance where assistive technologies complement rather than replace the expertise of teachers and special education professionals. This balance ensures that students receive holistic support tailored to their individual needs.

Ethical principles guiding the use of assistive technology include beneficence, nonmaleficence, justice, and autonomy. The use of assistive technology should aim to benefit students by enhancing their learning experiences and promoting independence while avoiding harm through improper implementation or oversight (Wangmo, Lipps, Kressig & Lenca, 2019). Furthermore, the distribution of AT resources must be equitable to ensure that all students have access to the tools they need for academic success. Additionally, students should have a voice in selecting the assistive technologies they use, fostering a sense of ownership over their learning process. Most importantly, long-term implications related to sustainability must be considered when implementing assistive technologies in educational settings. Schools need to evaluate the long-term sustainability of these resources, including funding for maintenance, upgrades, and training for educators on new tools. Effective implementation requires collaboration among educators, technologists, therapists, and families to create a comprehensive support system for students with disabilities. In conclusion, the ethical implications surrounding the use of assistive technology in educational settings are complex and multifaceted. Stakeholders must engage in ongoing discussions to address these issues thoughtfully, ensuring that the integration of AT aligns with principles of fairness, dignity, and respect for all learners. Educational institutions, by prioritizing ethical considerations in the development and implementation of assistive technologies can foster inclusive environments where every student has the opportunity to thrive.

CONCLUSION

Assistive technology (AT) and accessibility tools are fundamentally reshaping adaptive education, providing new pathways for inclusion, independence, and academic success for students with disabilities. As emerging technologies such as artificial intelligence, virtual and augmented reality, and wearable devices continue to evolve, their potential to enhance learning experiences and cater to individual needs expands significantly. These innovations, when integrated with universal design principles, help bridge the divide between specialized assistance and mainstream educational resources, making accessibility a standard feature in educational settings. However, to fully realize the benefits of AT, stakeholders must confront the financial, logistical, and attitudinal barriers that often impede its widespread adoption. Actionable steps are essential for creating a supportive environment where AT can flourish and remain accessible to all who need it. First, policymakers should prioritize inclusive policies that mandate the integration of AT into educational frameworks. This includes advocating for dedicated funding streams that ensure schools have the necessary resources to acquire and maintain assistive technologies.

Additionally, investment in professional development for educators is crucial. Training programs should equip teachers with the knowledge and skills to effectively implement AT in their classrooms. This can be achieved through partnerships with technology developers who can provide insights into the best practices and innovative uses of their products. Collaboration among educators, policymakers, technology developers, and community organizations is vital to ensure that AT solutions are not only relevant but also effective and adaptable to changing needs. Stakeholders should establish forums for ongoing dialogue where experiences and strategies can be shared to foster a culture of continuous improvement in the use of assistive technologies. As we look to the future of adaptive education, it is clear that AT has the potential not only to assist students with disabilities but also to transform learning experiences for all students. This vision of an inclusive, technology-enhanced educational landscape requires a steadfast commitment to both innovation and equity. Empowering students of all abilities to succeed, build independence, and contribute meaningfully to their communities, assistive technology emerges as more than just a tool for adaptation; it becomes a powerful catalyst for inclusivity. Ultimately, through collective action and dedication from all stakeholders involved, we can create educational environments that celebrate and support diverse learning needs, paving the way for a brighter future for every learner.

REFERENCES

Ahmed, A. (2018). Perceptions of Using Assistive Technology for Students with Disabilities in the Classroom. *International Journal of Special Education*, 33(1), 129–139. https://files.eric.ed.gov/fulltext/EJ1184079.pdf

Alam, A., & Mohanty, A. (2023). Educational technology: Exploring the convergence of technology and pedagogy through mobility, interactivity, AI, and learning tools. *Cogent Engineering*, 10(2), 2283282. Advance online publication. DOI: 10.1080/23311916.2023.2283282

Almgren Bäck, G., Mossige, M., Bundgaard Svendsen, H., Rønneberg, V., Selenius, H., Berg Gøttsche, N., Dolmer, G., Fälth, L., Nilsson, S., & Svensson, I. (2024). Speech-to-text intervention to support text production among students with writing difficulties: A single-case study in nordic countries. *Disability and Rehabilitation. Assistive Technology*, 19(8), 3110–3129. DOI: 10.1080/17483107.2024.2351488 PMID: 38776244

Alsolami, A. S. (2022). Teachers of Special Education and Assistive Technology: Teachers' Perceptions of Knowledge, Competencies and Professional Development. *SAGE Open*, 12(1), 21582440221079900. Advance online publication. DOI: 10.1177/21582440221079900

Bhat, N., Gurung, S., Gupta, M., Dhungana, N., & Thapa, R. K. (2022). Enhancing collaborative learning through peer-assisted learning. *Journal of Physiological Society of Nepal*, 3(1), 4–9. DOI: 10.3126/jpsn.v3i1.57762

Boot, F. H., Owuor, J., Dinsmore, J., & MacLachlan, M. (2018). Access to assistive technology for people with intellectual disabilities: A systematic review to identify barriers and facilitators. *Journal of Intellectual Disability Research*, 62(10), 900–921. DOI: 10.1111/jir.12532 PMID: 29992653

Chow, W. S. E., de Bruin, K., & Sharma, U. (2023). A scoping review of perceived support needs of teachers for implementing inclusive education. *International Journal of Inclusive Education*, 28(13), 3321–3340. DOI: 10.1080/13603116.2023.2244956

Chukwuemeka, E. J., & Samaila, D. (2020). Teachers' Perception and Factors Limiting the use of High-Tech Assistive Technology in Special Education Schools in North-West Nigeria. *Contemporary Educational Technology*, 11(1), 99–109. https://files.eric.ed.gov/fulltext/EJ1234819.pdf. DOI: 10.30935/cet.646841

Copley, J., & Ziviani, J. (2004). Barriers to the use of assistive technology for children with multiple disabilities. *Occupational Therapy International*, 11(4), 229–243. DOI: 10.1002/oti.213 PMID: 15771212

Creel, K., & Dixit, T. (2022). Privacy and Paternalism: The Ethics of Student Data Collection. *MIT Case Studies in Social and Ethical Responsibilities of Computing*, Summer 2022. https://doi.org/DOI: 10.1002/oti.213 PMID: 15771212

D'Andrea, F. M., & Siu, Y.-T. (2015), "Students with Visual Impairments: Considerations and Effective Practices for Technology Use", Efficacy of Assistive Technology Interventions (Advances in Special Education Technology, Vol. 1), Emerald Group Publishing Limited, Leeds, pp. 111-138. https://doi.org/DOI: 10.1108/S2056-769320150000001005

Elfaizi, Y., & El Aouri, Z.Zahra EL AOURI. (2024). Inclusion between Equality and Equity: A Balance Model to an Equitable Quality Education for All. *International Journal of English Language Studies*, 6(3), 42–52. DOI: 10.32996/ijels.2024.6.3.7

Ellikkal, A., & Rajamohan, S. (2024). AI-enabled personalized learning: empowering management students for improving engagement and academic performance. *Vilakshan - XIMB Journal of Management*, Vol. ahead-of-print No. ahead-of-print. https://doi.org/DOI: 10.32996/ijels.2024.6.3.7

Erdem, R. (2017). Students with Special Educational Needs and Assistive Technologies: A Literature Review. *The Turkish Online Journal of Educational Technology*, 16(1), 128–146. https://files.eric.ed.gov/fulltext/EJ1124910.pdf

Eziamaka, N. V., Odonker, T. N., & Akinsulire, A. A.Nnaemeka Valentine EziamakaTheodore Narku OdonkorAdetola Adewale Akinsulire. (2024). AI-Driven accessibility: Transformative software solutions for empowering individuals with disabilities. *International Journal of Applied Research in Social Sciences*, 6(8), 1612–1641. DOI: 10.51594/ijarss.v6i8.1373

Fernández-Batanero, J. M., Montenegro-Rueda, M., Fernández-Cerero, J., & Garcia-Martinez, I. (2022). Assistive technology for the inclusion of students with disabilities: A systematic review. *Educational Technology Research and Development*, 70(5), 1911–1930. DOI: 10.1007/s11423-022-10127-7

Fteiha, M., Al-Rashaida, M., Elsori, D., Khalil, A., & Al Bustami, G. (2024). Obstacles for using assistive technology in centres of special needs in the UAE. *Disability and Rehabilitation. Assistive Technology*, 19(8), 1–11. DOI: 10.1080/17483107.2024.2323698 PMID: 38436086

Gligorea, I., Cioca, M., Oancea, R., Gorski, A. T., Gorski, H., & Tudorache, P. (2023). Adaptive Learning Using Artificial Intelligence in e-Learning: A Literature Review. *Education Sciences*, 13(12), 1216. DOI: 10.3390/educsci13121216

Halpin, M. (2024). *Assistive Technology in Education: Tools for Disabled Students in the Classroom*. UK: Recite Me. https://reciteme.com/news/assistive-technology-in-education/

Hayes, A. M., & Bulat, J. (2017). *Disabilities Inclusive Education Systems and Policies Guide for Low- and Middle-Income Countries*. RTI Press Publication No. OP-0043-1707. Research Triangle Park, NC: RTI Press. https://doi.org/DOI: 10.3768/rtipress.2017.op.0043.1707

HCPSS. (2024). *Special Education Programs*. https://www.hcpss.org/special-education/programs/

Hecker, L., Burns, L., Katz, L., Elkind, J., & Elkind, K. (2002). Benefits of assistive reading software for students with attention disorders. *Annals of Dyslexia*, 52(1), 243–272. DOI: 10.1007/s11881-002-0015-8

Hsieh, Y. (2022). *Eye-gaze assistive technology for play, communication and learning: Impacts on children and youths with severe motor and communication difficulties and their partners*. Academic dissertation for the Degree of Doctor of Philosophy in Special Education at Stockholm University. https://su.diva-portal.org/smash/get/diva2:1688403/FULLTEXT03.pdf

Juma, R. K., & Ntulo, G. R. (2024). The Availability and Use of Assistive Technologies among Pupils with Hearing and Visual Impairments in Zanzibar. *International Journal of Education and Development Using Information and Communication Technology*, 20(1), 63–77. https://files.eric.ed.gov/fulltext/EJ1426581.pdf

Kambouri, M., Simon, H., & Brooks, G. (2023). Using speech-to-text technology to empower young writers with special educational needs. *Research in Developmental Disabilities*, 135, 104466. DOI: 10.1016/j.ridd.2023.104466 PMID: 36863156

Karki, J., Rushton, S., Bhattarai, S., & De Witte, L. (2021). Access to assistive technology for persons with disabilities: A critical review from Nepal, India and Bangladesh. *Disability and Rehabilitation. Assistive Technology*, 18(1), 8–16. DOI: 10.1080/17483107.2021.1892843 PMID: 33651968

Keelor, J. L., Creaghead, N., Silbert, N., & Horowitz-Kraus, T. (2020). Text-to-Speech Technology: Enhancing Reading Comprehension for Students with Reading Difficulty. *Assistive Technology Outcomes and Benefits*, 14, 19–35. https://www.atia.org/wp-content/uploads/2020/06/ATOB-V14-A2-Keelor_etal.pdf

Kirboyun, S. (2020). High-Tech or Low-Tech? Impact of Assistive Technology in School Settings for Students with Visual Impairments: Review of Research. [IJI]. *International Journal for Infonomics*, 13(1), 1945–1953. https://infonomics-society.org/wp-content/uploads/High-Tech-or-Low-Tech.pdf. DOI: 10.20533/iji.1742.4712.2020.0201

KISE. (2024). Making quality and equitable education and services accessible to persons with Special Needs and Disabilities. https://kise.ecitizen.go.ke/

Kunka, A., & Wahome, N. (2021). The Role of Assistive Technology in the Education of Children with Special Needs: Teacher's Perspectives. Unpublished Master Thesis submitted to Linkoping University. https://www.diva-portal.org/smash/get/diva2:1639908/FULLTEXT01.pdf

Lahm, E. A. (2003). Assistive Technology Specialists: Bringing Knowledge of Assistive Technology to School Districts. *Remedial and Special Education*, 24(3), 141–153. DOI: 10.1177/07419325030240030301

Le, H., Janssen, J., & Wubbels, T. (2017). Collaborative learning practices: Teacher and student perceived obstacles to effective student collaboration. *Cambridge Journal of Education*, 48(1), 103–122. DOI: 10.1080/0305764X.2016.1259389

Li, G., Zarei, M. A., Alibakhshi, G., & Labbafi, A. (2024). Teachers and educators' experiences and perceptions of artificial-powered interventions for autism groups. *BMC Psychology*, 12(1), 199. DOI: 10.1186/s40359-024-01664-2 PMID: 38605422

Lim, L. A., Dawson, S., Gašević, D., Joksimović, S., Fudge, A., Pardo, A., & Gentili, S. (2020). Students' sense-making of personalised feedback based on learning analytics. *Australasian Journal of Educational Technology*, 36(6), 15–33. DOI: 10.14742/ajet.6370

Loveys, M., & Butler, C. (2023). Teachers' and students' perspectives on the extent to which assistive technology maximises independence. *British Journal of Visual Impairment*, 0(0), 02646196231212736. Advance online publication. DOI: 10.1177/02646196231212736

Lynch, P., Singal, N., & Francis, G. A. (2022). Educational technology for learners with disabilities in primary school settings in low- and middle-income countries: A systematic literature review. *Educational Review*, 76(2), 405–431. DOI: 10.1080/00131911.2022.2035685

McNicholl, A. (2022). *Assistive technology outcomes and impacts among students with disabilities in higher education*. Unpublished PhD Thesis submitted to School of Psychology Dublin City University. https://doras.dcu.ie/27681/1/17212312_Assistive%20technology%20outcomes%20and%20impacts%20among%20students%20with%20disabilities%20in%20higher%20education.pdf

McNicholl, A., Casey, H., Desmond, D., & Gallagher, P. (2021). The impact of assistive technology use for students with disabilities in higher education: A systematic review. *Disability and Rehabilitation. Assistive Technology*, 16(2), 130–143. DOI: 10.1080/17483107.2019.1642395 PMID: 31335220

Mhlongo, S., Mbatha, K., Ramatsetse, B., & Dlamini, R. (2023). Challenges, opportunities, and prospects of adopting and using smart digital technologies in learning environments: An iterative review. *Heliyon*, 9(6), e16348. DOI: 10.1016/j.heliyon.2023.e16348 PMID: 37274691

Molina Roldán, S., Marauri, J., Aubert, A., & Flecha, R. (2021). How Inclusive Interactive Learning Environments Benefit Students Without Special Needs. *Frontiers in Psychology*, 12, 661427. DOI: 10.3389/fpsyg.2021.661427 PMID: 33995221

Moon, N. W., Baker, P. M., & Goughnour, K. (2019). Designing wearable technologies for users with disabilities: Accessibility, usability, and connectivity factors. *Journal of Rehabilitation and Assistive Technologies Engineering*, 6, 2055668319862137. Advance online publication. DOI: 10.1177/2055668319862137 PMID: 35186318

Muhsin, Z. J., Qahwaji, R., Ghanchi, F., & Al-Taee, M. (2024). Review of substitutive assistive tools and technologies for people with visual impairments: Recent advancements and prospects. *Journal on Multimodal User Interfaces*, 18(1), 135–156. DOI: 10.1007/s12193-023-00427-4

National Academies of Sciences, Engineering, and Medicine (1997). *Educating One and All: Students with Disabilities and Standards-Based Reform*. Washington, DC: The National Academies Press. https://doi.org/. DOI: 10.1007/s12193-023-00427-4

Nkomo, L. M., & Daniel, B. K. (2021). Providing students with flexible and adaptive learning opportunities using lecture recordings. *Journal of Open, Flexible and Distance Learning*, 25(1), 22–31. https://files.eric.ed.gov/fulltext/EJ1314246.pdf

Ogundaini, O., & Mlitwa, N. (2024). *Artificial Intelligence for assistive learning to support physically impaired learners in Sub-Saharan Africa. 16th International Conference on Education and New Learning Technologies*. 1-3 July, 2024, Palma, Spain, pp. 156-163. https://doi.org/DOI: 10.21125/edulearn.2024.0070

Okoye, C. C. (2024). Assistive Technology and Inclusion of Children with Disabilities in Nigeria. *African Journal of Social Sciences and Humanities Research*, 7(3), 218–228. DOI: 10.52589/AJSSHR-JPKFGOEW

Oldfrey, B., Holloway, C., Walker, J., McCormack, S., Deere, B., Kenney, L., Ssekitoleko, R., Ackers, H., & Miodownik, M. (2023). Repair strategies for assistive technology in low resource settings. *Disability and Rehabilitation. Assistive Technology*, 19(5), 1945–1955. DOI: 10.1080/17483107.2023.2236142 PMID: 37466362

Ontario Human Rights Commission. (2018). *Policy on accessible education for students with disabilities*. https://www3.ohrc.on.ca/en/policy-accessible-education-students-disabilities

Osorio-Saez, E. M., Eryilmaz, N., & Sandoval-Hernandez, A. (2021). Parents' Acceptance of Educational Technology: Lessons From Around the World. *Frontiers in Psychology*, 12, 719430. DOI: 10.3389/fpsyg.2021.719430 PMID: 34526938

Ozor, S., Dodo, M., & Bana, D. (2024). Digital literacy skills and assistive technology use as enabler for academic performance of visually impaired students at the Nigerian law school. *Information Impact: Journal of Information and Knowledge Management*, 15(1), 143–152. DOI: 10.4314/iijikm.v15i1.11

Parette, P., & Scherer, M. (2004). Assistive Technology Use and Stigma. *Education and Training in Developmental Disabilities*, 39(3), 217–226. https://www.jstor.org/stable/23880164

Priyadharsini, V., & Mary, R. S. (2024). Universal Design for Learning (UDL) in Inclusive Education: Accelerating Learning for All. *Shanlax International Journal of Arts. Science and Humanities*, 11(4), 145–150. DOI: 10.34293/sijash.v11i4.7489

Raffoul, S., & Jaber, L. (2023). Text-to-Speech Software and Reading Comprehension: The Impact for Students with Learning Disabilities. *Canadian Journal of Learning and Technology*, 49(2), 1–18. DOI: 10.21432/cjlt28296

Satapathy, P. (2019). Applications of Assistive Tools and Technologies in Enhancing the Learning Abilities of Dyslexic Children. *TechnoLEARN: An International Journal of Educational Technology,* 9(2), 117-123. https://ndpublisher.in/admin/issues/TLV9I2i.pdf

Schaaf, D. N. (2018). Assistive Technology Instruction in Teacher Professional Development. *Journal of Special Education Technology*, 33(3), 171–181. DOI: 10.1177/0162643417753561

Seo, K., Tang, J., Roll, I., Fels, S., & Yoon, D. (2021). The impact of artificial intelligence on learner–instructor interaction in online learning. *International Journal of Educational Technology in Higher Education*, 18(1), 54. DOI: 10.1186/s41239-021-00292-9 PMID: 34778540

Shanker, A. (2022). *Assistive Technology in Inclusive and Special Schools of Bihar: A Study of Availability, Readiness of Teachers and Learning Experiences of Students*. Unpublished PhD Thesis submitted to Department of Teacher Education, School of Education Central University of South Bihar, Gaya. http://dx.doi.org/DOI: 10.13140/RG.2.2.13864.03849

Sharma, A., Thakur, K., Kapoor, D. S., & Singh, K. J. (2023). Designing Inclusive Learning Environments: Universal Design for Learning in Practice. In Calhoun, C. (Ed.), *The Impact and Importance of Instructional Design in the Educational Landscape* (pp. 24–61). IGI Global., DOI: 10.4018/978-1-6684-8208-7.ch002

Simeoni, R., Pirrera, A., Meli, P., & Giansanti, D. (2023). Promoting Universal Equitable Accessibility: An Overview on the Impact of Assistive Technology in the UN, UNICEF, and WHO Web Portals. *Health Care*, 11(21), 2904. DOI: 10.3390/healthcare11212904 PMID: 37958048

Svensson, I., Nordström, T., Lindeblad, E., Gustafson, S., Björn, M., Sand, C., Almgrem-Back, G., & Nilsson, S. (2019). Effects of assistive technology for students with reading and writing disabilities. *Disability and Rehabilitation. Assistive Technology*, 16(2), 196–208. DOI: 10.1080/17483107.2019.1646821 PMID: 31418305

Tay-Teo, K., Bell, D., & Jowett, M. (2021). Financing options for the provision of assistive products. *Assistive Technology*, 33(sup1), 109–123. https://doi.org/DOI: 10.1080/17483107.2019.1646821 PMID: 31418305

Therasa, M. M. (2023). Adapting Assistive Technology to Diverse Learning Needs in Inclusive Education. *International Journal of Arts, Science and Humanities*, 11(1), 63-66. https://www.researchgate.net/publication/379938594_Adapting_Assistive_Technology_to_Diverse_Learning_Needs_in_Inclusive_Education

UNICEF. (2022). The use of Assistive Technology in Education: A Guide for Teachers and Schools. https://www.unicef.org/eca/media/30671/file/Teacher's%20guide%20for%20building%20capacity%20for%20assistive%20technology.pdf

Vincent, D. A., Okeowo, R. O., & Ariyo, S. (2024). The use of assistive technology in technical colleges for students with disabilities in Ondo State. *Journal of Educational Research and Practice*, 14, 52–67. DOI: 10.5590/JERAP.2024.14.1.04

Viner, M., Singh, A., & Shaughnessy, M. F. (2020). Assistive Technology to Help Students With Disabilities. In Singh, A., Viner, M., & Yeh, C. (Eds.), *Special Education Design and Development Tools for School Rehabilitation Professionals* (pp. 240–267). IGI Global., DOI: 10.4018/978-1-7998-1431-3.ch012

Wangmo, T., Lipps, M., Kressig, R. W., & Lenca, M. (2019). Ethical concerns with the use of intelligent assistive technology: Findings from a qualitative study with professional stakeholders. *BMC Medical Ethics*, 20(1), 98. DOI: 10.1186/s12910-019-0437-z PMID: 31856798

Weck, M., & Afanassieva, M. (2023). Toward the adoption of digital assistive technology: Factors affecting older people's initial trust formation. *Telecommunications Policy*, 47(2), 102483. DOI: 10.1016/j.telpol.2022.102483

Willings, C. (2022, June 18). *History of Visual Impairments.* https://www.teachingvisuallyimpaired.com/timeline-of-vi.html

Wood, S. G., Moxley, J. H., Tighe, E. L., & Wagner, R. K. (2018). Does Use of Text-to-Speech and Related Read-Aloud Tools Improve Reading Comprehension for Students with Reading Disabilities? A Meta-Analysis. *Journal of Learning Disabilities*, 51(1), 73–84. DOI: 10.1177/0022219416688170 PMID: 28112580

Yell, M. L., Rogers, D., & Rogers, E. L. (1998). The Legal History of Special Education: What a Long, Strange Trip It's Been! *Remedial and Special Education*, 19(4), 219–228. DOI: 10.1177/074193259801900405

Young, G., & MacCormack, M. (2014, June 10). *Assistive Technology for Students with Learning Disabilities.* Toronto: Learning Disabilities Association of Ontario. https://www.ldatschool.ca/assistive-technology/

Zdravkova, K., Krasniqi, V., Dalipi, F., & Ferati, M. (2022). Cutting-edge communication and learning assistive technologies for disabled children: An artificial intelligence perspective. *Frontiers in Artificial Intelligence*, 28(5), 970430. DOI: 10.3389/frai.2022.970430 PMID: 36388402

Zhao, X., Ren, Y., & Cheah, K. S. L. (2023). Leading Virtual Reality (VR) and Augmented Reality (AR) in Education: Bibliometric and Content Analysis From the Web of Science (2018–2022). *SAGE Open*, 13(3), 21582440231190821. Advance online publication. DOI: 10.1177/21582440231190821

Zwarych, F. (2023). *Inclusive Education with Assistive Technology.* Pressbooks. https://pressbooks.pub/techcurr2023/chapter/inclusive-educadtion-with-assistive-technology/

KEY TERMS AND DEFINITIONS

Assistive Technology (AT): A broad category of devices, tools, and services designed to enhance the functional capabilities of individuals with disabilities, particularly in educational settings. AT enables users to perform tasks that may be challenging or impossible without assistance.

Accessibility Tools: Resources and technologies that facilitate access to information and learning environments for individuals with disabilities. Examples include screen readers, closed captioning, ramps, and adjustable seating.

Universal Design: An approach to designing products and environments that are usable by all people, regardless of their age, ability, or status. In education, universal design principles aim to create inclusive learning experiences that accommodate diverse learners.

Low-Tech Assistive Technology: Simple, non-electronic tools that require minimal training to use. These devices are typically inexpensive and effective in helping students with specific challenges. Examples include graphic organizers and communication boards.

Mid-Tech Assistive Technology: Devices that incorporate basic electronics or battery-operated systems, requiring moderate training for effective use. Examples include audio recorders and talking calculators.

High-Tech Assistive Technology: Sophisticated electronic or computerized systems that often utilize advanced software and artificial intelligence to provide personalized support for students with complex needs. Examples include screen readers and speech-to-text software.

Informed Consent: The process by which individuals are fully informed about the data being collected about them, how it will be used, and who will have access to it. In educational contexts, obtaining informed consent is crucial when implementing AT that collects personal data.

Data Minimization: The principle of collecting only the data necessary to fulfill a specific purpose. This practice helps protect individuals' privacy and reduces the risk of misuse of sensitive information.

Beneficence: An ethical principle that emphasizes the obligation to act for the benefit of others. In the context of AT, it refers to the responsibility to enhance students' learning experiences and promote their independence.

Nonmaleficence: An ethical principle focusing on the duty to avoid causing harm. When implementing AT, it is essential to consider potential negative consequences and ensure that technologies do not inadvertently disadvantage users.

Justice: An ethical principle that calls for fairness in the distribution of resources and opportunities. In education, this principle underscores the importance of equitable access to assistive technologies for all students.

Autonomy: The right of individuals to make their own choices regarding their education and support needs. In the context of AT, it emphasizes the importance of allowing students a voice in selecting the technologies they use.

Collaboration: The process by which different stakeholders, such as educators, policymakers, technology developers, and community organizations work together towards common goals. Effective collaboration is essential for creating inclusive educational environments that leverage assistive technologies.

Chapter 7
The Role of Assistive Technology in Education:
A Study of Four SADC States

William Chakabwata
https://orcid.org/0000-0002-4224-5239
University of South Africa, South Africa

ABSTRACT

This chapter examines the availability and accessibility of assistive devices and technologies in four Southern African Development Community (SADC) states—Namibia, South Africa, Zambia, and Zimbabwe. While assistive devices hold great potential for enhancing learning and supporting people with disabilities, their accessibility remains limited due to high costs and reliance on imported products. Moreover, the distribution of these devices is predominantly focused in urban areas, leaving individuals with disabilities in rural settings without the essential educational and support tools they need. Grounded in the principles of Ubuntu and intersectionality, this chapter highlights the urgent need for governments to prioritize the development of locally produced assistive technologies. It also advocates increased investment in assistive devices to promote equitable access and advance the realization of inclusive education across the region.

INTRODUCTION

Technology has enabled many people who suffer from a disability to access support using assistive equipment, adaptive and assistive technology. Assistive equipment refers to equipment or technology that helps a person with a disability to lead a life with less constrictions (Topper & Arizzi, 2024). Assistive equipment subsumes adaptive equipment. Adaptive equipment refers to equipment that has been transformed to meet the needs of a person with a disability. Adaptive equipment tends to be more sophisticated. Assistive equipment and adaptive equipment assist in enhancing a person's movement, use of senses and communication. An architype of adaptive technology is the use of a magnifying glass to enhance sight so that a person can utilize a keyboard in a more effective way. Examples of assistive equipment are crutches, wheelchairs and hearing aids. There are numerous and multiple forms of devices that people with a disability can access, to receive support in their learning. A disability can impact a student's life in any intersectional way that makes them experience interlocking disadvantages, due to multiple intersecting identities based on polyvalent factors such as social class, race, ethnicity, age, gender, sexuality among many other factors. The chapters postulate the use of Ubuntu as an appropriate lens to inform the provision of assistive equipment and technology to people with a disability. In this chapter an appraisal of the state of assistive equipment in Namibia, South Africa, Zambia and Zimbabwe is done. The chapter noted that governments and community-based organizations and other agencies of United Nations such as United Nations Children's Fund (UNICEF) and United Nations and Scientific and Cultural Organization (UNESCO) are actively involved in availing assistive equipment to people with a disability A case study extracted from each of the four state is presented and best practices are highlighted, for other states to adapt and implement. The chapter also noted very limited research on the current state of assistive equipment and technology in each of these states. The chapter therefore calls for more research on the use of assistive equipment and technology, within each of these states in general and at SADC level in particular. The chapter also noted a very limited production of assistive equipment in each of these countries. Although assistive equipment and technologies can help to enhance learning for students with a disability, they still remain largely out of reach for the majority of the citizens of the four countries, who desperately need them. The chapter therefore recommended that the government engage in local reproduction of assistive equipment in order to meet the huge needs in their countries.

Background

World Health Organisation (WHO, 2024) stated that disability is a part of being human. It is estimated that 1.3 billion people in the world have a major disability, and this constitutes 16% of the global population. The number of people with a major disability is anticipated to escalate, due to the rise in aging population and also outbreaks of non-communicable ailments. WHO explicated causes of disability as a nexus between a person who is health and with the environment. United Nations Children's Fund (UNICEF, 2023) adduced that about 29 million children with disabilities live in Eastern and Southern Africa. In spite of the declared international declarations that such children must be cared for and access assistance, most of them confront stigma, dearth of much needed services and physical barriers to access services. The same report by UNICEF alleged that there is a lack of reliable data on children with a disability from countries such as Malawi, Madagascar and Zimbabwe.

Sustainable Development Goal (SDG) 4, foregrounded the significance of providing inclusive and equitable quality education for all. This is a part of the United Nations Agenda 2030, and it expanded the need to address issues confronting people from accessing education in schools, which include gender and disability. The Convention on the Rights of the Child (CRC) fronted the rights of children to special care and protection (United Nations UN,1989). The General Assembly (2006) declared that human rights are interrelated and indivisible and that the rights of people with a disability have to be upheld. The same declaration highlighted the importance of mainstreaming disability in sustainable development discourse. The declaration also underscored the importance of apprehending the diversity of disabilities and protecting the rights of people with a disability.

National Library of Medicine (NIM,2024) expounded that the term disability is a contested concept, that is fluid and multifaceted. In contemporary times there has been a transition from perceiving a disability from medical discourse to acknowledging the place of social and physical barriers in disability. This change from a medical discourse to a social discourse highlight how people are disabled with their society rather than by their bodies. (NIM,2024).

Chibaya et al. (2022) asserted that the United Nations General Assembly adopted the United Convention on the Rights of the People with a Disability (UNCRPD) ON 13 December 2006. The UNCRPD provides an appropriate framework for people to guarantee the rights of people with a disability. The convention has a monitoring process that is intended to facilitate implementation and monitoring of UNCRPD. The states are urged to ensure that there is adequate implementation and monitoring of UNCRPD which involves civil society. Article 20 of the Convention on the Rights of People with a Disability (CRPD), foreground the need to ensure that there is access to affordable assistive equipment and also ascertaining that professionals are trained to use assistive equipment to provide support.

There are a variety of types of disabilities. They are categorised in about fifteen forms which includes hearing impairment, physical disability, vision impairment, intellectual disability, mental illness, autism, attention deficit hyperactivity disorder (ADHD), cerebral palsy, learning disabilities, acquired brain injury, language disorder, epilepsy, blindness, mobility, multiple sclerosis, muscular dystrophy, neurological disorder, spinal cord injury, arthritis, cognition, dyspraxia, and impairment (Australian National University, 2024).

Different forms of disability require different forms of intervention such as assistive equipment for people with poor vision may use screen magnification software, different forms of keyboards or voice recognition software and devices for walking may include wheelchairs, walkers and canes. People who have hearing challenges may use personal amplification systems, amplified telephones and face to face dual keyboard communicating system (Minnesota Guide to Assistive Technology, 2024). The models grant academics a mental framework to conceptualize disability. Models can also be perceived as theoretical construct that helps us to comprehend reality. Zaks (2023) indicated that the models of disability have an effect on the way we perceive disability and life chances that the people with a disability can have.

THE BIOMEDICAL MODEL

The term medical model of disability was first used in the 1950s by a psychiatrist Dr Szasz, who explicated people with a disability were perceived as deviant and aberrant. Disability Nottinghamshire (2024) averred that people are disabled by society and not by disability. Zaks (2023) declared that the medical model of disability gained traction in the western world and the United States since 1800. The basic presupposition of the medical model is that the bodies of a person with a disability or their brain are not normal and that the person with a disability is held accountable for their state. This framework has focused on providing interventions that were intended to rectify the perceived abnormality.

The medical model conceptualizes disability as an aberration that requires medical intervention to address it. Sofokleous and Stylianou (2023) indicated that the biomedical model did not distinguish between disability and impairment. Disability was conceptualised as a personal challenge that required medical intervention to rectify it. This model also created a nexus with philanthropic activities as people with a disability were perceived as object of pity who needed help. The thinking that was reflected was that the people with a disability required support and help and the most impactful way to avail that help was through philanthropism.

Activists in the field of disability have pushed back at the use of the medical model of disability and rejected the prescribed treatments and surgeries and are embracing their physical differences. The medical model of disability had to a large extent impacted interventions regarding access to schools among people living with a disability in the four SADC states. The medical model created a perception that people with a disability required special schools, lacked the capacity to act in a responsible way and had constrictions in acquiring skills. Special Schools sustained the worldview that a person with a disability was incapable of functioning in a mainstream school and required special intervention. In each of the four SADC states there are special schools that were instituted and functions on the basis of the presuppositions of the medical model such as Tswellang Special School in Bloemfontein, school in South Africa and Zimcare Trust in Zimbabwe among many others. The social disability model evolved as a reaction to the medical model of disability and the way it conceptualised interventions for people with a disability.

THE SOCIAL MODEL OF DISABILITY

The social model of disability was premised on the presupposition that there is a distinction between a disability and an impairment. The model acknowledges that an impairment can refer to a person's physical, intellectual or mental health condition, while a disability is a social construction that imposes a barrier on the functioning in society of person with an impairment. The trajectory of the social disability model is to eliminate the social obstacles and infrastructure challenges affecting the functioning of people with any impairment.

Sofokleous and Stylianou (2023) declared that the philanthropic model was premised on different assumptions from the biomedical model which indicated that reality for people with a disability is socially created. The social model of disability argues that people with a disability are not limited by their impairment but by the society that places obstacles in their path to progress.

Thorneycroft (2024) expounds that the social disability model perceives disability as distinct from impairment. The social disability model avers that disability is not a pathological condition for people with impairment. The same framework argues that impairment is a physical condition, and it must not lead to disability. Disability Nottinghamshire (2024) adduced that disability is attributed to the way society is structured. The focus of this model is the elimination of impediments that constrict life choices for people with a disability. It is argued that this elimination of obstacles can help to actualize a society where people with a disability are able to realise equality of opportunity or rights in society.

The social model forefront that people with a disability are able to function in society provided there are inclusive measures put in place. Lawson and Beckett (2021) asserted that disability is perceived to be a socially constructed injustice that needs to be challenged.

The following sections present an overview of the scenario in each of the four states regarding disability. A brief history of each of the four states is presented prior to presenting an appraisal of the use of assistive equipment and technology in each of the states. The social model has gained ascendancy in most disciplines since the 1980s.

Namibia

The population of Namibia constitute 3, 2 million people (Namibia Statistical Agency, 2023). Chibaya et al. (2022) adduced that Namibia has ratified the UN-CRPD in 2007. The majority of people who live with a disability in Namibia reside in rural areas. The constitution of Namibia acknowledges the rights of people with a disability. A number of more innovative legislation were adopted by the government of Namibia to ensure the rights of people with a disability which includes National Policy on Disability of 1997, National Policy on Orthopaedic Technical Services of 2001 and National Policy on Mental Health of 2005. Namibia has adopted inclusive education and has put a policy framework in place in line with the Salamanca Statement and Framework of Action for Special Needs Education (1994) and also the World Conference on Education for All (EFA) and Dakar Framework of Action (2000) (United Nations Educational, Scientific and Cultural Organization, 1994; World Education Forum,2000). Centre for Human Rights University of Pretoria (2024) averred that the total number of people with a disability in Namibia is 108 992, constituting 4,7% of the national population.

Ntinda (2024) indicated that the most prevalent forms of disability in Namibia are:

- Lower limb impairment constituting 28745 people
- Impairment of the upper limb making up 22 450 people
- Visual impairment constitutes 31 968
- Hearing impairment making up 17 454
- Mental disability making up 16 609

Chibaya et al. (2022) indicated that Namibia embraced the African Decade of People with a disabilities (1999-2009). Abiatal (2019) conducted a study on a rural primary school in Namibia in order to appraise on the use of assistive technology for the deaf in mathematics. The study focalised on students with a hearing disability. The study also noted a paucity of resources to implement programmes that offer deaf learners support using assistive technologies.

Zambia

Worldometer (2024) declared that the population of Zambia is 21,517,661. United Nations Development Coordination Office (2024) averred that in Zambia, the people with a disability make up 11% of the population. Many of the people with a disability have to deal with stereotypes and discrimination. Zambia has also embraced inclusivity as a commitment to realise the Sustainable Development Goals (SDGs). Zambia has a national blueprint for development titled no one is left behind and the country 8th development plan which adopted a developmental approach that in addition to economic development goals seeks to enhance inclusivity and to reduce poverty.

Disability Rights Watch (2022) expounded that the constitution of Zambia, upholds the rights of children with a disability and outlaws' discrimination. Discrimination in Zambia is forbidden under the legislation Education Act of 2011 and People with a Disability Act of 2011. Muzata et al., (2021) conducted a study to determine the status of inclusive education in Zambia. The study generated both quantitative and qualitative data and drew a conclusion that learners with partial or moderate challenges were included in mainstream schools, while those who were considered as showing severe disability were sent to special schools. The practices of sending students to special schools was informed by the medical model.

South Africa

The population of South Africa is at 63 million people and 3million are acknowledged to have a disability (Stats SA Department of Statistics in SA Republic of SA, 2024). Disability in South Africa is higher among females than males. Given the socioeconomic disparity in South Africa, disability tends to impact more the underprivileged groups. Several policy initiatives were adopted by the government in order to improve the policy regime for people with a disability which includes the Disability Rights Charter of South Africa, a White Paper on the Rights of People Living with a disability and the Employment Equity Act which makes discrimination an offence.

Trafford et al., (2021) averred that South Africa has been a signatory to the UN-CRPD since 2007. The constitution of South Africa canonise the rights of people with a disability. In addition, the country upholds inclusive education. The country allows citizens to request tax refund costs linked to disability. The approach to addressing the needs of people with a disability in South Africa are impeded by a fragmented approach among various government ministries and agencies. Multiple policy proclamations regarding people with special needs have not been implemented.

Boot et al., (2021) the study that was conducted in western Cape Province of South Africa in order to explore factors that influence access to and persist use of assistive devices. The qualitative study noted that the attitude of the user had an effect on the continued use of assistive equipment. Trafford et al., (2021) noted that South Africa has an impressive array of legislation to guide the implementation of inclusive education in the world among the low and middle -income countries. The government has reasserted the rights of people with special needs in 2016 White Paper in the Rights of People with Disabilities by the 2020 the Department of Development had not developed a policy framework to actualise these rights. South

Africa has nine provinces and each of them has a different budget, organisational capability and guidelines leading to a variation in accessing support. There is also a national constriction in identifying people with a disability either for providing support to them or social security benefits.

Children in South Africa who have a disability are entitled to a government social fund amounting to R1850 which translate to about US$125,25 which is given to a parent or guardian. To secure the grant a person has to undergo medical assessment by a doctor that is framed within the medical model of disability. In South Africa people can access mobility devices in the private sector, while the public sector provides help to those who cannot afford private service. The public sector suffers from a paucity of devices such as wheel chairs and there are long waiting list in the public sector. The provision of assistive equipment requires the support of skilled professionals who are able to provide support on their use, and securing such skills is major limitation in South Africa. There community based groups in South Africa that are committed to the improvement of the lives of people with a disability by providing assistive equipment and technology which includes Shonaquip Social Enterprise (SSE), which has worked together with the government on a number of projects to support and facilitate network building. SSE was founded in Cape Town by a parent who had a child with cerebral palsy. The parent recognised the paucity of assistive equipment or technology to help children who had challenges to sit upright in South Africa. This led them to create devices that were intended to match the needs of each user and support children to seat upright.

Zimbabwe

The current population of Zimbabwe is estimated to be at 17 million people (Macrotrends, 2024). It is acknowledged that about 9,5% are people with disabilities (ZimRights, 2024). It is noted that the government is currently in the process of revamping the old legal framework on disability in order to align it with the revised constitution. UNDP Zimbabwe (2024) indicated that a number of United Nations Agencies which includes United Nations Development Programme (UNDP), United Nations Scientific and Cultural Organisation (UNESCO) and a representative of United Nations Partnership on the Rights of People with a Disability (UNPRPD) are collaborating with the government in order to help them realise the Sustainable Development Goals (SDGs) of inclusion of all people in the development agenda and ending poverty.

Tigere (2023) admitted that in Zimbabwe major hindrance in accessing assistive equipment is poverty, most of the devices are imported and there is a lack of access to the devices in the local market. It is noted that the highest use of assistive equipment in Zimbabwe occurs in the urban areas. Mokwetsi (2022) indicated that

UNICEF working through Global Partnership for Education (GPE) donated Brailles Embossers, voice recorders, magnifying glasses, and white canes to Margaretha Hugo Primary School. In the education system the paucity of assistive equipment and technology tends to constrict the chances of learners with a disability from attending school in Zimbabwe (Dube et al., 2021).

The constitution of Zimbabwe spotlights the importance of ensuring that people with a disability are not discriminated and receive support. Section 24(4) of the constitution urges agencies to adopt measures that ascertain that there is easy access by all people with a disability to buildings and transportation services to which all other members of the public have access. At-Infor-Map (2019) expounded that in a survey about 7% of the population constituting 7% of the population and translating to 990,000 individuals had a disability. The spectrum of disability ranged from 31% on physical disability, 26% visual impairment, multiple disorders 13% deafness, 12% intellectual challenge, 8% and mental illness 6%.

ASSISTIVE EQUIPMENT

Minnesota Guide Assistive Technology (AT) (2024) declared that assistive technology has been a part of human life going back a thousand years, for instance, eyeglasses were invented in Italy between 1268-1289 and the first recorded 5th century China. The assistive equipment can be grouped into two categories of low and high technology. Assistive equipment can range from a basic guide to an elevator where a person must follow a blue line to the elevator to more subtle ones such as devices that can generate speech by using eye gaze. Assistive equipment can also be manufactured or prepared at home or acquired from the shops. Devices that can help with visual impairment may include screen reading software, braille display, massive print resources, mobile devices with massive tactile buttons among many others. Devices that are designed to help with hearing impairment include personal amplification system, wireless TV listening system, amplified telephones and mobile devices that have special features.

Children with special needs may require support in the form of movement, communication, learning and interpersonal engagements with peers. Assistive technologies have been identified as a solution to help meet some of the needs of children with special needs.

There are multiple forms of assistive equipment that can be used to help a person with a disability to attend school and learn with limited impediment. Some of the assistive equipment is explored in this section. Physiopedia (2024) explained the forms of assistive equipment constituting the devices or technology that are designed to sustain or enhance a person's functioning and improve their autonomy and well-being. In addition, the assistive equipment includes wheelchairs, hearing aids, visual aids, properly designed computer software and hardware, that helps to enhance movement, hearing seeing, and communication.

The international classification of Functioning and Disability is a framework that describes functioning and health in conjunction to a health environment (Physiopedia, 2024). It provides a blueprint and language for what a person with a given health condition can do in a given environment and what they are able to accomplish in their usual context which is termed performance.

Wyeth et al. (2023) indicated that assistive technologies can help to equip children with special needs to participate at the same level with other learners in school. The next section discusses forms of assistive equipment by placing them into three categories which includes assistive equipment that improve communication devices that support social engagements and those that support general skills development. binti Nor Rashid et al., (2024) asserted that there are levels to hearing impairment. (World Health Organization (WHO, 2024) averred that an estimated 430million people require help to rehabilitate hearing loss. Hearing loss is explicated as a person who is unable to hear at 20 Db thresholds in both ears is perceived as displaying hearing loss. Students with severe hearing difficulties require special education.

Dimitrov and Gossman (2023, p.3) indicated the categories of hearing as

Slight hearing loss: 16-25 dB
Mild hearing loss: 26-40dB
Moderate hearing loss 41-55dB
Severe hearing loss 71-90Db
Profound hearing loss 90 dB

Fletcher (2021) expounded that haptic devices were employed in the 1920s using a desktop device that stimulated fingers was employed to support learning of deaf learners. The device was used by deaf learners who were also using lip reading and was noted to increase the number of words that they were able to recognize.

Assistive Equipment That Improves Communication

Erdem (2017) explicated equipment that assist to enable communication for students with special needs in a variety of contexts and environments. The strategy that is employed to enhance student communication is termed Augmentative/Alternative Communication (AAC). These devices also incorporate aided and unaided symbols. Assistive equipment supports communication skills for students who face a challenge in using speech and they can utilise communication boards or high technology electronic system.

A number of technologies are available to help students with communication challenges which includes communication boards/books with pictures, eye boards frames, devices with speech synthesise and picture exchange communication capability can be utilised to help overcome speech disorders among students in school. Research has adduced that the use of Power-Point to teach students vocabularly presentation can help students who had hearing impairment at primary school level.

Assistive Equipment That Supports Social Engagement

Students with special learning needs may face challenges of comprehending or recalling texts. A number of strategies were proposed to enhance reading skills and comprehension capacity, which includes low-tech modification to text, text reader and use of symbols with picture and text (Erdem, 2017).

Assistive Equipment That Promotes Mobility

There are multiple devices that can be used to enhance mobility. Some of the equipment includes walkers and canes, wheelchairs, prosthetic devices, home modifications or modfication of buildings at institution level to facilitate easy movement and stair lifts. These devices are invaluable for aiding people with a mobility challenge to navigate around.

Assistive Equipment and Technology Used for Learning

There are numerous devices that can be used for people with learning differences. For instance, the use of audio books can help to enhance understanding for students with challenges of reading the traditional text. Smartphones, tablets and digital devices can support audio books. There are multiple technologies that can be used for learning for people with learning and thinking differences. These technologies include highlighters, organizers and timers. Some of the tools use high technology, for instance the use of text to speech technology that can be utilized by people with dyslexia. Akpan and Beard (2014) declared that assistive devices can play a vital role in supporting students who have challenges in mathematics. Some of the equipment includes calculators with talking multiplication tables, scientific calculators with large numbers display and portable calculator with arithmetic functions.

THE USE OF ASSISTIVE EQUIPMENT IN THE FOUR SADC COUNTRIES

In this part of the chapter four case studies from the four SADC countries namely Namibia, South Africa, Zambia, and Zimbabwe are discussed.

The Case Study of Eros Girl High in Namibia

This case study examined the use of assistive equipment at Eros High school in Namibia. Veiko (2019) conducted a study on the use of assistive technology at a girl's high school among students who suffer from dyslexia in Namibia. Dyslexia is a hereditary disease that impacts the neurological system. Snowling et al. (2020) expounded that dyslexia is a challenge that is associated with failure to decode or read and write. Dyslexia seems to be an overarching term that could apply to a number of reading and writing challenges and tends to show different manifestations. Kunwar (2022) indicated that dyslexia are not attributed to social and economic conditions such as poverty, hearing impairment, developmental impediments although the presence of some of these factors may exacerbate the challenge of reading, writing and spelling. The students who tend to manifest signs of dyslexia may abound with energy and display hard work in school, but may face a challenge of precision in reading and spelling words or letters.

Veikos (2019) study admitted to a lack of assistive technology in Namibia to help learners with dyslexia, and the study represents one such effort to utilise assistive technology to help students at Eros Girls high to tackle challenges they confronted in reading and mathematics termed Assistive Technology for Children with Learning Difficulties (ATCLD) for students in 5th and 7th Grade. The study incorporated 300 students and 30 teachers and the study noted a prevalence of traditional modes of teaching, which doesn't take into account contemporary research on assistive equipment such as the use of audio books, use of alphabets that are speech enabled or content management software. Bonifatius and Haihambo (2022) conducted a study in order to appraise the use of assistive technology at two schools which incorporate inclusive learning, in the Oshana region. The study noted that among the sixteen teachers, twelve teachers used ICT tools in their teaching as well as audio recorders in teaching. ICT tools are an effective form of assistive equipment in enabling students to acquire communication skills. The same study urged that teachers need to be trained in the use of assistive technology in teaching and that they have to attend in-service orientation programmes. Paucity of computers tended to impact negatively on the use of technology as an assistive technology in teaching and learning.

A Case Study of Twellang Special School in South Africa

Tswellang Special School (2017) was instituted to meet the needs of students with a disability. The school accommodation facility is for 92 borders, and it also serves the 288-day school students. The annual fee for the school is a paltry R1000 and the school is sustained by a government subsidy and fundraising.

Visser, et al., (2020) noted that resource constrictions in South Africa have made it difficult for all students who require assistive equipment to access them. This means that learning and participation for students who have a disability is severely compromised in South Africa. Visser, et al., (2020) conducted a study at a Tswellang Special School in Bloemfontein, school in South Africa. The study spotlighted students with motor impairment at a primary school, who struggle with functioning in a prescribed curriculum, if they are not supported with assistive technology. The students with motor impairments confront challenges such as restricted motor capability, which is an outcome of weak physical capacity. In this study occupational therapists had designed devices to help students who had motor challenges in school and was funded by a Khanya for life a non –profit organisation. This study led to the development and use of a number of devices to help the students function in school, which included pointing devices and keyboards that were modified were used in the study to enhance the capacity of students with motor challenges to function.

A Case Study on the Use of Assistive Technology in Zambia

A case study of Zambia shows how assistive technology can be used to help students with visual impairment. World Vision Zambia (2023) working with funding provided by the European Union availed assistive equipment to school for the blind in Chipata Eastern Province to more than 70 students. The variety of assistive equipment consists of Prodigi Connect Tablets with camera and a facility for talkback, braille paper, calculators' handheld magnifiers.

Kaulu (2019) noted that there are a number of assistive technologies that are were developed for the people who are visually impaired which included Job Access with Speech (JAWS), which can help users who are unable to see the screen, Windows Eyes, which transforms the Widows operating system to synthesized speech facilitating access for people for people with visual impairment and Dolphin Super Nova, that functions by reading the screen interactively and then communicate through a speech device and can also display on braille. In Zambia this software for the visually impaired is located only at the library Zambia Library Cultural and Skills Centre (ZLCSCVI). This centre is registered with the governments agency which includes the Technical Education and Vocational Training Authority (TEVETA).

The centre helps the visually impaired to access assistive technology for academic and training purposes.

Muzata (2020) conducted a study at the university of Zambia to assess the availability of the assistive technology for the visually impaired students. The same study noted that students at university are required to type assignments and then submit them online. The study noted a dearth of resources to support visually impaired students, lack of computer skills on the part of the educators, lack of research on ways to enhance learning for visually impaired students and lack of human resource that has a capacity to manage the use of Information and Communication Technology for the visually impaired.

Case Study of the Local Rehabilitation Workshop in Zimbabwe

Zimbabwe instituted a local initiative to address the concerns of a lack of local initiative to manufacture assistive equipment locally called Local Rehabilitation Workshop (LOREWO). This entity helps to ensure the production of wheelchairs, walking aids, and hearing aids (Local Rehabilitation Workshops LOREWO, 2013). The more prominent device that is in use is walking aids making up 70%. Among the people with a disability 14,4% had access to an assistive device.

LOREWO represents a local and flexible strategy that is designed to address the needs in a given context. Five chief concepts drives the LOREWO rehabilitation workshop and these are:

- Facilitation the setting up of local workshop infrastructure
- Training and empowering local personnel to provide the infrastructure
- Provision of assistive equipment such as walking aids, wheelchairs and hearing aids that meet local needs
- Provision of delivery services, rehabilitation equipment and counselling functions

LOREWO workshops are designed with all the necessary tools that can help with the repair, adjusting and mending of assistive devices (Local Rehabilitation Workshops, LOREWO, 2013). The workshops may either be situated at a hospital, or a non-governmental institution or other institutions. The acquisition of assistive equipment is realized through local manufacture, securing through donations of secondhand equipment, and also purchasing.

LOREWO also forefronts the significance of raising awareness on disability issues, educating people on disability, providing awareness on assistive equipment and training and developing skills in this area.

BEST PRACTICES IN PROVIDING ASSISTIVE EQUIPMENT AND ASSISTIVE TECHNOLOGY

There are some best practices in the provision of assistive equipment in the education sector in the four SADC states which other countries can draw from and implement in their own programs. It was noted in the case of South Africa that a community-based organization was actively engaged in the provision of assistive equipment to students with a disability. This foregrounds the reality that community-based groups hold tremendous potential to make a difference in the provision of assistive equipment. In the case of South Africa, the community-based initiative was launched by a parent whose child had a challenge with mobility.

It is also paramount to produce assistive equipment locally. In this case Zimbabwe provided a model for manufacturing assistive equipment as demonstrated by the production of assistive equipment largely to address mobility challenges such as wheelchairs and hearing aids. Production of equipment locally can help to reduce the challenges of importing it and the costs of seeking foreign currency to fund the procurement process. In the case of Zambia partnership between the government and other development partners such as World Vision, collaborated with European Union to provide assistive technology for students in Zambia (Disability Rights Watch, 2022).

The technology was also located within a library to facilitate its usage by many people with challenges that are related to visual impairment. Given the massive demand for assistive equipment in the four countries, it is vital that a multi-stakeholder approach be employed in addressing the dire needs of students with a disability. South Africa has also experimented with the removal of taxes on assistive equipment as a measure to increase access by people who have a disability. It is a progressive measure that SADC countries may want to replicate. The implementation of assistive technology also requires the use well- trained educators who can work with students with an impairment. An architype of this type of practice was noted in Zimbabwe where a well-trained educator supported the students in primary school on the use of Braille in Gweru. The case study in Namibia at Eros high school showed that most of the teachers were able to use technology in teaching. This is the best practice when it comes to the use of assistive technology designed for use with people with a disability (Veiko, 2019).

THEORETICAL FRAMEWORK

The theoretical framework for this study is based on Ubuntu, a lens that is associated with the Bantu people in sub-Sahara Africa that enunciate solidarity and mutual personhood and intersectional theory

Ubuntu

This chapter is underpinned by the philosophical lens of Ubuntu. Mbazzi (2022) noted the dominance of global theory to explicate experiences of people in the global south. In the majority of countries with a colonial history the experiences of people with a disability were always articulated within the framework of western episteme and the provision of education for people with a disability was dominated by religious or charitable organisations. This chapter seeks to make a departure from that philosophical lens and postulate ubuntu as a framework for discussing disability in the four SADC countries. Ubuntu philosophy is a lens recognised as a capturing a cosmology of the indigenous people in sub-Sahara Africa prior to colonialism (Chakabwata & Mukazi, 2022; Swanson, 2007; Mutwarasibo & Adelheid, 2019). Ubuntu worldview foregrounds the importance of interdependency, relatedness, cooperation, empathy, sharing, and cooperation. In addition, this worldview or cosmology maintains that people have to act in a way that enhances the well-being of others.

It is complex to find an overarching statement of ubuntu that subsumes its essence, however, the closest is the proverb "I am because we are" and "a person is a person because of other people" (Poovan, Du Toit, & Engelbrecht 2006, p. 19). These two dictums illustrate that our lives are tied up with that of other people in our communities and we also share humanity together as a collective. The collective assumes primacy over individualism. Ubuntu has multiple elements that support the provision of care to learners with disability in a community setting which includes mutuality, reciprocity and a sense of community. Ubuntu foregrounds the communal living where a person is valued regardless of their status. The ubuntu lens informs the way we are supposed to treat each other in the society. Ubuntu is built on a foundation of respect for diversity and an appreciation of what it entails to be human.

Ubuntu does not just submit a description of this lens, but imposes normative ethical claims on society, to act in a way that is selfless to others. Berghs (2017) expounded that in sub-Sahara Africa, there are multiple forms of interpretation regarding disabilities, as articulated in songs, dance, folktales and culture. In the light of ubuntu the majority of South Africa rejected a biomedical view of disability outlined in the previous sections and argued that treating impairment as a pathology that needed to be treated is an act of oppression. This also contributed to political activism among people living with a disability, and they crafted an organisation that sought to challenge discrimination on the basis of disability. Ubuntu does not endorse discrimination against people based on any criteria.

Intersectional Theory

Intersectionality has its genesis in black feminist scholarship particularly the work of Kimberlee Crenshaw, who coined the term to describe the experience of black American women (Grabham et al., 2009; Carasthathis, 2016; Chakabwata, 2022). Intersectional theory explains ways in which the interaction of gender, race and disability impacts on student's learning outcome in inclusive schools (Forber-Pratt eta l., 2020). Romeo (2018)

expounded that intersectionality focalises on social justice and has its genesis in the social justice research. Intersectionality is an activist theory that seeks to present an analytical lens for scrutinising issues of exclusion and inclusion in education among people with a disability. Intersectionality also facilitates our understanding of privilege and how exclusion functions in different social locations. This concept is not only applicable to situations of destitution but is relevant to comprehending privilege and social location. In the 1980s race, class and gender were the primary focus of intersectional studies (Carasthathis, 2016; Collins & Bilge, 2019).

The children who have a disability tend to suffer from multiple intersecting disadvantages. Crenshaw was confronting the confounding challenges of disadvantage based on race, gender and other social markers in the United States. Crenshaw postulated that people could confront multiple layers of disadvantages due to their social positioning. The forms of disadvantage can be seen in the context of education, access to health, jobs and many others. Moodley and Graham (2015) explicated ways in which race, gender and disability intersected in South Africa, to deprive women with a disability to access education. It was also fore fronted in the same publication that women with poverty tends to experience a greater degree of poverty than their male counterparts. In addition, the authors averred that race, gender and disability interact to place women at a disadvantage in education, employment and access to health. Moodley and Graham (2015) study noted that race was a major contributor in accessing education among students with a disability in South Africa. Poverty creates a nexus with a disability to maintain the state of disadvantage among black South Africans.

Economics disadvantages may be impacted by social markers such as ableism, which is more pertinent to this chapter which can collaborate with other variables to create interlocking disadvantages. Loets (2024) noted that disadvantages that people face in their daily experiences may be due to the multiple identities that occupy in society. For instance, people who have an impairment may face discrimination on the basis of a variety of social identities which include ethnicity, race, gender, disability, social class, age among many others. Loets (2024) spotlighted three key canons of intersectionality namely specificity, which means certain identities place some people at a disadvantage. The second point is that intersectionality does not only bestow disadvantage, but it may also bring privilege and finally, inseparability. Intersectionality may bring privilege in the sense that there are cases where people can experience intersectional privilege due to social location and identities. Irreducibility which means that one cannot isolate intersectional disadvantages to a single variable which is also termed the non -additivity of intersectional disadvantages. Disadvantages that students with a disability experience stem from my social variables which intersect to giving them disadvantages in school.

Forber-Pratt et al., (2020) noted that in the United States students with a disability may face a number of challenges due to intersecting factors such as race, gender, identity, sexuality among many others. These students are likely to face bullying in school, peer victimisation, and most of tend to engage in suicidal ideation. Samuels et al., (2020) noted that not only may the students with a disability face disadvantage in accessing education, but they also face challenges in accessing health services in countries such as South Africa. Inequality has grown markedly in South Africa and the other three countries accentuating the disadvantages that students from less privileged groups have to contend with in accessing information, assistive device, health services and education. The legacy of apartheid has left South Africa as a very unequal country with a gini coefficient of 0,67, Namibia 0,58, Zambia 0,43 and Zimbabwe 0,51 (Statistica, 2024; Statisca, 2024, Statistica, 2024; Statistica, 2024).

It is noteworthy that most people with an impediment may be located in rural areas where they may not even have access to education, let alone assistive equipment. Eide et al., (2022) explicated poverty as the inability to attain certain standards which includes lack of shelter, education and health care. In addition, it was noted by the same authors that poverty is multifactorial. Literature demonstrated a close relationship between poverty and disability in southern Africa (World Bank Group, 2024). This trend where people with a disability live in poverty was noted even in developing countries where the state of poverty in countries such as Norway remained in spite of the general prosperity in the country. A high rate of illiteracy was noted among people with a disability in Zimbabwe and Namibia (Eide, et al., 2022). The people who were identified in the same study by Eide, et., (2022) were that the majority who had never attended school in Namibia, Zambia, and Zimbabwe had sensory impairment (vision, hearing or communication) and these were followed by physical impairment and mental and emotional impairment.

World Bank Group (2024) noted that women tend to experience higher levels of disability than men due to way that parents may place priority on the health of the male child as opposed to the female. Pregnancy, domestic violence and childbirth also has a contributory effect on disability in women. The same report asserted that people with a disability tend to attain low levels of academic attainment due to multiple factors such as experiencing bullying at school and paucity of resources to support children with a disability.

DISCUSSION

The study noted that the four countries generally use assistive technology to a limited degree to facilitate teaching and learning. However, there were some impediments that were also noted with the use of assistive technology in each of the four countries which included a lack of competencies on the part of the teachers to use technology for teaching and learning, a dearth of ICT hardware and software to support learning among other challenges. The research on the use of assistive equipment and technology in the four countries in this study is still in its infancy and is very fragmented. It is important to strengthen research and collaboration in research within the domain of the use of assistive technology within the four countries. In some countries such as South Africa the approach towards helping people with a disability has been very fragmented among government ministries and agencies. Multiple loft policy pronouncement in South Africa has not been converted into policy implementation. The use of assistive equipment such as wheelchairs requires ongoing support from skilled people who are able to train people on their proper use. In this chapter, it has been highlighted that there is a dearth of such skills in South Africa and the other three states. The study also noted that in Zimbabwe, there was an effort to manufacture local devices through a local initiative called LOREWO. This is a commendable effort that can help to reduce the massive demand for assistive equipment and technologies in the four countries.

It was also notable that in most of these countries there is an unduly emphasis on the donor community for funding inclusive education through the provision of assistive equipment in schools. While this is commendable, it is also vital that governments must begin to build their capacity in this area by providing assistive equipment and technology to their own citizens for sustainable provision of inclusive education.

This study was foreground on the two theoretical lenses of Ubuntu and intersectionality. Ubuntu as already noted supports an approach to placing the collective above individual needs, and valuing and supporting each other in the community to experience being human together. This means that upholding Ubuntu, a genre for African people who live in the sub-Sahara Africa can help to enhance the educational opportunities for people living with a disability. The chapter also discussed intersectionality as articulated by Kimblerlee Crenshaw, who perceived disadvantage as interlocking. This means that disadvantage is not additive, but multiplicative creating an interlocking web of disadvantage among people with a disability. Providing support to people living with a disability would require a caring approach such as Ubuntu and also an intersectional approach that takes into account how disadvantages can manifest as a matrix for people with a disability.

Recommendation

Based on the issues that were discussed in this chapter, it is recommended that:

i) The government and other stakeholders in the region help to facilitate on-going professional development of teachers in the use of assistive technology and assistive equipment which provides a basis for support for students with challenges such as dyslexia.
ii) Governments in the four countries must also ensure that there are adequate resources for local manufacture of assistive equipment and financial resources for assistive technology to support the use of assistive technologies and assistive equipment in schools, especially those that practice inclusive education and they have students with special needs.
iii) Governments in the four states must put in place clear policies regarding the implementation of inclusive education.
iv) Governments and other stakeholders working in assistive technology and devices for students with special needs must support research in this area in order to provide a holistic picture of developments within this field of inclusive education.
v) The four countries must work tirelessly to set- up and strengthen local manufacturing of local devices to help people with a disability in their countries, since the demand for the devices is high and many of them are imported and expensive.
vi) It is important to coordinate research within this area of the use of assistive equipment and technology within each country and across country in order to bridge the current fragmented status.
vii) In countries such as South Africa which has evolved a sophisticated legal framework to support people with special needs, it is important to ensure that the policy trajectory is actualized.
viii) It is important to ensure that there are trained people in the four states to help provide specialized support to people with disabilities using mobile equipment.

CONCLUSION

This chapter has highlighted the critical role of assistive technologies and devices in fostering inclusive education within the Southern African Development Community (SADC) states of Namibia, South Africa, Zambia, and Zimbabwe. Despite the progressive legislative frameworks and policy commitments in these countries, significant gaps remain in ensuring equitable access to assistive technologies for people with disabilities, particularly in rural areas. The challenges of high costs, reliance on imported devices, and fragmented implementation of inclusive education policies exacerbate the inaccessibility of these essential tools. Grounded in the principles of Ubuntu and intersectionality, this chapter underscores the importance of collective responsibility, mutual support, and addressing interlocking disadvantages to create a more inclusive society. Governments and stakeholders are urged to prioritize local production of assistive devices, strengthen professional development for educators, and enhance research collaboration to bridge the gaps in implementation. By adopting these measures, the SADC states can make significant strides toward actualizing inclusive education and improving the quality of life for people with disabilities, ultimately advancing the Sustainable Development Goals across the region.

REFERENCES

Abiatal, L. (2019). *Constructivist assitive technology in a mathematical classroom for the deaf: An experiement in a rural primary school Namibia.* University of South Africa.

Akpan, J., & Beard, L. (2014). Assistive technology and mathematics education. *Universal Journal of Educational Research*, 2(3), 219–222. DOI: 10.13189/ujer.2014.020303

At-Infor-Map. (2019, 01 12). *Summary Overview Disability and Assistive Devices in Zimbabwe.* Retrieved from At-Infor-Map: https://atinfomap.org/zimbabwe.html

Australian National University. (2024, 11 7). *Different types of disabilities.* Retrieved from Australian National University: https://services.anu.edu.au/human-resources/health-safety/different-types-of-disabilities

Berghs, M. (2017). Practices and discourses on ubuntu: Implications for an African modelof disability. *African Journal of Disability*, 6, 1–8. DOI: 10.4102/ajod.v6i0.292 PMID: 28730067

binti Nor Rashid, N., binti Asaari, A., & Rashid, S. (2024). Assistive Technology for The Deaf: A Literature Review. *International Journal of Academic Research in Business and Social Sciences vol14, Issue2*, 612-623. DOI: 10.4102/ajod.v6i0.292 PMID: 28730067

Bonifatius, S., & Haihambo, C. (2022). Assessing the utilization of Information and Communication Technologies in inclusive classes in the Oshana region of Namibia. *Namibia Educational Reform Forum Journal*, 30(1), 87–96.

Boot, F., Kahonde, C., Dinsmore, J., & MacLachlan, M. (2021). Perspectives on access and usage of assistive technology by people with intellectual disabilities in the Western Cape province of South Africa:Where to from here? *African Journal of Disability*, 10, 1–5. DOI: 10.4102/ajod.v10i0.767 PMID: 33824859

Carasthathis, A. (2016). *Intersectionality, origins, contestations and horizons.* University of Nebraska Press. DOI: 10.2307/j.ctt1fzhfz8

Centre for Human Rights University of Pretoria. (2024, 11 7). *Namibia: Updated Country Report.* Retrieved from Centre for Human Rights University of Pretoria: http://www.rodra.co.za/countries/namibia/21-countries/namibia/60-updated-country-report

Chakabwata, W. (2022). An Intersectional Study of the Funding Experiences of South African University Students After Majority Rule. In J. Keengwe, *Handbook of research on social justice and equity* (pp. 242-258). Dakota: IGI Global. DOI: 10.4018/978-1-7998-9567-1.ch012

Chakabwata, W., & Mukazi, F. (2022). Ubuntu Philosophy and Online Assessment in Higher Education Institutions. In J. Keengwe, *Handbook of research on transformative and innovative pedagogies in education* (pp. 257-275). Dakota: IGI Global. DOI: 10.4018/978-1-7998-9561-9.ch014

Chibaya, G., Naidoo, D., & Govender, P. (2022). Exploring the implementation of the United Nations Convention on the Rights of People with Disabilities (UNCRPD) in Namibia. Perspectives of policymakers and implementers. *South African Journal of Occupational Therapy*, 52(1), 16–23. DOI: 10.17159/2310-3833/2022/vol52n1a3

Collins, P., & Bilge. (2019). *Intersectionality as a critical social theory.* Duke: Duke University Press. DOI: 10.17159/2310-3833/2022/vol52n1a3

Dimitrov, L., & Gossman, W. (2023, 06 2). Retrieved from National Library of Medicine National Centre for Biotechnology Information: https://www.ncbi.nlm.nih.gov/books/NBK538285/#_ncbi_dlg_citbx_NBK538285

Disability Rights Watch. (2022, 01 24). *Commitments to create a more Disability Inclusive Zambia –Delivering Quality Inclusive Education.* Retrieved from Disability Rights Watch: https://disabilityrightswatch.net/commitments-to-create-a-more-disability-inclusive-zambia-delivering-quality-inclusive-education/

Dube, T., Ncube, S. B., Mapuvire, C. C., Ndlovu, S., Ncube, C. M., & Mlotshwa, S. (2021). Interventions to reduce the exclusions of children with a dsability in from education: A Zimbabwean perspective from the field. *Cogent Social Sciences*, 7(1), 1–10. DOI: 10.1080/23311886.2021.1913848

Eide, A., Loeb, M., Nhiwatiwa, S., Munthali, A., Ngulube, T., & van Rooy, G. (2022). Living conditions among people with disabilities in developing countries. In A. Eide, & B. Ingstad, *Disability and poverty: A global Challenge* (pp. 55-70). Bristol: Bristol University Press; Policy Press.

Erdem, R. (2017). Students with Special Educational Needs and Assistive Technologies: A Literature Review. *The Turkish Online Journal of Educational Technology*, 16(1), 128–146.

Fletcher, M. (2021). Using haptic stimulation to enhance auditory perception in hearing-impaired listeners. *Expert Review of Medical Devices*, 18(1), 63–74. DOI: 10.1080/17434440.2021.1863782 PMID: 33372550

Forber-Pratt, A., Merrin, G. J., & Espelage, D. (2020). Exploring the Intersections of Disability, Race, and Gender on Student Outcomes in High School. *Remedial and Special Education*, ●●●, 1–14.

Grabham, E., Herman, D., Cooper, D., & Krishnadas, J. (2009). Introduction. In Grabham, E., Cooper, D., Krishnadas, J., & Herman, D. (Eds.), *Intersectionality and beyond: Law, power and politics of location* (pp. 1–17). Taylor and Francis Group.

Guide, M. (2024). [AT]. *Assistive Technology*, 11, 3.

Islim, O., & Cagiltay, K. (2012). Disability and assistive technology. *6th International Computer & Instructional Technologies Symposium, October 4th - 6th 2012 Gaziantep* (pp. 1-6). Turkey: Gaziantep.

Kaulu, J. (2019). *Efficacy of assistive technology on the visually impaired learners' grasping of library information services: A case of Zambia library cultural and skills centre for the visually impaired (ZLCSVI) in Lusaka, Zambia*. A Dissertation submitted to the University of Zambia in Partial Fulfillment of the Requirements of the Degree of Master of Library and Information Science (MLIS): University of Zambia.

Kunwar, R. (2022). An overview of dyslexia: Some key issues and its effect on learning mathematics. *Turkish International Journal of Special Education and Guidance & Counseling*, 11(2), 82–98.

Lawson, A., & Beckett, A. (2021). The social and human rights models of disability: towards a complementarity thesis. *The International Journal of Human Rights vol 25 Issue 2*, 1-32.

Local Rehabilitation Workshops(LOREWO). (2013, 02 14). *LOREWO concept*. Retrieved from Local Rehabilitation Workshops (LOREWO): https://www.sintef.no/en/projects/2001/lokale-rehabiliteringsverksteder/

Loets, A. (2024). Intersectional disadvantage. *Australasian Journal of Philosophy vol 102 Issue No 4*, 857–878.

Macrotrends. (2024, 11 2). *Zimbabwe Population 1950-2024*. Retrieved from Macrotrends: https://www.macrotrends.net/global-metrics/countries/ZWE/zimbabwe/population

Mbazzi, F. (2022). *Disability and ubuntu*. Uganda Research Unit.

Minnesota Guide to Assistive Technology. (2024, 11 7). *Types of assistive technology*. Retrieved from Minnesota Guide to Assistive Technology: https://mn.gov/admin/at/getting-started/understanding-at/types/

Mokwetsi, J. (2022, 09 12). *UNICEF Zimbabwe helps to advance inclusive education at Margaretha Hugo*. Retrieved from UNICEF Zimbabwe: https://www.unicef.org/zimbabwe/stories/unicef-zimbabwe-helps-advance-inclusive-education-margaretha-hugo

Moodley, J., & Graham, L. (2015). The importance of intersectionality in disability and gender studies. *Agenda (Durban, South Africa)*, 29(2), 24–33. DOI: 10.1080/10130950.2015.1041802

Mutwarasibo, F., & Adelheid, I. (2019). I am because we are - the contribution of the Ubuntu philosophy to intercultural management thinking. *Online-Zeitschrift für interkulturelle Studien, 18(32)*, 15-32. DOI: 10.1080/10130950.2015.1041802

Muzata, K. (2020). The Utilisation of Computers to Improve the Quality of Learning for Students with Visual Impairment at the University of Zambia. [ZAJLIS]. *Zambia Journal of Library & Information Science*, 4(2), 34–44.

Muzata, K., Simui, F., Mahlo, D., & Ng'uni, P. (2021). Status of Zambia's Inclusive Education through the Lenses of Teachers. *African Journal of Teacher Education VOL*, 10(1), 1–20. DOI: 10.21083/ajote.v10i1.6338

Namibia Statistical Agency. (2023). *Namibia population and hosuing census main report*. Namibia Statistics Agency.

National Library of Medicine (NIM). (2024, 08 25). *World Report on Disability 2011*. Retrieved from National Library of Medicine (NIH): https://www.ncbi.nlm.nih.gov/books/NBK304082/

Nottinghamshire, D. (2024, 11 7). *Social Model versus medical model of disability*. Retrieved from Disability Nottinghamshire: https://www.disabilitynottinghamshire.org.uk/index.php/about/social-model-vs-medical-model-of-disability/

Ntinda, R. (2024, 11 1). *Centre for Human Rights University of Pretoria: Repository on Disability Rights in Africa*. Retrieved from Centre for Human Rights University of Pretoria: http://www.rodra.co.za/countries/namibia/21-countries/namibia/60-updated-country-report

Physiopedia. (2024, 11 2). *Assistive devices*. Retrieved from Physiopedia: https://www.physio-pedia.com/Assistive_Devices

Physiopedia. (2024, 11 2). *International Classification of Functioning, Disability and Health (ICF)*. Retrieved from Physiopedia: https://www.physio-pedia.com/International_Classification_of_Functioning,_Disability_and_Health_(ICF)

Poovan, N., Du Toit, M., & Engelbrecht, A. (2006). The effect of the social values of ubuntu on team effectiveness. *South African Journal of Business Management*, 37(3), 17–27. DOI: 10.4102/sajbm.v37i3.604

Romeo, M. (2018). *Introducing intersectionality*. Polity Press.

Samuels, A., Stemela, U., & Boo, M. (2020). The intersection between health and education: Meetings the interventions needs of children and youth with a disability. *South African Health Review*, 2, 170–181.

Snowling, M., Hulme, C., & Nation, K. (2020). Defining and understanding dyslexia: Past, present and future. *Oxford Review of Education*, 46(4), 501–513. DOI: 10.1080/03054985.2020.1765756 PMID: 32939103

Sofokleous, R., & Stylianou, S. (2023). Effects of Exposure to Medical Model and Social Model Online Constructions of Disability on Attitudes Toward Wheelchair Users: Results from an Online Experiment. *Journal of Creative Communications*, 18(1), 61–78. DOI: 10.1177/09732586221136260

Statisca. (2024, 11 7). *Socioeconomic indicators Zambia*. Retrieved from Statistica: https://www.statista.com/outlook/co/socioeconomic-indicators/zambia#:~:text=The%20gini%20coefficient%20in%20Zambia,to%200.43m%20in%202024

Statistica. (2024, 11 7). *Socioeconomic indicators for South Africa*. Retrieved from Statistica: https://www.statista.com/outlook/co/socioeconomic-indicators/south-africa#:~:text=The%20gini%20coefficient%20in%20South,to%208.41m%20in%202024

Statistica. (2024, 11 7). *Socioeconomic indicators Namibia*. Retrieved from Statistica: https://www.statista.com/outlook/co/socioeconomic-indicators/namibia#:~:text=The%20gini%20coefficient%20in%20Namibia,forecast%20to%2020.29%25%20in%202024

Statistica. (2024, 11 7). *Socioeconomic indicators Zimbabwe*. Retrieved from Statisca: https://www.statista.com/outlook/co/socioeconomic-indicators/zimbabwe#:~:text=The%20gini%20coefficient%20in%20Zimbabwe,forecasted%20to%2062.90%25%20in%202024

Stats SA Department of Statistics in SA Republic of SA. (2024, 11 2). *South Africa population surpuses 63 million*. Retrieved from Stats SA Department of Statistics in SA Republic of SA: https://www.statssa.gov.za/?p=17430

Swanson, D. (2007). Ubuntu: An African contribution to (re)search for/with a 'humble togetherness'. *Journal of Contemporary Issues in Education*, 2(2), 53–67.

Thorneycroft, R. (2024). Screwing the social model of disability. *Scandinavian Journal of Disability Research*, 26(1), 286–299. DOI: 10.16993/sjdr.1130

Tigere, D. (2023, 05 26). *Assistive devices a necessity for people with a disability*. Retrieved from Zimbabwe Independent: https://www.newsday.co.zw/theindependent/opinion/article/200012053/assistive-devices-a-necessity-for-people-with-disabilities

Topper, A., & Arizzi, R. (2024, 11 10). *Adaptive and assistive technology an overview & differences*. Retrieved from Study.com: https://study.com/academy/lesson/adaptive-assistive-technology-definition-uses.html

Trafford, Z., van der Westhuizen, E., McDonald, S., Linegar, M., & Swartz, L. (2021). More than just assistive devices:How a South African social enterprises supports an environment of inclusion. *International Journal of Environmental Research and Public Health*, 18(5), 1–15. DOI: 10.3390/ijerph18052655 PMID: 33800783

Tswellang Special School. (2017, 11 11). *Who we are*. Retrieved from Tswellang Special School: https://www.tswelangschool.co.za/

United Nations. (2006, 12 12). *UN Conventions on the Rights of People with Disabilities*. Retrieved from United Nations Human Rights Commission of People with disabilities: https://www.ohchr.org/en/instruments-mechanisms/instruments/convention-rights-people-disabilities

United Nations Children's Fund (UNICEF). (2023, 07 21). *Children with a disabilities in Eastern and Southern Africa: A statistical*. Retrieved from UNICEF for every child: https://data.unicef.org/resources/children-with-disabilities-in-eastern-and-southern-africa-a-statistical-overview-of-their-well-being/

United Nations Development Coordination Office. (2024, 11 2). *UN in Zambia doubles on inclusion down on disability inclusion*. Retrieved from United Nations Development Coordination Office: https://un-dco.org/stories/un-zambia-doubles-down-disability-inclusion

United Nations Educational, Scientific and Cultural Organization . (1994). *World Conference on Special Needs Education: Access and Quality*. Spain: UNESCO.

United Nations (UN). (1989). *Convention on the Rights of the Child (CRC)*. New York: UN.

Veiko, V. (2019). Assistive technology for students with dyslexia at Eros Girls High. A report submitted in partial fullfillment of the requirement for the Master of Science in Information Technology: University of Namibia.

Visser, M., Nel, M., De Klerk, M., Ganzevoort, A., Hubble, C., Liebenberg, A., Snyman, M., & Young, M. (2020). The use of assistive technology in classroom activities for learners with motor impairments at a special school in South Africa. *South African Journal of Occupational Therapy*, 50(2), 11–22. DOI: 10.17159/2310-3833/2020/vol50no2a3

World Bank Group. (2024, 11 7). *Challenges facing people with a disabilities in Sub-Sahara Africa- in 5 Charts*. Retrieved from World Bank Group: https://www.worldbank.org/en/topic/poverty/brief/challenges-facing-people-with-disabilities-in-sub-saharan-africa-in-5-charts

World Education Forum. (2000). *The Dakar Framework of Action*. Senegal: UNESCO.

World Health Organisartion (WHO). (2024, 02 02). *Deafness and hearing loss*. Retrieved from World Health Organisartion (WHO): https://www.who.int/news-room/fact-sheets/detail/deafness-and-hearing-loss

World Health Organisation (WHO). (2024, 08 25). *Disability*. Retrieved from World Health Organisation: https://www.who.int/health-topics/disability#tab=tab_1

World Vision Zambia. (2023, 07 27). *World Vision and the European Union donate assistive devices to Mangwiro school for the blind to promote quality*. Retrieved from World Vision Zambia: https://www.wvi.org/stories/zambia/world-vision-and-european-union-donate-assistive-devices-magwero-school-blind

Worldometer. (2024, 11 2). *Zambia population*. Retrieved from Worldometer: https://www.worldometers.info/world-population/zambia-population/#:~:text=The%20current%20population%20of%20Zambia,21%2C314%2C956%20p

Wyeth, P., Kervin, L., Danby, S., & Day, D. (2023). Digital technologies to support young children with special needs in early childhood education and care: A literature review. *OECD Education Working Papers No. 294*.

Zaks, Z. (2023). Changing the medical model of disability to the normalization model of disability: Clarifying the past to create a new future direction. *Disability & Society*, •••, 1–29.

Zimbabwe, U. N. D. P. (2024, 06 5). *Towards achieving sustainable and inclusive development*. Retrieved from UNDP Zimbabwe: https://www.undp.org/zimbabwe/news/towards-achieving-inclusive-sustainable-development

ZimRights. (2024). *Eights things that can be improved*. ZimRights.

KEY TERMS AND DEFINITIONS

Assistive Devices: Tools or technologies designed to enhance the functional capabilities of individuals with disabilities, enabling greater independence and access to education.

Assistive Technology: Specialized technological solutions that support individuals with disabilities in performing tasks they might otherwise find challenging, such as communication, mobility, or learning.

Biomedical Model of Disability: A framework that views disability as a medical condition requiring treatment or intervention to correct perceived abnormalities.

Inclusive Education: An educational approach that seeks to accommodate and integrate students of all abilities into mainstream classrooms, promoting equal access to learning opportunities.

Intersectionality: An analytical framework that examines how overlapping social identities, such as disability, race, and gender, contribute to unique experiences of disadvantage or privilege.

Local Manufacturing: The production of assistive devices within a specific region or country to reduce costs and improve accessibility for individuals with disabilities.

Social Model of Disability: A perspective that defines disability as a societal issue, focusing on removing environmental and systemic barriers to enable full participation for individuals with impairments.

Southern African Development Community (SADC): A regional organization of 16 Southern African countries that collaborates on economic development and integration, including efforts to support individuals with disabilities.

Ubuntu: A philosophical concept originating from sub-Saharan Africa, emphasizing community, interconnectedness, and mutual support, particularly in addressing social challenges like disability.

Universal Design: An approach to designing products, environments, and systems that are accessible to all people, regardless of age, ability, or status.

Chapter 8
VR Interventions for Students With Intellectual Disabilities:
Innovative Approaches and Practical Applications

Hüseyin Göksu
 https://orcid.org/0000-0003-4596-4922
İstanbul University-Cerrahpaşa, Turkey

Selami Eryilmaz
 https://orcid.org/0000-0002-6507-740X
Gazi University, Turkey

ABSTRACT

This chapter explores the development and evaluation of a virtual reality (VR) application designed to enhance learning for students with mild intellectual disabilities. The application focuses on teaching eight foundational concepts—"few," "many," "large," "small," "far," "near," "long," and "short"—through an adaptive, sequential learning approach. Each concept is unlocked only after the student demonstrates mastery of the preceding one, ensuring a structured and progressive learning experience. Developed using Unity software, the application leverages immersive technology and was tested with the Oculus Quest 2 headset. A pilot test was conducted at a vocational high school in Antalya with the participation of a student with mild intellectual disabilities under the guidance and supervision of their teachers. The findings contribute to understanding how VR technology can support personalized and accessible education for students with special needs.

DOI: 10.4018/979-8-3693-8227-1.ch008

INTRODUCTION

According to the statistics bulletin on disabilities and elderly individuals published by the Ministry of Family and Social Services of the Republic of Turkey in April 2023, the number of individuals with intellectual disabilities registered in the data system and currently alive is 385,313. Figure 1 illustrates the number of individuals with different types of disabilities living in the Republic of Türkiye.

Figure 1. Distribution of disability types, Ministry of Family and Social Services of Türkiye, 2023

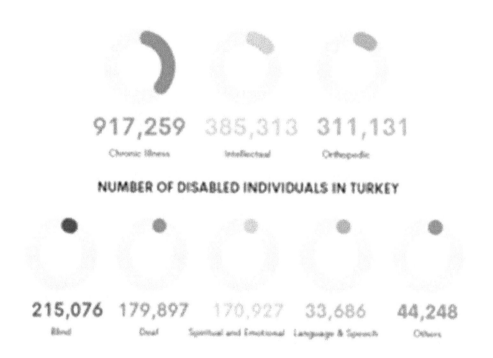

The graph above includes individuals who have obtained disability reports from health institutions or hospitals in Turkey and have contacted government institutions to receive state support or services. These individuals are often deprived of educational activities during natural disasters or the COVID-19 pandemic. Such events lead to the necessity of conducting education through remote or hybrid methods (where part of the educational activities is conducted remotely and part in person).

Considering both the current conditions and the potential for future pandemics or natural disasters, remote education is gaining increasing importance. However, students with intellectual disabilities are not fully benefiting from the planned educational activities during the remote education process. Moreover, many have been entirely excluded from these activities. Additionally, natural disasters resulting from climate change have led to school closures or hindered individuals with intellectual disabilities from accessing educational environments. To prevent individuals with intellectual disabilities from being deprived of educational activities during future natural disasters, virtual reality applications, and similar tools could be utilized. In such situations, teachers of students with intellectual disabilities often struggle with the use of technology. Furthermore, considering that parents also face difficulties in this area, it is evident that students with intellectual disabilities are often left to manage on their own. This study aims to enable students to continue learning concepts with the help of their families in situations where teachers and students cannot conduct educational activities in a physical classroom environment. Additionally, in cases where there is a shortage of teachers for students with intellectual disabilities, the virtual reality headsets shown in Figure 2, developed by various companies, can assist teachers in the classroom with appropriate software support for educational purposes.

Virtual reality technology can significantly contribute to the education of individuals with intellectual disabilities. However, to realize this potential, a comprehensive approach focusing on individual student needs, accessibility, and cost-effectiveness is required.

In March 2016, the Rift model was released by Oculus, followed by the introduction of Oculus GO in May 2018. The GO model was notable for its integrated operating system, advanced lenses, long-lasting battery, user-friendly strap, and high-resolution display. It quickly became one of the best all-in-one devices of its time. Building on this success, Oculus launched two additional devices in May 2019, named Quest and Rift S. These new models featured enhanced sensors and camera experiences, higher-resolution panels, options for wired or wireless use, and advanced capabilities such as screen mirroring (Facebook Meta, 2021). As with every technological advancement, each new device surpasses the capabilities of its predecessor, creating a continuous cycle of development and improvement.

With the developed virtual reality application, students with intellectual disabilities will be able to learn concepts such as "few," "many," "big," and "small" at any time and place they choose. They will also have the opportunity to practice repeatedly without limitations. During times when educational activities are disrupted, such as in the event of pandemics or natural disasters, this application will allow students to continue their education with the support of their parents. Consequently, the research indicates that virtual reality, one of today's most significant technological innovations, can be utilized more effectively in the educational activities of students with intellectual disabilities. This study aims to develop a virtual reality application for students with mild intellectual disabilities and to test the effectiveness of the developed application. The application will focus on concept teaching and will aim to teach eight different concepts.

Use of Technology

Technology is advancing at a dizzying pace, and this development is being effectively utilized in every conceivable field imagined in the twentieth century. In this context, individuals and fields that embrace technology gain a significant advantage over others. Therefore, it has become increasingly important to closely follow and master modern technology (Eryılmaz, 2021). The widespread use of the internet, the rapid growth in the use of smart devices, their integration into every sector, virtual and augmented reality technology, and most recently, artificial intelligence—one of today's most cutting-edge technologies—have all made our lives easier and provided solutions to many problems.

The new generation lives in close interaction with technology and sometimes uses it more than necessary. They are eager to use technology in all aspects of their lives, including educational activities. This generation is growing up with rapid access to information, the ability to research and explore, and a desire to multitask (Bilgiç, Duman, & Seferoğlu, 2011). Designing an educational environment without technology for these generations would be akin to standing in front of a flowing river. Therefore, integrating technology into educational activities and using it as effectively as possible will increase students' motivation and interest.

Emerging Technological Trends in Education

The technologies used in education today have also benefited from the rapid advancements in technology. A few years ago, discussions centered around computer-assisted or mobile-assisted learning, but today these technologies have been replaced by much more advanced ones. The most significant of these advanced technologies include augmented reality, virtual reality, robotics, and artificial intelligence applications. Virtual reality technology, which aims to create realistic three-dimensional sensory experiences in a virtual environment using various technological devices, is one of the newer technologies (Gao, 2023). Researchers have highlighted several advantages of virtual reality technology.

With the use of various virtual environments and display systems, the content that needs to be learned can be presented independently of schools and classrooms, while content from the outside world can also be brought to schools and classrooms cost-effectively and safely (Can & Şimşek, 2016, p. 360).

The integration of virtual reality into education allows for the inclusion of environments or objects that would otherwise be impossible to bring into educational settings, thereby greatly enhancing accessibility. Today, a significant portion of studies demonstrate the impact of virtual reality-supported technology. While these technologies offer numerous advantages for educational activities, potential risks also need to be considered.

Virtual Reality

Virtual reality (VR) can be thought of as a headset that completely disconnects a person from the outside world. It is a computer-generated simulation of a three-dimensional environment that can be interacted with using specialized equipment, such as a headset with a screen or gloves equipped with sensors. Users are fully immersed in a virtual world, where they can look around and interact with their surroundings as if they were real. This technology is now being used in almost every field, including military, gaming, healthcare, education, and therapy. In education, VR is used to create immersive learning experiences, such as virtual school trips or reenactments of historical events. In healthcare, VR is used for exposure therapy for phobias and treatments for conditions like post-traumatic stress disorder. As virtual reality technology continues to evolve, it is becoming a promising tool for various industries.

Potential Risks of Using VR Technology

The use of VR technology in education provides many advantages to students and teachers, but it also has disadvantages. The most important of these are:

Cost: Purchasing and installing VR Technology tools can create huge costs for students and schools. Maintenance and repair of these devices can also be costly.
Addiction: If students get used to VR technology, they may find it difficult to learn in environments without these tools. Students can become so addicted to these technologies that it can affect their social lives. Studies in the field show that technology has the risk of becoming addictive. Kumari (2023) states in his study that electronic devices have effects on the lifestyle of secondary school

students, including their effects on mental and physical health. Research by Endert (2021) has focused on the addictive use of digital devices, especially smartphones, tablets, and laptops, in young children. In this study, the relationships between the addictive use of digital devices, the duration of use declared by the person, delay reduction, self-control, and academic achievement in children between the ages of 10 and 13 were investigated.

Security and Privacy: Technological educational tools can also pose security and privacy risks to students and schools. Students may make unconscious use of the security and confidentiality of technological educational tools and therefore their personal information or school information may be stolen. Schools and teachers may have to take measures to protect the security and confidentiality of information provided to students. Azaabi (2022) investigated the digital security and privacy culture among students and emphasized that students should have security awareness.

Excessive Gamification: Studies in the field often mention the positive aspects of gamification. Özgür, Çuhadar and Akgün (2018) stated in their study that gamification increases motivation. However, excessive gamification can make students forget the importance and seriousness of real-world applications. At the same time, it can make students adopt the idea of learning while playing games and therefore negatively affect the learning process.

Current Eclipse Cost: It is emphasized that when the area is scanned, it will contribute positively in terms of cost in integrating VR technology into education (Simplicio, 2002). However, it should not be forgotten that the technology used is kept up-to-date. For example, schools have to pay for the purchase or rental of technological educational tools, and they can allocate resources to this once, and allocating a certain amount of resources every year to keep it up to date can negatively affect the limited budget of institutions.

Environmental Impacts: The production and disposal of VR technology tools can have negative effects on the environment. In his study, Escobar (2020) mentions the damage to the environment caused by the batteries produced for mobile devices, which are widely used today, after the end of their service life. The production of technological training tools can create the need for energy and raw materials and lead to negative effects on the environment.

As a result, Virtual reality technology provides many benefits to students and schools. However, it also brings some disadvantages. Therefore, schools and teachers have to plan and manage the use of virtual reality technology correctly.

BACKGROUND

Academic research is significantly influenced by current technological developments. The advancement and integration of information and communication technologies into education have made learning environments more dynamic and adaptable, providing innovative learning settings. The existing literature highlights the advantages, challenges, and best practices of integrating technology into education. In their study, Arnesen et al. (2020) focused on subtopics that can be explored in-depth within educational technologies. Pulham and Graham (2018) presented a synthesis of reports and research related to K-12 blended teaching competencies and K-12 online teaching competencies in their review study. Similarly, Lo and Hew (2017) provided an overview of flipped classroom studies in K-12 education, analyzing fifteen journal publications in terms of flipped learning activities, student achievement, student attitudes, and challenges encountered. According to their findings, various pre-class and in-class activities, in addition to educational videos and small group activities, had a neutral or positive effect on student achievement compared to traditional classrooms.

When examining research related to mobile learning, it is defined as education conducted via devices that can fit in a pocket or bag, have a reliable connection, and can be carried out individually (Göksu & Atmaca, 2019). Communication through a portable device facilitates the creation of knowledge, allowing for the development of more productive students. Xie, Basham, Marino, and Rice (2018) comprehensively reviewed 47 studies conducted between 2007 and 2016. Their review focused on the effectiveness of these studies on teaching and learning, finding that mixed methods and experimental studies were the most popular methodologies. The results generally reflected positive views on the potential of mobile learning to support the needs of students with disabilities in inclusive environments.

The use of virtual reality (VR) in education is not a new development. A review of the literature reveals that the first use of virtual reality was in 1966, in the form of a flight simulation designed for training purposes by the United States Air Force (Page, 2000). Until the game was released by the company Virtuality in 1991, VR applications were primarily confined to the public sector (Kushner, 2014; West, 1995). In 1993, SEGA designed a head-mounted display (HMD) for virtual reality, and several game studios began producing software for it, although these games were never released (Horowitz, 2004). In July 1995, Nintendo released its VR-based gaming system, the Virtual Boy (Kushner, 2014). Although it was not commercially successful, it paved the way for the use of VR technology in various fields, from entertainment to gaming. The number of studies on the use of VR technology in education is increasing every day (Huang, Rauch, & Liaw, 2010; Johnson et al.,

1998). However, it is still too early to say that VR technology has been widely adopted or used.

Within the framework of virtual reality applications, Lave and Wenger (1991) introduced a new perspective on learning, attempting to relate the interaction of factors such as student, expert, community, knowledge level, and practical application in determining the characteristics of existing authentic activities. From this perspective, VR technology enables students to navigate within a simulated world, providing a highly powerful environment for understanding lessons (McGonigle & Eggers, 1998). Virtual reality, used in the creation of new content, guides students from novice to expert, encouraging them to engage in the exchange of ideas in practice and communication. At this point, the educational effects of technology and the environmental factors that facilitate effective learning should be emphasized. The student's capacity to understand involves (1) comprehending the world and events, using tools and themselves, and (2) segmenting routine tasks specific to the culture of society to build a rich knowledge base (McLellan, 1994). Authentic learning activities in virtual reality are influenced by societal values and created characteristics (Ellis, 1994). With these features, evolving technology has made it possible in some educational institutions in the United States for babies to perform walking and speaking exercises in a virtual environment (Hay, 1997).

One of the primary challenges faced by individuals with intellectual disabilities is acquiring daily living skills. One of the earliest studies in this area examined the effectiveness of a video-based simulation application on individuals' shopping skills. The findings from the study, which involved three students with moderate intellectual disabilities, indicated that the participants learned to use the application and acquired the skill to shop for designated items (snacks). In another study, Davies et al. (2003) evaluated the effectiveness of a simulation application in teaching nine adults with intellectual disabilities how to use an ATM. The findings showed significant positive differences in pre-test and post-test results, with a decrease in the number of assistances needed and errors made. Additionally, it was reported that participants were able to generalize the skills acquired in the simulation application to real ATMs. Brooks et al. (2002) aimed to teach students with intellectual disabilities how to prepare food, and in addition to the effective findings, they noted that the method was more efficient compared to traditional teaching methods, as it did not require the use of real materials.

In another study aimed at supporting the independence of individuals with intellectual disabilities, Groenewegen et al. (2008) developed a virtual reality application to teach students navigation skills between locations. The participants were required to go to appropriate locations (e.g., going to the kitchen to prepare food) in a virtual environment to complete the tasks given to them. The findings indicated that participants acquired the necessary skills quickly. Lee and Huang (2007) developed a virtual reality application to improve students' pedestrian skills on their way to school, and the findings showed that students acquired the skills in a computer environment and were able to generalize them into real traffic environments.

In a study conducted by Akbıyık (2020), the effectiveness of virtual reality technology in improving communication initiation and maintenance skills in students with autism spectrum disorder (ASD) was examined. The results of the study revealed that virtual reality applications were effective in enhancing communication initiation and maintenance skills in students with ASD, that the learning was permanent, and that the skills were generally transferred to different environments. Based on these results, it was argued that virtual reality technology could be a useful method for improving communication skills in individuals with ASD (p. 56). Another study in the field of communication skills training was conducted by Sağdıç (2019), and similar results were obtained. Going further back, similar studies can be found. Didehbani et al. (2016) examined the effectiveness of a virtual reality application developed for teaching skills in the field of social cognition and obtained similar positive results. When examining the results of this study, it was found that students with intellectual disabilities made significant gains in acquiring skills such as recognizing emotions, attention and reasoning, and social interpretation in the field of social development.

In simpler terms, virtual reality technology has predominantly been used to improve communication skills in the education of students with intellectual disabilities, and positive results have been achieved. There are numerous studies in the literature that support this outcome (Lahiri et al., 2015; Ke & Im, 2013; Trepagnier et al., 2010; Cheng, Chiang, Ye, & Cheng, 2010).

In light of all this information, it can be said that virtual reality, one of today's most important technologies, can be particularly useful in the education of individuals with intellectual disabilities and can assist teachers. In situations where the number of teachers is insufficient, especially in the education of students with intellectual disabilities, where one-on-one teaching is essential, virtual reality technology can provide significant benefits.

VR APPLICATION[1]

Currently, there are two main operating systems, and platforms available in the marketplace. The majority of the VR devices are running on Android operating systems or iOS systems. Therefore, in this study, we would rather utilize these platforms. Android platform is more suitable for free application development. The VR application is created on Unity, based on the C++ programming language. It is built on the Oculus Quest 2 Android operating system. The application features a main page where students can select their lessons. On this main page, all lesson titles are listed, but students must progress sequentially. A student can move on to the next lesson only after completing the first module; otherwise, all other modules remain locked. Figure 2 displays the main page of the application.

Figure 2. Main page of the VR application

Data Set

In teaching each concept, 48 different 3D objects are utilized. These selected objects are also used to teach opposite concepts. For example, the 3D objects used to teach the concept of "long" are also used to teach the concept of "short." Each concept is taught using 24 3D objects in the learning module and 24 different 3D objects in the test module. The first 16 3D objects consist of two different quantities but are the same object, of the same type, color, and size. The next 16 objects vary in quantity and color but remain the same object, type, and size. The final 16 3D objects differ in quantity, color, and size.

First Data Set Concept

The concept covers 8 different 3D images which are animals with the inclusion of the same object, same type, same color, and same size but different numbers

Figure 3. VR application teaching module

3D objects in the test module. The first 16 3D objects consist of two different quantities but are the same object, of the same type, color, and size. The next 16 objects vary in quantity and color but remain the same object, type, and size. The final 16 3D objects differ in quantity, color, and size.

Teaching Module

This module is where students receive their lessons. When the student launches the application, they encounter two different 3D objects. At first, the objects are stationary. The first object is then animated and enlarged to teach the student. During this process, audio and text are utilized. Then, the second 3D object is similarly presented to the student, and both objects return to their initial positions. At this point, a question is posed to the student, both verbally and in writing, and the student is asked to select the correct object using the VR controller. If the student does not make a selection within five seconds, the correct object is automatically highlighted to assist the student, providing a hint. This positive discrimination is intended to teach the correct choice to students with intellectual disabilities. The algorithm describing the functioning of the teaching module is shown in Figure 4.

Figure 4. Flowchart of teaching module

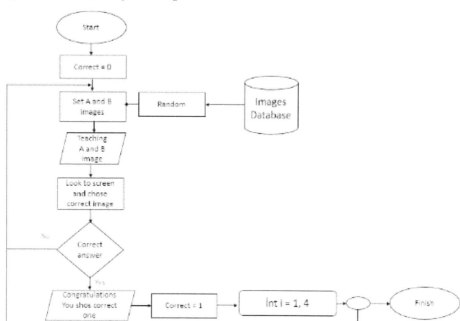

(Göksu, Karanfiller & Yurtkan, 2016)

As depicted in this figure, students must answer correctly to progress. If they fail to do so, the application repeatedly teaches the lesson until the student answers correctly. When the student provides the correct answer, the application rewards them with applause and confetti, a method used to capture the student's attention and motivation. Figure 5 shows the confetti effect displayed within the application upon selecting the correct answer.

Figure 5. Application display upon correct answer selection

Testing Module

This module is where students are assessed. After completing the teaching module, students proceed to the evaluation module. They are shown two different 3D objects, following the same concept as in the teaching module. At this stage, a question is posed to the student, both verbally and in writing, and the student is asked to select the correct object using the VR controller. If the student makes a selection, another question is posed, and this process continues until four questions are answered. If the student answers three out of the four questions correctly, they move on to the next stage. However, if they fail to answer three questions correctly, they must repeat the previous teaching module.

Figure 6. Flowchart of the testing module

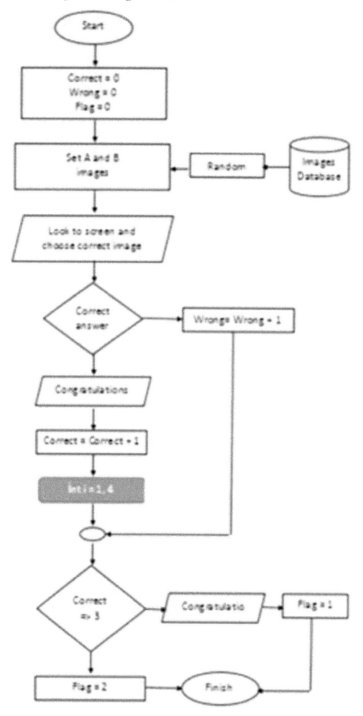

No hints are provided during the evaluation stage, as the purpose is to determine whether the student has truly learned the material. If the student remains inactive for more than five seconds, the application repeats the question.

SOLUTIONS AND RECOMMENDATIONS

Teaching conceptual skills, which are among the most fundamental abilities for individuals with intellectual disabilities to adapt to the real world and acquire a social environment, holds significant importance. In line with concept instruction, software (virtual reality application) has been developed, and sequential steps have been followed to teach specific concepts to students. This software will provide students with intellectual disabilities the opportunity to receive uninterrupted education on the concepts of "Less" and "More" during periods when they are away from school or when education has transitioned online due to pandemics, natural disasters, or similar circumstances.

Based on the results of this study, the following recommendations are provided for future research:

- This research is limited to students with mild intellectual disabilities. Therefore, future studies involving students with different levels of intellectual disabilities could contribute to the field.
- This research was developed to cover only the concepts. Future studies should focus on developing virtual reality applications that teach more concepts or are suitable for different topics in the education of individuals with intellectual disabilities. Conducting academic studies supported by these applications would contribute to the field.
- This research was conducted with individuals with mild intellectual disabilities. The subjects taught in the virtual reality application developed for this study are similar to those taught to students in normal preschool education. Therefore, the virtual reality application could be planned for use with preschool students in regular education.
- The effectiveness of this application, developed for individuals with mild intellectual disabilities, was measured using a between-subjects method. Future research could plan a study between concepts by adding different concepts alongside the "less" and "more" concepts within the application.
- A study focusing on determining how proficient teachers working in the field of special education and students receiving education in this field are in virtual reality technologies, and how improving their skills in this area, would contribute to the field.

CONCLUSION

The use of virtual reality applications in the education of students with intellectual disabilities is relatively new, but when examining the literature, it can be noted that this topic has been studied since the 1990s. Wissick, Lloyd, and Kinzie (1992) explored the effectiveness of video-based simulation in teaching shopping skills. The findings of the study, which involved three students with moderate intellectual disabilities, indicated that the participants learned to use the application and acquired the ability to shop for specific items (snacks). By the 2000s, we observed an increase in the use of virtual reality applications like their current usage, and these applications have increasingly supported the educational process, contributing positively to students' academic success. In a study conducted by Özdemir et al. (2019), research on special education was reviewed. The study concluded that interest in virtual reality applications in the field of special education has been evident since the 1990s, and applications in this area have been developed accordingly. Furthermore, it was found that these applications particularly provide opportunities for students with intellectual disabilities to access and experience environments that they may have difficulty accessing in the real world or may not have the chance to experience due to various reasons. Another finding is that virtual reality applications effectively support the education of students with intellectual disabilities, as one-on-one instruction is essential in this context. Specifically, these applications offer opportunities for students with mild intellectual disabilities to engage in independent learning under the supervision of a teacher within the classroom.

Throughout the study, several technical and physical issues were encountered. Both students and teachers were unfamiliar with this technology and had not spent sufficient time with virtual reality technology, leading to the need for technical support or expert assistance in solving these problems. The main technical challenges included the teacher's inability to solve emerging issues and guide the student, resulting in interruptions in the educational process until an experienced person in virtual reality technologies could intervene and resolve the problem (Göksu, Karanfiller, & Yurtkan, 2016). Additionally, when issues such as the school's internet infrastructure were considered, some teachers developed negative attitudes towards this new technology. In conclusion, it has been found that integrating virtual reality technology into the educational processes of students with intellectual disabilities, when developed per special education methodologies and supported by technological means, is significantly effective in the education of students with mild intellectual disabilities. Furthermore, when examining teachers' opinions on the use of this technology, a general sense of satisfaction and a positive attitude were identified.

REFERENCES

Akbıyık, M. (2020). *Otizm spektrum bozukluğu Olan Öğrencilere İletişim Başlatma-Sürdürerme Becerisinin Kazandırılmasında Sanal Gerçeklik Teknolojisinin Etkililiği. Yüksek Lisans Tezi*. Bolu Abant İzzet Baysal Üniversitesi Lisansüstü Eğitim Enstitüsü.

Arnesen, K., Walters, S., & Borup, J. (2020). Irrelevant, Overlooked, or Lost? Trends in 20 Years of Uncited and Low-cited K-12 Online Learning Articles. *Online Learning : the Official Journal of the Online Learning Consortium*, 24(2), 187–206. DOI: 10.24059/olj.v24i2.2080

Azaabi, C. (2022). Improving Digital Security and Privacy Of Students In Colleges Of Education: An Attitudinal Change Framework Based On Competence Learning Matrix. *European Journal of Education Studies*, 9(10). Advance online publication. DOI: 10.46827/ejes.v9i10.4501

Bilgiç, H. G., & Duman, D. ve Seferoğlu, S. S., (2011), Dijital yerlilerin özellikleri ve çevrim-içi ortamların tasarlanmasındaki etkileri, XIII. *Akademik Bilişim Konferansı (AB11) Bildirileri, İnönü Üniversitesi*, Malatya, s. 257-263. DOI: 10.46827/ejes.v9i10.4501

Brooks, B. M., Rose, F. D., Attree, E. A., & Elliot-Square, A. (2002). An evaluation of the efficacy of training people with learning disabilities in a virtual environment. *Disability and Rehabilitation*, 24(11-12), 622–626. DOI: 10.1080/09638280110111397 PMID: 12182802

Can, T., & Şimşek, İ. (2016). Eğitimde Yeni Teknolojiler: Sanal Gerçeklik. [Ankara: Ayrıntı Yayınları.]. *Eğitim Teknolojileri Okumaları*, 2016, 351–362.

Davies, D. K., & Stock, S. E., ve Wehmeyer, M. L. (2003). Application of computer simulation to teach ATM access to individuals with intellectual disabilities. *Education and Training in Developmental Disabilities*, 38(4), 451–456.

Didehbani, N., Allen, T., Kandalaft, M., Krawczyk, D., & Chapman, S. (2016). Virtual reality social cognition training for children with high-functioning autism. *Computers in Human Behavior*, 62, 703–711. DOI: 10.1016/j.chb.2016.04.033

Ellis, S. (1994, January). What are Virtual Environments? *IEEE Computer Graphics and Applications*, 14(1), 17–21. DOI: 10.1109/38.250914 PMID: 7757252

Eryılmaz, S. (2021). Compare Teachers and Students Attitudes According to Mobile Educational Applications. *The Turkish Online Journal of Educational Technology*, 20(1), 19–24.

Escobar, N. R. E. (2019). Las baterías como residuos tecnológicos contaminantes: Un reto de la educación ambiental. *ESPIRAL*, 9(1), 71–85. DOI: 10.15332/erdi.v9i1.2442

Gao, F. (2023). Research on VR equipment based on VR technology. *Journal of Innovation and Development*, 2(2), 44–47. DOI: 10.54097/jid.v2i2.5910

Göksu, H., & Atmaca, S. (2019). Öğretmenlerin Ve Öğretmen Adaylarının Mobil Eğitim Uygulamalarına Yönelik Tutumları. *Folklor/Edebiyat, 25(97)*, 105-115. DOI: 10.54097/jid.v2i2.5910

Göksu, H., & Karanfiller, T., ve Yurtkan, K. (2016). The Application of Smart Devices in Teaching Students with Special Needs. *Online Submission*. DOI: 10.54097/jid.v2i2.5910

Groenewegen, S., Heinz, S., Fröhlich, B., & Huckauf, A. (2008). Virtual world interfaces for special needs education based on props on a board. *Computers & Graphics*, 32(5), 589–596. DOI: 10.1016/j.cag.2008.07.002

Horowitz, K. (2004). Sega VR: Great Idea or Wishful Thinking? Retrieved 19 May 2015, from:http://web.archive.org/web/20100114191355/http://sega-16.com/feature_page.php?id=5&title=Sega

Huang, H.-M., Rauch, U., & Liaw, S.-S. (2010). Investigating learners' attitudes toward virtual reality learning environments: Based on a constructivist approach. *Computers & Education*, 55(3), 1171–1182. DOI: 10.1016/j.compedu.2010.05.014

Ke, F., & Im, T. (2013). Virtual-reality-based social interaction training for children with high-functioning autism. *The Journal of Educational Research*, 106(6), 441–461. DOI: 10.1080/00220671.2013.832999

Kumari, Shilpi. (2023). "AA study of the impact of electronic devices on the lifestyle of secondary school students.: A study of the impact of electronic devices on the lifestyle of secondary school students." *International Journal Of Humanities, Engineering, Science, And Management* 4.1, 01-07. DOI: 10.1080/00220671.2013.832999

Kushner, D. (2014). Virtual reality's moment. *IEEE Spectrum*, 51(1), 34–37. DOI: 10.1109/MSPEC.2014.6701429

Lahiri, U., Bekele, E., Dohrmann, E., Warren, Z., & Sarkar, N. (2015). A physiologically informed virtual reality-based social communication system for individuals with autism. *Journal of Autism and Developmental Disorders*, 45(4), 919–931. DOI: 10.1007/s10803-014-2240-5 PMID: 25261247

Lave, J., & Wenger, E. (1991). *Situated Learning: Legitimate Peripheral Practice*. Cambridge University Press. DOI: 10.1017/CBO9780511815355

Lee, S. L. ve Huang, C. Y. (2007). The effects of 3-D graphics-based virtual reality on the pedestrianized skills of elementary students with intellectual disabilities. *Paper presented at the meeting of the 18th Asian Conference on Mental Retardation*, Taipei, Taiwan. Paper retrieved from http://www.jldd.jp/gtid/acmr_18/pdf/57.pdf

Lo, C. K., & Hew, K. F. (2017). A critical review of flipped classroom challenges in K-12 education: Possible solutions and recommendations for future research. *Research and Practice in Technology Enhanced Learning*, 12(1), 1–22. DOI: 10.1186/s41039-016-0044-2 PMID: 30613253

McGonigle, D., & Eggers, R. M. (1998). Stages of Virtuality: Instructor and Student. The Association for Educational Communication and Technology. *TechTrends*, 43(3), 23–26. DOI: 10.1007/BF02824051

McLellan, H. (1994). Why focus on Virtual Reality? *HperNEXUS*, 4, 2, 8-9. DOI: 10.1007/BF02824051

Meta, F. (2021), Five Years of VR: A look at the greatest moments from Oculus: https://about.fb.com/news/2021/03/five-years-of-vr-a-look-at-the-greatest-moments-fromoculus/, [Ziyaret tarihi: 09.11.2023].

Özdemir, O., Erbaş, D., & Yücesoy Özkan, Ş. (2019). Özel eğitimde sanal gerçeklik uygulamaları. *Ankara Üniversitesi Eğitim Bilimleri Fakültesi Özel Eğitim Dergisi*, 20(2), 395–420. DOI: 10.21565/ozelegitimdergisi.448322

Özgür, H., Çuhadar, C., & Akgün, F. (2018). Eğitimde oyunlaştırma araştırmalarında güncel eğilimler. *Kastamonu Eğitim Dergisi*, 26(5), 1479–1488.

Page, R. (2000). Brief history of flight simulation. *Proceedings of the SimTecT*, 2000, 1–11. 10.1.1.132.5428

Pulham, E., & Graham, C. R. (2018). Comparing K-12 online and blended teaching competencies: A literature review. *Distance Education*, 39(3), 411–432. DOI: 10.1080/01587919.2018.1476840

Simplicio, J. S. (2002). The Technology Hub: A Cost Effective And Educationally Sound Method For The Integration Of Technology Into Schools. *Education*, 122(4).

Tim, S. (2021, June 22). van, Endert. (2021). Addictive use of digital devices in young children: Associations with delay discounting, self-control and academic performance. *PLoS One*, 16(6), e0253058. Advance online publication. DOI: 10.1371/journal.pone.0253058

Trepagnier, C. Y., Olsen, D. E., Boteler, L., & Bell, C. A. (2011). Virtual conversation partner for adults with autism. *Cyberpsychology, Behavior, and Social Networking*, 14(1-2), 21–27. DOI: 10.1089/cyber.2009.0255 PMID: 21329439

West, N. (1995). NEXT Generation Issue #6 June 1995: AOU: coin-op houses unveil '95 line-up. Retrieved 19 May 2015, from https://archive.org/details/nextgen-issue-006#page/n23/mode/2up

Wissick, C. A., Lloyd, J. W., & Kinzie, M. B. (1992). The effects of community training using a videodisc-based simulation. *Journal of Special Education Technology*, 11(4), 207–222. DOI: 10.1177/016264349201100405

Xie, J., Basham, J. D., Marino, M. T., & Rice, M. F. (2018). Reviewing research on mobile learning in K–12 educational settings: Implications for students with disabilities. *Journal of Special Education Technology*, 33(1), 27–39. DOI: 10.1177/0162643417732292

ADDITIONAL READING

Karanfiller, T., Göksu, H., & Yurtkan, K. (2017). A Mobile Application Design for Students Who Need Special Education. *Education & Science/Egitim ve Bilim*, 42(192). Göksu, H., Karanfiller, T., & Eryılmaz, S., (2020). Zihinsel Yetersizliği Olan Bireylerde Temel Kavramların Öğretimi İçin Mobil Uygulama Tasarımı. *Eğitim Teknolojileri Okumaları 2020 (pp.723-735)*, Ankara: Pegem A Yayıncılık. Can, T., & Şimşek, İ., (2016). Eğitimde Yeni Teknolojiler: Sanal Gerçeklik. [Ankara: Ayrinti Yayinlari.]. *Eğitim Teknolojlierli Okumalari*, 2016, 351–362.

Özer, F. 2023, *A case study on the use of virtual reality application in primary school science course*, PhD Thesis, Istanbul University-Cerrahpasa, İstanbul. https://tez.yok.gov.tr

Parsons, S., Beardon, L., Neale, H. R., Reynard, G., Eastgate, R., Wilson, J. R., ... ve Hopkins, E. (2000, September). Development of social skills amongst adults with Asperger's Syndrome using virtual environments: The 'AS Interactive' project. In Proc. *The 3rd International Conference on Disability, Virtual Reality and Associated Technologies*, (pp. 23-25), Alghero, Sardinia, Italy.

Raskind, M., Smedley, T. M., & Higgins, K. (2005). Virtual technology: Bringing the world into the special education classroom. *Intervention in School and Clinic*, 41(2), 114–119. DOI: 10.1177/10534512050410020201

Smith, J. D. (2016). Inclusive education and the development of social skills in children with intellectual disabilities. *The Journal of Special Education*, 50(3), 157–169. DOI: 10.1177/0022466916659131

Wissick, C. A., Lloyd, J. W., & Kinzie, M. B. (1992). The effects of community training using a videodisc-based simulation. *Journal of Special Education Technology*, 11(4), 207–222. DOI: 10.1177/016264349201100405

KEY TERMS AND DEFINITIONS

3D Objects: Digitally created items rendered in three dimensions, used in virtual reality to provide interactive and immersive educational experiences.

Adaptive Learning: A teaching approach that customizes educational content to the individual learner's progress and needs, ensuring mastery of specific concepts.

Intellectual Disabilities: A developmental condition characterized by limitations in intellectual functioning and adaptive behavior, affecting social and practical skills.

Oculus Quest 2: A standalone virtual reality headset used to deliver immersive experiences, commonly employed in educational and recreational applications.

Sequential Learning: An instructional method where learners progress through concepts in a specific order, ensuring foundational understanding before advancing.

Special Education: Tailored educational practices designed to meet the unique needs of individuals with disabilities, promoting inclusion and skill development.

Teaching Module: A structured part of an educational application where lessons are delivered and reinforced through guided instruction and practice.

Testing Module: An assessment component in an educational application that evaluates learners' understanding of previously taught concepts without hints or guidance.

Unity Software: A versatile game development platform used for creating interactive applications, including virtual reality educational tools.

Virtual Reality (VR): A technology that simulates realistic environments and sensory experiences, allowing users to interact with a computer-generated world.

ENDNOTES

[1] VR Interventions for Students with Intellectual Disabilities: Innovative Approaches and Practical Applications.

Chapter 9
Exploring the Perspectives and Expectations of Special Educational Needs Coordinators on the Use of Special iApps for Children

Samiullah Paracha
Xi'an Jiaotong-Liverpool University, China

Lynne Hall
https://orcid.org/0000-0001-5090-1980
University of Sunderland, UK

Gillian Hagan-Green
University of Sunderland, UK

Derek Watson
https://orcid.org/0000-0002-1944-3544
University of Sunderland, UK

ABSTRACT

The digitalization of education has significantly transformed special education practices and the roles of Special Education Needs Coordinators (SENCOs). One

DOI: 10.4018/979-8-3693-8227-1.ch009

area of rapid growth is the use of learning applications for children with severe intellectual disabilities, with many apps promising both new ways to engage and educational benefits. Despite this potential, research examining the impact of these tools remains limited. This chapter addresses this gap by exploring SENCOs' perspectives and expectations regarding learning apps, specifically Special iApps, for children with severe intellectual disabilities. Through qualitative research methods and an inductive approach, the study investigates the overarching question: "What do SENCOs perceive and expect from learning apps designed for children with severe intellectual disabilities?" The findings shed light on SENCOs' views on the educational effectiveness of these apps and offer critical recommendations to support the integration of mobile technologies in teaching practices.

INTRODUCTION

The rise of digital learning amidst pandemic lockdowns has the potential to become one of education's great levelers (Crampton & Billett 2021). Digital learning has so much to offer for the 21st century's learners, but it is the educators and wider learning communities who hold the keys for driving that positive change. With society getting increasingly digitalized comes rising expectations of the school to educate children to be able to work in and contribute to the digitalized society. Several arguments about the effects of this development have been published (Holmgren 2021) stating that school is going through a change of epistemology (Lund & Aagaard 2020), a change that challenges the traditional ways of teaching and learning (Bates 2019). If the view on knowledge and the ways of teaching and learning are changed, it is not bold to argue that the conditions for identifying, and organizing teaching and learning for students experiencing difficulties are changing as well (Holmgren 2022).

Children with Severe Intellectual Disabilities (SID) have delayed play and learning skills development (Edyburn 2020; Godin, Freeman & Rigby 2017). Characteristics of intellectual disabilities include a significantly reduced ability to understand new or complex information, a reduced ability to learn new skills, and a reduced ability to cope independently (Wyeth, Summerville & Adkins 2014). The body of research claims that use of digital technologies can have positive outcomes in special education is broad and still growing (Holmgren 2021). Previous work (Laurie, Manches & Fletcher-Watson 2022; Hof et al., 2010) suggests that introducing new technologies to autistic children's play provides opportunity for spontaneous social interactions as they create a shared understanding, which then drops off once the toy becomes less novel. A number of these studies have looked at the use of iPads or tablet computers to promote literacy skills amongst children with SID. For instance, Waddington et al. (2014), found that children with SID learned to perform a three-step communication sequence using an iPad. King et al. (2014) evaluated the use of the iPad involving children with SID and their results showed that training with device was effective for this purpose. Lorah et al. (2014) had success training children with SID to use the iPads as a speech generating device for labelling. Ganz et al. (2013) found that children with SID preferred to use the learning app as compared to the traditional PECS. Likewise, Kemp et al., (2016) found that children with SID were better engaged through using iPad apps than with picture books. Vandermeer et al., (2012) who examined the use of social stories on the iPad to increase on-task behavior and attention have found that children with SID demonstrated interest in using the iPad and an increase in attention in their study. Similarly, Chmiliar (2017) documented improvements in learning outcomes for children with SID using iPads in several areas including shape and colour recognition, letter recognition, and tracing letters.

Although there is evidence in the literature regarding the use of learning apps by children with SID, a voice that has yet not been heard about the digitalization of the school is the Special Educational Needs Coordinators or SENCOs (Holmgren 2021). A SENCO is the schoolteacher who is responsible for assessing, planning and monitoring the progress of children with special educational needs (SEN) and disabilities (Moloney 2019). Empirical enquiry into teacher agency for inclusion has focused on a variety of teaching roles, including general education teachers, special education teachers, subject teachers and pre-service teachers (Lin, Grudnoff & Hill 2022; Miller et al., 2020; Mu et al., 2015; Qu, 2021). However, little attention has been paid to SENCOs regarding their agency for disability inclusive education despite extensive international interest in the nature and enactment of the SENCO role (Lin, Grudnoff & Hill 2022; Klang et al., 2017; Maher & Vickerman, 2018; Rosen-Webb, 2011). This gap is what present study aims to create knowledge about, using the overarching research question: *"what do SENCOs perceive and expect from learning apps designed for children with severe intellectual disabilities"?*

SENCOs take a leading role in identifying SEN, coordinating inclusive practice, applying for resources related to SEN, advising classroom teachers, and liaising with families and outside agencies (Lin, Grudnoff & Hill 2022; Rosen-Webb, 2011). This suggests the important role SENCO agency plays in performing their service coordination role of ensuring students with SEN gain access to quality inclusive education. Although critical to the task of facilitating inclusion for children with SID, SENCO agency for disability inclusive education appears to be an under-researched area (Lin, Grudnoff & Hill 2022). With the digitalization of school, the special education practice and the roles of SENCOs change (Holmgren 2022). The use of learning apps specially designed to support children with SID is expected to increase rapidly with many claiming not only new ways to play, but also to have educational benefits. However, there is a lack of research examining this transformation, a gap which this exploratory study opens up for new understanding through the use of Special iApps as an exemplar.

To underpin and inform our interviews with SENCOs, a systematic review was carried out via reputable databases, including Scopus, Education Source, Education Resources Information Center (ERIC), PsycINFO, and Web of Science from 1997 onwards. These databases were selected for this study, because they were preferred in the systematic review studies related to the topic. Inclusion criteria for the review was guided by the selected research question. Considered criteria (Snyder 2019) were commonly used e.g., year of publication, language of the article, type of article (e.g., conceptual, randomized controlled trail, etc.), and journal. Key terms such as Special Educational Need Coordinators, Learning Apps, Playful Digital Learning, Intellectual Disabilities, Autism, Learner Engagement and Multimedia Learning were searched in full-text English articles. Studies related to play-based learning, learning apps and intellectually disabled children were identified and uploaded to Zotero. Two review authors independently applied the eligibility criteria. Data extraction was done by one author and checked by a second. The methodological quality of included studies was assessed independently by other authors. After providing an overview of the study's purpose, scope, and significance, we now the literature review.

RELATED WORK

Special education is a term that describes an educational alternative that has been implemented to meet the needs of children who are exceptional in some way. It refers to individualized programs, curricula, and instruction designed to address the needs of students with disabilities (WGU 2020). The intent of special education is to enable individuals with special needs to reach their fullest potential. Technology in special education has rapidly evolved and become more accessible to many teachers, parents, and students over the past couple of decades. Special education technology can improve learning by helping students engage with the material in new and interesting ways. The infusion of technology into special education programs predates even the invention of the microcomputer (Jeff et al., 2003). For instance, the first electrical amplifying device for the hearing impaired was invented in 1900. Later, Pressey developed a teaching machine that used programmed instruction in 1926. In 1928 Radios were distributed to blind citizens by the American Foundation for the Blind. Talking Books for the Blind were produced on long- playing records in 1934. The Waldman Air Conduction Audiometer was developed to detect hearing impairments in 1935. The megascope was invented to project and magnify printed material in 1953. The laser cane was developed for use by the blind in 1966. In

1968, a device was invented for compressing speech to more than 320 words per minute without distortion.

MACS (Multisensory Authoring Communication System) was distributed in the 1980's as public domain software by Johns Hopkins University that enabled teachers to create custom software for students with disabilities (Blackhurst & Edyburn 2000). During this early stage of interest in technology as an educational innovation, the main thrust of research was dedicated to how available technologies could be used to address the individual needs of students. Software programs were designed primarily for use as tutorials, to encourage drill and practice, or as enrichment in the form of games and simulations. From the beginning, there was a differentiation in the use of technology, which depended heavily on the exceptionality for which it was used. For example, in the areas that deal with students with disabilities, technology was viewed primarily as assistive, concentrating on facilitating student ability to communicate and promoting academic success (Jeff et al., 2003). As technology began to advance in the late 1980s and early 1990s, researchers working in the field of learning disabilities began to investigate the power of graphics, and multimedia for learning. Multimedia–a combination of graphics, video, animations, pictures, and sound provides diverse learning instruction and has been used for years in the classroom (Jeff et al., 2003). Similarly, word prediction software provided the student with learning disabilities a tool to make the writing process more approachable. In addition, the use of speech recognition to build remedial skills demonstrated an increase in word recognition, speed, accuracy, and reading comprehension. There have been tremendous advancements since 2000 in technological tools such as virtual agents, AI, VR, AR and the infusion of computers for instruction with students who are of special needs. With the advent of AI, the professionals in the field are at a critical juncture to move forward with future advancements for instruction and learning for students who are deaf/hard of hearing.

Play is central to early child development (Godin, Freeman & Rigby 2017), contributing to the development of motor, cognitive, social and emotional skills (Healey & Mendelsohn 2019; Weisberg, Hirsh-Pasek & Golinkoff 2013). Playfulness is the essence of play (Bross et al., 2008) as it captures the quality of children's play beyond the performance of play skills; it refers to the child's disposition and attitude towards play (Godin, Freeman & Rigby 2017; Bundy 1997). Today's children play with smart mobile devices that incorporate technology to provide play, thus, introduced a new concept i.e. Playful Digital Learning (PDL) into early childhood education and care (Hargraves 2022; Edwards 2018). Recent research conceptualizes PDL in two main ways. The first of these attends to the theorization of digital play. Much of this work adopts variations of existing play scholarship and applies these to observations of children's play with technologies (Marsh et al., 2016; Bird & Edwards 2015; Fleer 2014; Verenikina & Kervin 2011; Johnson & Christie 2009).

The second direction focuses on understanding the relationship between children's traditional play activities and their engagement with digital technologies (Edwards 2015; O'Mara & Laidlaw 2011; Marsh 2010).

A key reason for the popularity of smart mobile devices among children is related to technological features of these devices (Papadakis, Kalogiannakis & Zaranis 2016). Large screen displays, high resolution, lightweight, user-friendly and ergonomic design, short start-up time, multimedia content viewing ability, are just to name a few. Furthermore, smart device mobility and ease allow children to learn in a variety of settings instead of the traditional desk and chair (Ellingson 2016). Those features permit children the flexibility of laying the tablet in their lap, on the floor or moving with it to any area within their home (Papadakis & Kalogiannakis 2017; Wood et al., 2016). A mobile application or popularly known as 'app' is a computer program designed to run on mobile devices such as smartphones and tablet computers (Yusop & Razak, 2013; Bouck et al., 2016). Goodwin & Highfield (2012) distinguishes apps into three different categories (see Table 1).

Table 1. The 3-categories of apps (Goodwin & Highfield 2012)

Category	Example	Description
Constructive apps	Trello Evernote Forest	Characterized by an open-ended design that allows users to create their own content or digital artefact using the app e.g. cupcakes, robots, painting etc.
Instructive apps	Hangman Bingo Hot potato	Characterized by 'drill-and-practice' design whereby the app delivers a 'task' which elicits a homogenous response from the user e.g., game apps.
Manipulable apps	Toontastic Math Bingo Quizlet	Allow for guided discovery and experimentation within a predetermined context or framework e.g., apps for mathematics.

Research (Hirsh-Pasek et al., 2015; Papadakis & Kalogiannakis 2017) suggests that children learn best when they are cognitively active and engaged, when learning experiences are meaningful and socially interactive, and when learning is guided by a specific goal (Figure 1). Additionally, children progress quickly from novice to mastery when using a well-designed app (Cohen, Hadley & Frank 2011).

Figure 1. The 4-pillars of learning app

Children with SID have specific learning needs and requirements additional to mainstream learners (Paracha et al., 2023). Aspiranti, Larwin & Schade (2020) opine that educators should consider investing in tablets to use for students with autism as tablet interventions produce significantly higher scores than either traditional or computer-based instructions. Likewise, Sharma et al., (2022) have observed that tablet interventions improve children attention spans. Besides, learning apps provide opportunities for assessing learner progress with explicit feedback. Relevant learning apps for this population include picture-supported text, visual schedules, social skills training, video modeling and prompting, communication boards, and augmentative and alternative communication, audio books, alternative access, wearable AT, wayfinding etc. Some examples include Lola (Gupta 2020) which is web-based platform that works as a messaging and task management tool for special education students. ActivateTM (Bikic et al., 2015) is another example of a web-based platform that combines computer and physical exercises to develop the cognitive skills necessary to learn in the classroom and improve math and reading achievement. Similarly, Google Book (Keen, Webster & Ridley 2016) supports teachers in writing and teaching 'Common Core-based Individual Education Plans'. Likewise, MyChoicepad (Coulson & Doukas 2016), Brain Power (Charlton 2018) and Helpicto (Pertus, 2017) have shown significant progress in the areas of comprehension, attention and autonomy (Pertus, 2017).

Sports-based applications have also been developed, such as the work of Kartiko et al., (2020). Paulino et al., (2016) presents a music application for people with intellectual disabilities called "Piano Teacher." To validate the approach of the application, they evaluated the use of the application by a group of people with intellectual disabilities, without much user experience with mobile technologies, to measure effectiveness, efficiency, and satisfaction. An evaluation of the current state and characteristics of mobile applications was also carried out under this paradigm (Llerena Sarcco, Diaz Zegarra & Sulla-Torres 2023). Barta et al., (2017) created an Android-based app that helps children ages 6-9 living with autism spectrum disorder learn everyday tasks and acquire daily routines. The application consists of two parts: the first is an application of classic daily routines based on an agenda to be carried out; The second part of the application is for the practice of tasks to be carried out by the child. Cuascota et al., (2019) indicates the importance of assistant applications for people with intellectual disabilities in their social inclusion. They developed a tool for Android smartphones designed to help people with cognitive disabilities in tasks for their social inclusion using Beacon technology to locate the user's position and evaluate their functioning within an educational center. The result of the evaluation was that the application called Tk-Helper managed to reduce the time, errors, help and assistance in the tasks of a specific activity carried out by each user (Llerena Sarcco, Diaz Zegarra & Sulla-Torres 2023). Similarly, Lancioni et al., (2017) evaluated a smartphone-based program to promote independent leisure and communication engagement in participants with visual impairment and mild intellectual disability. Masruroh et al., (2014) described the effectiveness of the educational games Marbel Huruf and Belajar Membaca in helping children with ID in early-stage reading. This study is limited to reading only due to the complexity of this skill. The result showed the subject's enthusiasm through the learning activities, high motivation, and increased ability, although it has not yet reached an optimal stage. The interaction and participation of the family were also necessary.

Having explored the related work, we discuss the theoretical underpinnings in the next section.

THEORETICAL UNDERPINNINGS

The literature on the teaching theory, method, or technique used in special education are mainly influenced by the behaviorist and constructivist approach. The behaviorist approach pioneered by the ecole Ivan Pavlov (Özer Şanal & Erdem 2023) which reflects a positivist worldview that focuses on how people behave (right or wrong). In this approach, the emphasis is on observable behaviors. If something is visible, it can be evaluated, measured, and controlled (Picciano, 2021). Although behaviorism is criticized for general education, it is an approach that is defended as a practical approach to special education practices (Özer Şanal & Erdem 2023). The constructivist approach, on the other hand, is a philosophy of the subject and is concerned with how people make their own world, perceptions, interpretations, activities, and actions (Erdem, 2019). Constructivism focuses on the construction of knowledge, that is, while the learning process takes place and what the procedures mean for students and teachers (Akban & Beard, 2016).

Edyburn (2001) highlighted 12 models that have impacted the special education technology knowledge base (see Table 2).

Table 2. Special education technology models and frameworks

Model Name	Description	Reference
The SETT Framework	designed to aid the process of gathering, organizing, and analyzing data to inform collaborative problem solving and decision-making regarding assistive technology and appropriate educational programming for students with disabilities	Zabala, J. (2002). Get SETT for successful inclusion and transition. Available at http://www.ldonline.org/ld_indepth/technology/zabalaSETT1.html Zabala, J. (1995). The SETT Framework: Critical areas to consider when making informed assistive technology decisions. Available at http://www.joyzabala.Com.
Education Tech Points	Education Tech Points was created to facilitate decision-making regarding the utilization of assistive technology services and resources when planning educational programs for students with disabilities. The six key points are (1) referral, (2) evaluation, (3) extended assessment, (4) plan development, (5) implementation, and (6) periodic review.	Bowser, G., Reed, P.R. (1995). Education TECH Points for assistive technology planning. Journal of Special Education Technology, 12(4), 325-338. Education Tech Points. (2002). Available at: http://www.edtechpoints.org/
Chamber's Model	It is a flowchart of the consideration process that illustrates key questions and decisions that must be made when considering assistive technology.	Chambers, A.C. (1997). Has technology been consid- ered? A guide for IEP teams. Reston, VA: CASE/TAM.

continued on following page

Table 2. Continued

Model Name	Description	Reference
The AT CoPlanner Model	A groupware product that supports communication, collabora- tion, and co-planning. Additional content modules (i.e., Instruction CoPlanner, Transition CoPlanner, and Assistive Technology CoPlanner) provide electronic worksheets and planning systems that support specific applications of collaborative planning.	Haines, L., & Sanche, B. (2000). Assessment models and software support for assistive technology teams, Diagnostique, 25(3), 291-306.
The ABC Model	Technology benefits could be understood by noting that technology can Augment abilities and Bypass or Compensate for disabilities.	Lewis, R. B. (1993). Special education technology: Classroom applications. Pacific Grove, CA: Brooks/Cole, p. 7.
HATT Model	It involve the human, a person with a disability who controls a number of intrinsic enablers (sensors, central processing, and effectors or motor) as well as skills and abilities; activity (performance in areas such as self-care, work/school, leisure/play); Assistive technology (extrinsic enablers such as human/technology interface, processor, environmental interface, and activity output); and the Context (such factors as setting, social contexts, cultural context, and physical).	Cook, A.M., & Hussey, S.M. (2002). Assistive technol- ogy: Principles and practices (2nd ed.). St. Louis, MO: Mosby, pp. 34-53.
Wile's Model of Human Performance Technology	suggests that performance can be affected by seven variables: (1) organizational systems, (2) incentives, (3) cognitive support, (4) tools, (5) physical environment, (6) skills/knowledge, and (7) inherent ability. This model helps us understand that technol- ogy is not a simple panacea for remediating performance problems.	Edyburn, D.L. (2000). Assistive technology and students with mild disabilities. Focus on Exceptional Chil- dren, 32(9), 1-24. Wile, D. (1996). Why doers do. Performance and Instruction, 35(2), 30-35.
King's Adaptation of Baker's Basic Ergonomic Equation (BBEE)	key factors associated with the successful use, or not, of assistive technology include: the motivation of the assistive technology user to pursue and complete a given task (M), the physical effort (P), the cognitive effort (C), the linguistic effort (L) and the time load (T).	King, T.W. (1999). Assistive technology: Essential human factors. Boston: Allyn & Bacon, pp. 67-86.

continued on following page

Table 2. Continued

Model Name	Description	Reference
Stages	Stages is a theoretical framework which serves to organize resources and assessment materials for documenting student growth and development and its implications for technology use.	Pugliese, M.K. (2001). Stages: An alternative curricu- lum and assessment philosophy. Special Education Technology Practice, 3(4), 17-26.
Edyburn's Model of the Technology Integration Process	Edyburn's model of the integration process was developed to (a) describe the various tasks involved in integrating software into the curriculum, (b) provide a planning guide for individuals interested in technology integra- tion, (c) serve as a tool for discussing the process among the major stakeholders, and (d) assist in the identification of methods and resources for facili- tating the process.	Edyburn, D.L. (1998). A map of the technology integra- tion process. Closing the Gap, 16(6), pp. 1, 6, 40.
The Quality Indicators for Assistive Technology Services	A set of descriptors that can serve as over- arching guidelines for evaluating the quality of assistive technology services, regardless of service delivery model.	QIAT Consortium Leadership Team. (2000). Quality indicators for assistive technology services in school settings. Journal of Special Education Technology, 15(4), 25-36.
The A3 Model	A theoretical work that seeks to describe a developmental process associated with efforts to provide access for individuals with disabilities to facilities, programs, and information.	Schwanke, T. D., Smith, R. O., & Edyburn, D. L. (2001, June 22-26, 2001). A3 Model Diagram Developed As Accessibility And Universal Design Instructional Tool. RESNA 2001 Annual Conference Proceedings, 21, RESNA Press, 205-207.

Engagement theory (Kearsley & Shneiderman, 1998) served as the conceptual framework for the study that holds if students are involved and enmeshed intellectually, socially, and behaviorally leads to enhanced learning. According to O'Brien & Toms (2008), *"engagement is a quality of user experiences with technology that is characterized by challenge, aesthetic and sensory appeal, feedback, novelty, interactivity, perceived control and time, awareness, motivation, interest, and affect"*. The core principle of engagement theory talks about students being meaningfully engaged in learning activities through interaction with others and worthwhile tasks (Malik 2021). It is a framework for technology-based teaching and learning processes. Kearsley & Schneiderman (1998) believe that technology can be used to facilitate engagement in ways that might be difficult to achieve otherwise. Its fundamental underlying idea is that students must be meaningfully engaged in learning activities through interaction with others and worthwhile tasks. While in principle, such engagement could occur without the use of technology, Kearsley & Schneiderman (1998) believe that technology can facilitate engagement in ways which are difficult to achieve otherwise. This theory promotes working collaboratively, project-based learning, and having an authentic focus.

Engaged learning happens when active cognitive processes such as problem-solving, decision making, and evaluating are involved. The end goal of applying engagement theory to the teaching-learning process is to develop an intrinsic motivation in students to be better learners. Knowledge is no longer limited to books and classrooms. Education technology has developed massively, and student engagement in classrooms is now a significant focus of educators and students. Several factors, including economic, geographic, and social aspects, have led to the decline of student engagement. However, the growth of education technology has helped us understand the importance of student engagement in classrooms. The three principles relate, create and donate focus on developing meaningful situations, requiring students to use their cognitive processes involving problem-solving, decision making, and evaluating. *Relate* emphasizes teamwork (communication, management, planning, social skills). Similarly, *Create* emphasizes creativity and purpose. Students have to define (or at least identify in terms of a problem domain) and execute a project in context. Likewise, *Donate* stresses usefulness of the outcome (ideally each project has an outside "customer" that the project is being conducted for). The end goal of each of these three principles is to develop intrinsic motivation in the learner's mind (Malik 2021).

The related principle deals with making students trade points of view with their peers and relating with what they give and receive. This can be achieved through active and meaningful collaboration between students. Interactive tutorials can play a significant role in this approach. Educators should involve students in activities that emphasize team efforts, communication, management planning, and social skills. In an ideal situation, students would hear, see and relate to how their peers approach the topic at hand and what they take from it. Special iApps feature easy-to-use and intuitive tools and interfaces to help students present their ideas more expressively and helps them defend their views better. To the listener, a tangible example or concept is more relatable than an example or concept which is not. This one-way technology can activate an intrinsic motivation in students' minds to be engaged in the learning process by making the whole procedure more relatable to them. According to Malik (2021), the creation principle is about approaching the learning process in a project-based manner. It requires educators to design activities that are both creative as well as purposeful. When a student approaches the learning process through an innovative project that involves them defining things in their way, organizing and creating something that helps them express what they understand, they can develop a sense of ownership of their learning. When a student feels responsible for their education, intrinsic motivation is created. Special iApps is such a tool that SENCOs and students in this process can use. Likewise, donation to an outside focus is essential for engagement theory-based learning. Donation involves understanding the requirements of a third party and catering to them (Malik 2021). Technology grants them access to people, groups, and organizations that would otherwise be inaccessible to them. Communication is made more accessible by the internet, delivery of solutions or products that are virtual. Understanding the requirement and its specifics is also made easy by the vast amount of knowledge that is easily available on the internet.

We use Activity Theory (Engeström, 1987; Vygotsky, 1978) to examine SENCOs within various systems of activity that orient subjects toward a goal or object, broadly characterized as mastery of teaching or pedagogical expertise. Activity theory begins with the notion of activity. An activity is seen as a system of human "doing" whereby a subject works on an object in order to obtain a desired outcome. In order to do this, the subject employs tools, which may be external (e.g. an axe, a computer) or internal (e.g. a plan). Engeström, (1987) developed an extended model of an activity, which adds another component, community ("those who share the same object"), and then adds rules to mediate between subject and community, and the division of labour to mediate between object and community. Activity theory recognises that each activity takes place in two planes: the external plane and the internal plane. The external plane represents the objective components of the action while the internal plane represents the subjective components of the action. Kaptelinin, (1996) defines the internal plane of actions as *"a concept developed in activity theory that refers to the human ability to perform manipulations with an internal representation of external objects before starting actions with these objects in reality."* Human creativity plays an important role in activity theory, that "human beings... are essentially creative beings" in "the creative, non-predictable character". Tikhomirov, (1999) analysed the importance of creative activity, contrasting it to routine activity, and notes the important shift brought about by computerization in the balance towards creative activity. He focused on problems and prospects of creativity and creative activity in conditions of rapid development and pervasive implementation of information technology in various spheres of human activity.

Tikhomirov, (1999) posits that the delegation of certain human functions to computers presents the theory of activity with new problems. What is the nature of the activity performed by humans in the context of advanced computerization? How does human activity change when humans use computers? Computer science constantly uses the notions of routine and creative. Focusing on creativity reveals a large gap between psychological studies of activity and psychological studies of creativity. Theories of activity and theories of creativity have developed as separate domains of inquiry. It offers a developmental view of the ways that conceptual frameworks and technologies, practical actions in the world, individuals, and social institutions shape and are shaped by one another in the learning process Wiske &

Spicer (2010). This makes it particularly suitable for analyzing the roles of the SENCOs and networked technologies. Furthermore, the study also has a relational perspective on education (Holmgren 2021), where a human is understood by its relations to the context (von Wright, 2002; Persson, 2008). With this view, analyses of both the education (e.g. pedagogy, instructions, individual adaptions etc.) and the physical learning environment (e.g. classroom settings, teaching materials, audio-visual conditions etc.) are important for understanding how and why special needs occur (Nilholm, 2007).

Having discussed the underlying conceptual theories, models and frameworks that support the use of technology-based educational tools, we now describe our Special iApps in the next section.

SPECIAL iAPPS

Special iApps is a non-profit social enterprise, developing learning apps for children with special educational needs (Paracha et al., 2023), including autism, Down syndrome, cerebral palsy, hearing impairment and other learning disabilities. These apps are specially designed to provide support to children with special educational needs, fostering language and communication development. Special iApps are used by schools, parents, health care professionals and therapists in more than 100 countries with 28 different languages supported. With Special iApps, users can effortlessly create personalised learning resources in minutes, making it easier for children to access the educational tools they need. The technology they create helps children learn at their own pace, its designed to build their confidence and independence. Their flagship apps 'Special Stories' and 'Special Words' focus on, not only developing skills for literacy and vocabulary, but they also allow children to build their fine motor skills and short-term memory. To help children, families and the support team around them, Special iApps have introduced Special Words Plus that promotes speech, language and communication through word-picture card and sound matching activities. It also includes matching pictures, written and real human voices, in 28 languages (see Figure 2).

Figure 2. Special words plus

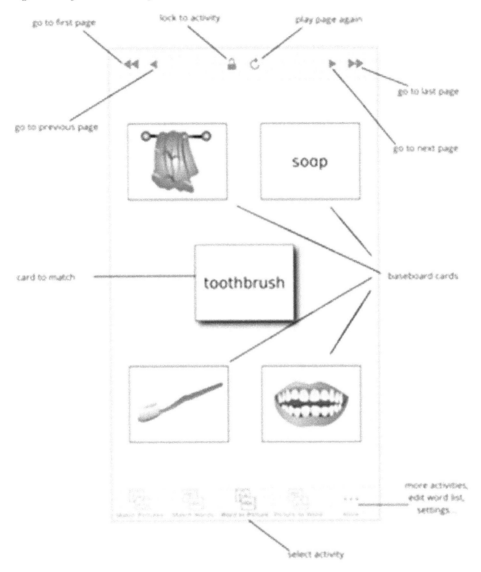

Special Stories Plus allows us to create personalized social stories (see Figure 3). These apps can be used to teach and assess recognition of written and spoken words, to encourage speech and communication. They are also helpful in improving fine motor control, hand-eye coordination and attention skills. The app includes six activities: Match Pictures, Match Words, Word to Picture, Picture to Word, Sound to Picture and Sound to Word, offering alternative setup options for teachers and parents. Teachers or parents can personalize resources by adding their own words, pictures and audio, reordering and deleting words, and they can be easily synchronized to other devices. Match & Find is an interactive game to help develop memory, matching, searching, and sequencing skills. Six different activities are included, with their own settings so the app facilitator can adjust the level to suit the learner's ability. Teachers and therapists can use this app to help develop and/or test audio or visible memory by adjusting presets. Similarly, Special Numbers contains a set of activities to help develop early number skills, including counting, matching, ordering, comparing and selecting. This app has been designed in collaboration with parents, children, teachers and educational psychologists, and with reference to research into how children acquire mathematics skills.

The next section presents the step-by-step approach taken in this study vis-à-vis collection and analysis of data.

Figure 3. Special stories plus

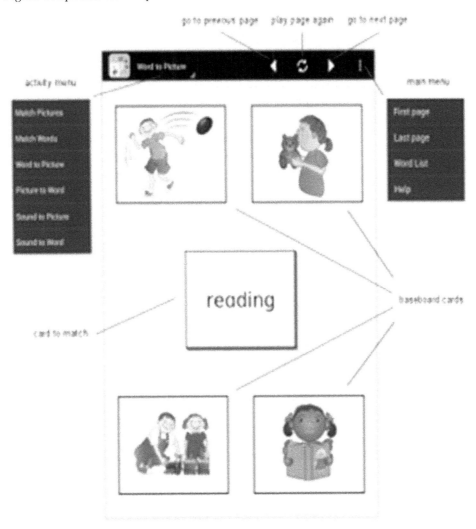

METHODOLOGY

The research question: *"what do SENCOs perceive and expect from learning apps designed for children with severe intellectual disabilities?"* was explored using a qualitative approach with an inductive perspective. The critical steps at this stage are described below:

Step I

Samples in qualitative research tend to be small (Vasileiou, Barnett & Thorpe 2018) in order to support the depth of case-oriented analysis that is fundamental to this mode of inquiry (Sandelowski 1996). Additionally, qualitative samples are purposive, that is, selected by virtue of their capacity to provide richly-textured information, relevant to the phenomenon under investigation. Cresswell (2007) suggests that semi- structured/in-depth interviews require a minimum sample size of between 5 and 25. Morse (2000) argues that the more useable data are collected from each person, the fewer participants are needed. A purposive sample of ten SENCOs, who were familiar with Special iApps, were identified, and invitation emails were sent to them. Of the ten, six of those invited responded positively and four declined due to pandemic and pressure of work (see Table 3). All interviewees opted for online interviews via Teams. The interviews lasted from 30-45 minutes and included a brief demonstration of the current version of the Special iApps products.

Table 3. Demographic details of SENCOs

Participants	Sex	Average Age	Ethnicity	Education	Location
6	3 male 3 female	30 years old	White	Graduate	North East England

Step II

Template Analysis (King & Brooks 2017) emphasizes the use of hierarchical coding and central to the technique is the development of a coding template, usually on the basis of a subset of the data, which is then applied to further data, and revised, refined and reapplied. The analysis began after all interviews were transcribed and uploaded to NVivo. The first step was to carefully read through the first set of responses and colour-code the data (using highlighters) for each participant. For example, if three participants shared that the students had difficulty using Special iApps, the researcher highlighted all similar statements with the same colour. The highlighted data were reviewed to ensure the research question is addressed. Unrelated data was set aside for later review and reconsideration. Sets of similar phrases were labelled to identify the patterns that emerged from the data. This step-by-step process was completed for each participant. Duplicate patterns were added to the categories and labelled novel statements as new patterns. Results of the pattern-development process yielded several themes discussed below. The themes were then reported with supporting patterns to elucidate the results. Although presented as a linear, step-by-step procedure, the research analysis was an iterative and reflexive process (Byrne 2022; Fereday & Muir-Cochrane 2006; King 2004). To maintain the overarching principle of "goodness" (Tobin & Begley 2004), this interactivity applied throughout the process of qualitative inquiry. In this study, the data collection and analysis processes were carried out simultaneously, and we reread the previous stages of the process before undertaking further analysis to ensure that the developing themes were grounded in the original data. Our objective for data collection was to represent the subjective viewpoint of SENCOs who shared their experiences and perceptions of Special iApps during interviews. Researchers coded data separately and then compared and combined their codes to evaluate their fit and usefulness. In the case of emerging different codes, the researchers, instead of dismissing the codes, scrutinized how differences among coders might generate new insights.

The following section reports the findings of our study based upon the information gathered as a result of the methodology we applied.

RESULTS

The research question: *"what do SENCOs perceive and expect from learning apps designed for children with severe intellectual disabilities?"* was explored using a qualitative approach with an inductive perspective. The interview data was collected using a semi-structured interview protocol and analysed through Template Analysis. The following broad themes emerged from the analysis, as discussed below:

Playfulness

SENCOs mentioned that *"children like Special iApps because they need something to play with, but they don't realize that they're learning even though they are." (KC)* *"They've got to be playful" (KF)*. However, some disagreed that merely the presence of animations and graphics does not add to anything if there is no meaningfulness in them. *"I think extraneous animations, sound effects, and tangential games might be appealing to kids when activated but do not add to their understanding of the primary content." (KR)*. Some suggested that teachers and parents should take the time to play and become familiar with apps to ensure that they suit their goals for learning with that particular age range of their children.

Fun

SENCOs opined that *"education should be fun anywhere! I think keeping these applications as fun and simple make learning enjoyable for children with severe intellectual disabilities. If something's falling in simple to them, they enjoy it." (KR)* Children like learning apps because they think they are entertaining and fun. SENCOs believed that fun is the major factor that attracts children to use learning apps: *"Yeah, they've got to be fun" (KF) "they want learning apps for fun. They'll sit and play with it all day long, but if it looks like it's hard work, they're just like not interested in that anymore. So definitely, fun is a major element for them, especially the ones who aren't working at the level that they should be at." (TJ)* SENCOs opined that digital play should involve some degree of agency, enabling children to take on an active role and ownership in their experiences: *"you know, the colorful images are fun for them if they're able to access them the way they want to manipulate those images and boxes around the screen at their own free will." (KC)* *"It's still good to use an app than a worksheet. It's still a novelty. I think that's one of the things they enjoy it. So, I think it's still fun." (MA)*

Engagement

SENCOs believed that engagement is key to learning and when a child is not engaged in a learning environment, the probability of child learning gets very low. Special iApps provide such affordances: *"I've seen children engaged (interacting with the Special iApps) and I think it's more child friendly." (KR)* The level of mental involvement for children increases when apps include symbolic systems that promote learning potential. SENCOs stated that Special iApps are engaging and quickly spark interest: *"The kids haven't got sick of it which is a good sign I think. They're still keen every time and even though there's that break in the middle, it's still a two hours' session." (MA)*

Interactivity & Accessibility

SENCOs expressed that the Special iApps are interactive and intuitive: *"children like learning apps, because they need something to interact independently." (KR)* *"the level of accessibility would be the only other thing really that would hinder the use of it." (KC)* *"allows to be accessible in so many more ways for children who struggle with mainstream ways of learning and in certain lessons." (MA),* *"Just watching her interact with apps. It was enough of an assessment to say, OK, she can't access this part and she's actually forming the sentence perfectly." (AA)* *"Definitely something quite being very interactive. Just thinking my two loved things that are interactive and like a sort of a story game type thing, that's what they're like." (KR). "It needs to be colorful and interactive, but it also needs to be able to be paired down to keep it simple." (TJ)*

Ease of Use

SENCOs indicated that children prefer simple and easy-to-use interfaces. *"Touch screen technology is useful as it allows children to move things around because again, for someone with a visually impaired child, it's hard to see the mouse, cursor on a screen and have to use the mouse to navigate around. So, touch screen is always used by our children as far as possible." (KC)* SENCOs also indicated that if an app is easy to set up for them, the easier it is for the children to use *"it's easier for the child because then we can set it. It's so easy to set up. It's then handed over. So, I think the easier it is for us, the easier it is for child." (MA) "It's got to be easy for me. So, I'm not spending 5 minutes with child sat next to me gotta go to that screen. Something that can be set up and ready to go as soon as I get into school." (KF) The touch screen technology is a lot easier for children as compared to moving a computer mouse for matching images and text." (TJ)*

Satisfaction

SENCOs emphasized that customization and personalization improve learner satisfaction: *"Special iApps makes things so much more accessible for so many different reasons. And I think constantly having the light background. If you got a vision impairment where you need that is really helpful, making font sizes larger, being able to change colour, backgrounds and font colors even." (KC)* SENCOs expressed that Special iApps are appealing because they are filled with curiosity, challenge, fantasy, and game play. *"I find children highly engaged if they're listening to something, watching something and actually participating in as well. So, there's a bit of everything in there. They like everything to be animated. They like it to be noisy, interactive, ready to poke around and figure something out." (KR)* SENCOs mentioned that tablets allow children to access a multitude of educational games, activities and more. *"So iPads are great! (AA)*

Personalized Learning

SENCOs pointed out that *"tailoring a lesson is for their wellbeing, especially for children actually feel like they've achieved something. I think Special iApps would actually work really well for them. And I think that would be nice for my students." (KR)* They also proposed some more options and choices that could be very useful e.g., animated introduction to letters, and more variety of vowels, numicon etc. *"That's the big thing, isn't it? That you've a variety of option to create lessons as you want in Special iApps and being able to change font sizes larger/small, colour, backgrounds and font colors even."* (KC) As curriculum aligned learning apps are difficult to find personalized learning options in Special iApps helps in tailoring a lesson in accordance with the curriculum. *"Obviously, we've got to teach to the curriculum. I think being able to tailor and app will be really good."* (KF)

Assessment

Tracking student progress over time is a daunting task for teachers, *"assessment is always hard, yeah. There's a traditional view of assessment, you know as well as digital, you know. It's all subjective on my part. It can't be objective."* (KF) *"Special iApps is a really valuable tool to put in with the other ways that we assess our children."* (AA) They wanted to link with curriculum and include Numicon: *"children really should be getting challenged a little bit more. So, I'm just thinking about your Special iApps as well as if you've got your tailored curriculum, you could be going in and checking to see what they're accessing and how they're getting on with it. And then obviously if they're not doing as much as they should be, you could be targeting them to do a little bit more."* (KR)

Active Problem-Solving

Our interviews with SENCOs indicated that Special iApps may be a useful resource for engaging children in active problem-solving activities e.g., *"Apps get their attention straight away. You know like you said William, he could work out what to do without being told which I think is a good skill to encourage."* (AA) Another teacher said: *"Problem Solving activities are perfect for kids on a rainy day, a long car ride, or a day off from school.* (KC)

Difficulty in Selecting Appropriate Apps

The choice of appropriate apps can be a difficult process for teachers and parents. SENCOs mentioned *"the reason is that little information on the quality of apps is available, beyond the star ratings published on retailers' web pages and reviewers' comments. Parents and educators do not know how the algorithms work but make decisions based on the projected number of downloads and ratings."* (MA) *"Often schools or parents choose an application if they find the activities enjoyable without worrying about the content of the apps."* (TJ)

Digital Divide

No participant mentioned that using digital apps was purposeless, however, they expressed the decision to use or not use these applications depended on the level of technological skills than on pedagogical knowledge in relation to SEN. For instance, *"on the wider school level, we've very limited influence on decisions about digital apps, and this causes obstacles for students in need of special support."* (MA) *"advising teachers how to use digital tools is something I do continuously, but I do not have that much knowledge nor received any professional training in it so, sometimes it is difficult to advise others."* (KC)

Evidence of Educational Claims

SENCOs also expressed that *"most of the top apps scored low, with free apps scoring even lower than their paid counterparts on some criteria."* (AA) *"Several top apps in the market have interactive yet repetitive game formats with content could not be extended by the learner. Such apps rely on low levels of thinking skills and often do little more than promote rote learning colours, numbers, shapes or letters."* (KF) However, as one teacher commented *"it would be hard to prove that educational apps didn't have a learning benefit, after all you can learn by playing with a toy.* (KR)

Summary of Key Results

SENCOs stated that Special iApps offer playful ways to engage children with SID in learning, without them even realizing it. For instance, Special Word Plus takes a fun playful approach to learning English language. They mentioned that the exercises in Special Word Plus are interactive and engaging and helping children learn new words and phrases. SENCOs accepted that the apps are purposeful and educational. The learning process happens in the form of quick quizzes that test children vocabulary and comprehension skills. Children with SID have difficulties staying engaged while learning, Special Stories Plus offers an active, enjoyable, and engaging context attuned to their educational needs. The apps encourage the child to be in control. They also mentioned that tailoring lessons to each individual student's needs is a challenging task. With the aid of technology, a lesson plan is no longer a bitter medicine, but a template with plenty of room for individual variations allowing children to find their own learning path. Some informants expressed that they were not influential in the school's decisions about the selection of apps which is an interesting finding of this study.

DISCUSSION

Overall, the results showed that SENCOs had positive beliefs regarding and experiences with using digital apps in special education. Still, not being involved and influential in the school's decisions about digital technology was something that the informants expressed raises the question of why digital tools are used infrequently in special education, causing obstacles for children in need of special support. SENCOs involvement in school decisions about which digital apps to invest in would be beneficial from a disability inclusive education perspective. With the digitalization of school, the special education practice and the roles of SENCOs change (Holmgren 2022). The strategic SENCO is at the heart of school improvement. Effective leadership for SEN means ensuring that all staff have the digital competence they need to provide high quality teaching and learning opportunities for children with SID. In relation to this, some participants expressed that they lacked digital competence. Although they all at some point have expressed positive experiences using digital apps, they also talked about lacking digital competence, highlighting a feeling of low professional confidence in this space. Thus, a question for future researchers to investigate is how these shortcomings can be addressed.

Children with SID enjoy and learn through play, just as typically developing children do. Supporting and developing the playfulness of these children is important given their deficits in social and play abilities (Bross et al., 2008). Playfulness is understood as a quality of a child's play involving flexibility and spontaneity rather than the child's skill in performing specific play activities (Hamm 2006). Playfulness can be determined within any transaction by the presence of four elements, namely, intrinsic motivation, internal control, the freedom to suspend reality and framing. SENCOs we spoke expressed that Special iApps encourage these four elements. The results also confirmed that play-based learning allows children to participate in purposeful activities additionally, the findings highlights simplicity, fun and playfulness as the most important determinants of a good learning app. In other words, simplicity and fun spark engagement and interest in children with SID to learn in a way most suited to their needs. Furthermore, the study supports the view that play should involve some degree of agency, enabling children to take on an active role and ownership in their playful learning journey.

The participants expressed that majority of the apps fail to keep their promises to support learning in a purposeful, effective, and enjoyable way. This study indicates that a bulk of apps being marketed to children as 'educational' have no or little educational value for children with SID. The choice of appropriate apps can be a difficult process for teachers and parents as very little information on the quality of apps is available, beyond the star ratings published on retailers' web pages and reviewers' comments. The findings also extend previous special education research

(Holmgren 2022; Lin, Grudnoff & Hill 2022; Olakanmi et al., 2020; Anderson & Putman 2019; Roberts-Yates & Silvera-Tawil 2019) adding new understandings about special education in a digitalized school, especially regarding digital playful learning and how they are expected to develop this practice not only for special education but also teachers at large in digitalized schools. The discussions with SENCOs confirmed the long-term effects of Special iApps. SENCOs noticed that Special iApps have positively influenced their children's disruptive behaviour. After play, they are not becoming aggressive or annoying doing things that should not be done. The study has shown that the skills and behaviors acquired through Special iApps tend to persist over time, with children maintaining and building upon their gains even after the interaction is over.

After describing, analysing, and interpreting our findings, we list some recommendations on what actions to take based on our findings and discussion in the following section.

RECOMMENDATIONS

- The results indicate if, and how, the SENCO profession is affected by school's increasing level of digitalization i.e., indicating new or changed competences needed for working in special education sector. Thus, highlighting the need of how higher education can adapt to train SENCOs capable of working in a digitalized school. The results are also of interest for school management and special teacher educators as important actors in the process of digitalizing schools and education.
- The study emphasizes the need for educational researchers, educators and software companies to find a common framework for consultation, given the growing demand for SENCOs to integrate mobile technologies and apps into their teaching to assist children in meaningful learning.
- There a significant need for interdisciplinary and intersectoral research exploring the educational claims and potential of learning apps for children with SID. Such research needs to be broad, covering a wide range of users, from experts as in this study others including stakeholders, policy makers, parents and children.
- Greater innovations in the learning apps sector require increased collaborations amongst the mobile apps sector, SENCOs, academia and researchers. The mobile app sector needs to consider the design and production of content creation in constructive apps, in order to capitalize on the unique functionality and capabilities of the tablets.

- Children with SID may face psychological distress in writing and reading comprehension and math. This can be addressed by standardizing training methods and system adaptations as per children needs.
- Keeping such applications fun-filled with graphics, animations, sounds and music, make learning more enjoyable for children with complex needs. To help visually impaired children, the future apps should increase the thickness of outlines and simplify the drawings, remove colors, make it more like Makaton symbols or simple thick black outlines for the images.
- A critical issue for children with SID is assessment. Integrating AI plug-in and eye-tracking technology offers an effective approach to supporting parents, carers and teachers in creating tailored learning experiences based on assessing children's comprehension, attention and autonomy when engaging in numeracy, literacy and social skills learning.
- In the realm of education, ethical practices are paramount for ensuring the well-being and development of students. However, when it comes to children with SID, though, the needs are more unique and not always straight forward. SENCOs must prioritize their ethical decisions in the best interests of all the students (inclusion) involved while treating each as individuals. Furthermore, the ethical use of technology in special education involves ensuring that digital tools are accessible and appropriate for each student's needs while respecting students' privacy and data security. Lastly, SENCOs must employ fairness strategies that address the personal needs of their students. This may include tailoring instruction, assessments and support services to each student. Aside from this, SENCOs must also be educated on the ethics and equity of differentiated instruction for some students and not others.

In the following section, we present the limitations of the study and set our priorities for the future.

LIMITATIONS AND FUTURE DIRECTIONS

Although the present study provides exploratory insights into the special education practice vis-à-vis PDL in a digitalized school environment, yet the findings have to be seen in light of some limitations: Firstly, the study was conducted during the COVID-19 pandemic, which means that results could look different before and after this period. Secondly, the small number of participants limits the results' generalizability. Lastly, the SENCOs all worked in school years K-6, so there still is a lack of in-depth knowledge about the practice in school years K-12. In addition, the SENCOs in this study were interested in integrating the iPad/ learning apps into the classroom. Others may not be as willing or as interested in investing the time, energy, or commitment implementation of learning apps require. One of the main dilemmas in the development process is to establish 'what to put in' and 'what to leave out', and what is necessary for learning and what could distract from the learning process. These are important considerations that have direct implications for those who create educational apps and for those who choose them for a specific educational purpose (Somerton 2022).

Given this, we suggest that future studies can add game-based approaches (Honorato et al., 2024) and technologies such as VR and AR. The use of technological advancements such as virtual agents, artificial intelligence, virtual reality, and augmented reality undoubtedly provides a comfortable environment that promotes constant learning for children with SID (Valencia et al., 2019). Closer collaboration between developers and educators in the design and development process could negate some of the difficulties associated with producing genuine educational apps. We suggest that future studies involve other professionals in observing children using learning apps approaches. Incorporating diverse professionals into studies and interventions can enhance understanding of children with SID's behaviour, thereby facilitating the development of effective approaches. We also suggest that future studies seek to go beyond conventional environments, proposing approaches that involve other types of environments. These studies and interventions can broaden the perspectives of children with SID, fostering greater engagement with their surroundings and potentially enhancing their social skills. As a result, more apps could be available that meet the educational needs of targeted populations or suitable across a range of contexts. This reinforces the importance of matching the user, the technology, and the activity (Edyburn, 2003; Odom et al., 2015; Somerton 2022) which are important considerations and can inform future research design.

CONCLUSION

This chapter has reported SENCOs' views and perspectives of learning apps. The findings reveal how SENCOs perceive the educational effectiveness of Special iApps. SENCOs stated that Special iApps offer playful ways to engage children with SID in learning, without them even realizing it. The apps encourage the child to be in control. They also mentioned that tailoring lessons to each individual student's needs is a challenging task. With the aid of technology, a lesson plan is no longer a bitter medicine, but a template with plenty of room for individual variations allowing children to find their own learning path. Still, not being involved and influential in the school's decisions about the selection of appropriate learning apps, and lack of digital competence were something that the SENCOs highlighted, raise the question of why digital tools are not commonly used in special education, causing obstacles for children in need of special support. Therefore, a question for future researchers to investigate is how these shortcomings can be addressed. Currently, in a world that is so connected and where technology innovatively mediates across most aspects of life, there remains a lack of novel learning apps for children with SID, with real opportunities available for playful learning using connectivity, the IoTs and voice-enabled interaction. To achieve this and to provide children with SID in new ways to play and learn demands increased collaboration between HCI researchers, teachers, technology corporates and innovators.

ACKNOWLEDGEMENTS

The study was supported by the Creative Fuse North East project <https://www.creativefusene.org.uk/> partially funded by the Arts and Humanities Research Council (AHRC), UK and European Regional Development Funds (ERDF).

REFERENCES

Akpan, J. P., & Beard, L. A. (2016). Using constructivist teaching strategies to enhance academic outcomes of students with special needs. *Universal Journal of Educational Research*, 4(2), 392–398. DOI: 10.13189/ujer.2016.040211

Anderson, S. E., & Putman, R. S. (2019). Special education teachers' experience, confidence, beliefs, and knowledge about integrating technology. *Journal of Special Education Technology*, 35(1), 37–50. DOI: 10.1177/0162643419836409

Aspiranti, K. B., Larwin, K. H., & Schade, B. P. (2020). iPads/tablets and students with autism: A meta-analysis of academic effects. *Assistive Technology*, 32(1), 23–30. DOI: 10.1080/10400435.2018.1463575 PMID: 29634456

Barta, E. A., Guzsvinecz, T., Sik Lanyi, C., & Szucs, V. (2017) Android-Based Daily Routine Organizing Application for Elementary School Students Living with ASD. In: Studies in Health Technology and Informatics. https://doi.org/DOI: 10.3233/978-1-61499-798-6-283

Bates, A. W. (2019). Teaching in a Digital Age – Second Edition. Vancouver, B.C.: Tony Bates Associates Ltd. Retrieved from https://pressbooks.bccampus.ca/teachinginadigitalagev2/

Bikic, A., Leckman, J. F., Lindschou, J., Christensen, T. Ø., & Dalsgaard, S. (2015). Cognitive computer training in children with attention deficit hyperactivity disorder (ADHD) versus no intervention: Study protocol for a randomized controlled trial. *Trials*, 16(1), 480. DOI: 10.1186/s13063-015-0975-8 PMID: 26499057

Bird, J., & Edwards, S. (2015). Children learning to use technologies through play: A Digital Play Framework. *British Journal of Educational Technology*, 46(6), 1149–1160. DOI: 10.1111/bjet.12191

Blackhurst, A. E., & Edyburn, D. L. (2000). A brief history of special education technology. *Special Education Technology Practice*, 2(1), 21–36.

Bouck, E. C., Satsangi, R., & Flanagan, S. (2016). Focus on inclusive education: evaluating apps for students with disabilities: supporting academic access and success. *Childhood Education*, 92(4), 324–328. DOI: 10.1080/00094056.2016.1208014

Bross, H., Ramugondo, E., Taylor, C., & Sinclair, C. (2008). Children need others: Triggers for playfulness in pre-schoolers with multiple disabilities living within an informal settlement. South African Journal of Occupational Therapy, 38(2), 3-7. Available at http://www.scielo.org.za/scielo.php?script=sci_arttext&pid=S2 310-38332008000200002&lng=en&tlng=en Bundy A. (1997). Play and playfulness. What to look for. In Parham LD, Fazio LS, editors. Play in Occupational Therapy for Children, USA: Mosby, 52-65.

Byrne, D. (2022). A worked example of Braun and Clarke's approach to reflexive thematic analysis. *Quality & Quantity*, 56(3), 1391–1412. DOI: 10.1007/s11135-021-01182-y

Charlton, E. (2018). This AI-powered app aims to help people with autism improve their social skills. World Economic Forum. < https://www.weforum.org/agenda/2018/11/ai-app-helps- autism-social-skills/>

Chmiliar, L. (2017). Improving Learning Outcomes: The iPad and Preschool Children with Disabilities. *Frontiers in Psychology*, 8, 660. DOI: 10.3389/fpsyg.2017.00660 PMID: 28529493

Cohen, M., Hadley, M., & Frank, M. (2011). *Young Children, Apps & iPad*. Michael Cohen Group.

Coulson, N., & Doukas, T. (2016). MyChoice Pad. Citizen Network. Retrieved May 06, 2024 from https://citizen- network.org/library/mychoice-pad.html

Crampton, E., & Billett, I. (2021). How can we better engage digital learning for SEN pupils? SEN. Available at: https://senmagazine.co.uk/content/tech/assistive-tech/14351/how-can-we-better-engage-digital-learning-for-sen-pupils/

Cresswell, J. (2007). *Qualitative Inquiry and Research Design: Choosing among five approaches*. Sage.

Cuascota, L., Guevara, L., Cueva, R., Tapia, F., & Guerrero, G. (2019). Assistance application of people with cognitive disabilities in tasks for their social inclusion. In: Iberian Conference on Information Systems and Technologies, CISTI (2019). https://doi.org/DOI: 10.23919/CISTI.2019.8760732

Edwards, S. (2015). New concepts of play and the problem of technology, digital media and popular-culture integration with play-based learning in early childhood education. *Technology, Pedagogy and Education*, 25(4), 513–532. DOI: 10.1080/1475939X.2015.1108929

Edyburn, D. (2001). Models, Theories, and Frameworks: Contributions to Understanding Special Education Technology. Special Education Technology Practice. 4. DOI: 10.1080/1475939X.2015.1108929

Edyburn, D. (2003). Measuring assistive technology outcomes: Key concepts. *Journal of Special Education Technology*, 18, 53–55. DOI: 10.1177/016264340301800107

Edyburn, D. L. (2020). Rapid literature review on assistive technology in education. Research Report Department for Education. University of Wisconsin-Milwaukee. https://assets.publishing.service.gov.uk/government/uploads/system/uploads/attachment_data/file/937381/UKAT_FinalReport_082520.pdf

Ellingson, K. (2016) Interactive Technology Use in Early Childhood Programs to Enhance Literacy Development & Early Literacy Development for Children with Cochlear Implants, Culminating Projects in Child and Family Studies, Paper 3. Available online at: https://repository.stcloudstate.edu/cfs_etds/3

Engestrom, Y. (1987). Learning by Expanding: An Activity Theoretical Approach to Developmental Research. Helsinki, Finland: Orienta-Konsultit. https://lchc.ucsd.edu/mca/Paper/Engestrom/Learning-by-Expanding.pdf

Erdem, M. (2019). *Yeniden Öğretmeyi Öğrenmek, Organizmadan Bireye Öğretim Süreçleri Tasarımı*. Pegem Akademi.

Fereday, J., & Muir-Cochrane, E. (2006). Demonstrating Rigor Using Thematic Analysis: A Hybrid Approach of Inductive and Deductive Coding and Theme Development. *International Journal of Qualitative Methods*, 5(1), 80–92. DOI: 10.1177/160940690600500107

Fleer, M. (2014). The demands and motives afforded through digital play in early childhood activity settings. *Learning, Culture and Social Interaction*, 3(3), 202–209. DOI: 10.1016/j.lcsi.2014.02.012

Ganz, J., Hong, E., & Goodwyn, F. (2013). Effectiveness of the PECS Phase III apps that the choice between the app and traditional PECS among preschoolers with ASD. *Research in Autism Spectrum Disorders*, 7(8), 973–983. DOI: 10.1016/j.rasd.2013.04.003

Godin, J., Freeman, A., & Rigby, P. (2017). Interventions to promote the playful engagement in social interaction of preschool-aged children with autism spectrum disorder (ASD): A scoping study. *Early Child Development and Care.* Advance online publication. DOI: 10.1080/03004430.2017.1404999

Goodwin, K., & Highfield, K. (2012). iTouch and iLearn: an examination of "educational" apps, Paper presented at the Early Education and Technology for Children Conference, 14– 16 March, Salt Lake City, Utah.

Gupta, P. (2020). A Comprehensive List of Edapps in Special Education. EdTechReview. Retrieved May 06, 2022 from https://edtechreview.in/trends-insights/insights/3924-a- comprehensive-list-of-ed-apps-in-special-education

Hamm, E. (2006). Playfulness and the environmental support of play in children with and without disabilities. *OTJR (Thorofare, N.J.), 26*(3), 88–96. DOI: 10.1177/153944920602600302

Hargraves, V. (2022). What is digital play? Digital technologies in ECE. The Education Hub. Published online Feb 1, 2022 https://theeducationhub.org.nz/what-is-digital-play/#_edn2

Healey, A., & Mendelsohn, A. (2019). Selecting appropriate toys for young children in the digital era. *Pediatrics, 143*(1), 1–10. DOI: 10.1542/peds.2018-3348 PMID: 30509931

Hirsh-Pasek, K., Zosh, J. M., Golinkoff, R. M., Gray, J. H., Robb, M. B., & Kaufman, J. (2015). Putting education in "educational" apps lessons from the science of learning. *Psychological Science in the Public Interest, 16*(1), 3–34. DOI: 10.1177/1529100615569721 PMID: 25985468

Hof, L., Pee, J., Sturm, J., Bekker, T., & Verbeek, J. (2010). Prolonged play with the ColorFlares: How does open-ended play behavior change over time? *Proceedings of the 3rd International Conference on Fun and Games,* 106. https://doi.org/DOI: 10.1145/1823818.1823829

Holmgren, M. (2021). The Inclusion of Special Education in School's Digitalization - a special educational perspective on the digitalization of schools. ECER 2021— European Educational Research Association. Available at: https://eera-ecer.de/ecer-programmes/conference/26/contribution/50694

Holmgren, M. (2022). Enacting Special Education in a Digitalized School: Opening for New Understandings of a Digitalized Special Educational Practice. *Journal of Special Education Technology,* 0(0). Advance online publication. DOI: 10.1177/01626434221131776

Honorato, N., Soltiyeva, A., Oliveira, W., Delabrida, S. E., Hamari, J., & Alimanova, M. (2024). Gameful strategies in the education of autistic children: A systematic literature review, scientometric analysis, and future research roadmap. *Smart Learn. Environ.*, 11(1), 25. DOI: 10.1186/s40561-024-00309-6

Jeffs, T., Morrison, W. F., Messenheimer, T., Rizza, M. G., & Banister, S. (2003). A Retrospective Analysis of Technological Advancements in Special Education. *Computers in the Schools*, 20(1–2), 129–152. DOI: 10.1300/J025v20n01_10

Johnson, J., & Christie, J. (2009). Play and digital media. Computers in the schools. *Interdisciplinary Journal of Practice, Theory, and Applied Research.*, 26(4), 284–289.

Kaptelinin, V. (1996). Activity Theory: Implications for Human Computer Interaction. In Nardi, B. (Ed.), *Context and Consciousness: Activity Theory and Human-Computer Interaction* (pp. 103–116). MIT Press.

Kartiko, D. C., Juniarisca, D. L., Tuasikal, A. R. S., Prakoso, B. B., & Nurhayati, F. (2020). Android - Based Sport Board Games for Intellectual Disabilities. Presented at the (2020). DOI: 10.2991/assehr.k.201201.191

Kearsley, G., & Shneiderman, B. (1998). Engagement theory: A framework for technology-based teaching and learning. Educational Technology, 38(5), 20-23. JSTOR. www.jstor.org/stable/44428478

Keen, D., Webster, A., & Ridley, G. (2016). How well are children with autism spectrum disorder doing academically at school? An overview of the literature. *Autism*, 20(3), 276–294. DOI: 10.1177/1362361315580962 PMID: 25948598

Kemp, C., Stephenson, J., Cooper, M., & Hodge, K. (2016). Engaging preschool children with severe and multiple disabilities using books and iPad apps. *Infants and Young Children*, 29(4), 249–266. DOI: 10.1097/IYC.0000000000000075

King, M., Takeguchi, K., Barry, S., Rehfeldt, R., Boyer, V., & Mathews, T. (2014). Evaluation of the iPad in the acquisition of requesting skills for children with autism spectrum disorder. *Research in Autism Spectrum Disorders*, 8(9), 1107–1120. DOI: 10.1016/j.rasd.2014.05.011

King, N. (2004). Using templates in the thematic analysis of text C. Cassell G. Symon Qualitative methods in organizational research: The definitive guide 256–270 London Sage.

King, N., & Brooks, J. (2017). *Doing Template Analysis: A Guide to the Main Components and Procedures*. SAGE Publications Ltd., DOI: 10.4135/9781473983304

Lancioni, G. E., Singh, N. N., O'Reilly, M. F., Sigafoos, J., Alberti, G., Perilli, V., Zimbaro, C., & Chiariello, V. (2017). Supporting leisure and communication in people with visual and intellectual disabilities via a smartphone-based program. *British Journal of Visual Impairment*, 35(3), 257–263. Advance online publication. DOI: 10.1177/0264619617715497

Laurie, M. H., Manches, A., & Fletcher-Watson, S. (2022).The role of robotic toys in shaping play and joint engagement in autistic children: Implications for future design, International Journal of Child-Computer Interaction, Volume 32, 100384, ISSN 2212-8689, https://doi.org/DOI: 10.1016/j.ijcci.2021.100384

Lin, H., Grudnoff, L., & Hill, M. (2022). Agency for Inclusion: A Case Study of Special Educational Needs Coordinators (SENCos). *International Journal of Disability Development and Education*. Advance online publication. DOI: 10.1080/1034912X.2022.2137110

Llerena Sarcco, P. A., Diaz Zegarra, P. F., & Sulla-Torres, J. A. (2023). Mobile App for the Learning of Children with Intellectual Disabilities. *CEUR Workshop Proceedings*, 3693, 130–140.

Lorah, E., Parnell, A., & Speight, D. (2014). Acquisition of sentence frame discrimination using the iPad as a speech generating device in young children with developmental disabilities. *Research in Autism Spectrum Disorders*, 8(12), 1734–1740. DOI: 10.1016/j.rasd.2014.09.004

Lund, A., & Aagaard, T.Lund & Aagaard. (2020). Digitalization of teacher education: Are we prepared for epistemic change? *NJCIE*, 4(3-4), 56–71. DOI: 10.7577/njcie.3751

Malik, C. (December 10, 2021). Engagement Theory of Learning An Overview. Self-CAD https://www.selfcad.com/blog/engagement-theory-of-learning-an-overview

Marsh, J. (2010). Young children's play in online virtual worlds. *Journal of Early Childhood Research*, 8(1), 23–39. DOI: 10.1177/1476718X09345406

Marsh, J., Plowman, L., Yamada-Rice, D., Bishop, J., & Scott, F. (2016). Digital play: A new classification. *Early Years Journal of International Research and Development*, 36(3), 242–253. DOI: 10.1080/09575146.2016.1167675

Masruroh, M., F.L., Hadiati, S.R., Budirahayu, T. (2014). Android Technology-Based Educative Games for Children with Intellectual Disability: A Case Study at Yayasan Peduli Kasih Anak Berkebutuhan Khusus. In: Proceedings of the 2014 International Conference on Advances in Education Technolog. https://doi.org/DOI: 10.2991/icaet-14.2014.25

Moloney, H. (2019). *'We must protect our SENCOs' time*. Early Years Educator., DOI: 10.12968/eyed.2019.20.11.8

Morse, J. M. (2000). Determining sample size. *Qualitative Health Research*, 10(1), 3–5. DOI: 10.1177/104973200129118183

Nilholm, C. (2007). *Perspektiv på specialpedagogik* [Perspectives on special education]. Studentlitteratur.

O'Brien, H. L., & Toms, E. (2008). What is user engagement? A conceptual framework for defining user engagement with technology. *Journal of the Association for Information Science and Technology*, 59, 938–955.

O'Mara, J., & Laidlaw, L. (2011). Living in the iworld: Two literacy researchers reflect on the changing texts and literacy practices of childhood. *English Teaching*, 10(4), 149–159.

Odom, S. L., Thompson, J. L., Hedges, S., Boyd, B. A., Dykstra, J. R., Duda, M. A., Szidon, K. L., Smith, L. E., & Bord, A. (2015). Technology-aided interventions and instruction for adolescents with autism spectrum disorder. *Journal of Autism and Developmental Disorders*, 45(12), 3805–3819. DOI: 10.1007/s10803-014-2320-6 PMID: 25468409

Olakanmi, O. A., Akcayir, G., Ishola, O. M., & Demmans Epp, C. (2020). Using technology in special education: Current practices and trends. *Educational Technology Research and Development*, 68(4), 1711–1738. DOI: 10.1007/s11423-020-09795-0

Özer Şanal, S., & Erdem, M. (2023). Examination of Special Education with Constructivism: A Theoretical and Review Study. *The European Educational Researcher*, 6(1), 1–20. DOI: 10.31757/euer.611

Papadakis, S., & Kalogiannakis, M. (2017). Mobile educational applications for children: What educators and parents need to know. *Int. J. Mob. Learn. Organisation*, 11(3), 256–277. DOI: 10.1504/IJMLO.2017.085338

Papadakis, S., Kalogiannakis, M., & Zaranis, N. (2016). Comparing tablets and PCs in teaching mathematics: An attempt to improve mathematics competence in early childhood education. *Preschool and Primary Education*, 4(2), 241. Advance online publication. DOI: 10.12681/ppej.8779

Paracha, S., Hagan-Green, G., Hall, L., & Macfarlane, K. (2023). Special iApps: Play-based Learning for Children with Severe Intellectual Disabilities. In *Proceedings of the 10th International Conference on Software Development and Technologies for Enhancing Accessibility and Fighting Info-exclusion (DSAI '22)*. Association for Computing Machinery, New York, USA, 100–106. https://doi.org/ DOI: 10.1145/3563137.3563163

Paulino, D., Amaral, D., Amaral, M., Reis, A., Barroso, J., & Rocha, T. (2016). "Professor piano": A music application for people with intellectual disabilities. In: ACM International Conference Proceeding Series. https://doi.org/DOI: 10.1145/3019943.3019982

Persson, B. (2008). *Elevers olikheter och specialpedagogisk kunskap* [Pupils diversities and special educational knowledge]. Liber.

Pertus, S. (2017). How Equadex used Cognitive Services to help people with language disorders. Technical Case Studies. https://microsoft.github.io/techcasestudies/cognitive%20servi ces/2017/08/04/equadexcognitives.html

Picciano, A. G. (2021). Theories and frameworks for online education: Seeking an integrated model. In *A Guide to Administering Distance Learning* (pp. 79–103). Brill., DOI: 10.1163/9789004471382_005

Roberts-Yates, C., & Silvera-Tawil, D. (2019). Better Education Opportunities for Students with Autism and Intellectual Disabilities through Digital Technology. *International Journal of Special Education*, 34(1), 197–210.

Rosen-Webb, S. M. (2011). Nobody tells you how to be a SENCo. *British Journal of Special Education*, 38(4), 159–168. DOI: 10.1111/j.1467-8578.2011.00524.x

Sandelowski, M. (1996). One is the liveliest number: The case orientation of qualitative research. *Research in Nursing & Health*, 19(6), 525–529. DOI: 10.1002/(SICI)1098-240X(199612)19:6<525::AID-NUR8>3.0.CO;2-Q PMID: 8948406

Sharma, S., Achary, K., Kinnula, M., Norouzi, B., Kinnula, H., Livari, N., Ventä-Olkkonen, L., & Holappa, J. (2022). To Empower or Provoke? Exploring approaches for participatory design at schools for neurodiverse individuals in India, International Journal of Child-Computer Interaction, Volume 34, 100521, ISSN 2212-8689, https://www.sciencedirect.com/science/article/pii/S2212868922000435DOI: 10.1016/j.ijcci.2022.100521

Somerton, M. (2022). Developing an educational app for students with autism. *Frontiers in Education*, 7, 998694. DOI: 10.3389/feduc.2022.998694

Tikhomirov, O. K. (1999). The theory of activity changed by information technology. In Y. Engeström, R. Miettinen, & R.-L. Punamäki (Eds.), Perspectives on Activity Theory (pp. 347–359). chapter, Cambridge: Cambridge University Press. DOI: 10.1017/CBO9780511812774.023

Tobin, G. A., & Begley, C. M. (2004). Methodological Rigour within a Qualitative Framework. *Journal of Advanced Nursing*, 48(4), 388–396. DOI: 10.1111/j.1365-2648.2004.03207.x PMID: 15500533

Valencia, K., Rusu, C., Quiñones, D., & Jamet, E. (2019). The Impact of Technology on People with Autism Spectrum Disorder: A Systematic Literature Review. *Sensors (Basel)*, 19(20), 4485. DOI: 10.3390/s19204485 PMID: 31623200

Vandermeer, J. M., Milford, T. M., Beamish, W., & Lang, W. T. (2012). "Using an iPad presented social story to increase on-task behaviors of a young child with autism," in *Proceedings of the 7th Biennial International Conference on Technology Education Research*, Surfers Paradise, QLD, 146–154.

Vasileiou, K., Barnett, J., Thorpe, S., & Young, T. (2018). Characterising and justifying sample size sufficiency in interview-based studies: Systematic analysis of qualitative health research over a 15-year period. *BMC Medical Research Methodology*, 18(1), 148. DOI: 10.1186/s12874-018-0594-7 PMID: 30463515

Verenikina, I., & Kervin, L. (2011). iPads, digital play and preschoolers. *He Kupu.*, 2(5), 4–19.

von Wright, M. (2002). Det relationella perspektivets utmaning: En personlig betraktelse. [The relational perspective's challenge: A personal consideration] In *Attarbeta med särskilt stöd: några perspektiv* (pp. 9–20). Skolverket.

Vygotsky, L. S. (1978). *Mind in society. The development of higher psychological processes*. Harvard University Press.

Vygotsky, L. S. (1978). *Mind in Society: The Development of Higher Psychological Processes*. Harvard University Press.

Waddington, J., Sigafoos, J., Lancioni, G., O'Reilly, M. F., van der Meer, L., Carnett, A., Stevens, M., Roche, L., Hodis, F., Green, V. A., Sutherland, D., Lang, R., & Marschik, P. B. (2014). Three children with autism spectrum disorder learn to perform a three-step communication sequence using an iPad® -based speech-generating device. *International Journal of Developmental Neuroscience*, 39(1), 59–67. DOI: 10.1016/j.ijdevneu.2014.05.001 PMID: 24819024

Weisberg, D. S., Hirsh-Pasek, K., & Golinkoff, R. M. (2013). Guided play: Where curricular goals meet a playful pedagogy. *Mind, Brain and Education : the Official Journal of the International Mind, Brain, and Education Society*, 7(2), 104–112. DOI: 10.1111/mbe.12015

WGU. (2020). Special Education: History, Resources, Advice. https://www.wgu.edu/blog/special-education-history-resources-advice2001.html

Wiske, M. S., & Eddy Spicer, D. H. (2010). Teacher education as teaching for understanding with new technologies. In Peterson, P. L., & Baker, E. L. (Eds.), *International encyclopedia of education* (3rd ed., pp. 635–641). Elsevier. DOI: 10.1016/B978-0-08-044894-7.00671-0

Wood, E., Petkovski, M., De Pasquale, D., Gottardo, A., Evans, M. A., & Savage, R. S. (2016). Parent scaffolding of young children when engaged with mobile technology. *Frontiers in Psychology*, 7, 690. DOI: 10.3389/fpsyg.2016.00690 PMID: 27242603

Wyeth, P., Summerville, J., & Adkins, B. (2014). Playful interactions for people with intellectual disabilities. ACM Comput. Entertain. 11, 3, Article 2 18 pages. DOI: http://dx.doi.org/DOI: 10.3389/fpsyg.2016.00690 PMID: 27242603

Yusop, F. D., & Razak, R. A. (2013) 'Mobile educational apps for children: towards development of i-CARES framework', *Annual International Conference on Management and Technology in Knowledge, Service, Tourism* & Hospitality, Jakarta, Indonesia.

ADDITIONAL READING

Paracha, S., Hagan-Green, G., Hall, L., & Macfarlane, K. (2023). Special iApps: Play-based Learning for Children with Severe Intellectual Disabilities. In Proceedings of the 10th International Conference on Software Development and Technologies for Enhancing Accessibility and Fighting Info-exclusion (DSAI '22). Association forComputing Machinery, New York, USA, 100–106. https://doi.org/ DOI: 10.1145/3563137.3563163

KEY TERMS AND DEFINITIONS

SENCOs: Acronym for Special Educational Needs Coordinators. SENCOs are teaching staff members responsible for overseeing and supporting special educational needs within a school, ensuring appropriate provisions and strategies are in place.

Children with Severe Intellectual Disabilities (SID): Individuals with neurodevelopmental deficits characterized by significant limitations in intellectual functioning, including challenges in intelligence, learning, and daily living skills necessary for independent living.

Educational or Learning Apps: Software applications designed to facilitate virtual teaching and learning for students, educators, and professionals, offering tools to enhance education, skill development, and knowledge acquisition.

Special iApps: Educational applications specifically developed for children with special educational needs, such as autism, Down syndrome, cerebral palsy, hearing impairments, and other learning disabilities. These apps aim to provide tailored and accessible learning experiences.

Chapter 10
Digital Literacy Among Students With Disabilities in India:
Pros and Cons

Madhavi Kilaru
VNR Vignana Jyothi Institute of Engineering and Technology, India

Rajasekhara Mouly Potluri
https://orcid.org/0000-0002-6935-1373
Kazakh-British Technical University, Kazakhstan

ABSTRACT

Digital literacy has emerged as a critical competency in the 21st century, particularly for students with disabilities in India. This chapter explores the unique challenges faced by this group and emphasizes the importance of adopting tailored strategies to integrate technology effectively into their education. Digital literacy empowers students with essential skills, enhancing their learning experiences, fostering independence, and improving access to information and services. Tools such as screen readers, voice recognition software, and accessible internet platforms enable greater engagement in academic and social activities, bridging gaps in learning and providing opportunities for remote education and specialized resources. Despite these advancements, the chapter highlights the significant barriers that persist, as many digital platforms in India remain inaccessible and fail to meet the needs of individuals with disabilities. Addressing these gaps is essential for creating an equitable and inclusive digital learning environment.

DOI: 10.4018/979-8-3693-8227-1.ch010

INTRODUCTION

Each primary pillar of Digital India promotes a widespread and inclusive technological revolution. Digital infrastructure, which is required to provide the foundation for universal connection and access, is one of the fundamental components demanded in India for the country's progress. To ensure that no person is left behind in the march towards progress, the program envisions a nation in which even the most distant locations are seamlessly integrated with the digital network. In 2015, the Indian government launched Digital India, a ground-breaking program aimed at driving the country into a new era of growth and innovation in a variety of disciplines. This enormous undertaking aspires to transform India into a knowledge economy society enabled by digital means, a significant step towards the future. The fundamental goal of this program is to empower citizens digitally. The initiative aims to provide Indians with the tools and skills they need to flourish in the digital age by incorporating technology into their daily life. The purpose is to enable people, particularly those living in rural regions, to take benefit of the digital transactions brought about by the revolution. This includes efforts in skill development and digital literacy. Furthermore, digital India emphasizes electronic manufacturing as a means of fostering creativity and independence. The initiative aims to minimize reliance on imports, develop the economy, and provide job opportunities in the fast-growing technology industry by supporting the domestic production of electronic goods (Pulicherla et al., 2022).

Digital literacy is critical for students during digitalization because it provides them with the skills necessary to navigate and prosper in an increasingly digital landscape. First and foremost, digital literacy improves student's capacity to obtain information. With so much material available online, digitally literate students may easily find credible resources to assist them with research and academic work. Furthermore, digital literacy promotes critical thinking. Students who learn to evaluate the authenticity of internet sources can distinguish between correct information and misrepresentation, which is a crucial skill in an age when fake news may spread quickly (Kong et al., 2014). This analytical capacity helps students achieve their academic goals and prepares them to be informed citizens. Creativity and communication are vital to survive in today's intense competition. This may be significantly achieved through digital literacy, which is a tool for boosting creativity. Students learn how to use various digital tools to create presentations, videos, and interactive content to achieve their objectives and effectively express their ideas. Furthermore, understanding how to interact utilizing digital platforms like cloud services and social media fosters collaboration. It improves interpersonal skills, which are essential in educational and professional settings. Digital literacy also helps students prepare for their future professions. Many businesses today rely on technology, and being familiar with digital technologies can provide students an advantage in the employment market. Employers are increasingly seeking candidates who can adapt to new technology and work in digital environments (Mishra et al., 2017). In today's technologically advanced society, digital literacy for students with disabilities is critical for fostering inclusion, independence, and opportunities for sustainability. As education becomes more reliant on digital resources, providing impaired students with the essential skills ensures their full participation in learning and life. Digital literacy empowers students with disabilities by offering access to educational tools that are not often available in traditional academic environments (Raja, 2016).

Assistive technology, such as screen readers, speech-to-text software, and communication devices, can improve learning experiences by allowing students with disabilities to engage with content, collaborate with classmates, and communicate their thoughts. Furthermore, gaining digital skills fosters independence; many impaired students encounter challenges traversing physical surroundings; digital platforms can provide them with alternate ways to communicate, access information, and complete tasks. It prepares impaired students for employment; businesses favor candidates who can traverse technology competently in an increasingly digital labor market. By learning these abilities, impaired students improve their employability and ensure they have a fair opportunity in a competitive environment. Additionally, digital literacy promotes social inclusion (Adams & Brown, 2006). Many social contacts nowadays take place online, and being digitally literate allows impaired students to connect with peers, engage in community activities, and participate in discussions. This connectivity is vital for developing social skills and building supportive networks. That is why this book chapter focuses on the relevance and significance of digital tools for disabled students in India.

COMPREHENDING DIGITAL ACCESS AND DISABILITIES

Digital India is an Indian government effort for the people and industries of India that has the potential to help India reach a worldwide platform. This project makes government services available to urban and rural populations via electronic or digital channels. It will contribute to digital innovation and positively influence people living in rural and urban locations. It will encourage investment in all product production businesses. The Digital India project aspires to transform India into a digital economy, with participation from both rural and urban individuals and enterprises. This will ensure that all government services and information are accessible from anywhere, at any time, on any device that is simple to use, reliable, and secure. Digital India Project closes the digital divide between rural and urban areas (Sharma, 2016). The National Institute of Electronics and Information Technology (NIELIT) in Ajmer is implementing courses as part of the National Digital Literacy Mission (NDLM), which aligns with the Prime Minister's vision of "Digital India." (Venkatesan, 2023). This initiative provides computer skills training to eligible households in chosen blocks of each state and union territory. The purpose is to equip trainees with fundamental ICT skills that are relevant to their needs, allowing them to effectively use IT and related applications, actively engage in the democratic process, and improve their employment possibilities. The program empowers individuals to access information, knowledge, and skills using digital devices. Human (2023) highlighted that the hierarchy defines disability. Regardless of culture or context, people with disabilities are almost always struggling at the bottom of the social hierarchy. With the initiation of the Convention on the Rights of People with Disabilities (2006), disability human rights seemingly provided a path forward for tearing down ableist social hierarchies and ensuring that all people with disabilities ubiquitously were pickled equally. Despite substantial progress, the disability human rights project not only remains incomplete but has often created new hierarchies among people with disabilities themselves or across the human rights it supports. Specified groups of people with disabilities have gained new voices. In contrast, others remain silenced, and certain rights are prioritized over others depending on what states, international organizations, or advocates want rather than what those on the ground need most.

The training framework includes stages such as appreciation and fundamental digital literacy. With this course structure, trainees are taught how to operate digital devices such as mobile phones or tablets, send and receive emails, and conduct internet searches for information at the first level. At the next level, known as the higher level, they learn how to effectively access various e-governance services provided to citizens. The syllabus includes topics such as digital device introduction and operation, internet usage, understanding digital technology safety and security, word processing, spreadsheets, presentations, and multimedia use. After completing this level, you can move on to the advanced level, which includes a thorough understanding of tools as well as the capacity to develop and create new digital solutions. Computational thinking, or problem-solving at this level, involves cognitive processes such as data representation, algorithmic work, information analysis, and the ability to generalize solutions that can be applied across various domains of learning (Haleem et al., 2022). Understanding disabilities and digital access is essential for supporting inclusive education. Physical, sensory, cognitive, and learning limitations all create specific problems when dealing with digital content. Students with vision impairments, for example, may struggle with text-heavy web pages, but those with motor limitations may have difficulty using typical input devices. Digital access refers to the availability of technology and the usability of digital platforms. Many educational resources are not built for accessibility, which creates barriers to learning. This can lead to students with impairments being excluded from digital literacy chances, which is critical in today's technologically driven environment (Leung, 2014). To overcome these issues, it is critical to incorporate accessible design principles into digital content, such as alt text for images, captioning for films, and easy navigation. Additionally, assistive technologies—such as screen readers and adaptive software—play an essential role in closing the digital gap. Ensuring that all kids, regardless of ability, can fully engage with digital resources is not only an issue of equity; it is crucial for developing a generation of digitally literate people prepared (Raja, 2016).

Students with impairments in India confront several challenges to internet access, limiting their educational possibilities and overall digital competence. One of the most significant difficulties is the absence of necessary accessibility features in many digital platforms and educational resources. For example, screen readers, alternative text for images, and video captioning are frequently unavailable, making it difficult for students with visual or hearing impairments to engage with content successfully. Furthermore, inadequate infrastructure is a significant barrier, especially in rural and deprived regions where poor internet connectivity and limited access to devices hinder many students from participating in online learning. Lack of training and awareness among educators causes the situation; many teachers are not prepared with the knowledge or abilities to implement inclusive teaching practices or to utilize assistive technologies effectively, resulting in a failure to accommodate the unique needs of students with disabilities. Social attitudes and prejudices also play an essential role, as unfavorable perceptions of disability may result in a lack of support from peers and educators, inhibiting children from fully utilizing digital tools (Rohwerder, 2018). Furthermore, the high cost of assistive devices can be prohibitively expensive, making it difficult for families and educational institutions to provide the resources pupils require to succeed in a digital environment. Finally, while policies exist to safeguard the rights of students with disabilities, effective implementation of these policies is frequently weak, with insufficient monitoring and accountability for accessibility requirements in digital education. Addressing these barriers demands a holistic approach that includes increased teacher training, enhanced infrastructure, and the development of more inclusive digital content to build a genuinely equitable learning environment.

The Importance of Adaptive Tools for Students With Disabilities

Assistive technologies can significantly improve the educational experiences of students with impairments in India. These technologies are primarily intended to meet a variety of demands, increasing access to education and boosting independence. One of the key advantages is increased accessibility; tools such as screen readers and speech recognition software allow students with visual impairments to interact with digital content, while hearing aids and captioning assist those who have hearing difficulties. Furthermore, assistive devices improve interactions for students with speech or language impairments. Augmentative and Alternative Communication (AAC) technologies enable these students to express themselves, participate in classroom discussions, and interact socially, all of which are essential for their emotional and social development. Assistive technologies also help students with learning difficulties, such as dyslexia, to learn and comprehend. Text-to-speech software and specialized educational apps help students with reading and comprehension, allowing them to learn at their own pace and on their schedule. This individualized approach contributes to a more inclusive educational environment. Furthermore, these tools foster students' independence. For example, smartphone navigation apps allow students with mobility issues to navigate their surroundings confidently. This increases not only their liberty but also their self-esteem.

Assistive technology has proven beneficial in recent educational moves toward online learning. They offer remote learning, allowing students with disabilities to continue their education despite physical limitations (Hashey & Stahl, 2014). Assistive Technology (AT) allows people with impairments to participate in activities that would otherwise be difficult or impossible for them. Assistive technology can make participating in play, school, community, and work activities easier and improve communication. It frequently serves as a game changer in assisting young children, teens, and people with disabilities to achieve success and independence. It can help students develop more autonomous reading, writing, math, and organizational skills. Additionally, AT can help offer access to the general education curriculum. AT tools range from low to high-tech (for example, laptops with reading and writing apps, voice-activated tablets, and an eye gaze communication system). AT can be utilized at any age and grade level with no requirements. AT use can vary over time depending on an individual's needs and available technology.

Role of Educators in Digital Literacy in India

Educators and support staff play a vital role in promoting digital literacy among students in India, particularly for those with disabilities. Their responsibilities encompass teaching digital skills and fostering an inclusive learning environment. Educators are crucial in implementing Universal Design for Learning (UDL) principles, ensuring that digital content is accessible and engaging for all students. They can adapt lessons using various multimedia tools and resources to cater to different learning styles. Support staff, including special education teachers and technology specialists, provide targeted assistance by helping students navigate assistive technologies and digital tools (Kunnath & Mathew, 2019). They also offer training sessions for educators and students, enhancing their proficiency in effectively using these resources. Collaboration among educators, support staff, and families is essential; sharing insights and strategies ensures that each student's unique needs are addressed. Additionally, ongoing professional development is critical for educators to stay updated on emerging technologies and best practices in digital literacy. By fostering a culture of inclusivity and continuous learning, educators and support staff can empower students to become confident digital citizens, equipping them with the skills necessary to thrive in a technology-driven world. Collaboration between educators, parents, and support staff is essential for enhancing digital literacy in India, especially for students with disabilities. When these stakeholders work together, they create a supportive network that addresses individual student needs and fosters an inclusive learning environment. Educators can share effective strategies with parents, while support staff can provide specialized training and resources. This teamwork ensures that students receive consistent guidance both at school and home, facilitating their engagement with digital tools. Ultimately, this collaboration empowers students, enhances their confidence, and equips them with essential skills for success in an increasingly digital world (Nascimbeni & Vosloo, 2019).

Successful Digital Literacy Initiatives for Disabled People in India

Digital India is a government initiative for the people and companies of India, with the potential to help India achieve a global platform. This project makes government services available to urban and rural communities through electronic or digital means (Tripathi & Dungarwal, 2020). It will help to drive digital innovation and have a good impact on both rural and urban populations. It will stimulate investment in all product-producing businesses. The Digital India project aims to transform India into a digital economy involving both rural and urban individuals and businesses. This will ensure that all government services and information are available from anywhere, at any time, on any device that is easy to use, dependable, and safe. The Digital India Project reduces the digital divide between rural and urban areas. It includes efforts to make digital resources accessible for people with disabilities. The levels of DL can be classified according to their primary usage, application, development, and transformation in three dimensions: cognitive, social, and technical. PWDs have DL levels similar to those of their age-matched healthy peers but confront additional obstacles and considerations. The use of accessible technology, such as screen readers or magnifiers for the visually impaired, can be challenging. Barriers, including unavailable websites, apps, and documents that are incompatible with AT, must be removed. Furthermore, there is a need for further training and support to help PWDs build DL skills, such as accessible training materials, one-on-one instruction, and peer monitoring. (Jamil, 2021). The Accessible

India Campaign (Sugamya Bharat Abhiyan) initiative focuses on making public spaces and digital platforms accessible to people with disabilities and ensuring they can access online services and information. The NASSCOM Foundation's digital literacy program provides training in digital skills that are specifically designed for people with disabilities. The program's principal goal is to help impaired people utilize technology and access online resources. In addition, NISH has developed digital literacy programs for hearing and speech-challenged people, focused on the use of technology in school and the workplace. Furthermore, the Enable India program provides a variety of digital literacy programs, including training in assistive technologies, to improve employability and independence for people with disabilities. The Sankalp Taru Foundation establishes a training program for disabled individuals to engage them in remote work and internet business. Accessible web design initiatives: This program's non-governmental organizations (NGOs) are developing accessible web platforms to improve information access for people with impairments. An initiative like eVidyaloka is one of the best platforms for providing quality education to children in rural areas, and it also helps disabled students by leveraging online teaching resources and volunteer educators. His Scheme's approach is to provide financial assistance to voluntary organizations to offer the full range of services required for the rehabilitation of people with disabilities, including early intervention, development of daily living skills, education, skill development geared toward employability, training, and awareness generation. Education and training programs would be prioritized to integrate people with disabilities into society and realize their full abilities (Babu et al., 2019).

Challenges in the Implementation of Digitalized Services in India

The digitalization of services and education in India has the potential to empower everybody, especially those with disabilities. However, several barriers prevent disabled people from fully participating in the digital realm. One of the most significant issues is a lack of accessibility to digital platforms and material. Many websites, programs, and online services fail to meet accessibility requirements, making it difficult for visually impaired people to navigate with screen readers. Similarly, content may not be provided in formats that are accessible to those with hearing or cognitive impairments. For example, movies frequently lack subtitles or audio descriptions, limiting access to information. Assistive solutions that improve accessibility, such as specialist software or hardware, are rarely integrated into mainstream digital platforms. Many disabled people in India continue to face financial barriers to accessing devices and assistive technology. High-end cell phones, laptops, and assistive devices such as braille displays or hearing aids might be prohibitively expensive. While some government initiatives seek to provide subsidies or free equipment, these attempts frequently fail owing to bureaucratic obstacles and insufficient outreach. Many disabled people are unable to make use of digital services because they lack cheap access to technology, thus marginalizing them in an increasingly digitizing world (Tripathi, 2012). Even when disabled people have access to technology, a considerable gap in digital literacy remains. Many disabled people are not adequately taught to utilize digital tools, limiting their capacity to interact with online information and services. Educational institutions frequently lack specialized programs designed to teach digital skills to students with disabilities. As a result, even people who have access to technology may struggle to use it for education or employment, perpetuating a cycle of exclusion. The potential benefits of digital tools are not well understood by schools, employers, and even disabled people themselves. Many educational institutions and businesses do not prioritize digital literacy training for impaired students or employees. This poor awareness can lead to a lack of investment in needed training, resulting in missed opportunities for impaired individuals to improve their abilities and employability. The obstacles that disabled people encounter during the digital era are also heavily influenced by societal views regarding impairments. Stigma and discrimination can prevent disabled people from receiving the support and encouragement they need to use technology (Fichten et al., 2009). In some circumstances, family members may underestimate impaired people's ability, preventing them from learning digital skills. This cultural attitude may reduce their drive to learn and interact with digital platforms. While the Indian government has launched a number of initiatives to promote digital inclusiveness, gaps in policy implementation and enforcement still exist. Many policies aimed at improving accessibility are rarely strictly implemented, resulting in inconsistent implementation across digital platforms. Furthermore, there is frequently a lack of interaction with disabled people throughout the development of digital services, resulting in solutions that do not fully meet their needs.

Case Study: Empowerment Through Digital Literacy – The Journey of Priya

Problem Statement: Priya is a 20-year-old woman from a small Uttar Pradesh, India town. She has a physical handicap that limits her mobility owing to a disorder called cerebral palsy. Despite her obstacles, Priya is motivated to pursue her educational and professional goals. However, she has experienced severe barriers to obtaining educational materials and technologies that are critical to her growth.

The primary objectives of this case study are:

1. Investigated how digital literacy may empower people with impairments.

2. Identify barriers for impaired individuals in accessing digital resources.
3. Emphasize the importance of community support and training in overcoming these problems.

Priya's family sought assistance from a local NGO specializing in disability services. The NGO conducted an assessment to determine Priya's needs and goals. They discovered that, while Priya was eager to learn, she lacked access to computers and the internet, limiting her capacity to participate in online classes and research. The NGO provided access to a laptop with assistive technologies like speech-to-text software and screen readers. They also ensured Priya had stable internet connectivity at home, which was essential for her online schooling. Priya enrolled in the NGO's digital literacy program. The curriculum was created to educate fundamental computer skills, such as internet usage, educational platform use, and digital communication. Priya received training that was targeted to her the training was tailored to Priya's specific needs, incorporating assistive technologies that accommodated her mobility challenges. Priya's family was involved throughout the process. The NGO organized workshops to educate her family on how to support her learning journey. This engagement was created as a part of the program; Priya was paired with a mentor who had experience in digital fields. The mentor guided her in exploring various career options and helped her build a network of contacts in the community. This connection provided Priya with insights into potential job opportunities in the future.

After completing the training, Priya became proficient in using digital tools. She could confidently navigate online resources, conduct research for her college assignments, and participate in virtual classes. With newfound skills, Priya's academic performance improved significantly. She began to excel in her studies and was able to access a wealth of knowledge that was previously out of reach. The training and support she received greatly enhanced her self-esteem. Priya became an advocate for disability rights in her community, inspiring others with similar challenges to pursue their educational goals. With the guidance of her mentor, Priya began exploring career options in digital marketing and content creation. She took on freelance projects, which helped her gain practical experience and build her portfolio.

Priya struggled to get started with digital tools, which required much help from family members, strong determination, motivation, patience, and practice. There are frequent power outages and a lack of internet access in the villages, significantly interfering with her ability to engage in online classes. Priya faced stigma and doubt from some of her peers about her ability, but community support enabled her to overcome these obstacles.

Priya's journey highlights the transformative power of digital literacy for individuals with disabilities. With the proper support and resources, she overcame significant challenges and is now well on her way to achieving her academic and career aspirations. This case study underscores the importance of community engagement, tailored training programs, and accessible technology in empowering disabled individuals in India. By addressing these areas, similar initiatives can foster greater inclusion and opportunity for disabled people across the country.

CONCLUSION

Digital literacy is a critical enabler for students with disabilities in India, providing them access to education, information, and opportunities for personal and professional growth. As India rapidly transitions into a digital economy, equipping these students with essential digital skills becomes imperative. Despite the significant potential for technology to enhance learning experiences, numerous challenges persist, including inaccessible digital platforms, limited availability of assistive technologies, and inadequate training tailored to their specific needs. Addressing these barriers requires a multi-faceted approach. Schools, government bodies, and NGOs must collaborate to create inclusive educational frameworks that prioritize accessibility. This includes developing digital content that adheres to accessibility standards and implementing training programs that empower students with disabilities to use technology effectively. Many families hesitate to send their children to mainstream schools, fearing discrimination or inadequate support. As a result, students with disabilities often miss out on vital educational and social experiences, leading to long-term consequences in terms of employability and independence. Furthermore, raising awareness among educators and families about the importance of digital literacy is essential in fostering supportive environments. Successful initiatives have shown that when students with disabilities receive proper support and resources, they can overcome obstacles and excel in their studies. In recent years, the Indian government has made notable strides toward promoting inclusive education through legislative measures, notably the Rights of People with Disabilities Act of 2016. This landmark legislation ensures equal opportunities for all children, emphasizing the right to education in an inclusive setting. It mandates that schools provide necessary support and reasonable accommodations for students with disabilities, fostering an environment conducive to learning. Despite these challenges, there is a growing movement towards inclusivity in education. NGOs, government initiatives, and grassroots organizations work tirelessly to promote awareness, provide resources, and develop inclusive practices within schools. The increasing availability of assistive technologies and specialized training for educators shows promise in transforming the educational landscape. Digital literacy not only enhances academic performance but also boosts self-confidence and prepares these individuals for future employment opportunities. In conclusion, promoting digital literacy among students with disabilities in India is vital for achieving inclusive education and social equity. By investing in accessible technology, targeted training programs, and community awareness, we can create a more equitable digital landscape (Joshi, 2021). This empowerment will enable students with disabilities to participate in society fully, contribute to the economy, and realize their potential, ultimately paving the way for a more inclusive future for all.

REFERENCES

Adams, M., & Brown, S. (Eds.). (2006). *Towards inclusive learning in higher education: Developing curricula for disabled students*. Routledge. DOI: 10.4324/9780203088623

Babu, R., Kalaivani, S., & Saileela, K. (2019). *Empowering India Through Digital Literacy (Vol. 1)*. Lulu. com.

Fichten, C. S., Ferraro, V., Asuncion, J. V., Chwojka, C., Barile, M., Nguyen, M. N., & Wolforth, J. (2009). Disabilities and e-learning problems and solutions: An exploratory study. *Journal of Educational Technology & Society*, 12(4), 241–256.

Haleem, A., Javaid, M., Qadri, M. A., & Suman, R. (2022). Understanding the role of digital technologies in education: A review. *Sustainable Operations and Computers*, 3, 275–285. DOI: 10.1016/j.susoc.2022.05.004

Hashey, A. I., & Stahl, S. (2014). Making online learning accessible for students with disabilities. *Teaching Exceptional Children*, 46(5), 70–78. DOI: 10.1177/0040059914528329

Human, O. D. (2023). *The Routledge International Handbook of Disability Human Rights Hierarchies*.

Jamil, S. (2021). From digital divide to digital inclusion: Challenges for wide-ranging digitalization in Pakistan. *Telecommunications Policy*, 45(8), 102206. DOI: 10.1016/j.telpol.2021.102206

Joshi, S. (2021). Rising importance of remote learning in India in the wake of COVID-19: Issues, challenges and way forward. *World Journal of Science. Technology and Sustainable Development*, 18(1), 44–63.

Kong, S. C. (2014). Developing information literacy and critical thinking skills through domain knowledge learning in digital classrooms: An experience of practicing flipped classroom strategy. *Computers & Education*, 78, 160–173. DOI: 10.1016/j.compedu.2014.05.009

Kunnath, S. K., & Mathew, S. N. (2019). Higher education for students with disabilities in India: Insights from a focus group study. *Higher Education for the Future*, 6(2), 171–187. DOI: 10.1177/2347631119840540

Leung, L. (2014). Availability, access and affordability across' digital divides': Common experiences amongst minority groups. *Journal of Telecommunications and the Digital Economy*, 2(2), 38–1. DOI: 10.7790/ajtde.v2n2.38

Mishra, K. E., Wilder, K., & Mishra, A. K. (2017). Digital literacy in the marketing curriculum: Are female college students prepared for digital jobs? *Industry and Higher Education*, 31(3), 204–211. DOI: 10.1177/0950422217697838

Nascimbeni, F., & Vosloo, S. (2019). Digital literacy for children: Exploring definitions and frameworks. *Scoping Paper, 1*. DOI: 10.1177/0950422217697838

Pulicherla, K. K., Adapa, V., Ghosh, M., & Ingle, P. (2022). Current efforts on sustainable green growth in the manufacturing sector complement "make in India" for making a "self-reliant India.". *Environmental Research*, 206, 112263. DOI: 10.1016/j.envres.2021.112263 PMID: 34695432

Raja, D. S. (2016). Bridging the disability divide through digital technologies—background paper for the World Development report. DOI: 10.1177/0950422217697838

Rohwerder, B. (2018). Disability stigma in developing countries. *K4D Helpdesk Report, 26*. DOI: 10.1177/0950422217697838

Sharma, J. (2016). Digital India and its Impact on the Society. *International Journal of Research in Humanities &. Soc. Sciences*, 4(4), 64–70.

Tripathi, M., & Dungarwal, M. (2020). Digital India: Role in development. *International Journal of Home Science*, 6, 388–392.

Tripathi, T. P. (2012). Deconstructing disability, assistive technology: secondary orality, the path to universal access.

Venkatesan, S. (2023). Digital literacy in people with disabilities: An overview and narrative review.

ADDITIONAL READING

Arslantas, T. K., & Gul, A. (2022). Digital literacy skills of university students with visual impairment: A mixed-methods analysis. *Education and Information Technologies*, 27(4), 5605–5625. DOI: 10.1007/s10639-021-10860-1 PMID: 35068987

Gupta, A., & Johri, T. (2022). ICT Tools & Implications for the Wellbeing of Divyangjan Working in Different Service Sectors. *Indian Journal of Psychological Science Vol, 15*(1).

Nedungadi, P. P., Menon, R., Gutjahr, G., Erickson, L., & Raman, R. (2018). Towards an inclusive digital literacy framework for digital India. *Education + Training*, 60(6), 516–528. DOI: 10.1108/ET-03-2018-0061

Petretto, D. R., Carta, S. M., Cataudella, S., Masala, I., Mascia, M. L., Penna, M. P., Piras, P., Pistis, I., & Masala, C. (2021). The Use of Distance Learning and E-learning in Students with Learning Disabilities: A Review on the Effects and some Hint of Analysis on the Use during COVID-19 Outbreak. *Clinical Practice and Epidemiology in Mental Health*, 17(1), 92–102. DOI: 10.2174/1745017902117010092 PMID: 34733348

KEY TERMS AND DEFINITIONS

Accessible Technology: Tools and platforms designed to ensure individuals with disabilities can effectively interact with digital resources, removing barriers to usability and access.

Assistive Technology: Devices or software such as screen readers and speech recognition tools that support individuals with disabilities in engaging with educational and digital content.

Digital Divide: The gap between those who have access to digital technologies and the skills to use them and those who do not, often exacerbate inequalities for individuals with disabilities.

Digital Literacy: The ability to effectively use digital tools, platforms, and resources for communication, information gathering, and problem-solving, essential for navigating modern educational and professional environments.

Inclusive Education: Educational practices designed to accommodate the diverse needs of all students, ensuring equitable access to learning opportunities, including those with disabilities.

Screen Readers: Assistive software applications that convert on-screen text into speech or Braille, enabling visually impaired individuals to access digital content.

Speech Recognition Technology: AI-powered tools that convert spoken words into text, offering accessibility solutions for individuals with physical or learning disabilities.

Universal Design for Learning (UDL): An educational framework that promotes flexible learning environments designed to accommodate diverse learner needs and preferences.

Voice Recognition Software: Tools that allow users to control digital devices and applications through voice commands, facilitating interaction for individuals with mobility or dexterity challenges.

Web Accessibility: The practice of ensuring websites and online platforms are usable by all individuals, including those with disabilities, through features such as alt text, captioning, and keyboard navigation.

Compilation of References

Abiatal, L. (2019). *Constructivist assitive technology in a mathematical classroom for the deaf: An experiement in a rural primary school Namibia*. University of South Africa.

Adams, M., & Brown, S. (Eds.). (2006). *Towards inclusive learning in higher education: Developing curricula for disabled students*. Routledge. DOI: 10.4324/9780203088623

Aggarwal, D. (2023). Integration of innovative technological developments and AI with education for an adaptive learning pedagogy. *China Petroleum Processing and Petrochemical Technology*, 23(2), 709–714.

Ahmed, A. (2018). Perceptions of Using Assistive Technology for Students with Disabilities in the Classroom. *International Journal of Special Education*, 33(1), 129–139. https://files.eric.ed.gov/fulltext/EJ1184079.pdf

Akavova, A., Temirkhanova, Z., & Lorsanova, Z. (2023). Adaptive learning and artificial intelligence in the educational space. In *E3S Web of Conferences* (Vol. 451, p. 06011). EDP Sciences. DOI: 10.1051/e3sconf/202345106011

Akbıyık, M. (2020). *Otizm spektrum bozukluğu Olan Öğrencilere İletişim Başlatma-Sürdürerme Becerisinin Kazandırılmasında Sanal Gerçeklik Teknolojisinin Etkililiği. Yüksek Lisans Tezi*. Bolu Abant İzzet Baysal Üniversitesi Lisansüstü Eğitim Enstitüsü.

Akpan, J. P., & Beard, L. A. (2016). Using constructivist teaching strategies to enhance academic outcomes of students with special needs. *Universal Journal of Educational Research*, 4(2), 392–398. DOI: 10.13189/ujer.2016.040211

Akpan, J., & Beard, L. (2014). Assistive technology and mathematics education. *Universal Journal of Educational Research*, 2(3), 219–222. DOI: 10.13189/ujer.2014.020303

Alam, A., & Mohanty, A. (2023). Educational technology: Exploring the convergence of technology and pedagogy through mobility, interactivity, AI, and learning tools. *Cogent Engineering*, 10(2), 2283282. Advance online publication. DOI: 10.1080/23311916.2023.2283282

Aldoseri, A., Al-Khalifa, K. N., & Hamouda, A. M. (2024). AI-Powered Innovation in Digital Transformation: Key Pillars and Industry Impact. *Sustainability (Basel)*, 16(5), 1790. DOI: 10.3390/su16051790

Almufareh, M. F., Kausar, S., Humayun, M., & Tehsin, S. (2024). A conceptual model for inclusive technology: Advancing disability inclusion through artificial intelligence. *Journal of Disability Research*, 3(1), 20230060. DOI: 10.57197/JDR-2023-0060

Almufareh, M. F., Tehsin, S., Humayun, M., & Kausar, S. (2023). Intellectual disability and technology: An artificial intelligence perspective and framework. *Journal of Disability Research*, 2(4), 58–70. DOI: 10.57197/JDR-2023-0055

Alnahdi, G., Dean, V., & Box, P. O. (2014). Assistive technology in special education and the universal design for learning. *The Turkish Online Journal of Educational Technology*, 13(2), 18–23.

Alowais, S. A., Alghamdi, S. S., Alsuhebany, N., Alqahtani, T., Alshaya, A. I., Almohareb, S. N., Aldairem, A., Alrashed, M., Saleh, K. B., Badreldin, H. A., Yami, M. S. A., Harbi, S. A., & Albekairy, A. M. (2023). Revolutionizing healthcare: The role of artificial intelligence in clinical practice. *BMC Medical Education*, 23(1), 689. Advance online publication. DOI: 10.1186/s12909-023-04698-z PMID: 37740191

Alsolami, A. S. (2022). Teachers of Special Education and Assistive Technology: Teachers' Perceptions of Knowledge, Competencies and Professional Development. *SAGE Open*, 12(1), 21582440221079900. Advance online publication. DOI: 10.1177/21582440221079900

Anderson, S. E., & Putman, R. S. (2019). Special education teachers' experience, confidence, beliefs, and knowledge about integrating technology. *Journal of Special Education Technology*, 35(1), 37–50. DOI: 10.1177/0162643419836409

Ankam, N. S., Bosques, G., Sauter, C., Stiens, S., Therattil, M., Williams, F. H., Atkins, C. C., & Mayer, R. S. (2019). Competency-Based Curriculum Development to Meet the Needs of People with Disabilities: A Call to Action. *Academic Medicine*, 94(6), 781–788. DOI: 10.1097/ACM.0000000000002686 PMID: 30844926

Arnesen, K., Walters, S., & Borup, J. (2020). Irrelevant, Overlooked, or Lost? Trends in 20 Years of Uncited and Low-cited K-12 Online Learning Articles. *Online Learning : the Official Journal of the Online Learning Consortium*, 24(2), 187–206. DOI: 10.24059/olj.v24i2.2080

Aspiranti, K. B., Larwin, K. H., & Schade, B. P. (2020). iPads/tablets and students with autism: A meta-analysis of academic effects. *Assistive Technology*, 32(1), 23–30. DOI: 10.1080/10400435.2018.1463575 PMID: 29634456

Assistive technology for children with disabilities: Creating opportunities for education, inclusion and participation: A discussion paper. (2015). UNICEF & WHO.

At-Infor-Map. (2019, 01 12). *Summary Overview Disability and Assistive Devices in Zimbabwe*. Retrieved from At-Infor-Map: https://atinfomap.org/zimbabwe.html

Australian National University. (2024, 11 7). *Different types of disabilities*. Retrieved from Australian National University: https://services.anu.edu.au/human-resources/health-safety/different-types-of-disabilities

Ayeni, O. O., Al Hamad, N. M., Chisom, O. N., Osawaru, B., & Adewusi, O. E. (2024). AI in education: A review of personalized learning and educational technology. *GSC Advanced Research and Reviews*, 18(2), 261–271. DOI: 10.30574/gscarr.2024.18.2.0062

Azaabi, C. (2022). Improving Digital Security and Privacy Of Students In Colleges Of Education: An Attitudinal Change Framework Based On Competence Learning Matrix. *European Journal of Education Studies*, 9(10). Advance online publication. DOI: 10.46827/ejes.v9i10.4501

Babu, R., Kalaivani, S., & Saileela, K. (2019). *Empowering India Through Digital Literacy (Vol. 1)*. Lulu. com.

Bachmann, N., Tripathi, S., Brunner, M., & Jodlbauer, H. (2022). The contribution of data-driven technologies in achieving the sustainable development goals. *Sustainability (Basel)*, 14(5), 2497. DOI: 10.3390/su14052497

Bäck, G. A., Mossige, M., Svendsen, H. B., Rønneberg, V., Selenius, H., Gøttsche, N. B., Dolmer, G., Fälth, L., Nilsson, S., & Svensson, I. (2024). Speech-to-text intervention to support text production among students with writing difficulties: A single-case study in Nordic countries. *Disability and Rehabilitation. Assistive Technology*, 19(8), 1–20. DOI: 10.1080/17483107.2024.2351488 PMID: 38776244

Bajwa, J., Munir, U., Nori, A., & Williams, B. (2021). Artificial intelligence in healthcare: Transforming the practice of medicine. *Future Healthcare Journal*, 8(2), e188–e194. DOI: 10.7861/fhj.2021-0095 PMID: 34286183

Baneres, D., Rodríguez, M. E., & Guerrero-Roldán, A. E. (2020). *Engineering Data-Driven Adaptive Trust-based e-Assessment Systems*. Springer International Publishing. DOI: 10.1007/978-3-030-29326-0

Barta, E. A., Guzsvinecz, T., Sik Lanyi, C., & Szucs, V. (2017) Android-Based Daily Routine Organizing Application for Elementary School Students Living with ASD. In: Studies in Health Technology and Informatics. https://doi.org/DOI: 10.3233/978-1-61499-798-6-283

Bates, A. W. (2019). Teaching in a Digital Age – Second Edition. Vancouver, B.C.: Tony Bates Associates Ltd. Retrieved from https://pressbooks.bccampus.ca/teachinginadigitalagev2/

Berghs, M. (2017). Practices and discourses on ubuntu: Implications for an African modelof disability. *African Journal of Disability*, 6, 1–8. DOI: 10.4102/ajod.v6i0.292 PMID: 28730067

Bhat, N., Gurung, S., Gupta, M., Dhungana, N., & Thapa, R. K. (2022). Enhancing collaborative learning through peer-assisted learning. *Journal of Physiological Society of Nepal*, 3(1), 4–9. DOI: 10.3126/jpsn.v3i1.57762

Bibri, S. E., & Krogstie, J. (2020). The emerging data–driven Smart City and its innovative applied solutions for sustainability: The cases of London and Barcelona. *Energy Informatics*, 3(1), 5. DOI: 10.1186/s42162-020-00108-6

Bikic, A., Leckman, J. F., Lindschou, J., Christensen, T. Ø., & Dalsgaard, S. (2015). Cognitive computer training in children with attention deficit hyperactivity disorder (ADHD) versus no intervention: Study protocol for a randomized controlled trial. *Trials*, 16(1), 480. DOI: 10.1186/s13063-015-0975-8 PMID: 26499057

Bird, J., & Edwards, S. (2015). Children learning to use technologies through play: A Digital Play Framework. *British Journal of Educational Technology*, 46(6), 1149–1160. DOI: 10.1111/bjet.12191

Blackhurst, A. E., & Edyburn, D. L. (2000). A brief history of special education technology. *Special Education Technology Practice*, 2(1), 21–36.

Bonifatius, S., & Haihambo, C. (2022). Assessing the utilization of Information and Communication Technologies in inclusive classes in the Oshana region of Namibia. *Namibia Educational Reform Forum Journal*, 30(1), 87–96.

Boot, F. H., Owuor, J., Dinsmore, J., & MacLachlan, M. (2018). Access to assistive technology for people with intellectual disabilities: A systematic review to identify barriers and facilitators. *Journal of Intellectual Disability Research*, 62(10), 900–921. DOI: 10.1111/jir.12532 PMID: 29992653

Boot, F., Kahonde, C., Dinsmore, J., & MacLachlan, M. (2021). Perspectives on access and usage of assistive technology by people with intellectual disabilities in the Western Cape province of South Africa:Where to from here? *African Journal of Disability*, 10, 1–5. DOI: 10.4102/ajod.v10i0.767 PMID: 33824859

Bouajila, A. (2023). Technological innovation at the service of the educational inclusion of children with disabilities: Digital education. *International Journal of Disability and Education*, 1(1), 1–15.

Bouck, E. C., Satsangi, R., & Flanagan, S. (2016). Focus on inclusive education: evaluating apps for students with disabilities: supporting academic access and success. *Childhood Education*, 92(4), 324–328. DOI: 10.1080/00094056.2016.1208014

Boyle, J. R., & Kennedy, M. J. (2019). Innovations in classroom technology for students with disabilities. *Intervention in School and Clinic*, 55(2), 67–70. DOI: 10.1177/1053451219837716

Bresciani, S., Ciampi, F., Meli, F., & Ferraris, A. (2021). Using big data for co-innovation processes: Mapping the field of data-driven innovation, proposing theoretical developments and providing a research agenda. *International Journal of Information Management*, 60, 102347. DOI: 10.1016/j.ijinfomgt.2021.102347

Brooks, B. M., Rose, F. D., Attree, E. A., & Elliot-Square, A. (2002). An evaluation of the efficacy of training people with learning disabilities in a virtual environment. *Disability and Rehabilitation*, 24(11-12), 622–626. DOI: 10.1080/09638280110111397 PMID: 12182802

Bross, H., Ramugondo, E., Taylor, C., & Sinclair, C. (2008). Children need others: Triggers for playfulness in pre-schoolers with multiple disabilities living within an informal settlement. South African Journal of Occupational Therapy, 38(2), 3-7. Available at http://www.scielo.org.za/scielo.php?script=sci_arttext&pid=S2 310-38332008000200002&lng=en&tlng=en Bundy A. (1997). Play and playfulness. What to look for. In Parham LD, Fazio LS, editors. Play in Occupational Therapy for Children, USA: Mosby, 52-65.

Byrne, D. (2022). A worked example of Braun and Clarke's approach to reflexive thematic analysis. *Quality & Quantity*, 56(3), 1391–1412. DOI: 10.1007/s11135-021-01182-y

Can, T., & Şimşek, İ. (2016). Eğitimde Yeni Teknolojiler: Sanal Gerçeklik. [Ankara: Ayrıntı Yayınları.]. *Eğitim Teknolojileri Okumaları*, 2016, 351–362.

Carasthathis, A. (2016). *Intersectionality, origins, contestations and horizons.* University of Nebraska Press. DOI: 10.2307/j.ctt1fzhfz8

Centre for Human Rights University of Pretoria. (2024, 11 7). *Namibia: Updated Country Report*. Retrieved from Centre for Human Rights University of Pretoria: http://www.rodra.co.za/countries/namibia/21-countries/namibia/60-updated-country-report

Chakabwata, W. (2022). An Intersectional Study of the Funding Experiences of South African University Students After Majority Rule. In J. Keengwe, *Handbook of research on social justice and equity* (pp. 242-258). Dakota: IGI Global. DOI: 10.4018/978-1-7998-9567-1.ch012

Chakabwata, W., & Mukazi, F. (2022). Ubuntu Philosophy and Online Assessment in Higher Education Institutions. In J. Keengwe, *Handbook of research on transformative and innovative pedagogies in education* (pp. 257-275). Dakota: IGI Global. DOI: 10.4018/978-1-7998-9561-9.ch014

Chalkiadakis, A., Seremetaki, A., Kanellou, A., Kallishi, M., Morfopoulou, A., Moraitaki, M., & Mastrokoukou, S. (2024). Impact of Artificial Intelligence and Virtual Reality on Educational Inclusion: A Systematic Review of Technologies Supporting Students with Disabilities. *Education Sciences*, 14(11), 1223. DOI: 10.3390/educsci14111223

Channa, A., Sharma, A., Singh, M., Malhotra, P., Bajpai, A., & Whig, P. (2024). Original Research Article Revolutionizing filmmaking: A comparative analysis of conventional and AI-generated film production in the era of virtual reality. *Journal of Autonomous Intelligence*, 7(4).

Charlton, E. (2018). This AI-powered app aims to help people with autism improve their social skills. World Economic Forum. < https://www.weforum.org/agenda/2018/11/ai-app-helps- autism-social-skills/>

Chary, M., Parikh, S., Manini, A., Boyer, E., & Radeous, M. (2018). A Review of Natural Language Processing in Medical Education. *The Western Journal of Emergency Medicine*, 20(1), 78–86. DOI: 10.5811/westjem.2018.11.39725 PMID: 30643605

Chibaya, G., Naidoo, D., & Govender, P. (2022). Exploring the implementation of the United Nations Convention on the Rights of People with Disabilities (UNCRPD) in Namibia. Perspectives of policymakers and implementers. *South African Journal of Occupational Therapy*, 52(1), 16–23. DOI: 10.17159/2310-3833/2022/vol52n1a3

Chisom, O. N., Unachukwu, C. C., & Osawaru, B. (2023). Review of AI in education: Transforming learning environments in Africa. *International Journal of Applied Research in Social Sciences*, 5(10), 637–654. DOI: 10.51594/ijarss.v5i10.725

Chmiliar, L. (2017). Improving Learning Outcomes: The iPad and Preschool Children with Disabilities. *Frontiers in Psychology*, 8, 660. DOI: 10.3389/fpsyg.2017.00660 PMID: 28529493

Chopra, A., Patel, H., Rajput, D. S., & Bansal, N. (2024). Empowering Inclusive Education: Leveraging AI-ML and Innovative Tech Stacks to Support Students with Learning Disabilities in Higher Education. In *Applied Assistive Technologies and Informatics for Students with Disabilities* (pp. 255–275). Springer Nature Singapore. DOI: 10.1007/978-981-97-0914-4_15

Chow, W. S. E., de Bruin, K., & Sharma, U. (2023). A scoping review of perceived support needs of teachers for implementing inclusive education. *International Journal of Inclusive Education*, 28(13), 3321–3340. DOI: 10.1080/13603116.2023.2244956

Chukhlomin, V. (2024). Conceptualizing AI-Driven Learning Strategies for non-IT Professionals: From EMERALD Framework to a Sample Course Design. *Available at SSRN* 4820332. DOI: 10.2139/ssrn.4820332

Chukwuemeka, E. J., & Samaila, D. (2020). Teachers' Perception and Factors Limiting the use of High-Tech Assistive Technology in Special Education Schools in North-West Nigeria. *Contemporary Educational Technology*, 11(1), 99–109. https://files.eric.ed.gov/fulltext/EJ1234819.pdf. DOI: 10.30935/cet.646841

Ciolacu, M., Svasta, P. M., Berg, W., & Popp, H. (2017, October). Education 4.0 for tall thin engineer in a data driven society. In *2017 IEEE 23rd International Symposium for Design and Technology in Electronic Packaging (SIITME)* (pp. 432-437). IEEE.

Cohen, M., Hadley, M., & Frank, M. (2011). *Young Children, Apps & iPad*. Michael Cohen Group.

Copley, J., & Ziviani, J. (2004). Barriers to the use of assistive technology for children with multiple disabilities. *Occupational Therapy International*, 11(4), 229–243. DOI: 10.1002/oti.213 PMID: 15771212

Costin, D. S., Cristian, A. F., Georgian, D. I., Ionu, C. S., & Alexandru, M. S. (2023). The implications of leveraging machine learning and artificial intelligence for the transformation of adult education and vocational training. Journal of Management and Quality, 14-20. DOI: 10.1002/aaai.12157

Coulson, N., & Doukas, T. (2016). MyChoice Pad. Citizen Network. Retrieved May 06, 2024 from https://citizen-network.org/library/mychoice-pad.html

Crampton, E., & Billett, I. (2021). How can we better engage digital learning for SEN pupils? SEN. Available at: https://senmagazine.co.uk/content/tech/assistive-tech/14351/how-can-we-better-engage-digital-learning-for-sen-pupils/

Cresswell, J. (2007). *Qualitative Inquiry and Research Design: Choosing among five approaches*. Sage.

Crotty, E., Singh, A., Neligan, N., Chamunyonga, C., & Edwards, C. (2024). Artificial intelligence in medical imaging education: Recommendations for undergraduate curriculum development. *Radiography*, pp. *30*, 67–73. DOI: 10.1016/j.radi.2024.10.008

Cuascota, L., Guevara, L., Cueva, R., Tapia, F., & Guerrero, G. (2019). Assistance application of people with cognitive disabilities in tasks for their social inclusion. In: Iberian Conference on Information Systems and Technologies, CISTI (2019). https://doi.org/DOI: 10.23919/CISTI.2019.8760732

D'Andrea, F. M., & Siu, Y.-T. (2015), "Students with Visual Impairments: Considerations and Effective Practices for Technology Use", Efficacy of Assistive Technology Interventions (Advances in Special Education Technology, Vol. 1), Emerald Group Publishing Limited, Leeds, pp. 111-138. https://doi.org/DOI: 10.1108/S2056-769320150000001005

Dash, S., & Bhoi, C. (2024). Exploring the Intersection of Education and Artificial Intelligence: A Comprehensive Review. *International Journal of Multidisciplinary Approach Research and Science*, 2(02), 601–610. DOI: 10.59653/ijmars.v2i02.637

Davies, D. K., & Stock, S. E., ve Wehmeyer, M. L. (2003). Application of computer simulation to teach ATM access to individuals with intellectual disabilities. *Education and Training in Developmental Disabilities*, 38(4), 451–456.

Denga, E. M., & Denga, S. W. (2024). Revolutionizing Education: The Power of Technology. In *Revolutionizing Curricula Through Computational Thinking, Logic, and Problem Solving* (pp. 167-188). IGI Global.

Didehbani, N., Allen, T., Kandalaft, M., Krawczyk, D., & Chapman, S. (2016). Virtual reality social cognition training for children with high-functioning autism. *Computers in Human Behavior*, 62, 703–711. DOI: 10.1016/j.chb.2016.04.033

Dimitrov, L., & Gossman, W. (2023, 06 2). Retrieved from National Library of Medicine National Centre for Biotechnology Information: https://www.ncbi.nlm.nih.gov/books/NBK538285/#_ncbi_dlg_citbx_NBK538285

Disability Rights Watch. (2022, 01 24). *Commitments to create a more Disability Inclusive Zambia –Delivering Quality Inclusive Education*. Retrieved from Disability Rights Watch: https://disabilityrightswatch.net/commitments-to-create-a-more-disability-inclusive-zambia-delivering-quality-inclusive-education/

Dube, T., Ncube, S. B., Mapuvire, C. C., Ndlovu, S., Ncube, C. M., & Mlotshwa, S. (2021). Interventions to reduce the exclusions of children with a dsability in from education: A Zimbabwean perspective from the field. *Cogent Social Sciences*, 7(1), 1–10. DOI: 10.1080/23311886.2021.1913848

Dumić-Čule, I., Orešković, T., Brkljačić, B., Tiljak, M. K., & Orešković, S. (2020). The importance of introducing artificial intelligence to the medical curriculum – assessing practitioners' perspectives. *Croatian Medical Journal*, 61(5), 457–464. DOI: 10.3325/cmj.2020.61.457 PMID: 33150764

Dunlap, P. B., & Michalowski, M. (2024). Advancing artificial intelligence data ethics in nursing: Future directions for nursing practice, research, and education (Preprint). *JMIR Nursing*, 7, e62678. DOI: 10.2196/62678 PMID: 39453630

Edwards, S. (2015). New concepts of play and the problem of technology, digital media and popular-culture integration with play-based learning in early childhood education. *Technology, Pedagogy and Education*, 25(4), 513–532. DOI: 10.1080/1475939X.2015.1108929

Edyburn, D. L. (2020). Rapid literature review on assistive technology in education. Research Report Department for Education. University of Wisconsin-Milwaukee. https://assets.publishing.service.gov.uk/government/uploads/system/uploads/attachment_data/file/937381/UKAT_FinalReport_082520.pdf

Edyburn, D. (2003). Measuring assistive technology outcomes: Key concepts. *Journal of Special Education Technology*, 18, 53–55. DOI: 10.1177/016264340301800107

Eide, A., Loeb, M., Nhiwatiwa, S., Munthali, A., Ngulube, T., & van Rooy, G. (2022). Living conditions among people with disabilities in developing countries. In A. Eide, & B. Ingstad, *Disability and poverty: A global Challenge* (pp. 55-70). Bristol: Bristol University Press; Policy Press.

Eid, N. (n.d.). *Innovation and technology for persons with disabilities*. Retrieved from. [https://www.un.org/esa/socdev/egms/docs/2013/ict/innovation-technology-disability.pdf]

Elendu, C., Amaechi, D. C., Elendu, T. C., Jingwa, K. A., Okoye, O. K., Okah, M. J., Ladele, J. A., Farah, A. H., & Alimi, H. A. (2023). Ethical implications of AI and robotics in healthcare. *Revista de Medicina (São Paulo)*, 102(50), e36671. DOI: 10.1097/MD.0000000000036671 PMID: 38115340

Elfaizi, Y., & El Aouri, Z.Zahra EL AOURI. (2024). Inclusion between Equality and Equity: A Balance Model to an Equitable Quality Education for All. *International Journal of English Language Studies*, 6(3), 42–52. DOI: 10.32996/ijels.2024.6.3.7

Ellingson, K. (2016) Interactive Technology Use in Early Childhood Programs to Enhance Literacy Development & Early Literacy Development for Children with Cochlear Implants, Culminating Projects in Child and Family Studies, Paper 3. Available online at: https://repository.stcloudstate.edu/cfs_etds/3

Ellis, S. (1994, January). What are Virtual Environments? *IEEE Computer Graphics and Applications*, 14(1), 17–21. DOI: 10.1109/38.250914 PMID: 7757252

Engestrom, Y. (1987). Learning by Expanding: An Activity Theoretical Approach to Developmental Research. Helsinki, Finland: Orienta-Konsultit. https://lchc.ucsd.edu/mca/Paper/Engestrom/Learning-by-Expanding.pdf

Erdem, M. (2019). *Yeniden Öğretmeyi Öğrenmek, Organizmadan Bireye Öğretim Süreçleri Tasarımı*. Pegem Akademi.

Erdem, R. (2017). Students with Special Educational Needs and Assistive Technologies: A Literature Review. *The Turkish Online Journal of Educational Technology*, 16(1), 128–146. https://files.eric.ed.gov/fulltext/EJ1124910.pdf

Eryılmaz, S. (2021). Compare Teachers and Students Attitudes According to Mobile EducationalApplications. *The Turkish Online Journal of Educational Technology*, 20(1), 19–24.

Escobar, N. R. E. (2019). Las baterías como residuos tecnológicos contaminantes: Un reto de la educación ambiental. *ESPIRAL*, 9(1), 71–85. DOI: 10.15332/erdi.v9i1.2442

Eziamaka, N. V., Odonker, T. N., & Akinsulire, A. A.Nnaemeka Valentine EziamakaTheodore Narku OdonkorAdetola Adewale Akinsulire. (2024). AI-Driven accessibility: Transformative software solutions for empowering individuals with disabilities. *International Journal of Applied Research in Social Sciences*, 6(8), 1612–1641. DOI: 10.51594/ijarss.v6i8.1373

Faresta, R. A. (2024). AI-Powered Education: Exploring the Potential of Personalised Learning for Students' Needs in Indonesia Education. *Traektoriâ Nauki*, 10(5), 3012–3022. DOI: 10.22178/pos.104-19

Fereday, J., & Muir-Cochrane, E. (2006). Demonstrating Rigor Using Thematic Analysis: A Hybrid Approach of Inductive and Deductive Coding and Theme Development. *International Journal of Qualitative Methods*, 5(1), 80–92. DOI: 10.1177/160940690600500107

Fernández-Batanero, J. M., Montenegro-Rueda, M., & Fernández-Cerero, J. (2022). Use of Augmented Reality for Students with Educational Needs: A Systematic Review (2016–2021). *Societies (Basel, Switzerland)*, 12(2), 36. DOI: 10.3390/soc12020036

Fernández-Batanero, J. M., Montenegro-Rueda, M., Fernández-Cerero, J., & Garcia-Martinez, I. (2022). Assistive technology for the inclusion of students with disabilities: A systematic review. *Educational Technology Research and Development*, 70(5), 1911–1930. DOI: 10.1007/s11423-022-10127-7

Fichten, C. S., Ferraro, V., Asuncion, J. V., Chwojka, C., Barile, M., Nguyen, M. N., & Wolforth, J. (2009). Disabilities and e-learning problems and solutions: An exploratory study. *Journal of Educational Technology & Society*, 12(4), 241–256.

Fleer, M. (2014). The demands and motives afforded through digital play in early childhood activity settings. *Learning, Culture and Social Interaction*, 3(3), 202–209. DOI: 10.1016/j.lcsi.2014.02.012

Fletcher, M. (2021). Using haptic stimulation to enhance auditory perception in hearing-impaired listeners. *Expert Review of Medical Devices*, 18(1), 63–74. DOI: 10.1080/17434440.2021.1863782 PMID: 33372550

Forber-Pratt, A., Merrin, G. J., & Espelage, D. (2020). Exploring the Intersections of Disability, Race, and Gender on Student Outcomes in High School. *Remedial and Special Education*, •••, 1–14.

França, R. P., Monteiro, A. C. B., Arthur, R., & Iano, Y. (2021). An overview of deep learning in big data, image, and signal processing in the modern digital age. In *Elsevier eBooks* (pp. 63–87). DOI: 10.1016/B978-0-12-822226-3.00003-9

Fteiha, M., Al-Rashaida, M., Elsori, D., Khalil, A., & Al Bustami, G. (2024). Obstacles for using assistive technology in centres of special needs in the UAE. *Disability and Rehabilitation. Assistive Technology*, 19(8), 1–11. DOI: 10.1080/17483107.2024.2323698 PMID: 38436086

Ganz, J., Hong, E., & Goodwyn, F. (2013). Effectiveness of the PECS Phase III apps that the choice between the app and traditional PECS among preschoolers with ASD. *Research in Autism Spectrum Disorders*, 7(8), 973–983. DOI: 10.1016/j.rasd.2013.04.003

Gao, F. (2023). Research on VR equipment based on VR technology. *Journal of Innovation and Development*, 2(2), 44–47. DOI: 10.54097/jid.v2i2.5910

Ghorashi, N., Ismail, A., Ghosh, P., Sidawy, A., & Javan, R. (2023). AI-Powered Chatbots in Medical Education: Potential Applications and Implications. *Cureus*. Advance online publication. DOI: 10.7759/cureus.43271 PMID: 37692629

Gil, M. J. V., Gonzalez-Medina, G., Lucena-Anton, D., Perez-Cabezas, V., Del Carmen Ruiz-Molinero, M., & Martín-Valero, R. (2021). Augmented Reality in Physical Therapy: Systematic Review and Meta-analysis. *JMIR Serious Games*, 9(4), e30985. DOI: 10.2196/30985 PMID: 34914611

Gligorea, I., Cioca, M., Oancea, R., Gorski, A., Gorski, H., & Tudorache, P. (2023a). Adaptive Learning Using Artificial Intelligence in e-Learning: A Literature Review. *Education Sciences*, 13(12), 1216. DOI: 10.3390/educsci13121216

Godin, J., Freeman, A., & Rigby, P. (2017). Interventions to promote the playful engagement in social interaction of preschool-aged children with autism spectrum disorder (ASD): A scoping study. *Early Child Development and Care*. Advance online publication. DOI: 10.1080/03004430.2017.1404999

Goodwin, K., & Highfield, K. (2012). iTouch and iLearn: an examination of "educational" apps, Paper presented at the Early Education and Technology for Children Conference, 14– 16 March, Salt Lake City, Utah.

Grabham, E., Herman, D., Cooper, D., & Krishnadas, J. (2009). Introduction. In Grabham, E., Cooper, D., Krishnadas, J., & Herman, D. (Eds.), *Intersectionality and beyond: Law, power and politics of location* (pp. 1–17). Taylor and Francis Group.

Gransden, C., Hindmarsh, M., Lê, N. C., & Nguyen, T.-H. (2024). Adaptive learning through technology: A technical review and implementation, *Higher Education. Skills and Work-Based Learning*, 14(2), 409–417. DOI: 10.1108/HESWBL-05-2023-0121

Groenewegen, S., Heinz, S., Fröhlich, B., & Huckauf, A. (2008). Virtual world interfaces for special needs education based on props on a board. *Computers & Graphics*, 32(5), 589–596. DOI: 10.1016/j.cag.2008.07.002

Guan, C., Mou, J., & Jiang, Z. (2020). Artificial intelligence innovation in education: A twenty-year data-driven historical analysis. *International Journal of Innovation Studies*, 4(4), 134–147. DOI: 10.1016/j.ijis.2020.09.001

Guide, M. (2024). [AT]. *Assistive Technology*, 11, 3.

Gupta, P. (2020). A Comprehensive List of Edapps in Special Education. EdTechReview. Retrieved May 06, 2022 from https://edtechreview.in/trends-insights/insights/ 3924-a- comprehensive-list-of-ed-apps-in-special-education

Haleem, A., Javaid, M., Qadri, M. A., & Suman, R. (2022). Understanding the role of digital technologies in education: A review. *Sustainable Operations and Computers*, 3, 275–285. DOI: 10.1016/j.susoc.2022.05.004

Halkiopoulos, C., & Gkintoni, E. (2024). Leveraging AI in E-Learning: Personalized Learning and Adaptive Assessment through Cognitive Neuropsychology—A Systematic Analysis. *Electronics (Basel)*, 13(18), 3762. DOI: 10.3390/electronics13183762

Halpin, M. (2024). *Assistive Technology in Education: Tools for Disabled Students in the Classroom*. UK: Recite Me. https://reciteme.com/news/assistive-technology-in-education/

Hamm, E. (2006). Playfulness and the environmental support of play in children with and without disabilities. *OTJR (Thorofare, N.J.)*, 26(3), 88–96. DOI: 10.1177/153944920602600302

Hargraves, V. (2022). What is digital play? Digital technologies in ECE. The Education Hub. Published online Feb 1, 2022 https://theeducationhub.org.nz/what-is-digital-play/#_edn2

Harmon, G. E. (2019). *Health care augmented intelligence: Where the AMA stands*. https://www.ama-assn.org/system/files/2019-08/ai-2018-board-policy-summary.pdf

Hashey, A. I., & Stahl, S. (2014). Making online learning accessible for students with disabilities. *Teaching Exceptional Children*, 46(5), 70–78. DOI: 10.1177/0040059914528329

Hawkins, R. E., Welcher, C. M., Holmboe, E. S., Kirk, L. M., Norcini, J. J., Simons, K. B., & Skochelak, S. E. (2015). Implementation of competency-based medical education: Are we addressing the concerns and challenges? *Medical Education*, 49(11), 1086–1102. DOI: 10.1111/medu.12831 PMID: 26494062

Hayes, A. M., & Bulat, J. (2017). *Disabilities Inclusive Education Systems and Policies Guide for Low- and Middle-Income Countries*. RTI Press Publication No. OP-0043-1707. Research Triangle Park, NC: RTI Press. https://doi.org/DOI: 10.3768/rtipress.2017.op.0043.1707

HCPSS. (2024). *Special Education Programs*. https://www.hcpss.org/special-education/programs/

Healey, A., & Mendelsohn, A. (2019). Selecting appropriate toys for young children in the digital era. *Pediatrics*, 143(1), 1–10. DOI: 10.1542/peds.2018-3348 PMID: 30509931

Healthcare Simulation Dictionary. (2020). *Agency for Healthcare Research and Quality eBooks.*, DOI: 10.23970/simulationv2

Hecker, L., Burns, L., Katz, L., Elkind, J., & Elkind, K. (2002). Benefits of assistive reading software for students with attention disorders. *Annals of Dyslexia*, 52(1), 243–272. DOI: 10.1007/s11881-002-0015-8

Heinen, M., Van Oostveen, C., Peters, J., Vermeulen, H., & Huis, A. (2019). An integrative review of leadership competencies and attributes in advanced nursing practice. *Journal of Advanced Nursing*, 75(11), 2378–2392. DOI: 10.1111/jan.14092 PMID: 31162695

Hersh, M., & Mouroutsou, S. (2015). Learning Technology and Disability: Overcoming Barriers to Inclusion: Evidence from a Multi-Country Study. *IFAC-PapersOnLine*, 48(24), 83–88. DOI: 10.1016/j.ifacol.2015.12.061

Hirsh-Pasek, K., Zosh, J. M., Golinkoff, R. M., Gray, J. H., Robb, M. B., & Kaufman, J. (2015). Putting education in "educational" apps lessons from the science of learning. *Psychological Science in the Public Interest*, 16(1), 3–34. DOI: 10.1177/1529100615569721 PMID: 25985468

Hof, L., Pee, J., Sturm, J., Bekker, T., & Verbeek, J. (2010). Prolonged play with the ColorFlares: How does open-ended play behavior change over time? *Proceedings of the 3rd International Conference on Fun and Games*, 106. https://doi.org/DOI: 10.1145/1823818.1823829

Holmes, W., & Littlejohn, A. (2024). 10. Artificial intelligence for professional learning. Handbook of Artificial Intelligence at Work: Interconnections and Policy Implications, p. 191.

Holmgren, M. (2021). The Inclusion of Special Education in School's Digitalization - a special educational perspective on the digitalization of schools. ECER 2021—European Educational Research Association. Available at: https://eera-ecer.de/ecer-programmes/conference/26/contribution/50694

Holmgren, M. (2022). Enacting Special Education in a Digitalized School: Opening for New Understandings of a Digitalized Special Educational Practice. *Journal of Special Education Technology*, 0(0). Advance online publication. DOI: 10.1177/01626434221131776

Honorato, N., Soltiyeva, A., Oliveira, W., Delabrida, S. E., Hamari, J., & Alimanova, M. (2024). Gameful strategies in the education of autistic children: A systematic literature review, scientometric analysis, and future research roadmap. *Smart Learn. Environ.*, 11(1), 25. DOI: 10.1186/s40561-024-00309-6

Horowitz, K. (2004). Sega VR: Great Idea or Wishful Thinking? Retrieved 19 May 2015, from: http://web.archive.org/web/20100114191355/http://sega-16.com/feature_page.php?id=5&title=Sega

How does AI Impact on Education? Top Ways to Use AI in Education. (n.d.) https://yourtechdiet.com/blogs/how-does-ai-impact-on-education-top-ways-to-use-ai-in-education/, accessed on 20.08.2024

Hsieh, Y. (2022). *Eye-gaze assistive technology for play, communication and learning: Impacts on children and youths with severe motor and communication difficulties and their partners*. Academic dissertation for the Degree of Doctor of Philosophy in Special Education at Stockholm University. https://su.diva-portal.org/smash/get/diva2:1688403/FULLTEXT03.pdf

Huang, H.-M., Rauch, U., & Liaw, S.-S. (2010). Investigating learners' attitudes toward virtual reality learning environments: Based on a constructivist approach. *Computers & Education*, 55(3), 1171–1182. DOI: 10.1016/j.compedu.2010.05.014

Huang, L. (2023). Ethics of Artificial Intelligence in Education: Student Privacy and Data Protection. *Science Insights Education Frontiers*, 16(2), 2577–2587. DOI: 10.15354/sief.23.re202

Human, O. D. (2023). *The Routledge International Handbook of Disability Human Rights Hierarchies*.

Hwang, G. J., Xie, H., Wah, B. W., & Gašević, D. (2020). Vision, challenges, roles and research issues of Artificial Intelligence in Education, Computers & Education. *Artificial Intelligence*, 1, 100001.

Ioerger, M., Flanders, R. M., French-Lawyer, J. R., & Turk, M. A. (2019). Interventions to Teach Medical Students About Disability. *American Journal of Physical Medicine & Rehabilitation*, 98(7), 577–599. DOI: 10.1097/PHM.0000000000001154 PMID: 30730327

Islim, O., & Cagiltay, K. (2012). Disability and assistive technology. *6th International Computer & Instructional Technologies Symposium, October 4th - 6th 2012 Gaziantep* (pp. 1-6). Turkey: Gaziantep.

Jain, A., Kamat, S., Saini, V., Singh, A., & Whig, P. (2024). Agile Leadership: Navigating Challenges and Maximizing Success. In Practical Approaches to Agile Project Management (pp. 32-47). IGI Global.

Jamil, S. (2021). From digital divide to digital inclusion: Challenges for wide-ranging digitalization in Pakistan. *Telecommunications Policy*, 45(8), 102206. DOI: 10.1016/j.telpol.2021.102206

Jeffs, T., Morrison, W. F., Messenheimer, T., Rizza, M. G., & Banister, S. (2003). A Retrospective Analysis of Technological Advancements in Special Education. *Computers in the Schools*, 20(1–2), 129–152. DOI: 10.1300/J025v20n01_10

Jeyaraman, M., Balaji, S., Jeyaraman, N., & Yadav, S. (2023). Unraveling the Ethical Enigma: Artificial Intelligence in Healthcare. *Cureus*. Advance online publication. DOI: 10.7759/cureus.43262 PMID: 37692617

Jian, M. J. K. O. (2023). Personalized learning through AI. *Advances in Engineering Innovation*, 5(1), 16–19. DOI: 10.54254/2977-3903/5/2023039

Jin, J., & Bridges, S. M. (2014). Educational Technologies in Problem-Based Learning in Health Sciences Education: A Systematic Review. *Journal of Medical Internet Research*, 16(12), e251. DOI: 10.2196/jmir.3240 PMID: 25498126

Johnson, J., & Christie, J. (2009). Play and digital media. Computers in the schools. *Interdisciplinary Journal of Practice, Theory, and Applied Research.*, 26(4), 284–289.

Joshi, A. K. (1991). Natural Language Processing. *Science*, 253(5025), 1242–1249. DOI: 10.1126/science.253.5025.1242 PMID: 17831443

Joshi, S. (2021). Rising importance of remote learning in India in the wake of COVID-19: Issues, challenges and way forward. *World Journal of Science. Technology and Sustainable Development*, 18(1), 44–63.

Juma, R. K., & Ntulo, G. R. (2024). The Availability and Use of Assistive Technologies among Pupils with Hearing and Visual Impairments in Zanzibar. *International Journal of Education and Development Using Information and Communication Technology*, 20(1), 63–77. https://files.eric.ed.gov/fulltext/EJ1426581.pdf

Kabudi, T., Pappas, I., & Olsen, D. H. (2021). AI-enabled adaptive learning systems: A systematic mapping of the literature, Computers and Education: Artificial Intelligence, Volume 2, 2021, 100017, ISSN 2666-920X, https://doi.org/DOI: 10.1016/j.caeai.2021.100017

Kambouri, M., Simon, H., & Brooks, G. (2023). Using speech-to-text technology to empower young writers with special educational needs. *Research in Developmental Disabilities*, 135, 104466. DOI: 10.1016/j.ridd.2023.104466 PMID: 36863156

Kaptelinin, V. (1996). Activity Theory: Implications for Human Computer Interaction. In Nardi, B. (Ed.), *Context and Consciousness: Activity Theory and Human-Computer Interaction* (pp. 103–116). MIT Press.

Karki, J., Rushton, S., Bhattarai, S., & De Witte, L. (2021). Access to assistive technology for persons with disabilities: A critical review from Nepal, India and Bangladesh. *Disability and Rehabilitation. Assistive Technology*, 18(1), 8–16. DOI: 10.1080/17483107.2021.1892843 PMID: 33651968

Kartiko, D. C., Juniarisca, D. L., Tuasikal, A. R. S., Prakoso, B. B., & Nurhayati, F. (2020). Android - Based Sport Board Games for Intellectual Disabilities. Presented at the (2020). DOI: 10.2991/assehr.k.201201.191

Kasula, B. Y., Whig, P., Vegesna, V. V., & Yathiraju, N. (2024). Unleashing Exponential Intelligence: Transforming Businesses through Advanced Technologies. International Journal of Sustainable Development Through AI. *ML and IoT*, 3(1), 1–18.

Kaulu, J. (2019). *Efficacy of assistive technology on the visually impaired learners' grasping of library information services: A case of Zambia library cultural and skills centre for the visually impaired (ZLCSVI) in Lusaka, Zambia*. A Dissertation submitted to the University of Zambia in Partial Fulfillment of the Requirements of the Degree of Master of Library and Information Science (MLIS): University of Zambia.

Kearsley, G., & Shneiderman, B. (1998). Engagement theory: A framework for technology-based teaching and learning. Educational Technology, 38(5), 20-23. JSTOR. www.jstor.org/stable/44428478

Keelor, J. L., Creaghead, N., Silbert, N., & Horowitz-Kraus, T. (2020). Text-to-Speech Technology: Enhancing Reading Comprehension for Students with Reading Difficulty. *Assistive Technology Outcomes and Benefits*, 14, 19–35. https://www.atia.org/wp-content/uploads/2020/06/ATOB-V14-A2-Keelor_etal.pdf

Keen, D., Webster, A., & Ridley, G. (2016). How well are children with autism spectrum disorder doing academically at school? An overview of the literature. *Autism*, 20(3), 276–294. DOI: 10.1177/1362361315580962 PMID: 25948598

Ke, F., & Im, T. (2013). Virtual-reality-based social interaction training for children with high-functioning autism. *The Journal of Educational Research*, 106(6), 441–461. DOI: 10.1080/00220671.2013.832999

Kemp, C., Stephenson, J., Cooper, M., & Hodge, K. (2016). Engaging preschool children with severe and multiple disabilities using books and iPad apps. *Infants and Young Children*, 29(4), 249–266. DOI: 10.1097/IYC.0000000000000075

Khalid, U. B., Naeem, M., Stasolla, F., Syed, M. H., Abbas, M., & Coronato, A. (2024). Impact of AI-powered solutions in rehabilitation process: Recent improvements and future trends. *International Journal of General Medicine*, 17, 943–969. DOI: 10.2147/IJGM.S453903 PMID: 38495919

King, N. (2004). Using templates in the thematic analysis of text C. Cassell G. Symon Qualitative methods in organizational research: The definitive guide 256–270 London Sage.

King, M., Takeguchi, K., Barry, S., Rehfeldt, R., Boyer, V., & Mathews, T. (2014). Evaluation of the iPad in the acquisition of requesting skills for children with autism spectrum disorder. *Research in Autism Spectrum Disorders*, 8(9), 1107–1120. DOI: 10.1016/j.rasd.2014.05.011

King, N., & Brooks, J. (2017). *Doing Template Analysis: A Guide to the Main Components and Procedures*. SAGE Publications Ltd., DOI: 10.4135/9781473983304

Kirboyun, S. (2020). High-Tech or Low-Tech? Impact of Assistive Technology in School Settings for Students with Visual Impairments: Review of Research. [IJI]. *International Journal for Infonomics*, 13(1), 1945–1953. https://infonomics-society.org/wp-content/uploads/High-Tech-or-Low-Tech.pdf. DOI: 10.20533/iji.1742.4712.2020.0201

KISE. (2024). Making quality and equitable education and services accessible to persons with Special Needs and Disabilities. https://kise.ecitizen.go.ke/

Klingenberg, C. O., Borges, M. A. V., & Antunes, J. A. V.Jr. (2021). Industry 4.0 as a data-driven paradigm: A systematic literature review on technologies. *Journal of Manufacturing Technology Management*, 32(3), 570–592. DOI: 10.1108/JMTM-09-2018-0325

Koedinger, K. R., Brunskill, E., Baker, R. S., McLaughlin, E. A., & Stamper, J. (2013). New potentials for data-driven intelligent tutoring system development and optimization. *AI Magazine*, 34(3), 27–41. DOI: 10.1609/aimag.v34i3.2484

Kong, S. C. (2014). Developing information literacy and critical thinking skills through domain knowledge learning in digital classrooms: An experience of practicing flipped classroom strategy. *Computers & Education*, 78, 160–173. DOI: 10.1016/j.compedu.2014.05.009

Köse, H., & Güner-Yildiz, N. (2020). Augmented reality (AR) as a learning material in special needs education. *Education and Information Technologies*, 26(2), 1921–1936. DOI: 10.1007/s10639-020-10326-w

Kumar, A., & Nagar, D. K. (2024). AI-Based Language Translation and Interpretation Services: Improving Accessibility for Visually Impaired Students. *As the editors of Transforming Learning. Power and Education*, 178.

Kunka, A., & Wahome, N. (2021). The Role of Assistive Technology in the Education of Children with Special Needs: Teacher's Perspectives. Unpublished Master Thesis submitted to Linkoping University. https://www.diva-portal.org/smash/get/diva2:1639908/FULLTEXT01.pdf

Kunnath, S. K., & Mathew, S. N. (2019). Higher education for students with disabilities in India: Insights from a focus group study. *Higher Education for the Future*, 6(2), 171–187. DOI: 10.1177/2347631119840540

Kunwar, R. (2022). An overview of dyslexia: Some key issues and its effect on learning mathematics. *Turkish International Journal of Special Education and Guidance & Counseling*, 11(2), 82–98.

Kushner, D. (2014). Virtual reality's moment. *IEEE Spectrum*, 51(1), 34–37. DOI: 10.1109/MSPEC.2014.6701429

Lahiri, U., Bekele, E., Dohrmann, E., Warren, Z., & Sarkar, N. (2015). A physiologically informed virtual reality-based social communication system for individuals with autism. *Journal of Autism and Developmental Disorders*, 45(4), 919–931. DOI: 10.1007/s10803-014-2240-5 PMID: 25261247

Lahm, E. A. (2003). Assistive Technology Specialists: Bringing Knowledge of Assistive Technology to School Districts. *Remedial and Special Education*, 24(3), 141–153. DOI: 10.1177/07419325030240030301

Lancioni, G. E., Singh, N. N., O'Reilly, M. F., Sigafoos, J., Alberti, G., Perilli, V., Zimbaro, C., & Chiariello, V. (2017). Supporting leisure and communication in people with visual and intellectual disabilities via a smartphone-based program. *British Journal of Visual Impairment*, 35(3), 257–263. Advance online publication. DOI: 10.1177/0264619617715497

Laurie, M. H., Manches, A., & Fletcher-Watson, S. (2022). The role of robotic toys in shaping play and joint engagement in autistic children: Implications for future design, International Journal of Child-Computer Interaction, Volume 32, 100384, ISSN 2212-8689, https://doi.org/DOI: 10.1016/j.ijcci.2021.100384

Lave, J., & Wenger, E. (1991). *Situated Learning: Legitimate Peripheral Practice*. Cambridge University Press. DOI: 10.1017/CBO9780511815355

Lawson, A., & Beckett, A. (2021). The social and human rights models of disability: towards a complementarity thesis. *The International Journal of Human Rights vol 25 Issue 2*, 1-32.

Lee, S. L. ve Huang, C. Y. (2007). The effects of 3-D graphics-based virtual reality on the pedestrianized skills of elementary students with intellectual disabilities. *Paper presented at the meeting of the 18th Asian Conference on Mental Retardation*, Taipei, Taiwan. Paper retrieved from http://www.jldd.jp/gtid/acmr_18/pdf/57.pdf

Lee, D., Pollack, S. W., Mroz, T., Frogner, B. K., & Skillman, S. M. (2023). Disability competency training in medical education. *Medical Education Online*, 28(1), 2207773. Advance online publication. DOI: 10.1080/10872981.2023.2207773 PMID: 37148284

Le, H., Janssen, J., & Wubbels, T. (2017). Collaborative learning practices: Teacher and student perceived obstacles to effective student collaboration. *Cambridge Journal of Education*, 48(1), 103–122. DOI: 10.1080/0305764X.2016.1259389

Leung, L. (2014). Availability, access and affordability across' digital divides': Common experiences amongst minority groups. *Journal of Telecommunications and the Digital Economy*, 2(2), 38–1. DOI: 10.7790/ajtde.v2n2.38

Li, G., Zarei, M. A., Alibakhshi, G., & Labbafi, A. (2024). Teachers and educators' experiences and perceptions of artificial-powered interventions for autism groups. *BMC Psychology*, 12(1), 199. DOI: 10.1186/s40359-024-01664-2 PMID: 38605422

Lim, L. A., Dawson, S., Gašević, D., Joksimović, S., Fudge, A., Pardo, A., & Gentili, S. (2020). Students' sense-making of personalised feedback based on learning analytics. *Australasian Journal of Educational Technology*, 36(6), 15–33. DOI: 10.14742/ajet.6370

Lim, T., Gottipati, S., & Cheong, M. L. F. (2023). Ethical considerations for artificial intelligence in educational assessments. In Keengwe, J. (Ed.), (pp. 32–79). Advances in educational technologies and instructional design. IGI Global., DOI: 10.4018/979-8-3693-0205-7.ch003

Lin, M., Baykasoglu, A., & Dominici, G. (2024). Artificial Intelligence Technology in Education, International Journal of Intelligent Computing and Cybernetics, https://emeraldgrouppublishing.com/calls-for-papers/artificial-intelligence-technology-education

Lin, H., Grudnoff, L., & Hill, M. (2022). Agency for Inclusion: A Case Study of Special Educational Needs Coordinators (SENCos). *International Journal of Disability Development and Education*. Advance online publication. DOI: 10.1080/1034912X.2022.2137110

Lipka, O., Sarid, M., Zorach, I. A., Bufman, A., Hagag, A. A., & Peretz, H. (2020). Adjustment to Higher Education: A Comparison of Students with and Without Disabilities. *Frontiers in Psychology*, 11, 923. Advance online publication. DOI: 10.3389/fpsyg.2020.00923 PMID: 32670127

Li, Q., & Qin, Y. (2023). AI in medical education: Medical student perception, curriculum recommendations and design suggestions. *BMC Medical Education*, 23(1), 852. Advance online publication. DOI: 10.1186/s12909-023-04700-8 PMID: 37946176

Liu, K. K., Thurlow, M. L., Press, A. M., Dosedel, M. J., & University of Minnesota, National Center on Educational Outcomes. (2019). *A Review of the Literature on Computerized Speech-to-Text Accommodations* (Report No. 414). University of Minnesota, National Center on Educational Outcomes. https://files.eric.ed.gov/fulltext/ED600670.pdf

Liu, D. Y. T., Bartimote-Aufflick, K., Pardo, A., & Bridgeman, A. J. (2017). Data-driven personalization of student learning support in higher education. *Learning analytics: Fundaments, applications, and trends: A view of the current state of the art to enhance e-learning*, 143-169.

Llerena Sarcco, P. A., Diaz Zegarra, P. F., & Sulla-Torres, J. A. (2023). Mobile App for the Learning of Children with Intellectual Disabilities. *CEUR Workshop Proceedings*, 3693, 130–140.

Lo, C. K., & Hew, K. F. (2017). A critical review of flipped classroom challenges in K-12 education: Possible solutions and recommendations for future research. *Research and Practice in Technology Enhanced Learning*, 12(1), 1–22. DOI: 10.1186/s41039-016-0044-2 PMID: 30613253

Local Rehabilitation Workshops(LOREWO). (2013, 02 14). *LOREWO concept*. Retrieved from Local Rehabilitation Workshops (LOREWO): https://www.sintef.no/en/projects/2001/lokale-rehabiliteringsverksteder/

Loets, A. (2024). Intersectional disadvantage. *Australasian Journal of Philosophy vol 102 Issue No 4*, 857–878.

Lorah, E., Parnell, A., & Speight, D. (2014). Acquisition of sentence frame discrimination using the iPad as a speech generating device in young children with developmental disabilities. *Research in Autism Spectrum Disorders*, 8(12), 1734–1740. DOI: 10.1016/j.rasd.2014.09.004

Lovett, B. J. (2021). Educational Accommodations for Students with Disabilities: Two Equity-Related Concerns. *Frontiers in Education*, 6, 795266. Advance online publication. DOI: 10.3389/feduc.2021.795266

Loveys, M., & Butler, C. (2023). Teachers' and students' perspectives on the extent to which assistive technology maximises independence. *British Journal of Visual Impairment*, 0(0), 02646196231212736. Advance online publication. DOI: 10.1177/02646196231212736

Lund, A., & Aagaard, T.Lund & Aagaard. (2020). Digitalization of teacher education: Are we prepared for epistemic change? *NJCIE*, 4(3-4), 56–71. DOI: 10.7577/njcie.3751

Lynch, P., Singal, N., & Francis, G. A. (2022). Educational technology for learners with disabilities in primary school settings in low- and middle-income countries: A systematic literature review. *Educational Review*, 76(2), 405–431. DOI: 10.1080/00131911.2022.2035685

Macrotrends. (2024, 11 2). *Zimbabwe Population 1950-2024*. Retrieved from Macrotrends: https://www.macrotrends.net/global-metrics/countries/ZWE/zimbabwe/population

Main barriers to education for students with disabilities (fact sheet) | Ontario Human Rights Commission. (n.d.). https://www3.ohrc.on.ca/en/main-barriers-education-students-disabilities-fact-sheet

Malik, C. (December 10, 2021). Engagement Theory of Learning An Overview. Self-CAD https://www.selfcad.com/blog/engagement-theory-of-learning-an-overview

Manzano-García, B., & Fernández, M. T. (2016). The inclusive education in Europe. *Universal Journal of Educational Research*, 4(2), 383–391. DOI: 10.13189/ujer.2016.040210

Marsh, J. (2010). Young children's play in online virtual worlds. *Journal of Early Childhood Research*, 8(1), 23–39. DOI: 10.1177/1476718X09345406

Marsh, J., Plowman, L., Yamada-Rice, D., Bishop, J., & Scott, F. (2016). Digital play: A new classification. *Early Years Journal of International Research and Development*, 36(3), 242–253. DOI: 10.1080/09575146.2016.1167675

Masruroh, M., F.L., Hadiati, S.R., Budirahayu, T. (2014). Android Technology-Based Educative Games for Children with Intellectual Disability: A Case Study at Yayasan Peduli Kasih Anak Berkebutuhan Khusus. In: Proceedings of the 2014 International Conference on Advances in Education Technolog. https://doi.org/DOI: 10.2991/icaet-14.2014.25

Mbazzi, F. (2022). *Disability and ubuntu*. Uganda Research Unit.

McDonald, P. L., Phillips, J., Harwood, K., Maring, J., & Van Der Wees, P. J. (2022). Identifying requisite learning health system competencies: A scoping review. *BMJ Open*, 12(8), e061124. DOI: 10.1136/bmjopen-2022-061124 PMID: 35998963

McGonigle, D., & Eggers, R. M. (1998). Stages of Virtuality: Instructor and Student. The Association for Educational Communication and Technology. *TechTrends*, 43(3), 23–26. DOI: 10.1007/BF02824051

McKee, M., Case, B., Fausone, M., Zazove, P., Ouellette, A., & Fetters, M. D. (2016). Medical Schools' Willingness to Accommodate Medical Students with Sensory and Physical Disabilities: Ethical Foundations of a Functional Challenge to "Organic" Technical Standards. *AMA Journal of Ethics*, 18(10), 993–1002. DOI: 10.1001/journalofethics.2016.18.10.medu1-1610 PMID: 27780023

McNicholl, A. (2022). Assistive technology outcomes and impacts among students with disabilities in higher education. Unpublished PhD Thesis submitted to School of Psychology Dublin City University. https://doras.dcu.ie/27681/1/17212312_Assistive%20technology%20outcomes%20and%20impacts%20among%20students%20with%20disabilities%20in%20higher%20education.pdf

McNicholl, A., Casey, H., Desmond, D., & Gallagher, P. (2019). The impact of assistive technology use for students with disabilities in higher education: A systematic review. *Disability and Rehabilitation. Assistive Technology*, 16(2), 130–143. DOI: 10.1080/17483107.2019.1642395 PMID: 31335220

Meeks, L. M., Jain, N. R., & Association of American Medical Colleges. (2018). Accessibility, Inclusion, and Action in Medical Education: Lived Experiences of Learners and Physicians with Disabilities. In *Association of American Medical Colleges*. https://sds.ucsf.edu/sites/g/files/tkssra2986/f/aamc-ucsf-disability-special-report-accessible.pdf

Mehta, P., Chillarge, G. R., Sapkal, S. D., Shinde, G. R., & Kshirsagar, P. S. (2023). Inclusion of Children With Special Needs in the Educational System, Artificial Intelligence (AI). In *AI-Assisted Special Education for Students With Exceptional Needs* (pp. 156-185). IGI Global.

Meşe, İ., Taşlıçay, C. A., Kuzan, B. N., Kuzan, T. Y., & Sivrioğlu, A. K. (2023). Educating the next generation of radiologists: A comparative report of ChatGPT and e-learning resources. *Diagnostic and Interventional Radiology (Ankara, Turkey)*, 30(3), 163–174. DOI: 10.4274/dir.2023.232496 PMID: 38145370

Meta, F. (2021), Five Years of VR: A look at the greatest moments from Oculus: https://about.fb.com/news/2021/03/five-years-of-vr-a-look-at-the-greatest-moments-fromoculus/, [Ziyaret tarihi: 09.11.2023].

Mhlongo, S., Mbatha, K., Ramatsetse, B., & Dlamini, R. (2023). Challenges, opportunities, and prospects of adopting and using smart digital technologies in learning environments: An iterative review. *Heliyon*, 9(6), e16348. DOI: 10.1016/j.heliyon.2023.e16348 PMID: 37274691

Minnesota Guide to Assistive Technology. (2024, 1 7). *Types of assistive technology*. Retrieved from Minnesota Guide to Assistive Technology: https://mn.gov/admin/at/getting-started/understanding-at/types/

Mir, M. M., Mir, G. M., Raina, N. T., Mir, S. M., Mir, S. M., Miskeen, E., Alharthi, M. H., & Alamri, M. M. S. (2023). Application of Artificial Intelligence in Medical Education: Current Scenario and Future Perspectives. *PubMed*, 11(3), 133–140. DOI: 10.30476/jamp.2023.98655.1803 PMID: 37469385

Mishra, K. E., Wilder, K., & Mishra, A. K. (2017). Digital literacy in the marketing curriculum: Are female college students prepared for digital jobs? *Industry and Higher Education*, 31(3), 204–211. DOI: 10.1177/0950422217697838

Mittal, S., Koushik, P., Batra, I., & Whig, P. (2024). AI-Driven Inventory Management for Optimizing Operations With Quantum Computing. In Quantum Computing and Supply Chain Management: A New Era of Optimization (pp. 125-140). IGI Global.

Miundy, K., Zaman, H. B., & Nordin, A. (2017). Review on data driven preliminary study pertaining to assistive digital learning technologies to support dyscalculia learners. In *Advances in Visual Informatics: 5th International Visual Informatics Conference, IVIC 2017, Bangi, Malaysia, November 28–30, 2017* [Springer International Publishing.]. *Proceedings*, 5, 233–246.

Mohammad Abedrabbu Alkhawaldeh, M. A. S. K. (2023). Harnessing The Power of Artificial Intelligence for Personalized Assistive Technology in Learning Disabilities. *Journal of Southwest Jiaotong University*, 58(4).

Moinuddin, M., Usman, M., & Khan, R. (2024). Strategic Insights in a Data-Driven Era: Maximizing Business Potential with Analytics and AI. *Revista Española de Documentación Científica*, 18(02), 117–133.

Mokwetsi, J. (2022, 09 12). *UNICEF Zimbabwe helps to advance inclusive education at Margaretha Hugo*. Retrieved from UNICEF Zimbabwe: https://www.unicef.org/zimbabwe/stories/unicef-zimbabwe-helps-advance-inclusive-education-margaretha-hugo

Molina Roldán, S., Marauri, J., Aubert, A., & Flecha, R. (2021). How Inclusive Interactive Learning Environments Benefit Students Without Special Needs. *Frontiers in Psychology*, 12, 661427. DOI: 10.3389/fpsyg.2021.661427 PMID: 33995221

Moloney, H. (2019). *'We must protect our SENCOs' time*. Early Years Educator., DOI: 10.12968/eyed.2019.20.11.8

Moodley, J., & Graham, L. (2015). The importance of intersectionality in disability and gender studies. *Agenda (Durban, South Africa)*, 29(2), 24–33. DOI: 10.1080/10130950.2015.1041802

Moon, N. W., Baker, P. M., & Goughnour, K. (2019). Designing wearable technologies for users with disabilities: Accessibility, usability, and connectivity factors. *Journal of Rehabilitation and Assistive Technologies Engineering*, 6, 2055668319862137. Advance online publication. DOI: 10.1177/2055668319862137 PMID: 35186318

Moreno-Guerrero, A. J., López-Belmonte, J., Marín-Marín, J. A., & Soler-Costa, R. (2020). Scientific development of educational artificial intelligence in web of science. *Future Internet*, 12(8), 124. DOI: 10.3390/fi12080124

Morse, J. M. (2000). Determining sample size. *Qualitative Health Research*, 10(1), 3–5. DOI: 10.1177/104973200129118183

Muhsin, Z. J., Qahwaji, R., Ghanchi, F., & Al-Taee, M. (2024). Review of substitutive assistive tools and technologies for people with visual impairments: Recent advancements and prospects. *Journal on Multimodal User Interfaces*, 18(1), 135–156. DOI: 10.1007/s12193-023-00427-4

Muzata, K. (2020). The Utilisation of Computers to Improve the Quality of Learning for Students with Visual Impairment at the University of Zambia. [ZAJLIS]. *Zambia Journal of Library & Information Science*, 4(2), 34–44.

Muzata, K., Simui, F., Mahlo, D., & Ng'uni, P. (2021). Status of Zambia's Inclusive Education through the Lenses of Teachers. *African Journal of Teacher Education VOL*, 10(1), 1–20. DOI: 10.21083/ajote.v10i1.6338

Nagel, D. A., Penner, J. L., Halas, G., Philip, M. T., & Cooke, C. A. (2024). Exploring experiential learning within interprofessional practice education initiatives for pre-licensure healthcare students: A scoping review. *BMC Medical Education*, 24(1), 139. Advance online publication. DOI: 10.1186/s12909-024-05114-w PMID: 38350938

Nakarmi, S., Ouazzane, K., Yu, Q., Gill, M., & Khemka, S. (2024). Leveraging data driven approach to empower assistive technology.

Namibia Statistical Agency. (2023). *Namibia population and hosuing census main report*. Namibia Statistics Agency.

Narayanan, S., Ramakrishnan, R., Durairaj, E., & Das, A. (2023). Artificial Intelligence Revolutionizing the Field of Medical Education. *Cureus*. Advance online publication. DOI: 10.7759/cureus.49604 PMID: 38161821

National Library of Medicine (NIM). (2024, 08 25). *World Report on Disability 2011*. Retrieved from National Library of Medicine (NIH): https://www.ncbi.nlm.nih.gov/books/NBK304082/

Nilholm, C. (2007). *Perspektiv på specialpedagogik* [Perspectives on special education]. Studentlitteratur.

Nimavat, N., Singh, S., Fichadiya, N., Sharma, P., Patel, N., Kumar, M., Chauhan, G., & Pandit, N. (2021). Online Medical Education in India – Different Challenges and Probable Solutions in the Age of COVID-19. *Advances in Medical Education and Practice*, 12, 237–243. DOI: 10.2147/AMEP.S295728 PMID: 33692645

Nkomo, L. M., & Daniel, B. K. (2021). Providing students with flexible and adaptive learning opportunities using lecture recordings. *Journal of Open, Flexible and Distance Learning*, 25(1), 22–31. https://files.eric.ed.gov/fulltext/EJ1314246.pdf

Nottinghamshire, D. (2024, 11 7). *Social Model versus medical model of disability*. Retrieved from Disability Nottinghamshire: https://www.disabilitynottinghamshire.org.uk/index.php/about/social-model-vs-medical-model-of-disability/

Ntinda, R. (2024, 11 1). *Centre for Human Rights University of Pretoria: Repository on Disability Rights in Africa*. Retrieved from Centre for Human Rights University of Pretoria: http://www.rodra.co.za/countries/namibia/21-countries/namibia/60-updated-country-report

Nuary, M. G., Judijanto, L., Nurliyah, E. S., Muriyanto, M., & El-Farra, S. A. (2022). Impact of AI in Education and Social Development through Individual Empowerment. *Journal of Artificial Intelligence and Development*, 1(2), 89–97.

O'Brien, H. L., & Toms, E. (2008). What is user engagement? A conceptual framework for defining user engagement with technology. *Journal of the Association for Information Science and Technology*, 59, 938–955.

O'Mara, J., & Laidlaw, L. (2011). Living in the iworld: Two literacy researchers reflect on the changing texts and literacy practices of childhood. *English Teaching*, 10(4), 149–159.

Odom, S. L., Thompson, J. L., Hedges, S., Boyd, B. A., Dykstra, J. R., Duda, M. A., Szidon, K. L., Smith, L. E., & Bord, A. (2015). Technology-aided interventions and instruction for adolescents with autism spectrum disorder. *Journal of Autism and Developmental Disorders*, 45(12), 3805–3819. DOI: 10.1007/s10803-014-2320-6 PMID: 25468409

Ogundaini, O., & Mlitwa, N. (2024). *Artificial Intelligence for assistive learning to support physically impaired learners in Sub-Saharan Africa. 16th International Conference on Education and New Learning Technologies*. 1-3 July, 2024, Palma, Spain, pp. 156-163. https://doi.org/DOI: 10.21125/edulearn.2024.0070

Okoye, C. C. (2024). Assistive Technology and Inclusion of Children with Disabilities in Nigeria. *African Journal of Social Sciences and Humanities Research*, 7(3), 218–228. DOI: 10.52589/AJSSHR-JPKFGOEW

Olakanmi, O. A., Akcayir, G., Ishola, O. M., & Demmans Epp, C. (2020). Using technology in special education: Current practices and trends. *Educational Technology Research and Development*, 68(4), 1711–1738. DOI: 10.1007/s11423-020-09795-0

Oldfrey, B., Holloway, C., Walker, J., McCormack, S., Deere, B., Kenney, L., Ssekitoleko, R., Ackers, H., & Miodownik, M. (2023). Repair strategies for assistive technology in low resource settings. *Disability and Rehabilitation. Assistive Technology*, 19(5), 1945–1955. DOI: 10.1080/17483107.2023.2236142 PMID: 37466362

Ontario Human Rights Commission. (2018). *Policy on accessible education for students with disabilities*. https://www3.ohrc.on.ca/en/policy-accessible-education-students-disabilities

Osorio-Saez, E. M., Eryilmaz, N., & Sandoval-Hernandez, A. (2021). Parents' Acceptance of Educational Technology: Lessons From Around the World. *Frontiers in Psychology*, 12, 719430. DOI: 10.3389/fpsyg.2021.719430 PMID: 34526938

Özdemir, O., Erbaş, D., & Yücesoy Özkan, Ş. (2019). Özel eğitimde sanal gerçeklik uygulamaları. *Ankara Üniversitesi Eğitim Bilimleri Fakültesi Özel Eğitim Dergisi*, 20(2), 395–420. DOI: 10.21565/ozelegitimdergisi.448322

Özer Şanal, S., & Erdem, M. (2023). Examination of Special Education with Constructivism: A Theoretical and Review Study. *The European Educational Researcher*, 6(1), 1–20. DOI: 10.31757/euer.611

Özgür, H., Çuhadar, C., & Akgün, F. (2018). Eğitimde oyunlaştırma araştırmalarında güncel eğilimler. *Kastamonu Eğitim Dergisi*, 26(5), 1479–1488.

Ozor, S., Dodo, M., & Bana, D. (2024). Digital literacy skills and assistive technology use as enabler for academic performance of visually impaired students at the Nigerian law school. *Information Impact: Journal of Information and Knowledge Management*, 15(1), 143–152. DOI: 10.4314/iijikm.v15i1.11

Page, R. (2000). Brief history of flight simulation. *Proceedings of the SimTecT*, 2000, 1–11. 10.1.1.132.5428

Panggabean, T. E., Paramansyah, A., Halim, C., & Maliha, S. (2024). Assessing the Effect of Online Learning Platforms in Promoting Inclusive Education for Students with Disabilities. *International Education Trend Issues*, 2(2), 287–297. DOI: 10.56442/ieti.v2i2.696

Pansara, R. R., Mourya, A. K., Alam, S. I., Alam, N., Yathiraju, N., & Whig, P. (2024, May). Synergistic Integration of Master Data Management and Expert System for Maximizing Knowledge Efficiency and Decision-Making Capabilities. In 2024 2nd International Conference on Advancement in Computation & Computer Technologies (InCACCT) (pp. 13-16). IEEE. DOI: 10.1109/InCACCT61598.2024.10551152

Papadakis, S., & Kalogiannakis, M. (2017). Mobile educational applications for children: What educators and parents need to know. *Int. J. Mob. Learn. Organisation*, 11(3), 256–277. DOI: 10.1504/IJMLO.2017.085338

Papadakis, S., Kalogiannakis, M., & Zaranis, N. (2016). Comparing tablets and PCs in teaching mathematics: An attempt to improve mathematics competence in early childhood education. *Preschool and Primary Education*, 4(2), 241. Advance online publication. DOI: 10.12681/ppej.8779

Papamitsiou, Z., Economides, A. A., Pappas, I. O., & Giannakos, M. N. (2018). Explaining learning performance using response-Time, self-Regulation and satisfaction from content: An fsQCA approach, ACM international conference proceeding series (2018), pp. 181-190

Paracha, S., Hagan-Green, G., Hall, L., & Macfarlane, K. (2023). Special iApps: Play-based Learning for Children with Severe Intellectual Disabilities. In *Proceedings of the 10th International Conference on Software Development and Technologies for Enhancing Accessibility and Fighting Info-exclusion (DSAI '22)*. Association for Computing Machinery, New York, USA, 100–106. https://doi.org/ DOI: 10.1145/3563137.3563163

Parette, P., & Scherer, M. (2004). Assistive Technology Use and Stigma. *Education and Training in Developmental Disabilities*, 39(3), 217–226. https://www.jstor.org/stable/23880164

Paulino, D., Amaral, D., Amaral, M., Reis, A., Barroso, J., & Rocha, T. (2016). "Professor piano": A music application for people with intellectual disabilities. In: ACM International Conference Proceeding Series. https://doi.org/DOI: 10.1145/3019943.3019982

Persson, B. (2008). *Elevers olikheter och specialpedagogisk kunskap* [Pupils diversities and special educational knowledge]. Liber.

Pertus, S. (2017). How Equadex used Cognitive Services to help people with language disorders. Technical Case Studies. https://microsoft.github.io/techcasestudies/cognitive%20servi ces/2017/08/04/equadexcognitives.html

Physiopedia. (2024, 11 2). *Assistive devices*. Retrieved from Physiopedia: https://www.physio-pedia.com/Assistive_Devices

Physiopedia. (2024, 11 2). *International Classification of Functioning, Disability and Health (ICF)*. Retrieved from Physiopedia: https://www.physio-pedia.com/International_Classification_of_Functioning,_Disability_and_Health_(ICF)

Pianosi, R., Presley, L., Buchanan, J., Lévesque, A., Savard, S.-A., & Lam, J. (2023). Canadian Survey on Disability, 2022: Concepts and Methods Guide. In *Canadian Survey on Disability* (Report Catalogue no. 89-654-X). Statistics Canada. https://www150.statcan.gc.ca/n1/en/pub/89-654-x/89-654-x2023004-eng.pdf?st= UVRCv8XU (Original work published 2022)

Picciano, A. G. (2021). Theories and frameworks for online education: Seeking an integrated model. In *A Guide to Administering Distance Learning* (pp. 79–103). Brill., DOI: 10.1163/9789004471382_005

Poovan, N., Du Toit, M., & Engelbrecht, A. (2006). The effect of the social values of ubuntu on team effectiveness. *South African Journal of Business Management*, 37(3), 17–27. DOI: 10.4102/sajbm.v37i3.604

Priyadharsini, V., & Mary, R. S. (2024). Universal Design for Learning (UDL) in Inclusive Education: Accelerating Learning for All. *Shanlax International Journal of Arts. Science and Humanities*, 11(4), 145–150. DOI: 10.34293/sijash.v11i4.7489

Procházková, D. (2014). The Human Factor and Its Handling. In *Elsevier eBooks* (pp. 199–223). DOI: 10.1016/B978-0-12-397199-9.00007-0

Pulham, E., & Graham, C. R. (2018). Comparing K-12 online and blended teaching competencies: A literature review. *Distance Education*, 39(3), 411–432. DOI: 10.1080/01587919.2018.1476840

Pulicherla, K. K., Adapa, V., Ghosh, M., & Ingle, P. (2022). Current efforts on sustainable green growth in the manufacturing sector complement "make in India" for making a "self-reliant India.". *Environmental Research*, 206, 112263. DOI: 10.1016/j.envres.2021.112263 PMID: 34695432

Raffoul, S., & Jaber, L. (2023). Text-to-Speech Software and Reading Comprehension: The Impact for Students with Learning Disabilities. *Canadian Journal of Learning and Technology*, 49(2), 1–18. DOI: 10.21432/cjlt28296

Recommendation on the ethics of artificial intelligence. (n.d.). https://unesdoc.unesco.org/ark:/48223/pf0000381137

Remote Proctoring Using Ai – Enabling Seamless Management of Online Examinations. (n.d.) https://www.leewayhertz.com/remote-proctoring-using-ai/#What-are-the-AI-technologies-used-for-Remote-Proctoring. Accessed on 28.08. 2024

Roberts-Yates, C., & Silvera-Tawil, D. (2019). Better Education Opportunities for Students with Autism and Intellectual Disabilities through Digital Technology. *International Journal of Special Education*, 34(1), 197–210.

Romeo, M. (2018). *Introducing intersectionality.* Polity Press.

Rosen-Webb, S. M. (2011). Nobody tells you how to be a SENCo. *British Journal of Special Education*, 38(4), 159–168. DOI: 10.1111/j.1467-8578.2011.00524.x

Ryan, G. V., Callaghan, S., Rafferty, A., Higgins, M. F., Mangina, E., & McAuliffe, F. (2021). Learning Outcomes of Immersive Technologies in Health Care Student Education: Systematic Review of the Literature. *Journal of Medical Internet Research*, 24(2), e30082. DOI: 10.2196/30082 PMID: 35103607

Saaida, M. B. (2023). AI-Driven transformations in higher education: Opportunities and challenges. *International Journal of Educational Research and Studies*, 5(1), 29–36.

Sajja, R., Sermet, Y., Cikmaz, M., Cwiertny, D., & Demir, I. (2024). Artificial Intelligence-Enabled Intelligent Assistant for Personalized and Adaptive Learning in Higher Education. *Information (Basel)*, 15(10), 596. DOI: 10.3390/info15100596

Samuels, A., Stemela, U., & Boo, M. (2020). The intersection between health and education: Meetings the interventions needs of children and youth with a disability. *South African Health Review*, 2, 170–181.

Sandelowski, M. (1996). One is the liveliest number: The case orientation of qualitative research. *Research in Nursing & Health*, 19(6), 525–529. DOI: 10.1002/(SICI)1098-240X(199612)19:6<525::AID-NUR8>3.0.CO;2-Q PMID: 8948406

Satapathy, P. (2019). Applications of Assistive Tools and Technologies in Enhancing the Learning Abilities of Dyslexic Children. *TechnoLEARN: An International Journal of Educational Technology,* 9(2), 117-123. https://ndpublisher.in/admin/issues/TLV9I2i.pdf

Schaaf, D. N. (2018). Assistive Technology Instruction in Teacher Professional Development. *Journal of Special Education Technology*, 33(3), 171–181. DOI: 10.1177/0162643417753561

Sehrawat, S. K., Dutta, P. K., Bhatia, A. B., & Whig, P. (2024). Predicting Demand in Supply Chain Networks With Quantum Machine Learning Approach. In Quantum Computing and Supply Chain Management: A New Era of Optimization (pp. 33-47). IGI Global. DOI: 10.4018/979-8-3693-4107-0.ch002

Seo, K., Tang, J., Roll, I., Fels, S., & Yoon, D. (2021). The impact of artificial intelligence on learner–instructor interaction in online learning. *International Journal of Educational Technology in Higher Education*, 18(1), 54. DOI: 10.1186/s41239-021-00292-9 PMID: 34778540

Seung, Y., & Seung, Y. (2024, October 17). Inclusive Intelligence Chapter 4: Envisioning AI's Impact on Special Education Research - CIDDL. *CIDDL - Center for Innovation, Design, and Digital Learning.* https://ciddl.org/inclusive-intelligence-chapter-4-envisioning-ais-impact-on-special-education-research/

Shafiq, W. (2024). Optimizing Organizational Performance: A Data-Driven Approach in Management Science. *Bulletin of Management Review*, 1(2), 31–40.

Shanker, A. (2022). *Assistive Technology in Inclusive and Special Schools of Bihar: A Study of Availability, Readiness of Teachers and Learning Experiences of Students.* Unpublished PhD Thesis submitted to Department of Teacher Education, School of Education Central University of South Bihar, Gaya. http://dx.doi.org/DOI: 10.13140/RG.2.2.13864.03849

Sharma, S. (2024) AI-Based Adaptive Learning: Revolutionizing Education. https://www.linkedin.com/pulse/ai-based-adaptive-learning-revolutionizing-education-shobha-sharma-ufrec/

Sharma, S., Achary, K., Kinnula, M., Norouzi, B., Kinnula, H., Livari, N., Ventä-Olkkonen, L., & Holappa, J. (2022). To Empower or Provoke? Exploring approaches for participatory design at schools for neurodiverse individuals in India, International Journal of Child-Computer Interaction, Volume 34, 100521, ISSN 2212-8689, https://www.sciencedirect.com/science/article/pii/S2212868922000435 DOI: 10.1016/j.ijcci.2022.100521

Sharma, A., Thakur, K., Kapoor, D. S., & Singh, K. J. (2023). Designing Inclusive Learning Environments: Universal Design for Learning in Practice. In Calhoun, C. (Ed.), *The Impact and Importance of Instructional Design in the Educational Landscape* (pp. 24–61). IGI Global., DOI: 10.4018/978-1-6684-8208-7.ch002

Sharma, J. (2016). Digital India and its Impact on the Society. *International Journal of Research in Humanities &. Soc. Sciences*, 4(4), 64–70.

Shrivastava, R. (2023). Role of artificial intelligence in future of education. *International Journal of Professional Business Review*, 8(1), 2. DOI: 10.26668/businessreview/2023.v8i1.840

Shute, V. J., & Zapata-Rivera, D. (2012). Adaptive educational systems. In Durlach, P. J., & Lesgold, A. M. (Eds.), *Adaptive technologies for training and education* (1st ed., pp. 7–27). Cambridge University Press., DOI: 10.1017/CBO9781139049580.004

Simeoni, R., Pirrera, A., Meli, P., & Giansanti, D. (2023). Promoting Universal Equitable Accessibility: An Overview on the Impact of Assistive Technology in the UN, UNICEF, and WHO Web Portals. *Health Care*, 11(21), 2904. DOI: 10.3390/healthcare11212904 PMID: 37958048

Simplicio, J. S. (2002). The Technology Hub: A Cost Effective And Educationally Sound Method For The Integration Of Technology Into Schools. *Education*, 122(4).

Singh, A. A., Shapter, F. M., Bernard, A., Whitworth, D. J., Holt, M. G., Waller, P. S., & Bond, S. L. (2024). Applying Iterative Student Feedback across Flipped Classroom and Flexible Teaching Approaches: Impact on Veterinary Students' Learning Experience. *Animals (Basel)*, 14(16), 2335. DOI: 10.3390/ani14162335 PMID: 39199869

Singh, R. J. (2023). Transforming higher education: The power of artificial intelligence. *International Journal of Multidisciplinary Research in Arts. Science and Technology*, 1(3), 13–18.

Snowling, M., Hulme, C., & Nation, K. (2020). Defining and understanding dyslexia: Past, present and future. *Oxford Review of Education*, 46(4), 501–513. DOI: 10.1080/03054985.2020.1765756 PMID: 32939103

Sofokleous, R., & Stylianou, S. (2023). Effects of Exposure to Medical Model and Social Model Online Constructions of Disability on Attitudes Toward Wheelchair Users: Results from an Online Experiment. *Journal of Creative Communications*, 18(1), 61–78. DOI: 10.1177/09732586221136260

Somerton, M. (2022). Developing an educational app for students with autism. *Frontiers in Education*, 7, 998694. DOI: 10.3389/feduc.2022.998694

Song, C., Shin, S., & Shin, K. (2024). Implementing the Dynamic Feedback-Driven Learning Optimization Framework: A Machine Learning Approach to Personalize Educational Pathways. *Applied Sciences (Basel, Switzerland)*, 14(2), 916. DOI: 10.3390/app14020916

Soori, M., Arezoo, B., & Dastres, R. (2023). Artificial intelligence, machine learning and deep learning in advanced robotics, a review. *Cognitive Robotics*, 3, 54–70. DOI: 10.1016/j.cogr.2023.04.001

Srinivasa, K. G., Kurni, M., & Saritha, K. (2022). Harnessing the Power of AI to Education. In *Learning, teaching, and assessment methods for contemporary learners: pedagogy for the digital generation* (pp. 311–342). Springer Nature Singapore. DOI: 10.1007/978-981-19-6734-4_13

Statisca. (2024, 11 7). *Socioeconomic indicators Zambia*. Retrieved from Statistica: https://www.statista.com/outlook/co/socioeconomic-indicators/zambia#:~:text=The%20gini%20coefficient%20in%20Zambia,to%200.43m%20in%202024

Statistica. (2024, 11 7). *Socioeconomic indicators for South Africa*. Retrieved from Statistica: https://www.statista.com/outlook/co/socioeconomic-indicators/south-africa#:~:text=The%20gini%20coefficient%20in%20South,to%208.41m%20in%202024

Statistica. (2024, 11 7). *Socioeconomic indicators Namibia*. Retrieved from Statistica: https://www.statista.com/outlook/co/socioeconomic-indicators/namibia#:~:text=The%20gini%20coefficient%20in%20Namibia,forecast%20to%2020.29%25%20in%202024

Statistica. (2024, 11 7). *Socioeconomic indicators Zimbabwe*. Retrieved from Statisca: https://www.statista.com/outlook/co/socioeconomic-indicators/zimbabwe#:~:text=The%20gini%20coefficient%20in%20Zimbabwe,forecasted%20to%2062.90%25%20in%202024

Stats SA Department of Statistics in SA Republic of SA. (2024, 11 2). *South Africa population surpuses 63 million*. Retrieved from Stats SA Department of Statistics in SA Republic of SA: https://www.statssa.gov.za/?p=17430

Svensson, I., Nordström, T., Lindeblad, E., Gustafson, S., Björn, M., Sand, C., Almgrem-Back, G., & Nilsson, S. (2019). Effects of assistive technology for students with reading and writing disabilities. *Disability and Rehabilitation. Assistive Technology*, 16(2), 196–208. DOI: 10.1080/17483107.2019.1646821 PMID: 31418305

Swanson, D. (2007). Ubuntu: An African contribution to (re)search for/with a 'humble togetherness'. *Journal of Contemporary Issues in Education*, 2(2), 53–67.

Tan, S. (2023). Harnessing Artificial Intelligence for innovation in education. In *Learning intelligence: Innovative and digital transformative learning strategies: Cultural and social engineering perspectives* (pp. 335–363). Springer Nature Singapore. DOI: 10.1007/978-981-19-9201-8_8

Tepgec, M., Heil, J., & Ifenthaler, D. (2024). Feedback literacy matters: Unlocking the potential of learning analytics-based feedback. *Assessment & Evaluation in Higher Education*, •••, 1–17. DOI: 10.1080/02602938.2024.2367587

Therasa, M. M. (2023). Adapting Assistive Technology to Diverse Learning Needs in Inclusive Education. *International Journal of Arts, Science and Humanities*, 11(1), 63-66. https://www.researchgate.net/publication/379938594_Adapting_Assistive_Technology_to_Diverse_Learning_Needs_in_Inclusive_Education

Thorneycroft, R. (2024). Screwing the social model of disability. *Scandinavian Journal of Disability Research*, 26(1), 286–299. DOI: 10.16993/sjdr.1130

Tigere, D. (2023, 05 26). *Assistive devices a necessity for people with a disability*. Retrieved from Zimbabwe Independent: https://www.newsday.co.zw/theindependent/opinion/article/200012053/assistive-devices-a-necessity-for-people-with-disabilities

Tikhomirov, O. K. (1999). The theory of activity changed by information technology. In Y. Engeström, R. Miettinen, & R.-L. Punamäki (Eds.), Perspectives on Activity Theory (pp. 347–359). chapter, Cambridge: Cambridge University Press. DOI: 10.1017/CBO9780511812774.023

Tim, S. (2021, June 22). van, Endert. (2021). Addictive use of digital devices in young children: Associations with delay discounting, self-control and academic performance. *PLoS One*, 16(6), e0253058. Advance online publication. DOI: 10.1371/journal.pone.0253058

Tobin, G. A., & Begley, C. M. (2004). Methodological Rigour within a Qualitative Framework. *Journal of Advanced Nursing*, 48(4), 388–396. DOI: 10.1111/j.1365-2648.2004.03207.x PMID: 15500533

Topper, A., & Arizzi, R. (2024, 11 10). *Adaptive and assistive technology an overview & differences*. Retrieved from Study.com: https://study.com/academy/lesson/adaptive-assistive-technology-definition-uses.html

Trafford, Z., van der Westhuizen, E., McDonald, S., Linegar, M., & Swartz, L. (2021). More than just assistive devices: How a South African social enterprises supports an environment of inclusion. *International Journal of Environmental Research and Public Health*, 18(5), 1–15. DOI: 10.3390/ijerph18052655 PMID: 33800783

Trepagnier, C. Y., Olsen, D. E., Boteler, L., & Bell, C. A. (2011). Virtual conversation partner for adults with autism. *Cyberpsychology, Behavior, and Social Networking*, 14(1-2), 21–27. DOI: 10.1089/cyber.2009.0255 PMID: 21329439

Tripathi, M., & Dungarwal, M. (2020). Digital India: Role in development. *International Journal of Home Science*, 6, 388–392.

Tripathi, T. P. (2012). Deconstructing disability, assistive technology: secondary orality, the path to universal access.

Tswellang Special School. (2017, 11 11). *Who we are*. Retrieved from Tswellang Special School: https://www.tswelangschool.co.za/

UNICEF. (2022). The use of Assistive Technology in Education: A Guide for Teachers and Schools. https://www.unicef.org/eca/media/30671/file/Teacher's%20guide%20for%20building%20capacity%20for%20assistive%20technology.pdf

United Nations (UN). (1989). *Convention on the Rights of the Child (CRC)*. New York: UN.

United Nations Children's Fund (UNICEF). (2023, 07 21). *Children with a disabilities in Eastern and Southern Africa: A statistical*. Retrieved from UNICEF for every child: https://data.unicef.org/resources/children-with-disabilities-in-eastern-and-southern-africa-a-statistical-overview-of-their-well-being/

United Nations Development Coordination Office. (2024, 11 2). *UN in Zambia doubles on inclusion down on disability inclusion*. Retrieved from United Nations Development Coordination Office: https://un-dco.org/stories/un-zambia-doubles-down-disability-inclusion

United Nations Educational, Scientific and Cultural Organization . (1994). *World Conference on Special Needs Education: Access and Quality*. Spain: UNESCO.

United Nations. (2006, 12 12). *UN Conventions on the Rights of People with Disabilities*. Retrieved from United Nations Human Rights Commission of People with disabilities: https://www.ohchr.org/en/instruments-mechanisms/instruments/convention-rights-people-disabilities

Valencia, K., Rusu, C., Quiñones, D., & Jamet, E. (2019). The Impact of Technology on People with Autism Spectrum Disorder: A Systematic Literature Review. *Sensors (Basel)*, 19(20), 4485. DOI: 10.3390/s19204485 PMID: 31623200

Vandermeer, J. M., Milford, T. M., Beamish, W., & Lang, W. T. (2012). "Using an iPad presented social story to increase on-task behaviors of a young child with autism," in *Proceedings of the 7th Biennial International Conference on Technology Education Research*, Surfers Paradise, QLD, 146–154.

Vasileiou, K., Barnett, J., Thorpe, S., & Young, T. (2018). Characterising and justifying sample size sufficiency in interview-based studies: Systematic analysis of qualitative health research over a 15-year period. *BMC Medical Research Methodology*, 18(1), 148. DOI: 10.1186/s12874-018-0594-7 PMID: 30463515

Vats, A. & Sharmistha Dey. (2022). Accommodation Strategies for Students with Disabilities in the Classroom. In G D Goenka University & Chandigarh University, *Technoarete Transactions on Applications of Information and Communication Technology (ICT) in Education: Vol. Vol-1* (Issue Issue-4, pp. 25–26). https://technoaretepublication.org/information-communication-technology/article/accommodation-strategies-students.pdf

Veiko, V. (2019). Assistive technology for students with dyslexia at Eros Girls High. A report submitted in partial fullfillment of the requirement for the Master of Science in Information Technology: University of Namibia.

Venkatesan, S. (2023). Digital literacy in people with disabilities: An overview and narrative review.

Verenikina, I., & Kervin, L. (2011). iPads, digital play and preschoolers. *He Kupu.*, 2(5), 4–19.

Vincent, D. A., Okeowo, R. O., & Ariyo, S. (2024). The use of assistive technology in technical colleges for students with disabilities in Ondo State. *Journal of Educational Research and Practice*, 14, 52–67. DOI: 10.5590/JERAP.2024.14.1.04

Vincent-Lancrin, S., & van der Vlies, R. (2020). Trustworthy Artificial Intelligence (AI) in Education: Promises and Challenges. OECD Education Working Papers, No. 218. *OECD Publishing*.

Viner, M., Singh, A., & Shaughnessy, M. F. (2019). Assistive technology to help students with disabilities. In Singh, A., Viner, M., & Yeh, C. J. (Eds.), *Advances in early childhood and K-12 education* (pp. 240–267). IGI Global., DOI: 10.4018/978-1-7998-1431-3.ch012

Visser, M., Nel, M., De Klerk, M., Ganzevoort, A., Hubble, C., Liebenberg, A., Snyman, M., & Young, M. (2020). The use of assistive technology in classroom activities for learners with motor impairments at a special school in South Africa. *South African Journal of Occupational Therapy*, 50(2), 11–22. DOI: 10.17159/2310-3833/2020/vol50no2a3

von Wright, M. (2002). Det relationella perspektivets utmaning: En personlig betraktelse. [The relational perspective's challenge: A personal consideration] In *Attarbeta med särskilt stöd: några perspektiv* (pp. 9–20). Skolverket.

Vygotsky, L. S. (1978). *Mind in society. The development of higher psychological processes*. Harvard University Press.

Vygotsky, L. S. (1978). *Mind in Society: The Development of Higher Psychological Processes*. Harvard University Press.

Waddington, J., Sigafoos, J., Lancioni, G., O'Reilly, M. F., van der Meer, L., Carnett, A., Stevens, M., Roche, L., Hodis, F., Green, V. A., Sutherland, D., Lang, R., & Marschik, P. B. (2014). Three children with autism spectrum disorder learn to perform a three-step communication sequence using an iPad® -based speech-generating device. *International Journal of Developmental Neuroscience*, 39(1), 59–67. DOI: 10.1016/j.ijdevneu.2014.05.001 PMID: 24819024

Wang, H., & Avillach, P. (2021). Diagnostic Classification and Prognostic Prediction Using Common Genetic Variants in Autism Spectrum Disorder: Genotype-Based Deep Learning. *JMIR Medical Informatics*, 9(4), e24754. DOI: 10.2196/24754 PMID: 33714937

Wangmo, T., Lipps, M., Kressig, R. W., & Lenca, M. (2019). Ethical concerns with the use of intelligent assistive technology: Findings from a qualitative study with professional stakeholders. *BMC Medical Ethics*, 20(1), 98. DOI: 10.1186/s12910-019-0437-z PMID: 31856798

Weck, M., & Afanassieva, M. (2023). Toward the adoption of digital assistive technology: Factors affecting older people's initial trust formation. *Telecommunications Policy*, 47(2), 102483. DOI: 10.1016/j.telpol.2022.102483

Weisberg, D. S., Hirsh-Pasek, K., & Golinkoff, R. M. (2013). Guided play: Where curricular goals meet a playful pedagogy. *Mind, Brain and Education : the Official Journal of the International Mind, Brain, and Education Society*, 7(2), 104–112. DOI: 10.1111/mbe.12015

Wesson, P., Hswen, Y., Valdes, G., Stojanovski, K., & Handley, M. A. (2021). Risks and Opportunities to Ensure Equity in applying Big Data Research in Public Health. *Annual Review of Public Health*, 43(1), 59–78. DOI: 10.1146/annurev-publhealth-051920-110928 PMID: 34871504

West, N. (1995). NEXT Generation Issue #6 June 1995: AOU: coin-op houses unveil '95 line-up. Retrieved 19 May 2015, from https://archive.org/details/nextgen-issue-006#page/n23/mode/2up

WGU. (2020). Special Education: History, Resources, Advice. https://www.wgu.edu/blog/special-education-history-resources-advice2001.html

Whig, P., & Kautish, S. (2024). VUCA Leadership Strategies Models for Pre-and Post-pandemic Scenario. In VUCA and Other Analytics in Business Resilience, Part B (pp. 127-152). Emerald Publishing Limited. DOI: 10.1108/978-1-83753-198-120241009

Whig, P., Kasula, B. Y., Yathiraju, N., Jain, A., & Sharma, S. (2024). Transforming Aviation: The Role of Artificial Intelligence in Air Traffic Management. In New Innovations in AI, Aviation, and Air Traffic Technology (pp. 60-75). IGI Global.

Whig, P., Mudunuru, K. R., & Remala, R. (2024). Quantum-Inspired Data-Driven Decision Making for Supply Chain Logistics. In Quantum Computing and Supply Chain Management: A New Era of Optimization (pp. 85-98). IGI Global. DOI: 10.4018/979-8-3693-4107-0.ch006

Whig, P., Remala, R., Mudunuru, K. R., & Quraishi, S. J. (2024). Integrating AI and Quantum Technologies for Sustainable Supply Chain Management. In Quantum Computing and Supply Chain Management: A New Era of Optimization (pp. 267-283). IGI Global. DOI: 10.4018/979-8-3693-4107-0.ch018

Whig, P., Silva, N., Elngar, A. A., Aneja, N., & Sharma, P. (Eds.). (2023). Sustainable Development through Machine Learning, AI and IoT: First International Conference, ICSD 2023, Delhi, India, July 15–16, 2023, Revised Selected Papers. Springer Nature. DOI: 10.1007/978-3-031-47055-4

Whig, P., Bhatia, A. B., Nadikatu, R. R., Alkali, Y., & Sharma, P. (2024). 3 Security Issues in. Software-Defined Network Frameworks: Security Issues and Use Cases, 34.

Whig, P., Bhatia, A. B., Nadikatu, R. R., Alkali, Y., & Sharma, P. (2024). GIS and Remote Sensing Application for Vegetation Mapping. In *Geo-Environmental Hazards using AI-enabled Geospatial Techniques and Earth Observation Systems* (pp. 17–39). Springer Nature Switzerland. DOI: 10.1007/978-3-031-53763-9_2

Whig, P., Kouser, S., Bhatia, A. B., Purohit, K., & Modhugu, V. R. (2024). 9 Intelligent Control for Energy Management. *Microgrid: Design, Optimization, and Applications*, 137. Rane, N., Choudhary, S., & Rane, J. (2023). Education 4.0 and 5.0: Integrating artificial intelligence (AI) for personalized and adaptive learning. *Available atSSRN* 4638365.

Whig, P., Madavarapu, J. B., Yathiraju, N., & Thatikonda, R. (2024). Interdisciplinary Data Analytics Transforming Influencer Marketing Strategies. In *Advances in Data Analytics for Influencer Marketing: An Interdisciplinary Approach* (pp. 103–124). Springer Nature Switzerland. DOI: 10.1007/978-3-031-65727-6_7

Willings, C. (2022, June 18). *History of Visual Impairments.* https://www.teachingvisuallyimpaired.com/timeline-of-vi.html

Wiske, M. S., & Eddy Spicer, D. H. (2010). Teacher education as teaching for understanding with new technologies. In Peterson, P. L., & Baker, E. L. (Eds.), *International encyclopedia of education* (3rd ed., pp. 635–641). Elsevier. DOI: 10.1016/B978-0-08-044894-7.00671-0

Wissick, C. A., Lloyd, J. W., & Kinzie, M. B. (1992). The effects of community training using a videodisc-based simulation. *Journal of Special Education Technology*, 11(4), 207–222. DOI: 10.1177/016264349201100405

Wood, E., Petkovski, M., De Pasquale, D., Gottardo, A., Evans, M. A., & Savage, R. S. (2016). Parent scaffolding of young children when engaged with mobile technology. *Frontiers in Psychology*, 7, 690. DOI: 10.3389/fpsyg.2016.00690 PMID: 27242603

Wood, S. G., Moxley, J. H., Tighe, E. L., & Wagner, R. K. (2017). Does the Use of Text-to-Speech and Related Read-Aloud Tools Improve Reading Comprehension for Students with Reading Disabilities? A Meta-Analysis. *Journal of Learning Disabilities*, 51(1), 73–84. DOI: 10.1177/0022219416688170 PMID: 28112580

World Bank Group. (2024, 11 7). *Challenges facing people with a disabilities in Sub-Sahara Africa- in 5 Charts*. Retrieved from World Bank Group: https://www.worldbank.org/en/topic/poverty/brief/challenges-facing-people-with-disabilities-in-sub-saharan-africa-in-5-charts

World Education Forum. (2000). *The Dakar Framework of Action.* Senegal: UNESCO.

World Health Organisartion (WHO). (2024, 02 02). *Deafness and hearing loss*. Retrieved from World Health Organisartion (WHO): https://www.who.int/news-room/fact-sheets/detail/deafness-and-hearing-loss

World Health Organisation (WHO). (2024, 08 25). *Disability*. Retrieved from World Health Organisation: https://www.who.int/health-topics/disability#tab=tab_1

World Vision Zambia. (2023, 07 27). *World Vision and the European Union donate assistive devices to Mangwiro school for the blind to promote quality*. Retrieved from World Vision Zambia: https://www.wvi.org/stories/zambia/world-vision-and-european-union-donate-assistive-devices-magwero-school-blind

Worldometer. (2024, 11 2). *Zambia population*. Retrieved from Worldometer: https://www.worldometers.info/world-population/zambia-population/#:~:text=The%20current%20population%20of%20Zambia,21%2C314%2C956%20p

Wu, H., Lee, S. W., Chang, H., & Liang, J. (2012). Current status, opportunities and challenges of augmented reality in education. *Computers & Education*, 62, 41–49. DOI: 10.1016/j.compedu.2012.10.024

Wyeth, P., Kervin, L., Danby, S., & Day, D. (2023). Digital technologies to support young children with special needs in early childhood education and care: A literature review. *OECD Education Working Papers No. 294*.

Xiao, L., Carroll, J. M., Clemson, P., & Rosson, M. B. (2008). Support of Case-Based authentic learning activities: a collaborative case commenting tool and a collaborative case builder. *Proceedings of the 41st Annual Hawaii International Conference on System Sciences (HICSS 2008)*, pp. *19*, 6. DOI: 10.1109/HICSS.2008.417

Xie, J., Basham, J. D., Marino, M. T., & Rice, M. F. (2018). Reviewing research on mobile learning in K–12 educational settings: Implications for students with disabilities. *Journal of Special Education Technology*, 33(1), 27–39. DOI: 10.1177/0162643417732292

Yandrapalli, V. (2024, February). AI-Powered Data Governance: A Cutting-Edge Method for Ensuring Data Quality for Machine Learning Applications. In *2024 Second International Conference on Emerging Trends in Information Technology and Engineering (ICETITE)* (pp. 1-6). IEEE. DOI: 10.1109/ic-ETITE58242.2024.10493601

Yell, M. L., Rogers, D., & Rogers, E. L. (1998). The Legal History of Special Education: What a Long, Strange Trip It's Been! *Remedial and Special Education*, 19(4), 219–228. DOI: 10.1177/074193259801900405

Young, G., & MacCormack, M. (2014, June 10). *Assistive Technology for Students with Learning Disabilities*. Toronto: Learning Disabilities Association of Ontario. https://www.ldatschool.ca/assistive-technology/

Yusop, F. D., & Razak, R. A. (2013) 'Mobile educational apps for children: towards development of i-CARES framework', *Annual International Conference on Management and Technology in Knowledge, Service, Tourism* & Hospitality, Jakarta, Indonesia.

Zaks, Z. (2023). Changing the medical model of disability to the normalization model of disability: Clarifying the past to create a new future direction. *Disability & Society*, •••, 1–29.

Zdravkova, K. (2022). The potential of artificial intelligence for assistive technology in education. In *Handbook on Intelligent Techniques in the Educational Process: Vol 1 Recent Advances and Case Studies* (pp. 61-85). Cham: Springer International Publishing. DOI: 10.1007/978-3-031-04662-9_4

Zdravkova, K., Krasniqi, V., Dalipi, F., & Ferati, M. (2022). Cutting-edge communication and learning assistive technologies for disabled children: An artificial intelligence perspective. *Frontiers in Artificial Intelligence*, 28(5), 970430. DOI: 10.3389/frai.2022.970430 PMID: 36388402

Zhao, X., Ren, Y., & Cheah, K. S. L. (2023). Leading Virtual Reality (VR) and Augmented Reality (AR) in Education: Bibliometric and Content Analysis From the Web of Science (2018–2022). *SAGE Open*, 13(3), 21582440231190821. Advance online publication. DOI: 10.1177/21582440231190821

Zimbabwe, U. N. D. P. (2024, 06 5). *Towards achieving sustainable and inclusive development*. Retrieved from UNDP Zimbabwe: https://www.undp.org/zimbabwe/news/towards-achieving-inclusive-sustainable-development

ZimRights. (2024). *Eights things that can be improved*. ZimRights.

Zwarych, F. (2023). *Inclusive Education with Assistive Technology*. Pressbooks. https://pressbooks.pub/techcurr2023/chapter/inclusive-educadtion-with-assistive-technology/

Zwoliński, G., Kamińska, D., Haamer, R. E., Coelho, L. F., & Anbarjafari, G. (2023). Enhancing empathy through virtual reality: Developing a universal design training application for students. *Medycyna Pracy*. Advance online publication. DOI: 10.13075/mp.5893.01407 PMID: 37695933

About the Contributors

Eriona Çela is a distinguished academic currently serving as a Full-Time Assistant Professor at the University of New York Tirana, where she is a member of the Faculty of Law and Social Sciences in the Department of Psychology. She earned her Ph.D. in Teaching Methodology of English for Specific Purposes (ESP) from the University of Bari "Aldo Moro" in Italy, enhancing her extensive background in language education, which includes earlier degrees in English Language and Law from the University of Tirana and Business Academy College in Albania. Dr. Çela's research interests are broad and interdisciplinary, focusing on Law, Business English, Artificial Intelligence, Machine Learning, Deep Learning, Natural Language Processing, Teaching Methodology, ESP, Academic Writing, Higher Education, Plagiarism, and European Integration among others. She is well-versed in teaching a range of subjects, including Academic Writing, ESL, Business English, Law, and Legal English. She also has significant expertise in translating legal, business, and educational documents. Her academic experience spans several respected institutions, including previous roles as an Assistant Professor at the University of Luarasi, University of Elbasan "Aleksandër Xhuvani", University of Tirana, and University of Durrës "Aleksandër Moisiu". In addition to her academic roles, Dr. Çela has held significant administrative positions within the Albanian Ministry of Education and Sport, contributing to integration, coordination, and project feasibility. Dr. Çela is active in the academic community as a member and managing editor of various editorial boards, including those for the European Journal of Arts, Humanities and Social Sciences, and the International Journal of Risk and Contingency Management. Her contributions to conferences and scholarly journals are numerous, underscoring her commitment to advancing research and practice in her fields of expertise. She also brings practical insights into her teaching and research from her experiences as a trainer and higher education expert involved in quality assurance and educational reforms in Albania. This rich background informs her ongoing contributions to academic discussions and policy-making in education, both in Albania and internationally.

Mathias M. Fonkam is an accomplished Associate Teaching Professor at Penn State University with over 20 years of experience in computer science education and industry. He holds a Ph.D. in Computer Science and an M.Sc. in Systems Engineering from Cardiff University, UK. His professional journey includes serving as the Dean at the American University of Nigeria (AUN), where he spearheaded numerous initiatives, such as developing the university's Open Source ERP System and establishing various postgraduate programs. Dr. Fonkam's research interests span AI, data science, blockchain, and systems dynamics, with over 30 publications in reputable conferences and journals. He has also contributed significantly to curriculum development and accreditation processes in Nigerian universities. Fluent in English, Portuguese, and French, Dr. Fonkam is dedicated to advancing computing education and professional development, leveraging his extensive expertise in teaching, mentoring, and research.

Narasimha Rao Vajjhala currently serves as the Dean of the Faculty of Engineering and Architecture at the University of New York Tirana in Albania. He previously held the position of Chair for the Computer Science and Software Engineering programs at the American University of Nigeria. Dr. Vajjhala is a senior member of both the ACM and IEEE. He is the Editor-in-Chief of the International Journal of Risk and Contingency Management (IJRCM) and a member of the Risk Management Society (RIMS) and the Project Management Institute (PMI). With over 23 years of experience, Dr. Vajjhala has taught programming and database-related courses across Europe and Africa at both graduate and undergraduate levels. He has also worked as a consultant for technology firms in Europe and participated in EU-funded projects. Dr. Vajjhala holds a Doctorate in Information Systems and Technology from the United States, a Master of Science in Computer Science and Applications from India, and a Master of Business Administration specializing in Information Systems from Switzerland.

Philip Eappen is an Assistant Professor of Healthcare Management at Cape Breton University. He is also a Director of Clinical Services and Transition to Community at the Breton Ability Center. With over a decade of experience in hospitals and healthcare management operations across different continents, Dr. Eappen is a seasoned professional. Before joining Cape Breton University, he taught at the University of Toronto, the Southern Alberta Institute of Technology, and Fanshawe College. He previously worked as a director of health services and chief administrator of healthcare operations at the American University of Nigeria.

Additionally, he has taught as an adjunct faculty member at the American University and several other universities and colleges for many years. Dr. Eappen holds a Doctorate in Healthcare Administration from Central Michigan University, a Master of Business Administration in Health Care Management, and a Bachelor of Nursing. He also has a post-graduate certificate in international health from Central Michigan University and several other certifications from reputed universities worldwide. Dr. Eappen's field of research interest is healthcare innovations, especially healthcare informatics. He has authored numerous publications, including journal articles, book chapters, and books.

***

William Chakabwata holds a PhD in Curriculum and Instruction, awarded by the University of South Africa on September 27, 2023. He also earned a Master's degree in Curriculum and Arts Education from the University of Zimbabwe. Dr. William has extensive teaching experience, having served as a faculty member at Midlands State University in Zimbabwe and the Namibia University of Science and Technology (NUST).

Sulagna Das is an accomplished Associate Professor at JIS University, Kolkata, with over 18 years of experience spanning corporate and academic domains. Her research expertise lies in Management and Social Sciences, with a strong focus on areas such as Banking, Microfinance, Digital Finance and Marketing, Blockchain and Finance, Cybersecurity in the Financial Sector, and Women Empowerment. Dr. Das earned her MBA and Ph.D. from KIIT School of Management, KIIT University, Bhubaneswar. She has published extensively in national and international peer-reviewed journals, including Scopus-indexed platforms and conferences organized by premier institutions such as the Indian Institutes of Management (IIMs) and Indian Institutes of Technology (IITs). Her scholarly contributions have been recognized with multiple Best Paper Awards at prestigious conferences and Innovation Awards from JIS University for the academic years 2020–21 and 2021–22, acknowledging her significant contributions to research. Currently, Dr. Das mentors five doctoral scholars and serves as a reviewer for Scopus-indexed and ABDC-A ranked journals published by Springer, Emerald, and IGI Global. She is also an external thesis evaluator for foreign universities and central universities in India.

Pushan Kumar Dutta is an Assistant Professor Grade III at Amity University Kolkata, part of the Amity Education Group, India. With five years of experience and extensive international exposure, he has demonstrated expertise in book editing, proofreading, research publication, and innovation programs. Dr. Dutta's academic contributions include IEEE Xplore conference publications, research collaborations, and organizing student workshops. He is actively involved as a mentor of change, focusing on skill-based and emerging courses, as well as serving on the Board of Studies. Dr. Dutta excels in designing and executing educational programs that prioritize student engagement, learning outcomes, and curriculum development. His commitment to fostering academic excellence and innovation underscores his impactful role in higher education.

Selami Eryılmaz is a distinguished academic at Gazi University, currently serving as a professor in the Department of Computer Education and Instructional Technologies. With extensive experience in education technology, his research focuses on integrating digital tools and methodologies to enhance learning outcomes and address contemporary challenges in education. Prof. Eryılmaz has contributed significantly to national and international projects, including Erasmus-funded initiatives, exploring digital education for diverse audiences, such as teachers, cancer patients, and palliative care providers. His scholarly work encompasses publications in peer-reviewed journals, book chapters, and conference proceedings, covering topics such as computational thinking, technology addiction, and information and communication technologies in education. Beyond his academic pursuits, Prof. Eryılmaz is actively involved in administrative leadership roles, serving as the head of multiple academic departments. He is a committed educator and mentor, supervising postgraduate and doctoral research while teaching courses ranging from instructional systems design to algorithm development. Prof. Eryılmaz's dedication to advancing education through technology continues to shape the field both in Turkey and internationally.

Hüseyin Göksu is a distinguished academic at Istanbul University-Cerrahpaşa, specializing in special education with a particular focus on integrating technology-driven solutions to support individuals with disabilities. His research centers on innovative educational methodologies designed to enhance learning outcomes and accessibility for individuals with intellectual disabilities. With extensive expertise in special education, he has contributed significantly to numerous projects aimed at improving inclusive education practices. Dr. Göksu is actively engaged in research, teaching, and the development of advanced educational tools, fostering inclusive learning environments and promoting professional growth among educators.

Gill Hagan-Green is the Research and Innovation Specialist of the Creative Fuse Sunderland team, she was also a Reader in Business Technology at the University of Bolton. She holds a first degree in Sociology and Social Policy and a PhD in Information Systems from Durham University. Her research area is around SMEs and their role in sociology-economic development, entrepreneurship and micro finance. She also looks at the opportunities in Creative and digital industries having started a programme of study for Music and Creative industries business and Management. Given her sociological background she also makes a significant contribution to the methodological integrity of the PhD students. Dr Hagan-Green has 25 years' experience as a researcher and academic. She has over 34 PhD completions and 28 examinations across the UK. She has more than 60 publications and her research outputs in journals such as the Journal of International Technology and Information Management, The Systemist and The Journal of End-User Computing. She acted as Chair at UKAIS (UK Academy of Information Systems) Conferences, been invited many times as Session Chair at the international European Conference for Research Methods in Business and Management (ECRM).

Lynne Hall is a Professor of Computer Science in the Faculty of Technology. She is an experienced user experience practitioner and researcher with considerable involvement in EU and UK projects and over 120 peer-reviewed publications in computing, psychology and education journals and conferences. She has considerable experience of external engagement, having been Project Manager for the Knowledge Transfer, Innovation and Enterprise strands of the Software City project; and Project Director of the Digital Media Network. Since 2009, she has directly interacted and collaborated with over 70 established SMEs and 35 start-ups (primarily in the software sector) through supporting business model development and evaluation, research opportunities, funding bid applications, innovation vouchers, consultancy, KTPs, etc. She has expertise in gaining EU, national and regional funding, and a track record in small and medium enterprise (SME) engagement and Knowledge Transfer Partnership (KTP) generation.

Madhavi Kilaru is an accomplished Assistant Professor in the Department of Humanities & Sciences at VNR Vignana Jyothi Institute of Engineering & Technology, Hyderabad, with approximately 17 years of teaching experience. She holds a BA in Mathematics and Statistics and an MBA in Marketing and HR from Andhra University, Visakhapatnam, where she also earned her Ph.D. in Marketing. Dr. Kilaru has an extensive research portfolio, including 25 publications in refereed international journals and over 30 contributions to national and international conference proceedings, along with patents to her credit. Her research interests span Supply Chain Management, Human Resource Management, Consumer Behavior, Artificial Intelligence, and Business Analytics. Additionally, she is an active member of the Commerce and Management Association of India (CMOAI), reflecting her commitment to advancing knowledge and practice in her field.

Indranil Mutsuddi holds a Ph.D. in Management from Amity University, Uttar Pradesh, India. He currently serves as an Associate Professor and Head of the Department at JIS University, Kolkata. With over 19 years of academic experience specializing in Human Resources (HR) and Organizational Behavior, Dr. Mutsuddi is a distinguished educator and researcher in his field. He is the author of three textbooks on Human Resource Management (HRM) and has published over 58 research papers in reputed journals. Dr. Mutsuddi has also chaired technical sessions on HR at several esteemed management conferences and seminars. A Double Gold Medalist from AIMA CME, he was honored with the Prof. Narendra Mohan Basu Award by Presidency College, Kolkata, in recognition of his academic excellence. Dr. Mutsuddi's research interests focus on employee retention and job skills, reflecting his dedication to addressing critical challenges in HR practices. His extensive contributions to teaching and research have established him as a respected figure in academia.

Sevinthi Kali Sankar Nagarajan is a versatile IT leader with over 20 years of experience in Data Architecture, Data Engineering, Business Intelligence (BI), and Artificial Intelligence/Machine Learning (AI/ML). Known for designing and implementing secure, scalable, and optimized data platforms, Sevinthi excels in leading end-to-end project lifecycles. With a strong focus on innovative and automated solutions, Sevinthi consistently drives business growth and efficiency, ensuring successful outcomes that meet the evolving needs of organizations.

Tunde Toyese Oyedokun is the Acting University Librarian at Thomas Adewumi University, Oko-Irese, Kwara State, Nigeria. A seasoned academic and researcher, Oyedokun specializes in integrating emerging technologies into library and educational systems. His work spans areas such as artificial intelligence in small businesses, Industry 5.0, immersive learning technologies, and digital transformation in academic libraries. Oyedokun has contributed significantly to scholarly literature, authoring articles and book chapters on topics like next-generation libraries, AI-driven education, and blockchain applications in supply chain management. He is also actively involved in fostering inclusive educational communities through collaborative learning spaces and technology-enhanced environments. In addition to his academic achievements, Oyedokun is known for his leadership in library innovation and his dedication to empowering learners and educators through advanced information services.

Samiullah Paracha's background is in creative technologies (VR/XR, Serious Games, AI, Eye-tracking, ITS, LMS, EdApps etc.) with a particular interest in Game Studies, Digital Humanities and Media, HCI, LCD and LXD, Educational

Robotics and Learning Analytic. Years of multidisciplinary work, with the United Nations (UN), Japan International Cooperation Agency (JICA), the Association of Southeast Asian Nations (ASEAN), and eminent educational establishments in Europe, Asia and Africa, has enabled him to embrace the discomfort and complexity involved in digital education space. He's employed field, lab, and lab-in- the-field experiments, developed systems, surveyed tools, and analyzed large panel data sets to better understand the intersection between education and technology. Thus, generating insights to inform theory and real-world decision-makers in the areas of digital education. His scholarly work has received Gold Medals, Silver Shields, Best Paper & First Prize Paper Awards from IEEE, IEEJ & IRES. Samiullah is also actively engaged in knowledge exchange activities particularly with the creative, digital, and IT sectors in order to bridge the gap between academia and industry.

Rajasekhara Mouly Potluri is a Professor of Management/Marketing with thirty-three years of industry/teaching experience in around ten countries and is currently working as a Professor of Marketing at the Business School of Kazakh-British Technical University of Almaty, Kazakhstan. Dr. Raj holds a Ph.D. and M. Phil. in Management/Marketing from Shivaji University, an MBA (Marketing), and a Master of Commerce (Banking) from Andhra University, India. He has published and presented around a hundred and thirty research articles, books, book chapters, and case studies in renowned peer-reviewed journals indexed in Scopus, ABDC, SSCI, IEEE, KCI, and International Conferences and won more than twenty Best Research Paper Awards and Academic Service Excellence Awards. Prof. Raj has extensive teaching and research experience in multicultural and multi-ethnic environments in India, Ethiopia, Kazakhstan, South Korea, Nigeria, and the United Arab Emirates (Golden Visa Received). His research interests are Marketing, Islamic Marketing, CSR and Sustainability, HRM & OB, and Entrepreneurship. He has professional memberships in the Eurasian Business & Economics Society, International Islamic Marketing Association, Social Responsibility Research Network, International Society for Development & Sustainability, Emerald Literate Network, and Consumer Guidance Society of India.

Nilanjan Ray is from Kolkata, India and presently associated as an Associate Professor at Department of Management Studies, JIS University. Prior joining to JIS University Dr Ray was at Institute of Leadership Entrepreneurship and Development as Associate Professor and HoD and additional responsibility as Director IQAC before that he was also associated at Adamas University as Associate Professor of Marketing Management and Centre Coordinator for Research in Business Analytics at Adamas University in Department of Management, School of Business and Economics, West Bengal, India. Dr Ray has obtained certified

Accredited Management Teacher Award from All India Management Association, New Delhi, India. He has obtained his PhD(Mktg); M.Com (Mktg); MBA (Mktg), STC FMRM (IIT-Kgp). He has more than 14 years teaching and 6 years Research experience, awarded 3 Doctoral Scholars and guided around 56 Post Graduate students' project also. Dr. Ray has contributed over 100 research papers in reputed National and International Referred, Peer Reviewed Journals, Proceedings and 13 Edited Research Hand Books from Springer, IGI-Global USA and Apple Academic Publisher CRC Press (A Taylor & Francis Group), USA. He has obtained 1 Patent from Germany and 3 Copyright from India. He has also associated himself as a reviewer of Tourism Management Elsevier, Journal of Service Marketing Emerald Group Publishing Limited, Journal of Business and Economics, Research Journal of Business and Management Accounting and as an Editorial Board Member of several referred Journals. Dr. Ray has organized several FDPs, National and International Conference, Management Doctoral Colloquium. Dr. Ray is a life-member of the International Business Studies Academia, Fellow Member of Institute of Research Engineers and Doctors Universal Association of Arts and Management Professionals (UAAMP) New York, USA Calcutta Management Association (CMA)

Munikrishnaiah Sundararamaiah is a versatile IT leader with over 17 years of experience in Data Architecture, Data Engineering, Business Intelligence (BI), and Artificial Intelligence/Machine Learning (AI/ML). Known for designing and implementing secure, scalable, and optimized data platforms, Sundararamaiah excels in leading end-to-end project lifecycles. With a strong focus on innovative and automated solutions, Sundararamaiah consistently drives business growth and efficiency, ensuring successful outcomes that meet the evolving needs of organizations.

Vismaya Vinod is a student and researcher at Cape Breton University. She is also a student assistant in the work-study program, contributing to campus healthcare projects. She is also a research project coordinator at the Nova Scotia Health Authority. With a Doctor of Pharmacy degree earned with high distinction from Kerala University of Health Sciences, Dr. Vinod has over three years of healthcare research experience, including a role as a Healthcare Data Analyst at Chisquare Labs, analyzing clinical trial data and patient outcomes. Her research interests focus on healthcare management, epidemiology, data analysis, and clinical research, with a passion for improving healthcare systems through evidence-based practices and innovation.

Derek Watson is an Associate Professor and Senior Fellow of the Higher Education Academy, founder of the Faculty 'Business Clinic' and the Doctoral lead for the University's 'Research Fridays' programme. Dr Watson has extensive links and networks as a result of sourcing and embedding external engagement opportunities across the curriculum, with an international portfolio of clients and contacts, such as the British Cabinet Office, Indian Government Council of Scientific and Industrial Research, Dubai Police and Canon International. His research focuses on Cultural Compliance and Academic-Industry collaboration, investigating the impact of knowledge exchange on practice in both the classroom and the workplace. In addition, his is also a Visiting Professor at the University of Panama in Food Culture and a Senior Research Fellow at the Cyprus Business School.

Pawan Whig is an accomplished IEEE Lifetime Member and the Country Head at Threws, with extensive experience as a Research Consultant in Machine Learning. He is Google Certified in Digital Marketing and formerly served as Dean of Research at VIPS-T. Dr. Whig holds a Ph.D. from Jamia Millia Islamia and has a robust research background in VLSI Design, Artificial Intelligence (AI), and Machine Learning (ML). With over 15 years of experience, he has published numerous papers in national and international journals and continues to contribute to cutting-edge advancements in technology and research.

Index

A

Accessibility 1, 5, 7, 14, 18, 27, 28, 30, 32, 44, 51, 52, 55, 62, 68, 73, 75, 76, 81, 84, 90, 95, 102, 104, 105, 108, 110, 118, 120, 122, 125, 126, 127, 128, 131, 132, 133, 139, 141, 147, 148, 149, 150, 151, 154, 157, 159, 161, 163, 191, 195, 197, 225, 234, 250, 252, 258, 259, 262, 263, 265, 269
Accessibility Tools 125, 126, 127, 128, 131, 147, 150, 151, 161
Accessible Technology 261, 265, 266, 269
Adaptive Education 1, 2, 3, 15, 16, 18, 21, 22, 24, 35, 73, 74, 75, 76, 77, 79, 80, 82, 101, 102, 103, 105, 125, 126, 127, 131, 133, 147, 148, 149, 150, 151, 152
Adaptive Learning 11, 14, 18, 21, 22, 23, 24, 25, 26, 27, 28, 36, 44, 45, 46, 47, 48, 49, 51, 57, 58, 60, 62, 65, 69, 71, 76, 77, 79, 80, 82, 83, 91, 92, 93, 94, 95, 97, 99, 102, 103, 107, 108, 113, 114, 115, 116, 117, 122, 132, 147, 154, 157, 213
AI-Driven Technologies 21, 73, 93, 95
Artificial Intelligence in Education 47, 48, 66
Assistive Devices 4, 7, 8, 15, 147, 163, 169, 173, 176, 183, 184, 187, 189, 190, 191, 259, 260, 262
Assistive Technology 2, 3, 4, 8, 9, 11, 12, 15, 17, 18, 56, 64, 67, 75, 77, 98, 99, 120, 122, 125, 126, 127, 128, 129, 130, 131, 132, 133, 134, 135, 136, 137, 138, 139, 140, 141, 142, 143, 144, 145, 146, 147, 148, 149, 150, 151, 152, 153, 154, 155, 156, 157, 158, 159, 160, 161, 163, 166, 168, 171, 174, 175, 176, 177, 181, 182, 184, 186, 189, 190, 191, 223, 224, 225, 243, 245, 257, 260, 262, 268, 269
Assistive Technology (AT) 174
Augmented Reality 6, 7, 19, 44, 51, 52, 53, 59, 65, 66, 70, 71, 95, 125, 133, 147, 148, 151, 160, 196, 241

B

Behavioral Data 78, 86, 101, 103, 110, 111, 112, 113, 114, 116, 117, 122

C

Concept Teaching 196
Cultural Stigma 8, 10, 18

D

Data-Driven Solutions 74, 75, 76, 77, 79, 82, 83, 85, 101, 102, 103, 105, 106, 107, 108, 122
Digital Literacy 158, 255, 256, 257, 258, 260, 261, 262, 263, 264, 265, 266, 267, 268, 269
Disability Support 73, 101, 108, 110

E

Educational Effectiveness 216, 241
Experiential Technology 53

H

Healthcare Management 52, 53, 54
Higher Education Institutions 21, 45, 68, 185
High-Tech Devices 4, 7, 19, 126

I

Immersive Learning 29, 53, 71, 197
Inclusive Education 1, 5, 7, 8, 17, 18, 19, 68, 71, 72, 76, 97, 123, 131, 144, 146, 153, 155, 158, 159, 160, 163, 168, 169, 181, 182, 183, 185, 187, 191, 213, 217, 238, 244, 258, 265, 266, 269
Inclusive Learning 2, 8, 51, 60, 84, 113, 130, 133, 142, 149, 159, 161, 174, 260, 261, 267
Intellectual Disabilities 153, 184, 193, 194,

195, 196, 200, 201, 203, 207, 208, 209, 211, 213, 216, 217, 218, 222, 231, 233, 234, 247, 248, 250, 252, 253
Intelligent Tutoring Systems 73, 75, 80, 83, 105
Interdisciplinary Research 1, 19
Intersectionality 163, 179, 180, 181, 183, 184, 185, 186, 187, 188, 191

L

Learning Analytics 60, 69, 74, 77, 78, 79, 101, 102, 106, 107, 108, 120, 122, 123, 156
Learning Applications 122, 150, 216
Low-Tech Solutions 7, 19, 131

M

Mobile Technologies 216, 222, 239

O

Oculus Quest 2 193, 201, 213

P

Personalized Learning 11, 22, 28, 30, 43, 49, 51, 56, 59, 60, 62, 65, 66, 72, 73, 74, 75, 76, 77, 79, 80, 82, 83, 84, 87, 88, 89, 91, 92, 95, 97, 101, 103, 105, 107, 109, 110, 111, 112, 113, 114, 115, 116, 117, 118, 122, 123, 135, 136, 139, 142, 150, 154, 235, 236
Personalized Learning Algorithms 73

R

Remote Learning 11, 260, 267

S

Screen Readers 7, 19, 75, 84, 102, 108, 126, 128, 130, 138, 143, 161, 255, 257, 259, 261, 262, 264, 269
SENCOs 215, 216, 217, 218, 226, 227, 228, 231, 232, 233, 234, 235, 236, 237, 238, 239, 240, 241, 248, 249, 253
Sequential Learning 193, 213
Severe Intellectual Disabilities 216, 217, 231, 233, 234, 250, 252, 253
Southern African Development Community 163, 183, 191
Special Education 4, 17, 18, 69, 77, 98, 104, 120, 122, 136, 138, 139, 142, 144, 146, 151, 153, 154, 155, 156, 158, 160, 172, 186, 207, 208, 212, 213, 215, 216, 217, 218, 222, 223, 224, 225, 238, 239, 240, 242, 243, 245, 246, 247, 249, 250, 252, 260
Special iApps 215, 216, 218, 226, 228, 232, 233, 234, 235, 236, 237, 238, 239, 241, 250, 252, 253
Speech Recognition Tools 73, 75, 269
Student Progress 21, 78, 81, 113, 115, 139, 236
Students with Disabilities 1, 2, 3, 4, 5, 6, 7, 8, 9, 11, 12, 13, 14, 15, 16, 17, 19, 51, 52, 53, 54, 55, 56, 59, 60, 62, 64, 67, 68, 70, 71, 73, 74, 75, 76, 77, 81, 84, 90, 97, 98, 101, 102, 103, 105, 107, 108, 109, 110, 123, 125, 126, 127, 131, 132, 133, 134, 135, 138, 139, 141, 142, 143, 145, 146, 147, 148, 149, 151, 152, 153, 154, 157, 158, 159, 160, 199, 212, 218, 219, 223, 244, 255, 257, 259, 260, 261, 263, 265, 266, 267

T

Teacher Training 19, 83, 147, 259
Technological Innovations 52, 53, 101, 102, 105, 108, 110, 195

U

Ubuntu 163, 164, 178, 179, 181, 182, 183, 184, 185, 186, 187, 188, 191
Unity Software 193, 213
Universal Design 3, 9, 15, 17, 19, 70, 84, 125, 142, 148, 149, 151, 158, 159, 161, 191, 225, 260, 269

V

Virtual Reality 29, 44, 51, 53, 59, 62, 64, 70, 71, 72, 119, 133, 148, 160, 193, 195, 196, 197, 198, 199, 200, 201, 207, 208, 209, 210, 211, 212, 213, 241

Voice Recognition Software 132, 166, 255, 269

www.ingramcontent.com/pod-product-compliance
Ingram Content Group UK Ltd.
Pitfield, Milton Keynes, MK11 3LW, UK
UKHW051942180125
453763UK00007B/36